Laurie Boucke

# INFANT POTTY TRAINING

a gentle and primeval method
adapted to modern living

Edited by Linda Carlson

WHITE
BOUCKE
PUBLISHING
LAFAYETTE, COLORADO

First published May 2000 (1-888580-10-0)
Reprinted with minor corrections December 2000
Second Edition April 2002 (1-888580-24-0),
Reprinted April 2003, March 2004 (minor changes),
September 2005, May 2006

**ISBN-10: 1-888580-24-0**
**ISBN-13: 978-1-888580-24-2**

**Printed in the United States of America**

**Library of Congress Cataloging-in-Publication Data**

Boucke, Laurie.
    Infant potty training : a gentle and primeval method adapted to modern
living / Laurie Boucke ; edited by Linda Carlson.-- 2nd ed.
        p. cm.
    Includes bibliographical references and index.
        ISBN 1-888580-24-0 (trade paper)
        1. Toilet training.  I. Carlson, Linda (Linda Frantzen), 1949-  II. Title.
HQ770.5.B68 2002
649'.62--dc21                                                    2002004268

PO BOX 400, LAFAYETTE, CO 80026, USA
www.white-boucke.com

## Permissions . . .

# CONTENTS

## PART 1
## THE CONCEPT & THE METHOD

# PART 2
## TESTIMONIALS – USA

# PART 3
## TESTIMONIALS – AROUND THE WORLD

# PART 4
# CROSS-CULTURAL STUDIES

# PREFACE

Potty training from birth or the early months of life? Most Westerners scoff at the very idea that an infant is able to work with adults in this respect. Doctors mistakenly associate this with the harsh and punitive type of "early toilet training" used in the United States and Europe until the 1950s. Yet observant visitors to the countrysides of Asia or Africa will invariably witness the wonder of infant potty training many a time. Anyone who pays attention will see mothers holding their infants in a relaxed, loving and natural manner as the babies pee and poo on cue. In many regions, fathers, siblings, other family members or caregivers such as child nurses sometimes assist in taking babies to the toilet. Whereas Westerners consider potty training to be both a "big deal" and an ordeal, it is as enjoyable and natural as caring for baby's other needs for millions who start the process in the early months of life.

The term "infant potty training" is a partial misnomer since small infants are not able to sit on a potty. As the term "potty training" is so prevalent in the West, it is used in the title of this book. The method of infant toilet learning discussed in this book consists of two different but directly related phases: (1) the in-arms phase, before baby can sit, and (2) the potty phase, when baby is able to sit and wants to use a potty or toilet rather than be held over a receptacle.

Part 1 of this book provides detailed guidelines on how to potty train an infant while living in a modern society. Chapters 1–7 (approximately the first

100 pages) explain exactly what the infant potty technique can achieve and how to achieve it. For parents in a hurry to get started, this is all you need to read for now—the rest of the book can be read at your leisure, when you'd like additional information, inspiration, background and assistance. Photos of various ways to hold baby are included. Part 1 also provides a general history of infant elimination training and an explanation of why toilet training infants was a seemingly taboo topic in North America throughout the second half of the 20th century and into the early 21st century. Part 1 also takes a look at some other gentle parenting practices and philosophies that are compatible with infant pottying. A chapter for late-starters ("Late-Starters: 6 Months & Older") is included for parents who learn about infant pottying after their babies have passed through the first sensitive period or window of opportunity. The good news is that many late-starters do extremely well with a slightly modified version.

In Parts 2 and 3, detailed testimonials by a number of mothers provide firsthand accounts and experiences. Part 2 consists of interviews with American mothers. Part 3 offers testimonials by and about families in other parts of the world. The testimonials were gathered from a cross-section of families representing different backgrounds, cultures, races, nationalities, lifestyles, income levels and education levels in order to demonstrate that this method is not limited to any particular society or group.

Part 4 takes a brief look at nurturant child-raising practices in other societies, then presents a selection of cross-cultural writings and commentary on infant elimination training techniques used in Sub-Saharan Africa, Asia, the Americas, the Arctic and Australasia. One of the reasons for presenting this cross-cultural information is to show that infant elimination training has long been and still continues to be fairly prevalent in a number of societies. The information will hopefully serve to counteract Western skepticism and unfounded fears about working with infants in this capacity.

Babies, parents and the environment are the three main beneficiaries of infant potty training. It enhances bonding and communication between parents and children and also provides infants with the ultimate hygienic respect. It can drastically reduce the amount of diapers needed, conserve resources, cut down considerably on dirty laundry and eliminate diaper rash. Admittedly, it is not the most convenient means of toilet learning, but practitioners generally understand this before beginning, still elect to use it, and are enthusiastic and satisfied with the outcome. The time is ripe to increase awareness, acceptance and usage of this gentle and age-old practice.

# Housekeeping

## Terminology

In this book, lay terminology is used with a view to reaching the average reader and family. Thus, the word "go" is frequently used to mean "eliminate." The term "pee" is used to mean "urinate" or "micturate," while the terms "poo" and "poop" are used to mean "defecate" and "defecation." The words "potty" and "toilet" are sometimes used as verbs in the generic sense of "pottying or toileting baby" and when used this way do not necessarily refer to any specific receptacles for elimination.

In the expression "infant potty training," the word "training" is used in the positive sense of a loving exchange between mother and baby. It refers to a reciprocal learning experience, a form of mother-baby training and synergy that should *never* be misconstrued in the negative sense of pressure, rigidity or coercion.

## Gender

Instead of awkwardly referring to baby as "s/he," "he or she" and "his/her," this book uses one single gender throughout a particular chapter unless there are obvious references where the opposite sex applies. Hence, Chapter 3 generically refers to baby in the feminine gender (she, her, hers), whereas Chapter 4 generically refers to baby in the masculine gender (he, him, his).

## Numbers

Ages in months and years are given in digits (2 months old) rather than words (two months old). This makes it easier to scan through the text and find a reference to a particular age. This applies everywhere except in quoted material where authors' original styles are preserved.

## Repetition

Each chapter is as complete a unit as possible. The book is designed to allow readers to turn to a chapter and obtain detailed information about a given topic without the need to flip back and forth from one page to another. For this reason, there is necessarily some overlapping of ideas and information among chapters. For example, Chapter 3, "The In-Arms Phase," outlines signals and cues used by baby and mother. These signals and cues are repeated and explained in far greater detail in Chapter 5, "Signals & Cues."

## Photographs

The majority of photos are natural in that they were taken during the actual course of potty training. Many of the photos depict baby in mid-micturition, but the urine stream is not always clearly visible in black-and-white renderings.

# About the Book

This book is the sequel to my first work on infant elimination training, *Trickle Treat: Diaperless Infant Toilet Training Method,* a small, 85-page work that was published in 1991 (now out of print). That book was written as a result of my own experience with infant toilet training and also was inspired by the fact that no other books existed on the topic.

Since that time, this gentle approach to toilet learning has grown in popularity. In addition, the attitude of Western medicine has started to change. There is now disagreement with the widely held premises about maturational readiness for toilet training and the age at which babies can start to gain some sphincter control. With interest steadily on the increase, parents are hungry for detailed information on this means of nurturing and enriching their relationships with their babies.

*Infant Potty Training* is intended to be a definitive guide for addressing parents' questions, providing encouragement and increasing awareness about this delicate topic. An abridged version of this book also exists. The title is *Infant Potty Basics: With or Without Diapers . . . the Natural Way*—a book published with frugal families, overseas customers, "time-challenged" readers and gifting in mind.

Parents must bear in mind that each baby is unique and will develop at her own personal pace. Anyone who desires to use infant pottying with a healthy baby in a stable home environment, who practices it correctly and exercises loving patience and diligence on a regular basis should be able to experience the many joys that ensue from this intimate and gentle practice.

Laurie Boucke
Lafayette, Colorado
March 2004

# INTRODUCTION

by Prof. Marten W. deVries, MD

Potty training is an important developmental milestone in all societies and therefore of universal interest to mothers and families. Cultures worldwide have given their signature to bowel and bladder training methods and back their approaches with specific ideas of what a baby is, can and should do.

Those who have studied and observed child-rearing practices across different cultural settings have been struck by the diversity of ideas, expectations and practices that guide parents and families in the day-to-day interactions with their babies and children. One observation by the influential anthropologist Caudill, who compared Japanese and American infant development and child-rearing practices during the 1950s and 1960s, has always loomed as a compelling wisdom. He was struck by the fact that the responses he observed in infants to child-care practices were in line with broad expectations for behavior in both cultures. For example, in the United States the expectation that the individual should be physically and verbally assertive, and in Japan, that the individual should be physically and verbally restrained, was observable in infant behavior as well as in child rearing. During my fieldwork in East Africa in the mid-1970s, I was similarly struck with how cultural values interacted with the constitutional characteristics of the baby.

From the cross-cultural perspective, two points emerge that are of interest regarding this volume. One is that the culture and the family project their ideas as to what an infant can actually do, often with very good evolutionary and social reasons, and thereby shape the infant's behavior. The other is that infants are capable of an immense repertoire of behavior at birth and during the first year, a fact borne out over 40 years of ethnographic and experimental study. These two aspects, that the infant is receptive to learning and can carry out an immense range of behavior, as well as being open to shaping by family and culture, provide the rationale for this book.

Ms. Boucke provides a practical update and guide to potty training, using observations of infants and maternal comments. In so doing she follows in the footsteps of earlier anthropological field studies dating to Geber. These cross-cultural studies have illuminated the diverse perspectives and the range of possibilities available to Western mothers. In photos, testimonials and descriptive material, Ms. Boucke brings this information to the Western reader in practical down-home language. The lesson from Ms. Boucke and traditional societies is that infant potty training is far more than just a chore or messy necessity, it is an important way for the family and baby to get to know one another. Boucke refutes the Western views that early training is coercive or potentially dangerous in terms of personality formation, using a world sample to show that potty training can indeed be a nurturant experience and help create a competent infant. Her selection of photos and comments make it clear that potty training can be anything but harsh.

Today, given the advance of diaper technology, it is not necessary for families to employ the time-tested method of infant toilet training. But this is a valid and effective alternative, as Ms. Boucke makes clear with examples from Asia, Africa and the USA. *Infant Potty Training* provides the opportunity for mothers to be with their infants in new, creative and loving ways. I find that the author's practical advice and clear descriptions constitute a nurturant contribution to families, pediatricians and child-rearing literature in general.

Marten W. deVries
Maastricht, 2000

THE CONCEPT
&
THE METHOD

# a wonderful discovery

This book is about working with infants towards accomplishing what is commonly known as "potty training." There is no English term to suitably describe "infant potty training" as a whole, since (a) an infant cannot sit on a potty and (b) the process is a gentle and nurturing form of reciprocal-communication teamwork and interconnectedness with your baby, and thus the usual definition of "training" does not apply.

*Infant Potty Training* is based on an elimination training technique used in much of Asia, rural Sub-Saharan Africa and South America. In this book, the method has been adapted to the Western urban lifestyle in various ways, including the use of a sink, potty, toilet or other container; variations in elimination positions; part-time use of the technique; and, where desired, part-time use of diapers.

Perhaps the most unique characteristic of this method is that parents typically begin working with a baby before she can even sit. Instead of beginning research on toilet training around the time a child takes her first steps, parents need to consider this method during pregnancy or the first weeks/months after delivery.

*Michael Smalley*

The best time to research infant potty training is during pregnancy.

## Who Can Use This Method?

This book is intended for parents of infants, parents-to-be, grandparents, nannies and anyone else interested in lovingly and patiently working with an infant towards accomplishing potty training at the earliest possible age. "Infant" is the operative word here, as opposed to "toddler," in that a caregiver begins working as a team with an infant in the early months of life.

This method does not claim to be *the* method for everybody, but parents should at least know the facts about it when considering how to toilet train their children. Pediatricians and other members of the medical community should be knowledgeable enough to discuss this method with inquisitive parents. Infant potty training is best used by:

- a parent who spends at least the first 1-2 years caring for baby
- a working parent with a trustworthy and reliable helper (family member, nanny or friend) or team of helpers readily available

## What Does It Take?

Time, diligence, patience and practice. If you cannot devote these qualities or arrange for any assistance you may need, this is not the method for you or your baby.

## How Long Does It Take?

Infant potty training is a gradual developmental and communication process that carries on for many months, similar to learning to walk or talk. As with other major skills, it takes months of practice. Parents who start sometime before their baby is 5 months old should expect to finish around the age of 2 years. Many finish around 18 months, but in order to have a relaxed and patient mindset, parents should be prepared to spend the maximum number of months. If you finish earlier, it will be a bonus. Consider this method as something akin to breastfeeding in terms of time, intimacy and bonding. It takes a dedicated caregiver. This is not a method for parents in a hurry. Expecting too much too soon can lead to giving up.

Mothers who don't limit themselves to the standard Western definition of "toilet trained" are more open to recognizing, appreciating and enjoying different degrees and stages of evolution along the way—and this new outlook yields a different answer to the question of how long it takes. Depending on circumstances (age started; individual learning curve; good health; positive environment; consistency of caregiver(s); control of voluntary muscles; cultural attitudes and expectations) and one's definition of the term "potty trained" (ability to release on cue; ability to retain and wait to go; importance or lack of clothing factors; total potty independence, including nighttime), it generally takes from 6 months to 2 years.

## Is It Safe?

Of course! Every effort has been made to provide proper and safe guidelines for holding and working with your baby. If the guidelines are followed correctly, no psychological or physical harm can occur to your baby. Punishment, anger and control are *not* a part of this method. Instead, parents must exercise patience and gentleness; observe and respond to baby's signals on time whenever reasonably possible; and use intelligent, caring and loving caution when handling their infants.

## How Do I Know When My Baby Needs to Go?

You can know when baby needs to go by one or more of the following, which form the blueprint of infant potty training:

- timing (by the clock)
- signals and cues (including body language and sound)
- patterns in elimination timing
- intuition and instinct

## Does It Really Work?

Yes, but not without practice and effort. Success does not just happen on its own. It takes at least one committed adult and several months of perseverance to complete infant potty training. In most situations, there are daily rewards for both baby and caregiver right from the very first days or weeks. Baby's communication is acknowledged and encouraged. Parents are amazed at the degree of their infant's awareness and are thrilled when experiencing this special form of communication and responsiveness with their infant.

## Does My Baby Have to Be Naked?

This is not a requirement. Many parents keep a diaper or training pants on their baby in between potty visits, while others prefer to leave their baby bare-bottomed or naked most of the time. In short, it is a matter of preference and a lifestyle choice.

## Can I Still Start If My Baby Is 6 Months or Older?

If this method resonates, if it sounds right for you and your baby, yes, it is fine to give it a try (despite all the scare tactics to the contrary). Although the first and most effective window of learning generally ends around age 4–5 months, some babies remain receptive beyond this. And other windows of opportunity open at different times during a child's development. For example, many babies are again ready for toilet learning around the age of 8–12 months, 18 months and/or 24 months. Since each child is unique, there is no way to know for sure when yours will again be receptive to toilet learning once she is older than 5 months.

Depending on the age of your baby, you may have to slightly modify some approaches. For more on starting infant potty training with an older baby, see Chapter 10, "Late-Starters."

## Will People Think I'm Crazy?

There are people who object to every lifestyle imaginable, so don't let this deter you. Since the 1950s, the Western world has been indoctrinated to fear and reject any form of early toilet learning. In fact, infant elimination training has been suppressed and eradicated from our national psyche, so in this sense, we face an uphill battle. Even when our own parents or grandparents tell us that they had all of their children potty trained by 8–12 months, we tend to disbelieve them and assume they are exaggerating.

Happily, the tide is turning and word is spreading. Many new and expecting parents are open and objective enough to weigh the pros and cons of this method. They are extremely excited when they hear about it and do not appreciate the fact that they have been kept in the dark for so long. There are now pediatricians and other medical professionals who support infant potty training. More and more Westerners are beginning to recognize the fact that there is a lot of money, rather than truth and sound research, behind some big product endorsements (diapers and best-selling books come to mind) and are less frightened by the lobbying against infant elimination training. As awareness spreads, there will be less resistance to, and consternation about, this gentle method.

## A Wonderful Discovery

When my first child was born, I knew almost nothing about babies. And so, as happens with many new mothers, I was trained to train my first son to use diapers. I dutifully followed suit with my second son. Both experienced conventional potty training. They started at ages 18 months and 15 months, and they stayed dry during the day at ages 3¼ and 3½ years, respectively. Both wet their beds at night until approximately 10 years of age.

When my third son was born, I dreaded the thought of another bout of conventional toilet training which would entail additional years of diapers and began seeking a better solution. I learned the basis for an alternative technique through a mother visiting us from India. She was horrified when I told her the way Westerners handle the "waste disposal issue" and explained to me the way things are done "back home" in her culture. I was skeptical when she told me that there is no need to use "the cloths" on an infant unless it is "ill of the stomach," feverish or wets the bed most nights. I had been to India several times and had noticed families peeing and pooing their babies around the countryside, but had not paid close attention. Like many others, I mistakenly assumed that Westerners could not use this technique.

I begged my new friend to tell me more and to teach me how to hold my son and get him to "go" for me, which she gladly and effortlessly did. I was spellbound watching her communicate with my tiny 3-month-old son, who somehow instinctively knew what she wanted him to do. I can only describe the exchange and instant understanding between them—a stranger and an infant—as a wonderful discovery.

I used the technique she demonstrated, slightly modifying and adapting it to a Western lifestyle, and found it to be far superior to conventional diaper-to-potty-training. From the day I started working with my 3-month-old son, he rarely needed a diaper, day or night. He stayed dry during most of the day at age 18 months and was finished with all aspects of potty training at age 25 months. Our lifestyle and economic situation remained constant during the childhood of all three sons. A detailed account of my personal experience is found in Part 2 of this book.

# chapter 2

# philosophy

Babies are smarter and more receptive than we think. The big mistake we make is to presume that a newborn baby is unaware of going to the toilet. We assume an infant is incapable of toilet learning since he is small and uncoordinated and because he cannot walk or talk. An infant is helpless in so many ways that it is hard for Westerners to imagine such a tiny being could be aware of peeing and pooing. It is even harder for us to believe that an infant has some control over his elimination. With these preconceived and narrow views, we encourage and teach our babies to be unconcerned about wetting and soiling diapers. In short, we teach our infants to use diapers as a toilet.

A normal, healthy infant is indeed aware of the bodily function of elimi-nation and can learn to respond to it from infancy. By using diapers, we con-dition and thereby train baby to go in them. Later the child must unlearn this training. This can be confusing and a traumatic experience for the child.

If you do not believe that an infant is aware of elimination, take his dia-per off and observe him as he pees or poos. From his facial expressions to his body language and vocalizations, you will see and hear that he is aware of what is going on. He is in touch with these muscles and sensations, and it is your job to help keep him in touch and to encourage further muscular development. Like any other muscle, the more a baby consciously experi-ences and begins to exercise his sphincter muscles, the more control he can gain. At first it may just be a sensation on his part, but he will inevitably experiment with contracting and relaxing the muscles. The earlier you ac-knowledge this and encourage him to continue, the earlier he can gain some control. When you work with this control, instead of against it by ignoring or denying it, toilet learning can usually be completed much sooner than ex-pected in the West.

An infant does his best to communicate his awareness to you, but if you don't listen, he will stop communicating and gradually lose touch with the elimination functions. He will be conditioned not to care and will learn that you want him to use his diaper as a toilet.

Babies are creatures of habit and instinct. The younger you teach them something they are ready to learn, the easier it is for them to learn it. In-fants send signals and are very receptive to your communication about their elimination, unless this awareness is suppressed by the constant use of dia-pers. By way of comparison, consider how easily and fast a newborn asso-ciates being held in a certain position with nursing. Anyone holding a breastfed infant in that particular position will see baby's natural reaction is to attempt to nurse. On the other hand, babies who are bottle-fed do not learn the nursing position and will not search for a breast when held in the breastfeeding position. This is because that natural instinct has been sup-pressed or replaced by a different behavior, and one that works just as well for survival. Both behaviors illustrate how easily, quickly and naturally baby becomes aware and responds to certain cues in infancy and how easily they can be suppressed if not used.

Studies of conditioning in babies demonstrate that newborns are able to learn and remember things. In 1928, Anderson Aldrich sounded a bell as he used a pin to prick a baby on the sole of his foot. The infant pulled his foot away from the pinprick. After repeating the association of the ringing bell with the pinprick 12 times, the sound of the bell alone resulted in the baby withdrawing his foot.[1]

A 1966 study by Ernest Siqueland and Lewis Lipsitt illustrated the quick learning ability of newborns and the power of positive conditioning in reinforcing learned behaviors in the first few weeks of life. Just one day after birth, babies mastered the ability to turn their heads to one side 83 percent of the time in response to an offering of sugar water. Next the newborns were taught to turn their heads to the left at the sound of a bell or to the right at the sound of a buzzer (bell-left, buzzer-right) in response to the offering of sugar water when the head was turned the correct direction. The task was then complicated by switching bell and buzzer, with reinforcement provided only for turning the opposite way (bell-right, buzzer-left). This called for discrimination between the different sounds, turning the head left and right and learning the new pattern in order to get the sugar water. It only took the infants 30 minutes to accomplish this.[2]

T. Berry Brazelton, MD, and Bertrand Cramer, MD, state that "None of these laboratory studies can be as effective in reinforcing an infant's memory as are the times when parent and infant are involved in spontaneous, reciprocal interaction, each giving and receiving rewarding cues from the other."[3] Although neither of these doctors are advocates of infant elimination training, this principle of positive reinforcement between mother and infant exists in the spontaneous and reciprocal interaction between mother and baby during infant toilet learning. And the baby-mother dyad fits this mold better than any other toilet training approach used by Westerners in the past century:

- parent-directed—based on parent leading, 1900–1960s
- child-directed—based on child leading, from 1962
- baby-mother-directed—based on reciprocal interaction between baby and mother

Brazelton argues that parents must wait until their kids initiate toilet training sometime after the age of 2 years. But *infants do* initiate toilet training—and from birth. The problem is that we ignore their signals and don't respond, causing (training) them to lose interest. An infant is a very social being. Instead of ignoring his elimination instincts and innate propensity for learning by waiting years for him to "get it" on his own, a mother can instead be an active participant in a shared symbiosis. In this way, she acknowledges and encourages his capacity for early learning. It is far more fulfilling, cozy and fun for a baby to do this "together with someone" at the moment he is ripe for it, and in most families, this will at first be with his favorite person and companion, his mother. A cooperative and caring partnership shapes the heart of infant potty training.

Another way to look at an infant's natural ability to respond to elimination communication is to compare it to a Montessori "sensitive period" in that the optimum learning time for many things is in infancy when the brain is open and receptive. "A sensitive period refers to a special sensibility which a creature acquires in its infantile state, while it is still in a process of evolution."[4] An infant can learn potty techniques effortlessly and with joy, just as children can learn foreign languages with no effort and no accent at a young age, something that later becomes an arduous process. "There is for each developmental phase a particular and specially suited period. These are times when a child is ready to make a developmental step. If it misses the timing of this learning step, the child will make up for it much later and with a lot of struggle."[5]

Most Westerners begin teaching toilet habits when it is difficult and awkward for both child and parent. It is hard for the child because:

- the child's instinctive awareness of elimination has been suppressed for months or years
- the child has been encouraged and allowed to use diapers as a toilet
- the child was not encouraged to use his "toilet muscles" in infancy
- the child was not encouraged to communicate the need to go in infancy
- a toddler is mobile and typically does not like to spend the necessary time sitting on the potty

It is difficult for the parent because:

- a toddler typically is not interested in potty training
- a toddler eats solid foods and makes bigger, smellier messes in his pants
- a toddler is more likely to "play ego games" and "test" his parents
- a toddler is mobile and usually does not like to spend the necessary time sitting on the potty

Babies in non-Western societies typically complete toilet learning far earlier than Western babies. In some respects, Western mothers using infant potty training face an uphill battle. The very concept strikes many as ridiculous, impracticable or impossible, so a mother opting for this method does not have the societal support and examples that teach, inspire and sustain mothers in traditional societies. Most women abroad have experienced infant elimination training themselves. It is and has long been the norm for them, so that women and children have a life experience of loving support from both their families and communities. Due to many generations of unwavering acceptance and positive acculturation in their societies, the attitude towards infant toilet learning is nurturing and tranquil. No one finds it unusual or strange. No doctors or psychologists frighten families with stories of psychological damage caused by infant pottying. In these cultures, babies generally don't wear diapers and are not subjected to anger, impatience, punishment or worries about keeping carpeting or fancy clothing clean and dry. They do not have to undergo diaper untraining and are free to run and play as toddlers, without interruption by boring and confining diaper changes and potty sessions.

Not only is toilet teaching from infancy basically unheard of in the United States, it also strikes many as inconvenient. With relatively few exceptions, however, toilet training is by definition inconvenient no matter when you begin.

One of the first mistakes is letting a baby become comfortable with his wetness. If he is allowed to wear his toilet by experiencing a wet diaper on a regular basis, he will grow accustomed to feeling wet and lose his natural aversion to this sensation. This will make toilet teaching a more difficult task, no matter when you begin. If you use super-absorbent disposable diapers that always make baby feel dry by absorbing the urine into a gel, he will not learn to associate urination with wetness. When he finally begins toilet learning in earnest, whether at age 15 months or 4 years, it is likely to be difficult for him to make the cause-and-effect connection between peeing and feeling wet.

Diapers, especially disposable ones, are a convenient but temporary solution to the toilet situation. We attempt to "plug up" our child's disposal system with diapers in the same way as we temporarily stop the flow from a leaking pipe. How many parents have pondered whether or not this is a caring, hygienic solution for the child? How many parents care about the effects of diapers on the environment? How many would care if they knew of an alternative to full-time diapers?

Training from infancy is time consuming, but dealing with elimination, cleanliness and toilet training take time no matter when you begin. If you plan to let your child self-train at the age of 2, 3 or 4 years (or even older—no one knows if or when a child will self-train), you will spend a lot of time changing diapers and dealing with laundry until that time comes. If you remain at home with your infant, you will be with him many hours a day anyway, so why not use some of the time to potty train instead of delaying the task? Take the time to learn and respond to his signals instead of bundling him up and ignoring his communications.

If you use diapers, remove his diaper as soon as he wets, to avoid his becoming accustomed to wetness. Whenever possible, use cloth diapers without a waterproof cover in order to immediately feel any dampness and remove the wet diaper. Let him remain bare-bottomed at intervals throughout the day. He will be more comfortable without a constant bulk between his legs. This will make it easier for him to maneuver, which in turn may speed up his learning of some motor skills. For example, if there is no diaper bulk to contend with, imagine how much easier it is for an infant trying to turn over for the very first time.

Infant potty learning, like many things in life, begins with conditioning and can be approached in a rational and scientific manner as well as an intuitive and spiritual one—or a combination of both—depending on what works best for you and your baby. The rational approach involves timing and observation of elimination patterns and baby body language. The more spiritual approach involves intuition and "tuning in" to your baby in more subtle ways. Both are covered in detail in this book. *Remember, it is teamwork, something you do together. It is not something you are doing to your baby, and it is not something your baby can do without you.* It is the forming of a mesh network, the joint achievement of a mutual state.

And never underestimate the intelligence and awareness of an infant. Another striking example demonstrating that infants are more intelligent and aware than most adults think is seen in deaf babies of deaf parents. These babies hardly make any noise, especially compared with hearing babies. Instead of crying to get their parents' attention, deaf babies use facial expressions and then learn gesturing and sign language as soon as they can coordinate their hands. The natural instinct to cry is replaced by communicating in (near) silence with the face and hands.

As they grow older, most babies dislike being held down and changed throughout the day but still love being held in-arms and receiving the attention they get during infant pottying. By responding to their natural timing and signals, you reinforce their instinctive awareness of and communication about elimination. Both of you will benefit greatly from the time you devote to this technique. If you are willing and able, your baby is ready for you.

chapter **3**

# the
# in-arms phase

T he two main phases of infant potty training are the:

- in-arms phase[6] (anytime from birth, for as long as baby needs considerable physical support at potty time)
- potty/toilet-seat phase (begins when baby can sit comfortably on a potty or toilet)

The in-arms phase is the most crucial and, for Westerners, unique part of infant pottying. Since an infant cannot sit, she should be cradled securely and comfortably in your arms over a receptacle or other toilet place for this phase.

The optimum time to begin this phase is anytime from birth through 3 to 4 months of age since this is the first window of opportunity. Starting at birth or before the 4th or 5th month generally yields faster and better results than starting at the age of 6 months or older (See Chapter 10, "Late-Starters," for starting with older babies). If you begin after 6 months, you will most likely need to modify some of the techniques. In short, there is no definite cutoff point, but typically, the earlier you start, the better.

Infant pottying is much more intense and demanding at the start, gradually becomes easier and less time consuming over the months and is often completed sooner than traditional methods. In the long run, it takes no more time than full-time diapering methods and in some cases takes (considerably) less time. But it's not about breaking any records or doing better than your neighbor or sister. It's about you and your infant entwining through mutual adoration and intrinsic involvement with each other, and unfolding from there.

The six steps of the in-arms phase of infant potty training are:

1. Choosing Your Basic Signal
2. Timing and Elimination Patterns
3. Selecting a Location and/or Receptacle
4. Positions
5. Signals and Cues
6. Understanding and Commitment

## STEP 1: Choosing Your Basic Signal

The first step involves selecting a signal to use to cue baby to go for you. Your signal can be any sound you choose. The most common signal for voiding is to imitate the sound of running water or urination, "sssss" or "pssss." For defecation, you can use a grunting or straining sound such as "hmmmm," or just use "sssss" for both forms of elimination. Some parents prefer baby talk such as "pee pee" while others like to use a sentence with recognizable voice intonation, "Do you have to pee?" Some mothers rely on the position to be the "cue de grace" and do not use any audible signal. Use whatever feels most natural and comfortable to you. Infants can learn to associate their elimination with your cues in just a few days if you start early enough.

## STEP 2: Timing and Elimination Patterns

Step 2 involves familiarization with baby's natural timing and elimination patterns. You can gain a general feeling for baby's elimination timing during one or more sessions of about 30 minutes to an hour or two, whatever feels right for you.

Select a warm, comfortable, well-lighted place for observing the child. Lay some protective material on the carpet or mattress. Suggestions include a layer of waterproof material covered with a sheet and either a few towels or a cloth diaper. If the fountain effect proves to be a problem with a baby boy during this exercise, you can put a diaper, flannel blanket or soft towel over his groin area. Bear in mind that if you cover his penis, you may have to pay closer attention to ascertain exactly when he pees.

If you find it helpful to make notations (not everyone does), you will need a pen, watch and writing paper (or copies of the form provided overleaf). Make a note of when you feed your baby. It's easier, but not essential, to start with a feeding which is not directly followed by a nap. Jot down the times you start and finish the feeding.

When baby pees or poos during and/or after the feeding, make the "sssss" sound and jot down the time. Making the "sssss" sound helps baby learn to associate your basic signal with elimination. If she makes a sound or you notice a physical body signal just before she eliminates, use this to help you anticipate future elimination. Remove the wet cloth and replace it with a clean, dry one. Repeat the process for as many times as baby pees after the feeding. The object of the exercise is to eventually use your notes to determine the frequency of your baby's need to urinate and any patterns in relation to feeding and sleeping.

If so desired, repeat the process after another feeding, but this may not be necessary since the frequency of urination is fairly regular in most babies. In general, boys pee more often than girls.

If you're observing a newborn and still recovering from delivery, or if you don't want to leave your baby (partially) unclothed for observation, another way to study your baby's elimination timing is to place a diaper on your chest, lay baby on the diaper, wait for her to go, give your basic signal when she pees or poos and jot down the time of elimination. Replace the wet or soiled cloth with a clean, dry one, and repeat this process as many times as necessary.

| OBSERVATION DATE: _____  NAME: _____ | | | |
|---|---|---|---|
| FEEDING TIME | EVENT | | NOTES |
| | PEE | POO | |
| | | | |
| | | | |
| | | | |
| | | | |
| | | | |
| | | | |
| | | | |
| | | | |
| | | | |
| | | | |
| | | | |
| | | | |
| | | | |
| | | | |
| | | | |
| | | | |

Sample Form

You can also study timing and patterns while using a sling. Baby-wearing is one of the best ways to become familiar and stay in tune with your baby's elimination timing and patterns since you know straightaway when she goes. It is especially beneficial in cold climates or rooms without sufficient heating. Some mothers keep their babies naked in the sling, carrying them skin-to-skin, which keeps baby at a perfect body temperature. If so desired, you can keep a cloth diaper under her while in the sling. It is, of course, not a requirement to keep your baby naked in the sling. Even if she is wearing some clothing and/or a cloth diaper without a waterproof cover, you will know when she goes.

As a demonstration of how quickly infants learn by association, some mothers who spend more than a day or two studying their babies' timing find that their infants learn to go in unusual places. One mother who started out by laying her baby on the changing table and making the "sssss" sound every time the little girl peed was baffled and discouraged when she later could never get her baby to go in the sink. She knew it was time for her baby to go, but the baby refused to pee in the sink. Then as soon as she lay her baby down on her back, she would pee. It finally dawned on the mother that she had inadvertently taught her daughter to pee when laying on her back rather than in-arms over the sink. A mother starting out with her 4-month-old son soon found that every time she placed him on the changing table and removed his diaper, he would immediately pee or poo—he associated both the positioning and diaper removal with a cue to eliminate.

Mothers who use their intuition to know when baby needs to go may only need to rely on timing to get started. Some may even skip this step altogether and instead rely exclusively on the intuitive connection with their babies. Trust your instincts and abilities. If you feel, have a hunch or simply *know* it is time for baby to pee, offer her a chance to go for you. Most mothers sense other things by instinct and intuition, such as when their baby is tired, hungry or ill. In a way similar to automatically knowing when to respond to these things for baby, you can help her relieve herself at the right moment too.

As you observe your baby, you will likely begin to note that there are "toilet patterns" in relation to when she eats and sleeps. Many babies urinate at fairly regular intervals, depending on the time of eating and sleeping. For example, newborns and small infants might pee once every 5–15 minutes for a number of times after a feeding. As babies grow older, they go less frequently. A 3-month-old might pee every 15–20 minutes three or four times after nursing, and then the interval between pees might increase to 30 minutes, or else baby might just pee once after 30 minutes and then not need to go again until she eats again. Other toilet patterns to expect are peeing or pooing upon waking and also during or soon after a feeding—although some babies don't need to go for 10–15 minutes after nursing.

In India, mothers non-coercively get their babies to poo first thing in the morning. "A physiologic aid for bowel training, called the gastrocolic reflex, may help predict when your baby will have a BM. A full stomach stimulates the colon to empty around 20–30 minutes after a meal. . . . Best odds for a predictable daily BM is after breakfast. Another benefit of this daily routine is that it teaches baby to listen to his bodily urges. It's a physiologic fact that bowel signals not promptly attended to will subside, and this can lead to constipation."[7]

Always remember that the timing used in infant potty training is based on baby's timing and patterns, rather than on your own. If you potty her every 15–20 minutes after feedings, it is because you have learned this from her. Even if you feel that potty visits are hit-or-miss based on an educated guess, your guess should be based on your observations and feelings about when your baby needs to go. And other factors can come into play here. For example, if baby is tired, ill or cold, she may pee more often. If in a warm climate or if dressed warmly, she may pee less frequently than usual.

Bear in mind that baby's timing and patterns will change from time to time as she grows and as her bladder capacity increases. Every so often, try waiting a little longer between toilet visits—maybe stretch it from going every 20 minutes to going every 30 minutes. If she does okay, use the new timing. If she isn't ready, go back to the earlier pattern for a while longer.

If you feed and put baby to sleep on a fairly regular schedule, it is usually easier to determine a regular timed pattern of discharge. Mothers who breastfeed on demand should bear in mind that continuous breastfeeding can at first make it tricky—especially for a beginner—to find a recognizable elimination timing pattern. This is especially true if you start with a tiny infant who is nursing and eliminating almost continuously during the first weeks of life—the bowel movements tend to be irregular for a while. A solution for this is to hold baby over a receptacle, such as a small bowl or small potty, while nursing her. Find a position that is comfortable. Later in this chapter you'll see a photo showing how to breastfeed while holding baby over a little mixing bowl. In Chapter 4, there is a photo of a potty-nursing position, with both baby and the potty oriented sideways. Or you can sit on the floor or bed with both the potty and baby facing you, wrap your legs around the potty and wrap your arms around baby as you nurse her. The key to learning baby's timing is to relate elimination to feeding and waking. An

attentive mother will instinctively sense or eventually recognize a correla-
tion between these components.

Finally, there are exceptions to every rule. Not all babies have a regular
or predictable elimination pattern, so don't be alarmed or discouraged if
you can't find a pattern. It can be a challenge for beginners to catch an elusive and enigmatic pee or poo. The first catches may seem like pure chance.
Some mothers start out by relying on the clock. Using a timer can be helpful
for this until timing becomes second nature. Others do really well the first
day or week, then seem to lose the knack for a while. Some mothers have
an easy time with pees but not poos, while others do well with poos but
can't seem to get their baby to pee for them for days or even weeks. Some
babies have very irregular or infrequent bowel movements (breastfed babies
might only poo once every 7–10 days), which can make it difficult or impossible to "score" for a while. You may have to rely more on signals, cues,
body language, intuition and/or a combination of (some of) these to first get
in sync with your baby. And later you may find yourself using some or all of
them to different degrees as your baby changes over time.

## STEP 3: Selecting a Location and/or Receptacle

Before proceeding any further, you will have to select a "toilet place" and
receptacle. For the first few days or weeks, it is advisable to use the same
place and receptacle(s) whenever possible so baby associates these with
the functions of elimination. Using different receptacles for urine and bowel
movements is acceptable (but not mandatory) for reasons of hygiene and
also because the receptacle used to catch a bowel movement may be less
accessible or less convenient to use.

A myriad of receptacles and locations are functional, and here you can
bring your creativity into play. Select whatever container and location suit
you, your child and your situation best. One of the most popular places for
urination is the bathroom sink. For peeing, you can also use the shower.
Receptacles for both urination and bowel movements include a potty, small
baking/mixing bowl, plastic rectangular basin, toilet, bidet, pet bowl, food
container, bucket (ideally with a tight-fitting lid), ice cream pail, plastic
sweater box, bedpan, chamber pot or any other catchall that works. For
boys, you can also use containers with smaller openings such as a quart
canning jar, plastic cup or (portable) urinal. If you seat your baby on a vessel, it should be "baby-bottom friendly" in terms of size, comfort and temperature. Whenever possible, containers should be rinsed or cleaned after
each use and disinfected when needed. Use mild cleaning products that do

not irritate baby's soft skin. If you live or camp in the wilderness, mother nature offers many an interesting toilet place for infants.

Some babies develop a strong preference for a specific location and/or receptacle and refuse to go anywhere else. If your baby cries or arches her back in certain places, this is one possible cause—she may prefer a different toilet place or receptacle. The easiest way to find out is to "test the waters" by trying different locations and receptacles. Most infants don't have a preference and will gladly go anywhere peaceful and warm. Some are happy using a variety of receptacles. Baby's taste in receptacles may suddenly and inexplicably change one day, so be prepared to offer options. After a while, most babies evolve to where they occasionally like a "change of scenery" and appreciate your putting their potty in varied and interesting places such as the back porch or balcony, in front of a window, near their books and toys, or in a special room.

You can also take your own preferences into account as long as your baby is content with your selection. For example, many mothers prefer the toilet since they can instantly flush the waste away without having to clean a receptacle. In addition, it is easy to hear when your baby goes in the toilet. If you use a training seat, it is convenient to carry with you when you go out.

As you venture out of the house on walks, local drives, day trips and long-distance travel, explore your surroundings for clean and comfy pit stops. In urban areas, learn which department stores offer facilities. Use your discretion in public restrooms. If you are carrying your own potty, you can use the changing table, a counter top or toilet stall. If using the toilet, you can sit on the seat and let your baby sit on your lap for warmth, sanitation, comfort and security. If your baby dislikes using a toilet or is frightened by the loud and unpredictable automatic flush (they tend to flush every time you move), you may have to resort to using the sink.

At home, I held my infant son over the bathroom wash basin when he had to pee. I aimed his penis downward so there was no mess or splashing. I washed the sink out after each use and disinfected it as needed. There was a mirror above the sink, and he enjoyed looking at our faces while we were waiting for him to pee. It was a cozy occasion to bond and communicate while holding him close to me, gazing and smiling at each other in the mirror, having him pat my face, talking to him and awaiting/achieving elimination success.

Most babies enjoy the mirror, but like everything else, this is subjective. In some cases it may prove to be (or eventually become) too distracting for a baby to watch her reflection. With every phase of infant potty teamwork, parents find that certain approaches work well for a while, then need to change as their babies change and grow. And certain approaches work with some children but not with others. *There is not a fixed way to "do" infant potty training.* Everyone progresses it in the way that works best for their own family. For many, it is an instinctive relationship that develops gradually and naturally over time. In the end, it is up to the mother or other caregiver(s) to learn, adapt to, and flow with all the nuances and changes that occur.

## STEP 4: Positions

The classic "elimination position" resembles sitting in a chair or squatting in-arms. For neonates, let baby lie flat on her back in your arms, with her head touching your chest or abdomen (depending on the height of your sink or receptacle). For both of these positions, hold baby's thighs in your hands, spreading the thighs slightly apart while "aiming" her over the sink or other toilet place. Take care not to pull her knees up too high and also not to squish or otherwise apply pressure to her belly. As baby grows, you'll need more arm space to accommodate her height, and you can cradle her in your arms by resting her back between your forearms and leaning her head against your chest. Most babies find this position relaxing. Many variations are possible. It is your responsibility to provide the following:

- comfortable, secure and relaxing position
- proper support for the neck, head and spine
- warm, hygienic and peaceful surroundings
- positive attitude

With boys, more attention is needed for aiming since urination lifts the penis. One means is to use a fingertip to aim him downward when the stream starts to rise. Another is to aim baby's body as best you can, then cup your hand to direct the stream, in effect using your palm as a splash-guard. Or you can place a container at a slight angle between your thighs or calves and direct the fountain there. With a toilet or bucket, hang baby's bottom deep enough so that the stream remains in the receptacle. Small boys, and even some girls, generally enjoy watching their stream, and this reinforces awareness. When old enough to sit well on a toilet, boys can straddle the seat further back and shoot into the bowl without assistance.

Caregivers with physical limitations can seek alternative ways to hold or support baby. If you experience back pain or if a young sibling finds baby heavy to hold in position, one solution is to hold and sit baby on a towel (for warmth and padding) which is draped over the edge of the bathtub. Another solution is to hold baby in your lap while you sit on the toilet, serving as a warm human cushion and taking the weight off your back. A variation is to sit on the toilet and hold baby between your legs. For this position, you can hold baby in either a squatting or sitting position, with her back against your abdomen or thighs. You can face either way on the toilet; some babies like to face the back of the toilet while others prefer facing forward.

Some mothers find it is easier on their backs if they squat or sit on a stool in front of the toilet and let the toilet support the weight of their baby. For this position, you can hold baby's thighs while resting your hands, elbows or arms on your knees or on the toilet seat. This allows baby to avoid contact with the cold seat, relieves pressure on your back and prevents your arms from getting tired. You can also place a small toilet seat over the larger seat and provide support in any of the ways already mentioned.

You can, of course, squat over any other type of receptacle. Parents living in rural areas often enjoy squatting outdoors with baby in-arms. If you are a passenger in a car, you can squeeze a bucket or other container tightly between your knees while holding your baby slightly above the rim. For tired arms or to avoid straining your back, you can rest your arms on your thighs or somewhere safe on the side of the vehicle.

Another popular position is to let baby stand while peeing and sometimes even while pooing—the latter being a temporary preference for some babies. This applies to both boys and girls. In the case of girls, it is usually short-lived and more likely if they have one or more brothers. And some boys don't like to stand for quite a while. One baby boy who would spit up when the slightest pressure was applied to his belly was not comfortable in the traditional squatty position. His parents found an "in-arms standing" position that applied no pressure to his belly, provided adequate support and was comfortable for all concerned.

Some babies spit up in a certain position but not in others. Standing might alleviate this. There are babies who work their abdominal muscles while trying to eliminate, and this extra pressure can cause them to spit up or even vomit. This doesn't seem to bother babies, as evidenced by their cooing and smiling during the experience, and it is generally not a cause for alarm. These clever little ones soon learn to distinguish which muscles they need to void the bladder and empty the colon, and then the problem disappears. There are also babies who spit up on a regular basis no matter what, and you simply have to wait for this phase to end.

If you find that the positions depicted in this chapter are not right for you and your baby, gently experiment until you find one that works well for both of you. Bear in mind that a favorite position can one day be unexpectedly rejected by your baby, in which case you'll need to find an alternative. And some babies are comfy and happy in a number of different positions.

Different positions are used in different societies around the world. The positions used in various lands are suited to the local customs, environment and living standards. Mothers in some lesser-developed lands typically squat outdoors or in a toilet place and hold baby in their arms, aiming the baby and the elimination away from them. Another common position involves sitting on the ground or floor with legs outstretched, forming a little seat for baby—not only for comfort and security but also to keep the child away from the mud and filth on the ground. Baby straddles her mother's legs and eliminates between the legs into the ground or in a designated area in the house. Some mothers form a little potty seat with their ankles or with the sides of their feet. After baby eliminates, the mother or caregiver buries or covers any mess with soil, sand or ashes, or else leaves it for the dogs to clean.

For baby-wearing mothers, the simplest solution is to quickly remove baby from the sling, aim her away from the mother, then return her to the sling after she has eliminated. For Vietnamese lap babies, mothers walk to the edge of the porch or home and pee baby away from the dwelling. If a simple bathroom consisting of four walls, a floor and a bucket is used, as is typical in India, the mother squats with baby in her arms, then rinses the waste down the drain. While traveling by bus, a mother will exit with her baby at bus stops and pee her along the side of the road. In family trucks or tractors, baby is held in position to pee out the back or to the side.

Many Chinese and Eskimos use split pants on their babies. This enables parents to hold the baby in a squatting position just above the ground as she eliminates. Once the child can squat on her own, she can independently squat and go on her own. In arctic climates, caregivers catch elimination in a can or other container, then toss it outside the igloo. Accidents are of little concern since excreta can be buried in the snow.

As your infant gets older and stronger, you will find different ways to provide the necessary support until finally she is strong enough sit on her potty unassisted. A series of photos depicting positions, receptacles and locations popularly used with Westerners follows. For photos and descriptions of positions, locations and receptacles used in non-Western societies, see Parts 3 and 4.

*Laurie Boucke*

3 months old — Classic squatting position for both mother and baby. Caregiver squats. Baby's head and neck are supported by caregiver's chest and arm, baby's back rests against adult's knees. Baby is held in position by the thighs. In Western countries, it is more common for the mother to stand at the sink, holding baby in the same position.

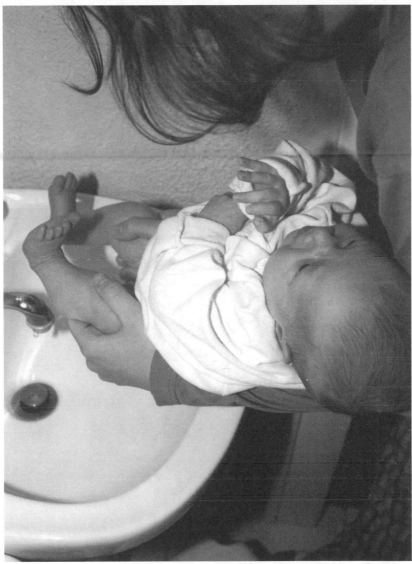

*Dana Pace*

Newborn Adaline, just 3 weeks old, making eye contact
as she rests comfortably in her mother's arms.

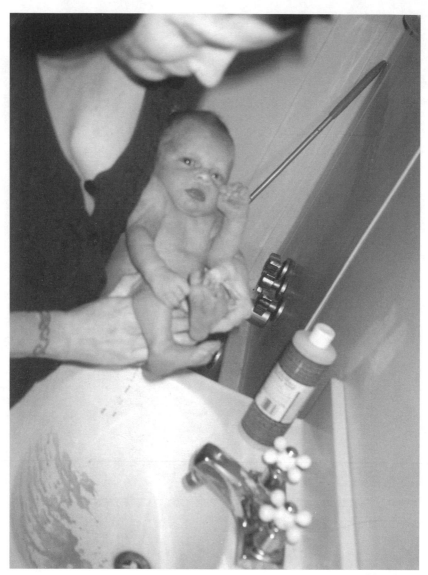

*Matt Jasper*

Little newborn Albion has "that look" on his face
and is already filling the sink at age 2 weeks . . .

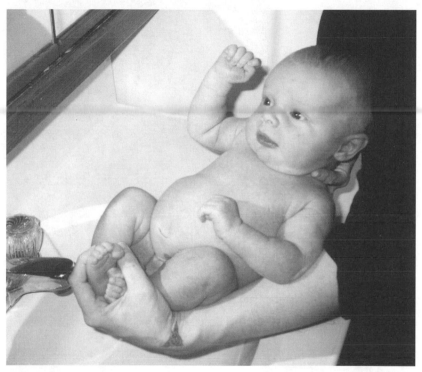

*Matt Jasper*

For newborns, it may be more comfortable to rest baby on one arm
while grasping his feet with the same arm
and supporting his head with the other hand.
Here 3-week old Albion is in a more laid-back pose, admiring
himself in the mirror. His mother discovered it was a good idea
to hold his feet together because:
(a) holding him under each thigh was making his legs turn purple and
(b) it was easier to hold his legs up and aim his stream downward.

*Tom Griggs*

2 weeks old — Holding a small baking bowl under Sara's bottom allows her to nurse uninterrupted while her mother becomes familiar with her timing and elimination patterns.

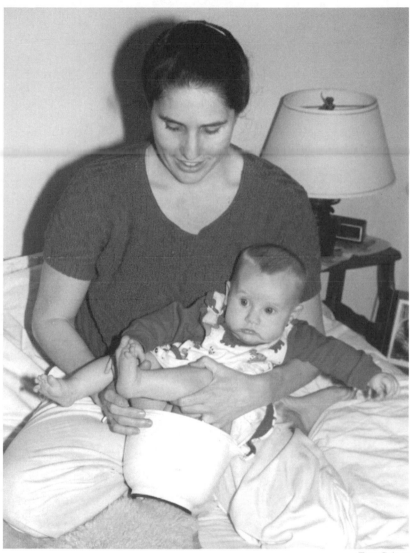

*Tom Griggs*

5 months old — Sara has graduated to the medium-sized baking bowl.
She has a look of concentration on her face as she poos in the baking bowl.

*Laurie Boucke*

Waiting for 4-month-old baby sister to go.

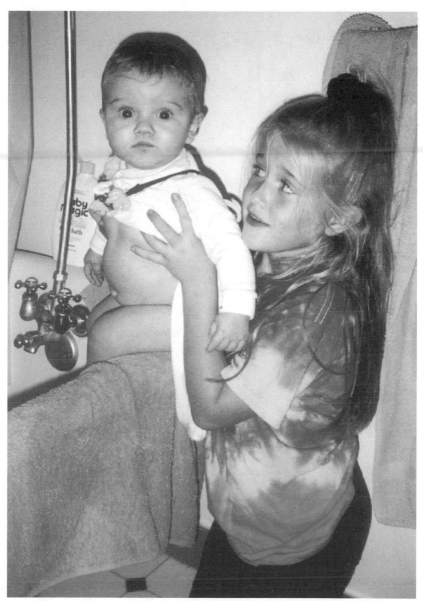

*Vanessa Lorentzen*

Siblings can also help.
In cases such as this where baby's weight is a concern, one solution is to use the bathtub rim as a support when it's time to pee (works better with boys!).

*Laurie Boucke*

Canadian Kitty's 4-month-old son in mid-pee amid nature's perfect potty place
in the Rocky Mountains. The squatting position helps alleviate back strain
and can also be used indoors, when holding baby over a receptacle.

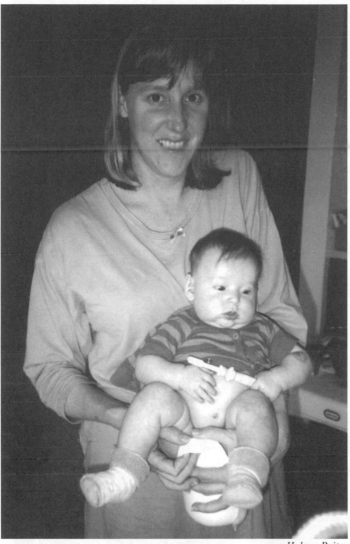

*Holger Reiter*

"Potty walking" — Holding 3-month-old Erika on her tiny potty.
The receptacle is an insert potty from a larger potty chair. Erika rests comfortably against
her mother's chest. Extra support and security are afforded by her mother's arms.

*Vanessa Lorentzen*

4 months old — Looking in the mirror is great fun!
Zion's favorite position is "in-arms standing" rather than squatting.

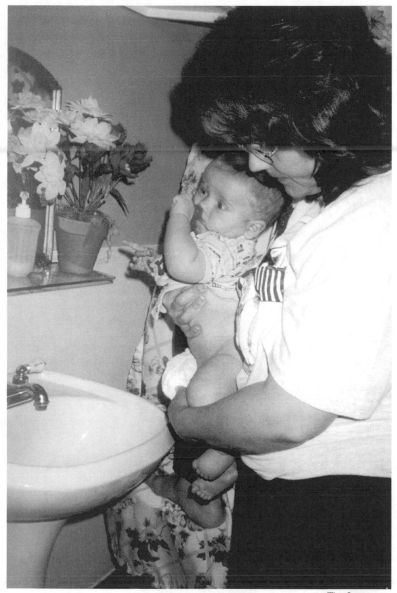

*Tim Lorentzen*

4 months old — Zion peeing in his preferred position.
By age 8 months, Zion was using just 1–2 diapers a day
and frequently remained dry all day.

Multitasking!

This 4-month-old baby girl is equally content with a potty held between her mother's legs (right) and . . .

*Shivalila*

*Shivalila*

. . . a potty on the ground (left)

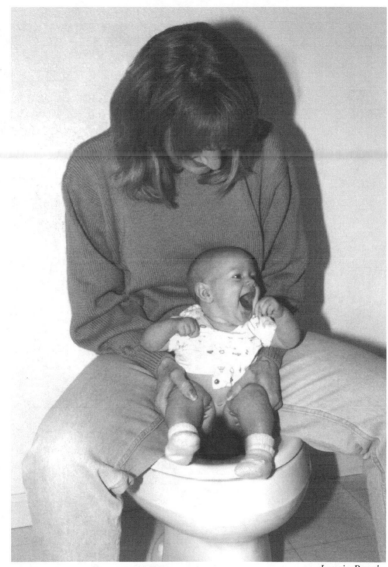

*Laurie Boucke*

This 4-month-old baby is more than happy to demonstrate how she can use the "big kids' potty" (with a little help from her "domestic engineer" mom)

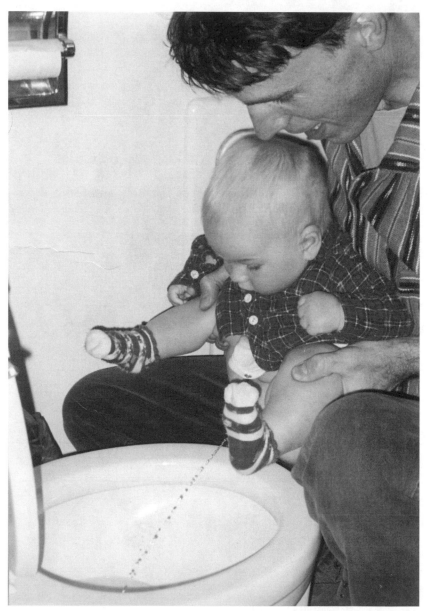

*Tom Strawn*

5-month-old Aidan is right on target.

## STEP 5: Signals and Cues

The next step is for caregiver and baby to develop the ability to read and respond to each other's cues and clues. This can be done on various levels and differs from child to child and parent to parent. In this phase, you continue to teach baby to associate certain things with elimination time and strive to learn her own particular signals. You become more communicative, coordinate your behavior with each other, and develop a sensitive and loving responsiveness as the following exchange of information takes place:

- Based on baby's signals and/or timing, cue her just before or during elimination.
- Baby (eventually) informs you in advance of when she needs to go.

The reciprocal sharing of information and feelings funnels itself into a positive feedback loop that fluctuates and flows at its own sweet tempo.

### Signals from Caregiver to Baby . . .

Pick a time when you think your baby might need to go. If helpful, you can refer to your notes for this. The important thing to remember is that a baby will not usually respond to your signals if she doesn't need to pee or poo. For many babies, the most predictable times to eliminate are upon waking first thing in the morning, upon waking up from a long nap, while nursing or a certain amount of time after nursing or eating.

When you think or feel it is a likely time for baby to eliminate, take her to the toilet place and give your signal. You will be amazed how quickly she learns to associate your signal with elimination, especially if you are consistent. Soon you can start getting her to go for you.

The main types of signals that infants respond to are:

- vocal or verbal cues ("sssss" or "do you have to pee?")
- physical cues (in-arms position, location, receptacle, etc.)
- intuitive cues
- manual cues such as gestures or sign language

If you are consistent and fairly intense at first, your baby will associate your specific vocal, verbal and physical signals with toilet activity within a week or less. If it's time for her to go but there is no response to your signal, try running a little water in the sink or bathtub.

The sound of running water may prompt her to go. You can also try running a little water over her feet, dipping her feet in water or sprinkling a little water on her tummy. The water can be warm or else slightly cooler than her body temperature but not cold. If you think it is time for your baby to urinate but she is resisting, the sound, temperature change and contact with water will help her relax and urinate. If she still doesn't go, it means she doesn't need to go. Try again in 5–10 minutes or whenever her natural timing suggests.

In general, you should not have to signal baby for longer than 1–2 minutes. If there is no reaction, she probably doesn't need to go. Do not continue to hold baby in position unless she is comfy, happy, relaxed or wants to remain there. Sometimes she will want to remain in your arms longer, in which case you can continue trying to get her to go. If she resists and you cannot quickly distract and relax her, respect her wishes and try again later.

The concept of intuitive cues may sound unusual at first, but this develops naturally and without much effort as you become more and more conscious of the extent of your baby's amazing awareness, and as you awaken and open up to her elimination needs. Manual cues can be started as early as you like. For a detailed explanation of the various types of signals and cues from caregiver to baby, see Chapter 5, "Signals and Cues."

## Baby's Signals and Cues . . .

You'll need to learn to read your baby's cues and signals. You can do this by observing her natural timing and/or monitoring her body language and other cues. These cues may be audible, inaudible, visible or invisible. The main types of signals that babies send are:

- body language
- vocal cues
- intuitive cues
- manual cues such as gestures or sign language

Body language is the easiest way for most parents to read their baby's cues. If you observe your baby just before and also during elimination, you'll start to notice physical indicators. Then watch for baby's body language and natural timing to coincide.

The easiest cues to read are the vocal ones. For example, babies typically grunt before and/or during defecation. Infants too young to consciously babble or speak sometimes signal impending or completed elimination by way of other vocal sounds such as crying, yelling, squealing, gurgling, cooing, chirping or breathing with a sigh or whimper.

Intuitive cues are hard for many Westerners to detect but are prevalent in cultures where mothers are able to sense exactly when to pee and poo their babies. These women are well bonded and in tune with their little ones. They take a casual approach to toilet training; if baby goes in the wrong place, they clean it up without emotion and get back to what they were doing. Once you start paying attention to your baby's elimination and responding to those needs, your instincts will be heightened and the intuitive connection and bond with your baby will deepen.

Silent signals, such as hand gestures, are most often used by deaf infants or infants of deaf parents. These babies begin what is known as "manual babbling" around the same age hearing babies start with vocal babbling. For a detailed explanation of signals and cues from baby to caregiver, see Chapter 5, "Signals and Cues."

## STEP 6: Understanding and Commitment

After you have tried and fully understood the first five steps of the in-arms phase, the next step is to determine whether or not you are prepared to do what it takes to move forward with this method of toilet learning. You'll need to make a further commitment and an increased investment of time if you decide to continue. From this point on, it will be necessary to observe and adhere to baby's natural rhythm whenever reasonably possible. If you do not have the opportunity to take baby to the toilet place throughout much of the day, strive to spend a minimum of one hour a day using this method, preferably at the same time everyday. Even if you can only concentrate on it in relation to a few feedings a day, this can keep her elimination awareness alive.

Some parents start by making a halfhearted attempt, perhaps due to skepticism, self-doubt or fearing a lack of time to do it properly, only to be amazed and pleasantly surprised at how well their babies respond. They soon find themselves using the method on a regular basis and breeze through the process. Others have a difficult time synchronizing with their babies from the very start. It may take several days or even a few weeks to be able to coordinate with their babies' timing and signals. It's fine to ease your way into this gradually. There is no hurry. It is going to take time and practice. Your confidence will build as you start to make more and more catches in the potty.

It is important to always remember that an infant will automatically urinate whenever her bladder is full. In no case should you direct anger at her if you arrive too late to take her to the toilet, nor should you feel guilty for not being on time. Both baby and caregiver need to be relaxed while using this natural method.

There is nothing complex or mysterious about infant pottying. This book contains a lot of information and tips. The idea is for you to pick and choose whatever helps and encourages both you and baby. Keep this thought with you throughout your pottying days: *Whatever works best is the best approach.* And your approach will need to change over time, as your baby grows and changes. During this very special time of life, you'll experience the thrill of discovering new and inventive ways to connect. And each time things change, remember that whatever works best is the best approach.

## Expectations

The goal of infant pottying isn't to speed toilet learning. A lot of parents start out expecting too much. Expecting too much too soon can lead to giving up. The best approach is to not have any time-critical expectations. Deadlines and expectations set us up for disappointment and feelings of failure if our child doesn't meet our arbitrary goals. In some situations, this leads to pressuring the child and ourselves, and is thus counterproductive. One mother put it succinctly, "The biggest lesson parenting has taught me is not to expect but to discover."

Of course, certain basic expectations must be in place before you begin, such as "infant potty training is possible," but aside from the obvious starting premises, it is unrealistic to expect anything specific at any stage. For example, no one should expect to get most pees and poos in the potty for many months. Likewise, newcomers may go days with few or no "catches." Infant potty training takes many months to complete—in most cases, longer than a year—and there are plenty of rewards along the way. Some babies catch on quickly; others take longer, but they all make the journey at their own innate rate, and the best you can do is be there for them when they need you and when you are able to assist without yourself becoming too overwhelmed.

Each child is unique. There is no way to know at what age a child will be toilet trained or when a baby will begin to consciously signal her elimination needs. It is possible that she won't signal you until she is nearing completion of toilet training and that this might happen around the age of 24 months. If this is the case, you can use the other tools discussed in this chapter: timing, patterns and intuition. It doesn't matter how you figure out your baby's toilet times. The important point to remember is this: If a child doesn't give clear signals, you can still move forward as a team.

The fact that a child doesn't give conscious signals or take the initiative to potty does not mean that she is unaware or that you have done something wrong. Rather, it is the pace and design of her natural development. If your baby doesn't get upset by going in a diaper, there is nothing wrong with this fact either. Some babies just naturally aren't bothered by dirty diapers. Others are so busy all the time (especially once mobile) that they don't notice or care. And of course, many *do* care and can't stand it. It's an individual thing. By dropping fixed and rigid expectations, new channels of appreciation and communication will open and flourish.

Parents who use this method can easily fall into the trap of being too hard on themselves. It's easy to feel like have failed when you miss one or more pees or poos. If you reverse the way you view this à la "Is the glass half empty or half full?" it is easier to appreciate your efforts. If you catch just one or a few pees a day, don't be discouraged. Things will pick up in due course. Realistic expectations include an increase in communication, responsiveness, hygiene and bonding from the start, along with a gradual gaining of control over the months.

Take care that you do not become too obsessed with pottying. Keep a balance in your activities. If you get to the point that you feel you can hardly do anything else but potty your baby, you are trying too hard. If you find that you are constantly looking for signs and signals, or that you are imagining that every little movement or sound is a signal, you are overdoing it and headed for burnout. If you constantly worry about when you will finish, you will miss a lot of the "magic" and likely become frustrated. If you are thrilled at each little deposit in the potty and enjoying the closeness with your baby, you are gaining far more than potty progress.

## No Showing Off

Once you start using this method on a regular basis, it will be tempting to try to impress friends and relatives by giving live demos with your adorable and amazing baby. You will soon learn that showing off is a no-no. Your baby is so in tune with you and her potty routine that she will sense a change or disruption in communication if you suddenly try to show her off to others. If she wakes up from a nap to find your guests oohing and aahing at her while you try to get her to pee for you, she is likely to be distracted by the people staring at her and lose her connection with you and her elimination functions. In short, it is generally best to keep toilet visits private and relaxed.

## Squirts and Spurts

Many infants urinate and defecate in 2–3 intermittent squirts and spurts. Once you're aware of this pattern, it's easy to notice. If possible, avoid diapering or dressing baby until she has truly finished going. If the wait between spurts is long and baby is impatient, take a short break, then bring her back to the sink, potty or other toilet place in time to complete elimination. If she has diarrhea, a cold or is suffering from another ailment, do not expect to capture all the spurts and squirts in a receptacle until she has recovered.

There are a variety of ways the squirt phenomenon can happen. The "warning pee" involves letting out a few drops of pee as a signal that more pee is about to follow. You'll either feel the warmth and dampness or see a small trickle of pee. This gives you time to take your baby to the sink, potty or toilet and demonstrates that babies gain some bladder control early in life. Or you could be dressing your baby after she pees for you, and she might start to signal you by crying. Try giving her the opportunity to go again before you dress her.

Other manifestations include the "pre-poop pee" (starting to push the poo out first sends out a little pee) and the "post-poop pee" (whereby baby invariably has to pee shortly or several minutes after pooping, whether or not she peed before the poo). And some experience the dynamic duo or tandem pee and poo.

"Skid marks" can be caused by releasing gas or else by pooing in stages. The spotting can go on for several months. If your baby is a poop dribbler, try longer poo sessions on the potty, or else come back for a second round after a short break. You can also try wiping. If you wipe your baby after what seems like the end of a poo, this might stimulate another spurt. If you don't wipe, you may end up waiting 5 minutes or longer—even up to 20 or 30 minutes—until the next spurt or "explosion" (newborns!) happens. If your baby is a poo spurter, the easiest way to tell if she has truly finished is to look at her anus in the mirror. If it is still a little open or contracting, she probably hasn't finished. When the complete bowel movement is out, the anus will close firmly and remain that way. When your baby has truly finished with a BM, wiping will not stimulate more evacuation.

Diapers can accentuate squirts and spurts. This can be especially baffling for mothers who use a lot of diapers. It is not uncommon for a diapered baby to poo (or pee) a little, then hold back when she feels the sensation of excrement (or urine) against her body. Her mother dutifully changes the diaper, then soon finds poo in the clean diaper. She changes baby again, and shortly thereafter notices a familiar red-faced grimace or perhaps hears grunting or gas passing, and ends up with yet another poopy diaper. This cycle can continue through more changes. Babies (including newborns) who are allowed to eliminate freely into a receptacle sometimes learn to regulate their BMs within a few weeks or months, to the point that they have just one or two poos a day instead of a continual stream of small poops.

## Changes in Timing

Sometimes due to illness, a change in diet, an emotional situation (arrival of a new baby, an upset in the home, etc.), travel, a change in routine (moving, hosting out-of-town guests, spending the night outside your home, etc.), milestones or any major life change, baby's elimination timing may fluctuate. Do not feel discouraged. A regular or recognizable rhythm will likely return once baby's situation is back to normal. The only time this will not be the case is when baby outgrows one pattern and adopts a new one. This, of course, will happen from time to time throughout infancy and toddlerhood. When this occurs, tune into your little one for clues, then observe and adjust to her new rhythms.

It is normal for the body to sometimes deviate from its usual pace on a temporary basis. Someone may occasionally feed your baby when you do not know about it, such as a well-meaning "older" toddler or grandparent (sound familiar?). On other occasions, baby may happen to "find" some food and in this way, unbeknownst to you, eat between meals. A sick, distraught or hysterical child's body rhythms usually go out of synchronization for a while. In such situations, expect to "miss" some pees and poos. These are reasons why it is helpful to monitor baby's body language and listen to your instincts, in addition to adhering to her natural timing.

Travel can disrupt baby's regular routine, especially if she misses or is awakened from naps. Travel sometimes throws parents off schedule more than it affects baby's natural timing. If it's not too disruptive or stressful, it's fine to continue with infant potty training while traveling. If this proves too difficult, use a diaper on such occasions. I managed to persevere in cars and airplanes; at airports and train stations; on camping trips and picnics; at family functions; in department stores and other shops; in foreign countries and hotels—in short, everywhere I took my child. When traveling or visiting friends, take along a small vessel. For children old enough to use a potty, take along a portable potty.

Timing can change with the occurrence of developmental milestones such as learning to crawl, walk and talk. Teething can throw things off course for a while. Many babies pee more often while teething. For more details on all of the above situations, see "Potty Pauses and Potty Strikes" in the next chapter.

If you experience some difficult days, the best way to break through is to remain "cool, calm and collected"—don't let it get to you. Keep an even keel and you'll find your way. If you are feeling frustrated, angry or guilty, perhaps you are trying too hard. You may reach a plateau and feel "stuck" for a while. *Infant potty training is not an exact science.* We adults tend to want things to progress logically and uninterrupted, but infant pottying moves more as a subtle ebb and flow where the tide is always slowly but surely advancing at its own unpredictable pace. It takes trial and error, and improves with experience and practice. If you try this with more than one child, you'll be more confident with the next. As with all aspects of child-rearing, it tends to get easier and you are more relaxed with each additional child.

As long as you are receptive to communication from your baby and remain patient and relaxed during the in-arms phase, your baby will be responsive to your prompts, providing it is (nearly) time to eliminate. Bearing in mind that there are bound to be "accidents" and mismatches in communication between you and your infant, if you can for the most part maintain a positive and patient mindset, you will create and sustain a bond of mutual understanding, knowledge and trust between you and your baby.

## Going Out Diaperless

Some mothers don't dare take their babies out diaperless, fearing embarrassing accidents. As with all other facets of infant potty training, going diaperless is a matter of preference and "what works best." If you are going out and she hasn't peed recently, potty your baby before departing. Offer her elimination opportunities at logical times when you are out. Devise a plan for finding toilet places, whether it be outdoors or in public facilities. If you are driving, take a receptacle in the car. Take your preferred equipment—a portable potty, child-size toilet seat or other device. Some mothers prefer to simply carry a diaper and hold their baby over the diaper at toilet times. Select whatever works best in a car, airplane, train or bus. If you are walking or cycling, become familiar with your surroundings so you can quickly find a toilet place. When pottying in shops or restaurants, you can seat your baby on the potty on top of the changing table or take your child-sized toilet seat along for use on the adult toilet. Your potty "route and routine" will soon become second nature and not require a lot of strategic planning.

Many mothers find that they are more attentive and more in tune with their babies when they go out—especially if wearing baby in a sling or other body carrier—without the usual household distractions. They find that they miss significantly fewer infant eliminations when outside the home. And some babies will do their best to "hold it" when out and about. Many will simply refuse to pee if they are in a car seat. If this happens, don't make your child wait too long as it could cause a bladder infection. On the other hand, there are mothers and babies who temporarily disconnect from their elimination awareness when they are out, due to involvement with their surroundings—and some babies at first always pee in their car seats. If this proves to be the case for you, you may prefer to use diapers on outings, until you feel more confident, tuned in and sure of yourself and your baby.

If you are using a sling and want to go diaperless but would like some extra security, place a diaper or soft cloth under baby in the sling. No matter how you are transporting baby, if so desired, it is fine for her to wear training pants or a diaper, either with or without a waterproof cover. The important thing is for you to feel relaxed and not worry about impending accidents, all the while being mindful of baby's elimination communication.

## Dress for Success

Use clothing that is quickly and easily removable. Expect accidents and messes with whatever styles you use. The way you dress your baby is a matter of personal preference and a lifestyle choice and can range from naked to bare-bottomed, from training pants to diapers, from onesie or dress to stretchy shorts or pants with an elastic waist. Climate and seasons are factors to be considered. Although easier to implement in warm climates, infant potty training is used in all climates around the globe, including the coldest places on earth. Find ways to modify and adapt to your local weather. To save money, consider visiting thrift shops and garage sales. Here is a short list of some of the most popular and economical items of clothing for infants:

- Homemade pants—use wool or warm fleece for winter and cool fabrics such as cotton knit for summer; trace around some baby sweatpants or PJ bottoms and use elastic in the waistband
- Poquito Pants—side-snap cotton underpants custom made in sizes to fit all babies, from tiny newborns to stocky toddlers; http://wonderbabydesigns.com
- Snug-to-Fit Diapers—one size fits babies from 8–30 pounds
- Knit pants—for cooler weather; if helpful, turn inside out so seams don't irritate baby's skin
- Chinese open-crotch pants—for home use and warmer weather; make your own, buy from www.weebees.com or check the links at www.timl.com/ipt for more options such as the "discreet Chinese pants."

The most complete online shop for "all things IPT" is called The EC Store. Here you can find tiny cotton training pants (newborn sizes and up) and other hard-to-find clothing, small potties including a portable transparent potty, attachable toilet seats for infants and toddlers, books on infant potty training/elimination communication, a variety of waterproof pads for nighttime and naps, baby carriers, gentle cleaning products, and more. Use this link to visit The EC Store www.theecstore.com.

If you like to see before you buy or are anxious to meet other IPT families, the nonprofit organization Diaper Free Baby has a list of playgroups and mentors who can be contacted in many locations around the world. In addition to being able to check out clothing, potties and more, you can also see demos of how to hold and potty your small infant in-arms, ask any questions you have, and learn from more experienced parents and babies. Check the DFB website for further details at www.diaperfreebaby.org.

Another good source of information and links is the Infant Potty Training Webring at www.timl.com/ipt. (Note: that's "timl" with the letter L.) Here you can find the latest links for IPT websites and online shops selling small training pants, open pants, specialized IPT clothing, cloth diapers, woolens and other useful items. This web page is translated into several languages.

chapter **4**

# the
# potty phase

The potty phase begins when baby can sit comfortably on a potty or toilet—at first with moderate "loving live support" during the transition, then later on his own—and continues until he completes toilet training. This chapter covers both:

- unstable sitters, for babies who cannot yet sit proficiently on their own and who need some physical support to steady them on the potty or toilet
- stable sitters

## Unstable Sitters

Many parents start using a potty before their babies can sit well on their own. Since potties are generally designed for toddlers rather than infants, small babies may at first need support while they are on the potty. The coziest and safest way to assure baby remains comfortably and securely on the potty is to support him with your hands or arms and let him lean against your chest. This will keep him steady and secure, prevent him from falling in or off the potty and be reminiscent of the in-arms phase. It will also allow you to focus on him and notice the moment he eliminates.

It is not easy to find a potty that fits a tiny baby bottom since most potties are designed for bigger bottoms. Two brands that have models small enough for infants are BabyBjörn® and Graco. More models are available in Europe. If you use the toilet, BabyBjörn®, Flip-N-Flush, Graco, Cushie-Tushie and others sell attachable child-sized seats that fit dinky bottoms. You can find these products online.

The potty you select should be readily available. When you start this phase, it's a good idea to either have more than one or else move the potty from room to room with baby. This is in order to avoid any unnecessary delay at this stage. In many cultures, tiny children simply squat and go, on the spot. The fact that they don't have to waste precious seconds looking for a potty or bathroom is one reason these children toilet train so young. Learning to go to a specific room (the bathroom) is something that can be accomplished at a later time.

Small children sitting on a full-sized toilet, even one with a smaller seat attached, need constant supervision and companionship. If left alone, they could fall off or into the toilet. Most small children need help descending from the toilet when they are finished. A footstool can be helpful in this regard and also provide support for his feet while sitting on the toilet. Children unfamiliar with a toilet may at first fear that they will be flushed away. Others are frightened by the sound of the toilet flushing as they sit on it. Still others imagine that monsters or strange creatures live in a toilet and can attack them from behind, so to speak, until they grow accustomed to an adult toilet.

On the other hand, many children enjoy graduating to the big toilet that everyone else in the house uses. These children are usually content to use a detachable child-size toilet seat and enjoy flushing the toilet. An alternative use of the big toilet seat, especially for small children, is for the mother to sit on the toilet seat and hold baby in her lap, aiming baby so that his

*Laurie Boucke*

Supporting 4½-month-old Sophie on the potty.
Stability is provided by mother's arms clasped at the front of baby's chest.
(Trickle Treat playgroup, San Jose, California)

*Laurie Boucke*

Supporting 5-month-old Sacha on the potty.
Stability is provided in two ways:
1) baby supported by mother's chest and
2) mother steadies baby's legs in position.
(Trickle Treat playgroup, San Jose, California)

*Gabi Reichert*

Supporting 5-month-old Amy on the potty
Polly is on father's lap. Stability is provided in two ways:
1) baby supported by father's arm and shoulder and
2) father steadies baby in position with his hands.
(Bubenheim, Germany)

Potty on mother's lap.
Mother supports baby around
baby's chest and waist.

*Gunter Reichert*

Potty rests on sofa between
mother's legs. Baby's back is
supported by mother's chest and
arm while mother's hands
balance baby on the potty.

*Gunter Reichert*

Supporting 5-month-old on potty.

*Lois Baas*

17-month-old Zachary fending for himself.

elimination goes directly into the toilet. This way he is sitting comfortably and securely on the big toilet, using mom as a warm cushion. A variation on the big toilet theme is for mom and baby to sit facing the back of the toilet, with baby seated comfortably on his mother's legs and between mother and the toilet tank (This applies to American toilets which have a toilet tank with flat surface at the back but may not be the case abroad). Some babies feel more secure facing the toilet tank rather than an open space at the front of the toilet. In addition, they can place a toy or book on the toilet tank. And as discussed earlier, another option is for the caregiver to hold baby in-arms while squatting in front of or standing over the toilet.

Babies typically graduate easily from the in-arms phase to a potty or toilet. The same basic method used during the in-arms phase works as you start the potty phase, the only changes being (a) a change in receptacle, (b) a change in position—sitting rather than in-arms squatting and (c) a possible change in location of the receptacle. At first you will likely need to continue tuning in and monitoring his timing, signals, body language and/or other communications in order to get him to the potty on time. Once baby is accustomed to the potty, you can gradually phase out signaling him to eliminate since he will understand that this is the purpose of the potty.

Make potty time as easy and simple as possible. Avoid clothing that will slow down the process. Buttons, snaps, buckles, zippers and tight-fitting outfits can cause delay and anticipatory accidents. The idea is for baby to be free to go as soon as you know it's time for him to go, or as soon as he signals you.

Find quick and easy ways to maintain good toilet hygiene. Never leave a small child alone at toilet time, as he may decide to sample his own excrement while you aren't looking. For quick rinsing of baby, potty, toilet, diapers, liners, clothing or bedding, install a water sprayer in the bathroom—either at the sink (if you want warm water) or else link directly to the toilet water supply.

As your baby becomes more aware of his environment and more able to explore his surroundings, he may at times be difficult to take to the potty or may forget to signal when he has to go—a situation that arises with most methods of toilet training. The solution is to stay connected, communicate, take him to the potty on time and be sure he is comfortable and relaxed. Use fun and creative ways to keep him seated long enough, while maintaining a balance between the following:

- Keep baby happy and entertained at potty time.
- Don't make unreasonable, ridiculous concessions or bribes to keep him on the potty or toilet.
- Don't require him to stay on the potty too long.

Since each parent and baby pair has different and individual needs, the more resourceful and creative you can be, the better. For example, during the transition-to-potty period, you may want to nurse your baby on or over the potty, just as you did during the in-arms phase.

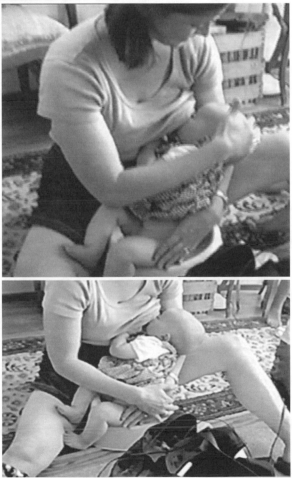

*Laura Diane Moore (from video)*

Nursing a 4½-month-old on the potty.

## Potty Comfort

Sitting on the potty or toilet should be as comfy as possible. Assess your overall situation and make any adjustments that will improve baby's comfort and level of contentment. If you live in a cold climate, for example, the awaiting potty or toilet seat is likely to be cold. Babies do not like being plopped onto a cold seat. This can cause them to dislike toilet time and rebel. Keep the potty or child's toilet seat near a source of heat such as a floor heating vent, or find another way to ensure that it is at body temperature or a little warmer. Other possibilities include placing a hot water bottle, heating pad, electric blanket, flannel diaper or other soft cloth on the potty. You can also warm it with your thigh, keep your hands between your baby and the cold seat, or hold baby in-arms above the seat. Some other aspects of potty comfort are the size, height, shape and seat diameter. These are discussed in "Selecting a Potty," later this chapter.

For most, sitting on a potty is relaxing and comfortable. It is certainly easier—since it requires less pushing—for a baby to poo into a potty or other receptacle than while sitting in a diaper seated on his rear end or while lying on his back or stomach. In addition, some mothers report that infant pottying relieves constipation and indigestion problems. A teenage mother named Linda started sitting her 8-month-old on the potty out of desperation, due to serious constipation problems. Not only did the constipation problem cease for the most part, but much to Linda's surprise, her infant never pooed in her diaper from the day they started using the potty.

An open-door policy helps children feel relaxed about visiting the potty or toilet. Familiarity with toilet use by others via live demos on the big toilet—dad for boys, mom for girls and siblings for siblings—creates a comfort level when small children are first introduced to the toilet. It is natural for children to want to imitate their older family members. The mother of a 6-month-old boy explains, "He loves to go with visual encouragement. His dad demonstrates, his brothers demonstrate and he loves it. He will usually go while they are demonstrating, even if it's just a quick pee. It has shown me that he can go when he wants to."[8]

## Genital Groping

Small children tend to occasionally grope and explore their genitals to some degree when sitting on a potty or toilet. A baby boy will typically touch his penis before or during urination. In fact, once he understands why he is on the potty and what he is supposed to do there, a small boy also figures out that touching his penis makes him pee sooner than just sitting there. It is not uncommon for a boy to use this trick to speed up the process so he can get on with other activities. For many boys, this is a passing phase. There is no need to be alarmed, and it is not good to react with negativity or morality.

Every male, once toilet trained, touches his penis in order to urinate. This is a normal part of urination for all males. There is nothing sexual or perverted about it. It is conceivable that a little boy's discovery and groping of himself on the potty is in part a precursor to normal male toilet behavior in that the little boy will eventually hold his penis each time he urinates.

Once he has peed, his interest will often shift to other things. If he continues to grope himself, you can either let him off the potty (if he is finished), or if you know he has not finished using the potty, gently distract him. Examples of ways to shift his attention include playing hand games such as Pat-a-cake or Itsy-bitsy Spider, playing clapping games or placing a book, toy, radio, gadget or anything else of interest in his lap. A sibling, friend, caretaker or pet can make a sudden appearance to divert his attention. The same distraction techniques apply to girls, although girls are less likely to engage in much genital exploration.

## Stable Sitters

Once baby can sit steadily on his own, you no longer need to physically support him on the potty or toilet. Although he is becoming less dependent on you, your presence, commitment and care are still essential.

As he begins to walk on his own and gains more bladder and bowel control, one of the last aspects of the potty phase is for him to learn and remember to pull down his pants at potty time. This task, along with wiping, can require fairly sophisticated coordination, and these are often the last hurdles to attaining complete toilet independence.

Families living in warm climates, rural areas or the wilderness often let their babies remain bare-bottomed or naked during part or all of the day. They find it simplifies and speeds up toilet learning. For one thing, it eliminates the problems of dealing with fasteners and pulling pants up and down. Using this method of toileting does not mean your baby has to run around naked. If you choose for your baby to be bare-bottomed, that is fine, but it is not a requirement for infant potty training. Many families use part-time diapers and/or training pants on their babies.

This chapter could also be called "The Potty or Squatty Phase" since families in Asia, Africa and many other places typically do not use a potty or toilet with their babies. Families in these areas live a relatively simple, natural and/or primitive lifestyle compared to life in the West and teach their babies to squat and go in allocated toilet places. Using a potty and toilet is one way the infant potty technique has been adapted to a Western lifestyle.

## Selecting a Potty

There are many factors to take into consideration when selecting a potty for children under 1 or 2 years of age. Choose a suitable size for your child. The potty should be of the correct dimensions to fit baby's anatomy. Bear in mind the following when making your selection:

- height
- seat diameter
- seat shape
- stability
- portability
- transparency

### Height

Most potties are designed for older and bigger children than your baby. His feet should rest squarely on the floor for comfort, support, security and extra pushing power. If his feet cannot reach the floor and his legs stick out straight, this position can eventually reduce or cut off the circulation to his legs and feet, causing discomfort or other problems. The weight of dangling feet and legs can cause his rectal muscles to tighten, making pooing difficult or even leading to constipation.

He should be able to sit down directly onto his potty, without using a step and without having to climb up onto it. If he is in a hurry to reach the potty, he could injure himself using a step. Climbing up onto a full-sized toilet for the first time can be frightening and dangerous for some children; however, many little ones are so glad to be invited and allowed on the big toilet that they don't hesitate at all.

### Seat Diameter

The seat should be of small diameter. Ideally, your child should be able to sit comfortably with a straight back at all times. Be certain that his buttocks does not sink into the potty, as this is not good for

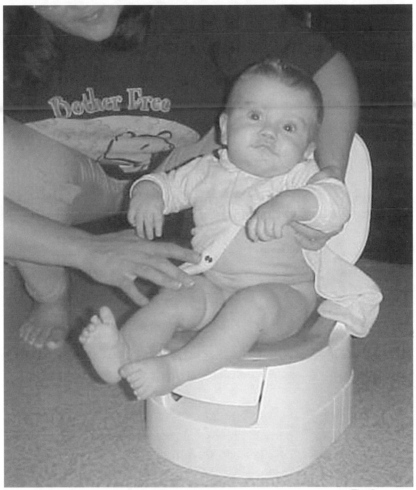

*Tim Lorentzen*

Concentrating on success —
The potty is too large for this 6-month-old baby boy because:
(1) his legs cannot reach the floor for support and pushing power
(2) the circulation in his legs can be reduced or cut off.

his spine and can be unhygienic. Smaller babies will need to be supported and held in place by their caregivers.

Some potties come with two sizes of seat: a tiny one and a larger one. These are fine, but not necessary unless you plan to have your child use the potty instead of the toilet when he is bigger.

## Seat Shape

Boys require a potty with a small, raised lip at the front. When they pee while seated, they will "squirt" in unexpected directions without protection. The lip directs the pee into the potty. If you are ever caught in a situation where a lipped potty is not available, either you or the child can "aim" him in the right direction.

Avoid using a potty with a relatively large shield or guard (urine deflector). The possibility exists that both girls and boys can injure themselves when sitting down or standing up. A flat potty seat without a shield is the safest shape for girls.

## Stability

Although you are likely to at first support your baby on his potty, when he becomes more independent, he will start to find his way to the potty on his own. Choose one that doesn't tip easily when he squirms. The BabyBjörn® Splash-Proof Potty (available in Europe) is ideal for this, since the bottom edges extend out on the floor far enough so that baby's feet hold the potty in position. An added benefit is that when he stands up, the potty won't stick to his buttocks and then tip and spill.

## Portability

A small, portable potty is very useful as you can take it with you wherever you go. Instead of carrying a diaper bag, take a potty purse with you. If the potty you select is not portable and you must travel or be out of the house for some time, take along an attachable toilet seat or any sort of vessel that will serve the purpose.

## Transparency

A transparent or semitransparent potty is useful in that you know instantly when your child goes and can provide immediate feedback by praising him while he is going, or immediately thereafter. He is then free to leave the potty as soon as he is finished. This type of positive reinforcement encourages him to use the potty on a regular basis. If he has diarrhea, you will know not to let him get up right away and can tell or read him stories, play games or otherwise entertain him until he has finished tending to business.

If you can't find a transparent potty, another way to get instant feedback is to feel the bottom of the potty. It will change temperature when baby eliminates—unless you are in a very warm room or climate, or unless the potty is too thick to feel the warmth.

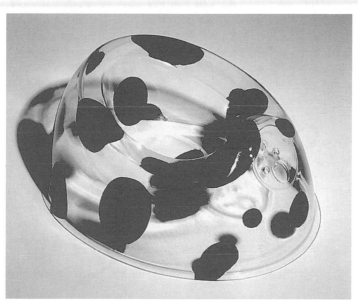

*Profile / Urchin*

The "Spotty Potty" (semitransparent potty)

## Nighttime and Naps

The second major area you will need to monitor is visits to the toilet before and after sleep. As a general rule, take baby to the toilet place before his last feeding or before going to sleep at night, immediately after every nap and immediately upon waking in the morning. His bladder usually fills up as he sleeps and will likely need emptying once he is awake and active again, especially where younger babies are concerned. Note that after a few months, some babies can "hold it" for a while after a nap and do not need to be peed immediately upon waking.

## Potty Pauses and Potty Strikes

Some babies go on potty pause or potty strike. The main reasons for setbacks in toilet training are usually developmental or emotional, when baby experiences distraction, intense learning, discomfort, upset or pressure (in these ways, a potty strike is similar to a nursing strike). More specifically, causes include developmental milestones and problems with health, family, physical comfort, daily routine or (breast)feeding. A potty pause is a temporary "phaseout" or hiatus from potty learning, while baby is working out an issue. It is not a conscious thing that a child does to be naughty or to manipulate you, whereas a potty strike can be a means of purposefully striking back at you for something that is bothering your little one. Strikes can last a day or longer, even up to a number of months, whereas pauses are usually less intense. In both cases, it is up to you to ascertain what is upsetting or distracting your baby.

Typical behavior for both potty pauses and strikes includes arching the back and straightening the legs, crying, screaming, holding back or refusing to sit on the potty. Note that these same behaviors can at times manifest for reasons other than a strike, such as misreading baby's signals or incorrect timing, in which case baby is simply letting you know he does not need to go potty. And be careful not to equate accidents with a potty strike—all babies experience numerous accidents during infant toilet learning.

The main reasons for potty pauses are:

- physical discomfort due to teething, illness, diarrhea or the need to pass gas
- developmental milestones (learning to crawl, walk or talk or mastering another major skill)
- temperamental reasons such as protesting the unwanted interruption of an activity, a change in schedule/routine or suddenly receiving less care and attention

If your baby is not feeling well, he might stop signaling and responding to your cues for as long as it takes for him to recover from his physical ailment. Viewed another way, infant communication can also help you find out about your baby's other needs. If he refuses to go on cue several times a day, this could be a sign that something is amiss, and you can look for ways to comfort him.

Diarrhea, the common cold and other illness can wreak havoc with potty training. Teething is another thing that can throw your baby off kilter and cause him to shut down for a while. With teething, there is the added complication that it may take days for you to even realize your baby is cutting teeth, plus babies cut lots of teeth over many months. If your child is not feeling well, he may need extra sympathy and understanding, and he is likely to lose interest in pottying for a while. Be sensitive to his needs. Do not view his refusals as rebellion or defiance. If you use force or punishment, it will backfire on you, and you could prolong the situation.

Developmental milestones tend to disrupt pottying for a number of reasons. Generally, as mobility begins to increase, so do accidents. Otherwise stated, during the learning of mobility, as mobility increases, bladder control decreases for a while. This is perfectly normal and to be expected. With mobility come freedom and independence. Babies are fascinated by their surroundings, and some have such a love affair with all the new discoveries that they lose interest in pottying for weeks or months. In this situation, continue to offer opportunities to use the potty or toilet at times that do not upset your little one. If life is too stressful, it doesn't hurt to use diapers again for a while until the potty interest returns.

Some activities put pressure on the bladder, and this pressure can cause babies to unexpectedly pee. For example, when baby is creeping around on his belly during attempts to scoot or crawl, he tends to pee without warning. When learning to stand and walk, new sets of muscles are contracting in the back and abdominal regions, again pressuring the bladder. One elimination communication ("ec") veteran mom and expert refers to this as the "learning to walk, don't bother me with ec phase" and explains:

"I'm watching my 9.5 month old learn to walk, and watching the accidents pile up with a relaxed eye. I've done this before and thankfully have no worries, knowing he'll be more capable of ec in a few short weeks. If you're out there watching your baby learn to crawl and walk, and wondering why babies seem so surprised to see pee pouring out of them when they get upright, let me explain. When baby is learning to stand, there is a lot of muscular activity happening in the back and stomach. Standing up, we have to keep our backs straight, right? Or we'd bend forward and flop over. So we have muscles that pull our back up. If these muscles are used to capacity, our backs arch. So what stops baby from arching and falling over backwards? Stomach muscles—they pull baby back forward. . . . What does this do to the belly? Well, if you have a partially full bladder and then tighten your belly muscles . . . this puts pressure on the bladder and BAM, baby pees on the rug with that 'Gee, where'd all that water come from' expression.

"Standing upright and walking . . . demand extraordinary muscle co-ordination, concentration, and lots of trial and error. That alone would be distracting enough. Add to that the muscular squeezing of the belly and the urge to be independent and influence their environments, and it's amazing any ec happens at all!"[9]

Learning the use and power of "no" is another milestone that can distract for a while. Children seem especially fascinated and empowered when they start signaling "no" or using the word "no." They like experimenting with the consequences. Sometimes it's possible to learn the difference between a negative no and an affirmative no, but be aware that the meaning can change over time. If need be, reduce peeing opportunities or take a break for some days or weeks until you find a more receptive time for your child. One mother discovered that, for a period of time, the older her baby got, the more often she would signal "no":

"At 6 months, Kate would signal 'no' very clearly and only signaled 'no' when she didn't need to go. At around 7 months, however, she started signaling when she didn't WANT to go. There were times where I was sure she needed to pee, but she would arch her back and refuse, so I decided to back off, even if it meant she went in her pants. Then from 9–10 months, she still occasionally signaled 'no' even though she needed to go—sometimes just to be mischievous, because she was tired, sometimes just because she could or else (our latest discovery) in order to get something. For example, she would often signal to go, then signal 'no' the minute we got to the toilet. We found out that 'no' often meant 'No, not until you give me a toy.' Even when we got up at night, in her groggy state she signaled 'no' until we put a toy in her hand. Then she'd pee and fall back to sleep. Around 11 months, she stopped signaling 'no' unless she really meant it and did not need to go."[10]

Here is what the mother of a 16-month-old said about the "no to everything" phase:

"I asked if she needed to go, and my daughter said, 'No, no, no!' (her current response to just about any question). Five seconds later, she RAN into the bathroom and peed. I've learned that she just likes saying 'no' and that often it means 'yes' or doesn't mean anything at all."[11]

Another mother thought her 21-month-old son was on strike for a while, until she figured out his meaning of "no":

"I learned that his 'no' didn't mean, 'No, I don't have to go,' but rather, 'No, don't take me. I can do it myself.' I also think he disliked me asking, 'Do you have to go potty?' after he had said 'poo.' If he didn't have to go, he wouldn't be saying 'poo' to me. So now if he announces his need to go, we just go, and I only help him as much as necessary."[12]

When experiencing an "I'm busy learning something else" phase, a baby's "brain power" is temporarily diverted elsewhere. At this time, children have better things to do than deal with pottying. If you don't respect their "space" and determination, they can turn hostile in an effort to get you to back off for a while. In other words, adults can be the catalyst that turns a potty pause into a potty strike.

There are many other things that can cause a potty pause and/or lead to a strike. Travel, moving house, hosting overnight guests, divorce, quarreling or other tension in the household, arrival of a new baby in the family, adjusting to a new nanny or babysitter, switching from the family bed to his own bed and room, discomfort on a (new) potty or toilet, constipation, urinary tract infections, dislike of a new toilet position or location, preference for one location only (perhaps in the bathroom where adults go), significant change in house temperature or noise level, construction in the house, receiving less care and attention (for example, at Christmas when you devote lots of time to shopping, cooking, guests, decorations, gifts, etc.)—all of these and more can trigger toileting trouble.

Strikes can start out for the same reasons as pauses but manifest themselves differently in that baby is sending an SOS message of discontent or disapproval and is awaiting resolution. If you are going through emotionally difficult times, your baby will sense this and may go on strike—a pee strike, poop strike or both. You might have to wait until you sort out your own problems before resuming potty training. On the other hand, solutions can seem amazingly simple once you figure things out. For example, you may be offering too many toilet opportunities in a quest for potty perfection. If so, repeat after me: "Reduce and relax!"

One way to view communication with your baby is to see yourself as a translator. You are the one who needs to read and interpret the meaning of your baby's communications and to then do some troubleshooting and solution seeking. Examples that have worked for mothers include letting baby sit on an adult toilet rather than a potty; using different toilet places to cut down on boredom; letting boys stand to pee; letting baby be diaperless for a while after pottying (he may resent being put back in a diaper right after pottying for you); or helping him adjust to a new nap routine or to napping alone.

During a potty pause or strike, it is easy to mistakenly assume that baby has forgotten everything he once knew about toileting. This is not the case. Your baby is simply preoccupied and too busy doing other things—hence the term "potty pause." The best thing to do at this time is to either take a break for a day or longer and wait it out, or else cut down on potty visits and only make them at strategic times for a while. If you sense that your baby needs a break from toilet learning, respect his wishes. It will not hurt to take a break. Or offer him potty occasions when it isn't likely to interrupt or upset him, at times when it seems the least likely to cause conflict. Don't hesitate to put him back in diapers or training pants to take some pressure off both of you. By relaxing about the situation and letting go of your expectations, everyone will be happier, and baby will get back to pottying when he is ready. It is helpful to remind yourself of the reasons you started infant potty learning in the first place—to communicate, to help your baby maintain awareness of his body, to keep him comfortable and dry naturally, and to help him take care of his needs until he is able to do so himself. And never lose sight of the cardinal rules: no pressure and no punishment!

At some point with toddlers (this tends to work near graduation), it can help to use an incentive for a day or two—a sort of "brief bribe" that is so short-lived that a child doesn't see it as a bribe because it only serves to help the child break through a barrier. This can help with potty pauses and other related situations. One mother helped her son overcome a fear of pottying anywhere but on his own potty at home. She offered him a small treat each time he used a different place or receptacle. This help him transcend his inhibitions, and within a few days, he was relaxed enough to pee anywhere she took him, without the need for a treat. My niece experienced a potty pause with her toddler daughter and found that offering her a sticker each time she used the potty helped her regain interest within a day. This got her daughter firmly back on track, and she graduated in a few days.

Potty pauses and strikes are not unusual and should not discourage you from continuing. If after a sincere attempt you cannot find a cause, don't worry. Babies tend to advance and retreat as a part of normal development—three steps forward and a step or two back. Be patient as you wait for the synergy between you to return.

Longer-term potty setbacks can happen at any stage or even after what seems to be total completion of toilet training. This type of potty regression can happen to children using all types of toilet training methods.

## Multiple Miniphases

Your baby will experience a variety of phases throughout toilet training. He is likely to test and try different behaviors which might cause temporary disruptions to the process. A common scenario is for a baby who has made considerable progress to suddenly start to "hold back" on the potty, then pee in his diaper or pants as soon as you dress him. A baby who normally waits to be taken potty when he awakes in the morning may suddenly shift to secretly peeing in his bed in the morning for a week or longer.

Some babies go through a phase of crawling behind furniture or into another room, rather than signaling you, when they need to poop. Others will come to you immediately *after*, rather than before, going in their diaper or pants. Most babies will start uttering one or more toilet words such as "pee" or "poo" months before they can distinguish the two functions from each other and long before they are able to regularly inform you before they need to go.

An important factor to bear in mind throughout all of infant potty training is the fact that your baby is very sensitive to everything you say, do and experience. While using this method, your baby is so closely tied to you that in some ways it is almost like still being joined by the umbilical cord. As you and your baby go through various changes, so will the rhythm and schedule you use with potty training. Do not despair if your good or nearly perfect routine is disrupted for a while. See the section called "Corrupted Cues" in Chapter 5 for more on this subject.

## Definition of "Toilet Trained"

One of the most common questions asked about infant potty training is, "At what age will my baby be toilet trained?"

In one sense, Westerners do not consider a child to be toilet trained until he can perform all toilet functions independently, without reminders. This happens when a child knows and can remember where to find the potty or bathroom, walk to the potty or toilet on his own, pull down his pants without help, do the job, wipe, get off the potty, pull up his pants and remain dry all day and night. Seen in this light, a child would not be considered 100% toilet trained until his coordination is developed to such a degree that he needs no help locating and using the potty or toilet, and wiping and dressing himself. Temporary and short-lived setbacks after seeming success can delay completion even longer. Taking all these factors or endpoints into consideration yields the strictest definition of "toilet trained." Most parents—no matter what method they use—claim their children are toilet trained before absolute perfection, per this strict definition, is achieved.

In another sense, a child can be considered toilet trained at a much younger age, as long as you get him to the toilet on time and offer the obvious assistance. The basis of this is that baby has reasonable control over the sphincter muscles and understands the concept of going to a toilet place to eliminate but needs help and/or reminders to get there on time. In short, there are different definitions of endpoints in determining when a child is toilet trained and "because studies use different endpoints (independent control versus child indication of need with caregiver attending to the need), they cannot be compared directly."[13]

A motto of some mothers using elimination communication ("ec") is that it is more about the "c" of communication than the "e" of elimination. They are not striving to "finish" earlier than other babies but are instead simply taking care of their babies' needs "in the moment." Just as they do not breastfeed with the goal of weaning their babies as soon as possible, so they do not potty their infants with the goal of having them "trained" as soon as possible. Maintaining this type of devoted and relaxed attitude often results in relatively early completion, although this is not the main focus.

While conducting extensive research on this method, I asked many mothers to tell me at what age their children were toilet trained. The most common reply in Western countries was 12 to 18 months for reasonable daytime dryness. In Asia and Africa, most mothers will tell you their babies are toilet trained at 6 to 12 months of age. These claims of being "toilet trained" allow for the fact that baby is still partially dependent on someone to transport him on time to the toilet place.

To some, such claims do not represent an acceptable definition or degree of "being toilet trained" since the child is still semi-dependent on help from a caregiver. They argue that a child has not learned to control his bladder or bowels; but that instead, he has merely established a conditioned reflex and the parents have been trained to "catch" his elimination. Parents who begin infant pottying in the early months of life all know for a fact that their baby soon gains some control over retaining and releasing elimination, and that this control gradually increases over the months. They all know for a fact that their baby can for the most part stay clean and dry with assistance from a caregiver.

As for the "catching" argument, is this not also the case when parents begin any type of potty training? It was certainly the case with my first two sons when we first sat them on the potty at age 18 months and 15 months. They had absolutely no idea why they were on the potty or what they had to do there. In the first weeks, it was a matter of luck to "catch" a pee or poo in the potty. It took them weeks to learn to associate being on the potty with elimination, whereas it takes an infant just a few sessions or days to learn the very same thing. For those who feel a child is too young to start toilet training until he takes the initiative himself, the alternative is to let the diaper "catch" everything for 2–4 years.

If you were asked, "At what age did your baby learn to feed himself?" (snacks or meals) you might say, "At about 2 years. He was too young to know how before then." The fact is, a baby can feed himself but is dependent on you to find, obtain and prepare the food; to give the feeding on time and to clean up the mess. In this sense, a child is dependent on you for all feedings for many years.

Why don't parents apply the same logic to toilet learning? The answer is, of course, that baby cannot live without food, so we must deal with that aspect of his life every day. But with toileting, we can "get away" with ignoring the topic until the child is older and the mess becomes too unbearable and embarrassing for anyone to ignore.

Parental and cultural expectations must also be taken into account when considering the age of toilet readiness. Like many things in life, parental expectations can have both a positive and a negative effect on a child, depending on parental behavior. Encouragement and wishful thinking applied in a positive manner can lead to early development and early maturity in some physical skills. Where physical development is concerned, you're never expecting too much as long as you don't punish your baby for not living up to expectations. No feelings of disappointment, please!

An example of the influence and importance of parental and cultural expectations is seen in a study by William Caudill, an influential anthropologist who compared Japanese and American infant development and child-rearing practices. "He was struck by the fact that responses observed in infants were in line with broad expectations for behaviour in both cultures. For example, in the USA the expectation that individuals should be physically and verbally assertive and in Japan that the individual should be physically and verbally restrained were present in infant behaviour."[14]

In some areas of Africa, certain activities are prized, praised and encouraged from the very first weeks or months of life, activities that are not deemed nearly as important or that are considered impossible in early infancy by Westerners. These include sitting, smiling and toilet training. In rural Africa, babies are generally taught to sit and smile months before Western babies. Babies from several Asian and African societies learn and hone elimination skills in early infancy. The point is that if a behavior or skill is culturally important and encouraged by the parents, a baby is likely to be precocious in that behavior or skill when compared to babies who do not receive similar early teaching and opportunity for sufficient practice. For more on the cultural relativity of toilet training readiness, see Part 4.

## When Can Baby Be Diaperless?

There is no fixed time for this. The best time for your little one to start going diaperless is a matter of preference and of what is possible, practical and desirable with respect to your own individual situation. Being diaperless can be helpful or even indispensable for some, while for others it doesn't seem to make much difference. There are mothers who feel tense and nervous if their babies are diaperless all the time. They constantly watch their babies (or their privates) and tend to interpret every little sound or body movement as a signal. In this situation, it is better to relax and use a diaper as a backup. The point is, infant pottying works with or without diapers, and many mothers use diapers in between potty visits.

In Asia, Africa, South America and other areas, millions of parents never use diapers, but in North America and Europe where sanitation and hygiene are perhaps the best in the world, the tendency is to keep baby bottoms covered until a baby has good or complete control of elimination. In a cold climate or in winter, parents are more likely to keep their babies warmly clothed and use training pants or a diaper. In warmer climates, the percentage of bare-bottomed babies rises.

As for when a baby is able to control the bladder and bowels enough to go diaperless, this again depends in large part on the parents' lifestyle as well as on the individual baby's physiology, "learning" and development. Some babies pee every 10 minutes while others pee every 3 hours, depending on the functional capacity of the bladder, infant age and intake of fluids. At age 4 months, some babies urinate every 2–3 hours and others still go every 10–15 minutes. At 6 months, some babies pee 6 times a day while others will void 20 times. Relatively frequent voiding is a normal condition for many and may continue into adulthood. In more severe cases, however, a small functional bladder capacity can result in long-term bedwetting (enuresis).[15]

In Israel, the process of toilet training is called "weaning from diapers," and this is precisely what you are doing at this point. Once you get to know your baby's patterns, you can figure out a realistic time frame for letting him remain diaperless. You might want to do this in stages, starting with a half hour or morning session, then increasing the time over the days, weeks or months. You are the expert for your baby in this department. No one knows your baby better than you.

The age range for totally ditching diapers can vary considerably. The important thing to bear in mind is that each baby is different. Some are easier to work with than others. Similarly, some mothers are more receptive, perceptive and able to open up than others. Every family situation varies and must be taken into consideration. Since there is no fixed length of time in which one should complete the process, there are no feelings of failure. The ability of a mother-infant pair to coordinate and synchronize their behavior (tune into each other) improves steadily over time as they hone their interactive skills. This method of toilet learning provides a means for you and your baby to function as a close and loving unit for however long it takes.

## The Transition to Diaperlessness

Treat the transition to diaperlessness as you would any other day. Do not make a "big deal" out of the occasion. Some mothers start to feel and behave more seriously about potty training once they remove the diapers. Your baby will sense the change in your demeanor and may balk at responding to your signals. He may feel you are nervous or pressuring him—and he may well be right, even though you are unaware of the change in yourself. You could even trigger a potty strike by the subtle differences in your behavior.

It is also helpful to bear in mind that making the transition to going diaperless can cause accidents. For example, if your baby is accustomed to wearing a diaper in his high chair and suddenly one day he is bare-bottomed in the chair, the new and different feeling—perhaps from experiencing a temperature change or chill when you seat him—may be enough to make him pee unexpectedly. If he is not accustomed to wearing training pants or underwear, or to being naked or bare-bottomed throughout the day, he may initially interpret a transition to diaperlessness as carte blanche to pee in his pants or anywhere he happens to be. He may be used to the feel of a diaper, and it could take a while to adjust to the switchover.

Some babies make more of an effort to "hold it" when wearing a diaper or pants, as opposed to going bare-bottomed; they need to wear *something* or else they pee everywhere. In this situation, the transition from diapers to pants may be fairly easy. Moreover, it is a relief to no longer have to diaper a squirmy baby. Some mothers feel they are more tuned in without the safety net of diapers. And most babies prefer to go diaperless as it gives them more freedom.

If you are worried about your carpets, one solution is to buy a fairly large, natural-fiber piece of remnant carpet and place it over your permanent carpeting. If your baby has accidents, you won't need to worry about your regular carpets. You can roll up the remnant whenever you like. If it starts to smell, let it air out in the sun.

## Latecomers

Many parents don't even hear about infant pottying until their children are 6 months or older and thus past the first window of opportunity. This early window represents the time when the brain is most naturally receptive and unobstructed by any "diaper training" that may have taken place during the early months of life. While there is no definite cutoff time for beginning, in general it is true that the later you start after that first window, the more difficult it tends to be, although this is not always the case. Some children remain receptive beyond 6 months of age. In other cases, new windows of learning open after 6 months of age. And it is possible that some babies remain in a constant state of readiness.

In one sense, it is never too late to begin, although some different tactics may be needed after a certain age. Newcomers whose babies are over 6 months of age will find plenty of tips and support in the modified approach outlined in Chapter 10, "Late-Starters."

# chapter 5

# signals &
# cues

This chapter reviews and expands the topic of signals and cues. From the very start, mother and baby need to develop the ability to read and respond to each other's cues. This will improve communication and bonding. It will also increase your chances of getting baby to the toilet place on time. Some cues are blatantly obvious, while others are far more subtle and tricky to detect. The more tuned in to your baby you are and the more you practice, the easier it will be for you to read her various types of signals. But don't make a big production or mystery of it! Just as you know when your baby is hungry and wants to nurse, in a similar way you can learn to recognize her elimination cues, if you just relax, watch and listen. If you can't detect signals for a while, there are other effective ways to proceed.

Don't feel guilty if you miss some signals. Bear in mind that some babies don't signal before every elimination and that others may not be signalers in infancy at all. If you miss a pee or poo, clean up without emotion, move on and wait for the next signal or moment to take baby to go.

Each child is different and unique. Some are easier to read and work with than others. Sometimes it is a struggle for parents to recognize and respond to signals in a timely manner. If you work with more than one baby, you'll need to make allowances for differences in temperament and timing. This means you'll need to respond appropriately to each baby's individual cues, personality, physical abilities, limitations and needs. As a result, baby will become more communicative and you will be able to understand each other's signals better.

Just how important is communication? Infant development specialist Dr. Michael Lewis has found that the responsiveness of a mother to the cues of her baby is the single most important influence on a child's intellectual development.[16] Anthropologist Edward Tronick writes that infants possess self-directed regulating systems that take over once their communication signals have not been read, resulting in a system that is out of balance. When signals are missed, babies stop signaling and withdraw. They try to repair the system by not sending out anymore signals.[17] Ainsworth and Bell found that when a mother (or other primary caregiver) is unresponsive, her baby eventually loses interest in regaining contact with her and turns inward.[18] Although none of these experts specifically referred to elimination communication in their studies, there is no reason to discount or diminish the importance of this type of communication in the overall repertoire of signals a baby transmits to her mother or other caregiver(s).

## Baby's Signals and Cues

Babies are aware of the elimination functions from birth, but this awareness can fade within months if she doesn't continue to associate it with anything. Parents can help her preserve and heighten this awareness by learning and responding to her natural and spontaneous elimination signals. Some parents find it easy to recognize these signals, while others can't detect any signals for a while. Either way, do your best to recognize, read and acknowledge your baby's own particular signals and cues as soon as you can, whenever that may be. If you are responsive and consistent, your baby will likely begin and continue to signal you in advance. If you have help from anyone else, you and your caregiver(s) can benefit by exchanging information on the types of, and interval between, signals received from baby.

As your little one grows and matures, try teaching her some specialized toilet signals. Babies love to mimic, and they respond well to encouragement. If you teach and/or reinforce signal behavior, your child will at some point begin to communicate her needs after, during and then before elimination.

Baby's cues may be audible, inaudible, visible or invisible. These were listed and introduced in Chapter 3 and are discussed here in greater detail. The main types of signals that babies send are:

- body language
- vocal and verbal communications
- intuitive communication
- manual cues

## Baby Body Language

Your baby makes facial expressions and uses other body language just prior to or while urinating or defecating. Through careful observation, you can learn to recognize your baby's toilet body language. For example, she may use her eyes to point towards the bathroom. If you are walking past her toilet place and she needs to go, she may lean or throw her weight in that direction. If she needs to poo, she might squirm as you walk past the bathroom. These are attempts to point before she can use her arm, hand and finger to point. Some body language is extremely subtle and hard to decipher. There are mothers who swear that their infants do not signal at all. If you are in this situation, use the other forms of communication for now, and watch for body language to become apparent as she matures. And be prepared for signals to change over time. Also, some body language is so blatant that it can be misunderstood. This happened with my son; while nursing, he would twist, grunt, turn red in the face and seem to struggle at the breast. For a while, I assumed it was a problem with nursing rather than a desperate plea to be taken to go.

The list below contains examples of both spontaneous and learned body language signals. Your baby may use just one, a few or several or even her own unique cues not mentioned here.

### Behavior:
- quieting: slows down or remains still and silent momentarily
- quick mood change from smiling and happy to grumpy or sullen
- stops or refuses to nurse, perhaps with a special "look"
- suddenly stops or loses interest in activity (including babbling)

- becomes animated, lively, energetic or hyper
- assumes special posture
- hides or goes to private place to be alone
- stirs or is restless in sleep, sometimes with head rocking
- awakes
- gets excited when looks at potty or bathroom
- throws a fit if signals ignored
- bites or gnaws your fingers, clothing, nipple or other body part
- bangs head on potty or toilet
- undoes own clothing fasteners
- removes diaper
- pulls down pants or undresses
- when in sling or other carrier, wriggles or kicks to get down
- stands with feet apart, looking down before or during elimination

**Eyes:**
- stares into the distance at nothing
- looks or stares at bathroom, potty or other toilet place
- looks at your hand, then towards bathroom, as you sign "toilet"
- stares at own genitals
- eyes twitch or eyelids flutter

**Face:**
- pulls faces, grimaces, wrinkles face
- has look of concentration on the face
- assumes blank, hard, piercing, dreamy or imploring expression
- has a thoughtful look or expression
- face turns red/flushes
- looks uncomfortable
- makes a special face before or during elimination
- tenses throat, chin and/or face
- twitches mouth or blows raspberries
- smiles before pooing or when you give cue to go

**Abdomen:**
- tenses abdominal muscles
- contracts abdominal region when "pushing"

**Whole Body (Physical):**
- squirms, wriggles or twists body, or arches back
- tenses or stiffens body
- shivers
- at night, squirms to awaken you

- squirms in your arms as you walk past or towards toilet place
- leans towards toilet place as you walk past it
- climbs into, or stands up in your arms or lap
- taps, grabs, or pulls self up on your leg
- moves (scoots, wiggles, crawls or walks) towards toilet place

- looks back at you at least once as moves towards toilet place
- crawls towards you
- stands in a funny or special position
- squats and turns quiet or concentrates (often in a corner or behind furniture)

## Legs:
- kicks or pumps one or both legs in the air (sometimes frantically)
- pushes against you with legs
- kicks you
- pushes up to standing position in your lap
- wiggles leg(s) or foot/feet
- engages in unique leg position or movement
- squeezes legs together

## Breathing:
- changes rate of breathing
- takes a sudden deep breath
- breathes heavier or exhales loudly

## Buttocks area:
- passes gas before defecation
- assumes special buttocks posture (newborns)
- pats diaper, butt or pants

## Arms and Hands:
- points at or touches self (points at diaper, groin or bottom; places or holds hands between legs; places hand on head or face; rubs face)

- points at or touches mother (reaches for you; pats, taps or slaps you; hits you on the head; pulls your hair; scratches you)
- points at or touches toilet, potty, etc. (points at bathroom, potty or other toilet place; reaches for or grabs potty; pats or bangs on toilet or potty; plays with toilet lid or potty)
- uses sign language (pats your hand as you use sign language cue; makes crude attempt at signing; waves in a special way with one or both arms or hands; gives clear sign language cue)

**Genitals:**
- grabs or looks at crotch area
- pats genitals
- points at genitals
- pulls on penis
- scrotum contracts or swells slightly before urination
- penis wiggles shortly before urination
- penis becomes slightly erect

There is also body language that tells you when your baby does *not* need to go or when she does not *want* to go for you. The most obvious signals are arching her back and straightening her legs, or shaking her head "no." However, there are times where these forms of communication are used to "test the waters" or in playful gesture rather than as a means of true protest. As always, it is up to mother to be the great communications expert and figure out the meaning. If your baby arches and stiffens when you know she has to go, try to distract her into relaxing out of the position. For example, scoop her into your arms and cuddle playfully, then retry pottying her

### Vocal and Verbal Communication

Infants cannot speak, but this doesn't mean they cannot communicate. Before they can speak, one of the ways infants communicate is to make vocal sounds. This does not imply that every sound a baby makes contains a message, but an attentive and discerning parent will soon learn which sounds have meaning. Some of the sounds, such as crying, grunting, gurgling, squealing and yelling, are familiar to all parents since these sounds are universal. Grunting invariably signals defecation, but crying can indicate a number of different things. There are different types of cries consisting of different pitch, volume, intensity and duration. It may take a while to figure out exactly why a baby cries or what a particular cry means. Elimination needs should be considered a possible cause. The more attentive and responsive a mother is to baby's vocalizations from birth, the better for both. This mother-infant interaction is an important step in creating a successful and satisfying communication system.

For newborns, crying is the most effective signal (except, of course, in the case of deafness). A newborn quickly learns that making sounds brings caregiver attention. She learns in the first few months of life that different sound patterns bring different results.[19] There are at least four types of cries that are distinguishable in infancy—cries caused by pain, hunger, boredom and general discomfort. Babies seem predisposed to test communication by crying in these various ways to see what the result will be. Mothers can distinguish between these four types of crying by the end of the second week, and fathers recognize them by three weeks.[20]

Non-cry vocalizations are produced for the first time during the third week. At first, they only occur when an infant starts to fuss but before she breaks out crying, as if discovered by accident. Once she has discovered how to make a new sound, she will practice it when she is content and in no distress.[21]

Most infants will cry if they are in a wet or soiled diaper. This instinct is often suppressed early in life, in which case baby's elimination awareness diminishes then disappears altogether. Other vocal communications, such as gurgling, grunting, chirping, inhaling or exhaling with a unique sound, are less obvious and not as easy to read. If you closely observe, carefully monitor and promptly respond to your baby, you'll learn the meaning of many of her personalized sounds.

Some babies vocally summon their caregivers by crying, screaming, grunting or making a unique sound such as a little yelp, in an effort to *announce* that they need to go. Parents of babies who vocally signal are especially fortunate since this type of signal is so easy to detect—that is, as long as they are paying attention and are responsive.

In societies where infant elimination training is the norm, babies typically signal to be pottied. They are also in constant physical contact with their mothers or caregivers, co-sleep, are breastfed and are immediately taken care of or soothed if they cry. In these intimate ways, signals and responses are innately coordinated by and between baby and mother. "There is extensive scientific evidence that the accepted Western caretaking style repeatedly, and perhaps dangerously, violates the adaptive system called crying that evolved to help babies communicate with adults." In addition, it has been found that there is little or no colic in many of these traditional societies.[22] It is tempting to ask if making babies wear their waste contributes to colic in the West, due to the discomfort in the diaper or due to holding in the elimination in an effort to avoid this discomfort. In both situations, cries for help go unheeded.

Another sign to watch for could take place as you walk past the bathroom or other "pot spot." Listen closely and you may hear a grunt or other vocalization signaling you to make a visit to the bathroom.

For a while, most babies will signal you "after the fact" (as in the case of crying when wet). The message starts out as a distress call to be changed. Then at some point it transforms into an announcement: "Hey, I went!" After a while, all children switch over to signaling *before* they need to go, but the age for this can vary a lot.

As babies develop the ability to produce specific sounds or words, they advance from meaningless vocalizations to simple one-syllable verbalizations such as "ba," "da" and "ma." These then progress to two-syllable or multi-syllable versions such as "dada," "mama" and "bababa." Next, more complicated sounds such as "poo," "poop," "pee" and "go" are attempted. At this point, some babies are able to verbally tell you if they need to go or if they already went. It is not uncommon for a child around 12–15 months old to assume that a word such as "pee" or "poop" refers to both types of elimination. If your baby signals you by saying "poop" and you end up with a pee in the potty, consider this good progress. She will eventually learn to distinguish between the words.

Here is a summary of some of the most common vocalizations and verbalizations:

- cries, screams or squeals before, during or after elimination
- fusses
- grunts before or during defecation
- makes a special, unique toilet sound (e.g., "pfff")
- laughs before pooing
- sighs or whimpers
- makes imploring sound such as "eh, eh, eh" or "uh, uh, uh"

- gives learned toilet cue such as "sssss"
- utters own sound (e.g., "eeew" or "ba") before or after pooing
- says "mama" while looking intently at you
- says "pee" before or after pees or poos
- says "poo" before or after poos or pees

There are also vocalizations and utterances that tell you your baby does *not* need to go, or that she does not *want* to go for you. The most obvious are crying, screaming or saying "no." Yet sometimes these vocalizations and words are used to mean "yes," for fun or simply to see how you react. It takes tuning in and practice before you learn how to interpret them correctly. Even more fun (or confusing), the meaning can change over time, so you need to keep your senses heightened. For more on the meaning of "no," see "Potty Pauses and Potty Strikes" in Chapter 4.

## Intuitive Communication

For many, intuitive communications from baby are the hardest to detect. These signals are subtle in that they are not visible or audible. They require an instinctual relationship with baby. Many Westerners do not believe there is such a thing as telepathic communication between caregiver and child. Others believe this type of communication exists but that they are not able to achieve it. If you cannot relate to or experience this type of communication with your baby, don't worry about intuition for now. You can be just as responsive by using the other forms of communication.

If you feel that you are mainly guessing your baby's timing and that it is often merely a matter of luck if you get baby to go on cue, carry on using timing, patterns, baby body language, baby vocalizations and even "guessing." One day you may be surprised to suddenly hear or feel something that tells you, "It's time to pee her," and your intuition will kick in. Another way to view it, your guessing might just be your intuition kicking into gear. If you ever all of a sudden think your baby might need to go, act on it rather than ignoring it, and you may be pleasantly surprised. After getting results this way, you may be able to supplement or change from relying on the clock to relying on intuitive timing. It's as if an alarm goes off in your head and alerts you, "It's time to toilet her now!"

Intuition is a subliminal phenomenon that is always functioning in your subconscious. For scientific-minded folks, it is like DSL, constantly streaming in the background, and you just have to tap into the current to access it.

Many mothers report that their babies send out pee signals on an intuitive level. The most common sensation is a feeling of spreading (wet) warmth, as if their babies were peeing on them. One couple calls this phenomenon a "chi pee" (per the Chinese word for energy) as they notice their baby has a warm burst of energy when she is about to pee. Others smell urine, hear the word "pee" in their minds, dream their babies need to "go," or subtley feel a full bladder in their own bodies. But in all these situations, when they check their babies, they find that they are clean and dry! When the mothers then hold them in position to go, the babies respond by peeing. Some mothers report the same with defecation—a warm sensation or the smell of baby poo precedes the actual movement. But not all babies communicate in this way. Some families have reported that while one child communicated intuitively, a sibling did not.

Mothers in so-called "primitive" cultures see baby as an extension of their own body. If you ask an Asian or African mother who uses infant potty training, "How do you know when your baby needs to go?" don't be surprised if her reply is that her intuition tells her. "I just know. Mothers just *know*." Many of these mothers do not possess or use watches, clocks or timers to alert them to baby's timing. Instead, they simply sense when it's the right moment for baby to go, implying that there is a psychic connection and communication between mother and baby. It's similar to knowing when your child needs to breastfeed—through various means, you learn and instinctively know when to offer the breast (or potty).

Customs of Western culture preclude an instinctive relationship with baby on certain levels. For Westerners, pottying by intuition requires relearning or simply accepting an art and type of communication long ago forgotten by our culture and in this sense may seem foreign or strange. The remnants are there, though, as seen in situations where Western parents experience a feeling of foresight where their babies are concerned. This prescience is often discerned as "a little voice" or feeling in the head that tells parents to do or not do something for their baby at a certain time. It's not uncommon to ignore and suppress this feeling when the message is weak but is considered a miracle when it leads parents to prevent or stop a life-threatening event.

It is easy for skeptics to logically argue away the concept of intuitive communication. For one thing, skeptics cannot communicate telepathically with their babies since their skepticism blocks this sensitive channel of communication, thus creating a self-fulfilling prophecy. They analyze the concept of intuitive communication with logic, questions and doubt. For example, if you tell a baby to pee and she pees, was she picking up a psychic signal, or was she responding to your verbal communication or in-arms positioning? Is it intuitive communication, a mother's tone of voice, her intonation or being held in a certain way that first prompts an infant to eliminate at the right time? In other words, which happens first, association coupled with conditioning or a more subtle form of communication?

As long as a caregiver succeeds in getting baby to go in the right place at the right time, it doesn't matter if the means of communication is intuitive or of another nature. All that really matters is that baby and caregiver communicate.

## Manual Cues

Manual cues are especially (but not exclusively) important in deaf families where communication is visual-gestural rather than auditory-vocal.[23] These cues consist of gestures, manual babbling and sign language. Before an infant can manually sign, she uses gazing, body movement and facial expressions (also called "facial grammar") to communicate.[24]

A hearing baby with deaf parents quickly learns that crying brings little or no results (unless the parents have a flashing light or vibrating baby monitor installed and notice the signal that way) and finds other ways to get her parents' attention. Deaf journalist Henry Kisor tells an amusing story of how his pet cat quickly learned that meowing would not elicit a morning meal from his sleeping owner. The cat cunningly devised another way to get his owner's attention. He would roust him by jumping onto his chest and licking his eyelids with his rough, feline tongue. Unfortunately, the cat assumed that all humans were deaf and would treat houseguests to a morning sandpapering of the eyelids too.[25]

Gestures or mime, such as raising the arms to be picked up, are used by both hearing and deaf infants. Some other early gestures and manual signals include pointing at an object, extending an object toward the mother and openhanded reaching toward an object.[26]

*Laurie Boucke (from video)*

Big sister Sara (7 years) initiates the "poop sign" her family uses with 11-month-old Beau who is sitting on a baking-bowl makeshift potty. The "poop sign" in question (not taken from ASL) is a "moving sign" which goes from a closed fist to an open fist and back several times. Sara's fist is closed and Beau's is open.

*Laurie Boucke (from video)*

Sara has stopped signing, but Beau continues. Here both of his fists are starting to close.

*Laurie Boucke (from video)*

Both of Beau's fists are now closed as he continues to make his "poop sign."

*Lois Baas (from video)*

10-month-old graduate Zachary making ASL sign for "toilet."
In this photo he is using his right hand; on next page,
he uses his left hand.

*Lois Baas (from video)*
10-month-old graduate Zachary making the ASL sign for "toilet"

Manual babbling is used more frequently by deaf babies and babies of deaf parents than by hearing babies, since babies with deafness in the family typically depend on their hands rather than sound to communicate. Just as hearing babies babble before they speak, so deaf babies use manual babbling before they sign.[27]

Babies start moving their hands in a crude mimic of sign language as soon as they develop some hand coordination. Manual babbling becomes more sophisticated in deaf babies between 7 and 10 months of age (coinciding with the age at which hearing babies become more adept at vocal babbling). At this time, syllabic manual babbling progresses to specific hand shapes and movements (at the same age that vocal babbling progresses to specific syllabic vocal babbling such as "bababa" and "dadada" in hearing babies).[28]

In comparison with the progress of learning a spoken language, sign language can be learned somewhat earlier in life. The mean age at which signing children make their first recognizable sign is 8.6 months—some have reported starting as early as 3 months—whereas most infants do not purposefully utter their first intelligible word until age 24–25 months.[29] Of course, babies can haphazardly pronounce several short words long before this time, but to make the direct connection between a specific word and concept generally takes longer.

Both deaf and hearing babies can be taught to associate manual signs and signals with elimination. Indeed, this can speed up the learning process for most. Here is a way to gradually introduce sign language. Make your toilet sign when asking her if she needs to go, when seating her on the potty or toilet, and while she is peeing or pooing. Then expand the meaning. Reinforce the sign by saying "potty" or "toilet" while signing. Next, begin to sign as you point and walk towards the bathroom, toilet or potty. Then signal her in silence when you think she may need to go. Finally, sign your offer while in a different room.

Parent and child can define their own particular manual cues or use ASL (American Sign Language) or another sign language—many countries have their own. To the untrained eye, when an infant first uses the ASL sign for "toilet," it may resemble a wave rather than an intentional sign, but an adoring mother can usually distinguish between a "toilet wave" and a "bye bye wave." And be ready for your baby to at first practice the hand coordination of signing at times when she doesn't need to go.

## Signals from Caregiver to Baby

Before signaling, bear in mind that baby will only respond to your signals if she has to go. If her bladder is full or nearly full, or if she needs to poo soon, she has the ability to *release* the contents upon receiving your cue(s). If she does not need to go, she will not respond to your cues, and you should not insist. There are exceptions in that some infants will listen to your cue, then grunt, bear down, thrust their pelvis or concentrate and release a small amount of urine even if their bladder is not very full.

With small infants, 1–2 minutes is long enough to signal. If baby doesn't pee within a few minutes but seems happy and comfortable in your arms, you can continue to signal if you so desire. Babies who are able to sit on a potty comfortably for a while should generally not be kept on the potty for longer than 5–10 minutes, unless they are content to remain there.

When you think or feel it is a likely time for baby to go, take her to her toilet place and signal her to go. For infants in the in-arms phase, pick a time when you think your baby might pee or poo. If necessary, refer to your notes for this. For many babies, the most predictable times are upon waking first thing in the morning, upon waking up from a long nap, during a feeding or a certain amount of time after a feeding. Parents of babies in the potty phase should already be well versed in sensing when baby needs to sit on the pot. Your job is to be sure she gets to the potty either with or without your help. Babies or toddlers with less potty experience will usually still need to be prompted by your signal(s) once they are on the potty.

Here are some cues you can use when you think or feel it is a likely time for baby to go:

- vocal and verbal cues
- physical cues
- intuitive cues
- manual cues

## Vocal and Verbal Cues

At the start of the in-arms phase, parents and caregivers should consistently use a basic signal such as "sssss," "psssss," "Do you want to pee?" "You're peeing" or "You peed," before, during or immediately after each elimination. Baby will associate this signal with elimination and soon transition to peeing or pooing upon hearing the signal. If so desired, you can use a different sound, word or sentence if you think baby needs to poo, but this is not required. Most families use one signal for both types of elimination. If a short sentence is your basic signal, consider using a unique intonation with that particular sentence. Again, the basic rule is to choose a signal that feels natural and comfortable to you.

After a while, your child may no longer want you to ask if she needs to go, or she may be irritated if you ask too often. An overzealous or overanxious mother isn't fun for anyone. Be sensitive to changes in receptivity to your cues.

It is usually beneficial to show your satisfaction with baby after completing a toilet session. Most parents feel excited and extremely pleased with their babies after getting baby to pee or poo on cue. Your natural reaction is the best reaction. If you are exuberant and want to verbally praise your baby, that is fine. If you are less outgoing and prefer to just state the facts of what happened, that is fine. If you have more than one child and feel less enthusiastic with the second or third, this is fine. The important thing is to let the child know that you are aware she has responded and done the right thing. She will sense that you are pleased, feel rewarded and be encouraged to continue her behavior.

If a toilet session yields no tangible results, simply move onto another activity. Do not direct disappointment, anger or frustration at the child. You might be feeling these emotions, but keep them to yourself. Strive to eliminate your negative feelings and replace them with positive ones, bearing in mind that there will be plenty more opportunities to work and communicate with baby. If helpful, reprogram yourself to "go with the flow" and stop viewing "misses" as failures or something to feel guilty about.

## Physical Cues

Baby quickly learns to associate the way you hold her with elimination. This is similar to a breastfed baby associating being held a certain way with nursing. During the in-arms phase, not only is the actual position a cue but also the feeling of being held in position against your body. Once you've found a suitable and comfortable position to use for pottying, be careful not to inadvertently hold baby in that position for any other purpose, or you may wind up wet!

Another physical cue is to (at first) use the same location each time you take your infant to go. She will soon recognize the location and translate being there as a cue for her to go. This also applies to consistently using the same receptacle. Your baby will come to recognize the look and feel of whatever receptacle you decide to use. Once she develops a conditioned response to your various signals and cues (or a specific combination of cues—position, location and sound all used together can at first serve as "the cue to go"), it's fairly easy to introduce other toilet places and graduate to a different receptacle as she grows.

Other physical cues can be used in addition to basic positioning, although they are not essential in the equation. For example, if you nurse mainly in one favorite spot, keep the receptacle in the same location (such as to the right or to the left) relative to you and baby, and perhaps she will one day start to look towards the receptacle when she needs it. When reaching for the potty or bowl, hold your baby's hands in yours so that she reaches for it and touches it too. This encourages her to turn and reach in the direction of the potty to signal you when she needs to go.

If it's time for baby to go but there is no response to your signal, try running a little water in the sink or bathtub. The sound of running water may prompt her to go. You can also try running a little water over her feet, dipping her feet in water or sprinkling a little water on her tummy. The water should be just slightly cooler than her body temperature. A signal as subtle as "feeling mama breathe" as you hold her against your belly can trigger elimination from an in-arms baby—if helpful, inhale, then tighten and relax your abdominal muscles. Another approach is to give her something to suck (e.g., your thumb), chew on (e.g., a teething toy) or drink, and she may suddenly relax enough to go. If she is able to sit on a potty, a gentle back or foot rub might help her relax and release. If she doesn't respond to your cues, take a break and try again later.

## Intuitive Cues

Intuitive cues from mother to baby work in the same way as from baby to mother. This phenomenon is explained earlier in this chapter.

Parents who feel they can communicate on an intuitive level with their babies can either purposefully direct specific thoughts towards their babies ("Do you have to pee?") from time to time or let the thought process flow, knowing that the right thoughts will go to baby at the right time. Intuitive communications can happen in different frames of mind and in different locations, such as while you're dreaming, relaxing, working or away from baby.

Tuning in does not mean that all you think about is baby's elimination. It is an awareness in the back of your mind that your baby needs to go every once in a while. Watching for signals becomes second nature, and your conscious focus remains on other things most of the time. It is similar to breastfeeding on demand. You instinctively offer the breast when you know your baby wants to nurse. You do not watch her constantly for signs of being hungry, yet still you realize when she is.

Siblings are often in tune with each other and sometimes have the ability to communicate through intuition or other subtle means that only they can understand. Let your toddler or older child try cueing baby at toilet time, and you may be in for a surprise.

## Manual Cues

You can teach your baby to associate manual cues with elimination. This can be handy at times and is essential with deaf babies.

Manual cues are most often used with deaf babies, but hearing babies are equally as capable of understanding them as deaf babies. Most hearing parents of hearing babies do not know any sign language and thus never consider using it. Verbal and physical cues provide a sufficient enough means for them to communicate with their babies. They don't realize that using manual cues and sign language with babies can be fun and useful. It opens up a new and personal channel of communication. If an official sign language is used on a regular basis, it will allow a hearing child to communicate with deaf children and adults later in life, and afford easier access to the deaf culture.

For obvious reasons, gesturing, manual babbling and sign language naturally play a much more important and necessary role in the development of deaf babies. An attentive and responsive mother can make a tremendous difference in the quality of life of a deaf infant.

Deaf mothers tend to be better communicators than hearing mothers. A deaf mother must be in close physical contact with her deaf infant when communicating. A lot of touching goes on, such as tapping, stroking and tickling, initially to get the baby's attention and then to communicate or play. Deaf mothers spend 70–80% of their interaction time with a positive affective expression on their faces compared with 50% for hearing mothers with hearing babies.[30]

A wide variety of facial expressions, body language, gesturing and other specific body movements are coupled with manual signing to communicate. For example, to ask her baby if she has to pee, a mother could use a combination of:

- a manual sign for "toilet," such as the ASL sign formed by placing the thumb between the index and middle fingers, then twisting the hand from side to side

- mouthing whatever word(s) she has elected to use to communicate potty time to her baby
- pointing to the bathroom, toilet place or potty
- holding her baby in their favorite in-arms position or placing her on the potty or toilet

## Corrupted Cues

Cues from caregiver to baby can become corrupted in a number of ways discussed throughout this book. Anything that causes a caregiver's normal demeanor to change can interrupt or corrupt the flow of communication to baby. Some of the ways signals and cues can become corrupted include showing off while potty training, loud noise, anger, impatience, distractions, sudden changes in room or body temperature, interruptions, illness, physical discomfort, changes in daily routine, emotional upsets and changes in environment.

Signals from baby can be corrupted by illness, diarrhea, teething, milestones, hunger, discomfort, emotional upsets, major life change and pain. Physical positioning can also affect cueing and can serve as a clue to puzzling accidents. If you know your baby needs to go but she does not respond to your cues and instead pees the moment you finally lay her down, this could simply be due to her anatomy. The sphincter muscles automatically clamp shut when there is pressure on them. There is more pressure on the sphincters in an upright position, and when you lay your baby down, the muscles tend to relax and release the contents of the bladder. Try putting her down briefly to help her relax those muscles, then offer another pee opportunity.

# chapter 6

# nighttime

Staying dry at night often takes longer to accomplish than staying dry during the day. The degree of difficulty of staying dry at night depends on your baby's elimination frequency and patterns, as well as on your diligence and ability to be in tune with your little one. At night, there is the added stress and complication of waking up from sleep, and the various aspects and consequences of this should be weighed and considered. It is important to do what seems best for both baby and the family as a whole.

Keep the bedding and clothing dry and clean, even if you have to change them at night. This encourages baby to remain dry. In the event of accidents, quietly and nonchalantly clean up, with as little fuss and disturbance as possible.

Many babies remain dry all night only to be left in bed to wet their bed or diaper in the morning. Babies generally need to be taken to the toilet as soon as they wake up. Bear in mind that they often wake up before everyone else in the house. Remember to base the "first thing in the morning" pee on *his* timing rather than yours. If you do not take him to pee immediately upon waking, it will probably be difficult for him to wait more than 1 to 5 minutes before he goes. The result will be a wet bed or diaper, not because he wet it during the night but because no one made the effort to take him to pee when he woke up in the morning. As he grows and his bladder gains more capacity, he will be able to "hold it" somewhat longer after waking. Don't wait too long, though. Even most adults need to relieve themselves upon waking in the morning.

If you take baby to pee soon before he goes to sleep for the night and then get him to the toilet place when he wakes in the morning, there is a good chance he will stay dry all night. The reason baby can remain dry all night is because certain hormones cause urine production to decrease at night, so his kidneys produce less urine while he is asleep than during his waking, active hours. If you let him eat something with a high liquid content such as watermelon before bed, you can expect him to need to pee during the night. Babies who nurse or drink a lot before bed or during the night are also likely to pee once or even several times at night, especially when they are very young.

Bedwetting is fairly common among infants, and one solution is to pee them at night. How do you know when to pee your baby? Many stir, kick, cry or otherwise (partially) wake at night if they have to go. As with daytime signals, nighttime signals can be either blatant or subtle. Many babies are restless in their sleep. They might toss and turn, with or without sound effects such as grunting, or perhaps just turn their heads from side to side. They might roll over or raise their rear ends in the air in an attempt to get the pressure off their bladders. Mothers often assume that if babies wake at night, it is to nurse, and they quickly offer the breast. But many babies stir or wake at night to pee. Through observation, you will know if this is the case with yours. Some are adamant about fussing and waking you and will even refuse to nurse before they have relieved themselves. Others will eliminate then drift back to sleep without any nursing. And of course many will want to nurse themselves back to sleep after going.

But what if you aren't forewarned at night? Perhaps your baby doesn't squirm or wake before he pees. Maybe he went to bed hours before you, and you aren't present when he stirs or whimpers. Perhaps he just wakes up and lies quietly waiting. Or maybe he is a deep sleeper and sleeps through just about anything. If your baby wets the bed and you want to do something about it, figure out the optimal time to take him for a "preventive pee" at night and see if he will go for you.

You can let him go in a portable receptacle (bucket, potty, bowl, etc.) kept near the bed, or else take him to the sink, toilet or bathtub. You can also let him pee on a diaper, a cotton changing pad with a waterproof backing or anything else that works in your situation. A newborn can be placed on a diaper, towel, etc., on your chest or on the bed. After he pees, just toss the wet item into a container and replace it with dry one. As a general rule, do whatever is the least disruptive at night.

Keep baby warm and comfortable. Darkness or dim lights, silence or quiet surroundings, gentle and minimal movement or changing of clothing can all be helpful. Some babies only half wake up to go, keeping their eyes closed the whole time, then fall back into a deep sleep in your arms after peeing. If yours likes to wake up slowly, respect this tendency and let him wake at his own pace. But there is usually no need to fully wake baby or otherwise disturb his slumber, as illustrated by this tip from one mother: "I wondered for a time, if by taking Zachary to pee in his sleep I might inadvertently train him to potentially go in his sleep. I was concerned at his being so relaxed that he slept through my toileting him in response to his restlessness or when I took him preventively before my bedtime. But he began to awaken more and more on his own, and would cry out and get up on his knees while waiting to be taken to the bathroom. And when he could sign, he would also wave the ASL toilet sign as I arrived. My experience with Zachary led me to conclude that my attentiveness at nights led to his learning to awaken fully on his own to go to the bathroom."[31]

If he is awake after he goes, nurse him back to sleep. You may soon find that both you and your baby remain in a light stage of sleep while taking care of his nighttime toileting needs. Do whatever lets you both fall peacefully back to sleep.

Some babies respond well to your signals in the middle of the night while others do not like being moved or awakened to go. Nighttime pottying can be more difficult with deep sleepers in that it may be harder to elicit a pee on cue.

It can take a few nights to become accustomed to a nighttime routine and isn't unusual to meet with a little resistance at first. One mother discovered that candlelight mesmerizes and relaxes her baby—he stares at the glow, and out comes the pee. Try different strategies such as rocking baby in your arms, nursing him over a receptacle or nursing while walking around. Or it might be helpful to nurse him for a few minutes, then pee him and then nurse him back to sleep. After some nights, you'll get into a routine and will both grow accustomed to staying more relaxed during nighttime potting. And of course things will change over time as your child physically matures and develops new habits.

Some parents find it easy to get up at night, while others find it extremely difficult. You'll soon ascertain whether or not it's a good idea for you and your baby to take him to pee at night. If you and baby don't find it too unsettling or tiring, carry on pottying at night. If it makes you negative or worn out during the day, or if disturbing your rest at night makes you susceptible to illness, it is better to sleep through the night. If your little one protests being pottied at night, it might be wise to "let sleeping babies lie" for some nights before trying again. If it goes well most of the time except for phases where his patterns change or when he is ill—he may temporarily nurse and pee a lot more at night—don't worry about getting up for every pee during that time. And always bear in mind that the infant potty technique is an ever-changing thing. Just when you think you have something figured out really well, your baby might transition to new timing, patterns and trends.

An important factor in the nighttime equation is clothing. Find something that is super fast and easy to remove with as little fuss as possible. A pajama top, long-sleeved T-shirt or sweater might be all you need for warmth. If diapering, fitted diapers are excellent in terms of keeping the bed dry.

But using diapers at night can actually encourage bedwetting, especially once a child has reasonable daytime control. This is particularly true with toddlers since having to remove a diaper adds to the time and complexity of using the potty or toilet independently, and this may be enough to discourage the attempt. Also, association with diaperlessness and/or the power of projection can have a positive effect on nighttime toileting with both infants and toddlers. One mother ran out of disposables and told her infant son not to pee in his sleep; another mother forgot to diaper her son one night. Both were happy to find their babies dry the next morning. They never diapered at night again and their babies stayed dry. Another mother found that when her baby was diaperless at night, he remained dry, but whenever she diapered him at night, he wet the diaper. Once she noticed this pattern, she stopped diapering him at night. And let us not forget how disposables suppress feelings of wetness that might otherwise wake a child at night and encourage him to use the toilet or potty rather than his disposable diaper.

Diapers can be especially uncomfortable for boys. If your boy cries at night for no apparent reason, his discomfort could be caused by diapers restricting penis movement and swelling/expansion during a nighttime erection.

Once your child begins to walk, use one or more nightlights so he can see in the dark. Place the potty near the bed. Invite him to wake you when he has to go, even if you are co-sleeping. The thought of you waking up to accompany him might be just the encouragement he needs to get up at night.

If one parent remains at home with baby during the day, it is helpful if the other parent takes on the task of getting up at night whenever possible and reasonable. Some fathers are glad to make this sacrifice, while others flatly refuse to make the effort. Each family has to weigh their total situation in order to determine who does what, if anything, about nighttime pottying.

If you want your baby to be diaperless at night but are worried about your mattress and bedding, there are a number of ways to protect them. Natural wool is one of the best solutions since wool is resistant, doesn't grow bacteria or fungus, absorbs a lot of liquid before feeling wet and is a natural deodorizer. You can let baby sleep diaperless by placing a sheepskin rug (shorthaired is preferable, to reduce the risk of suffocation and also for cleaning purposes) or wool mattress pad under soft and natural material such as a cotton or flannel sheet. If the wool starts to smell after some days, let it air out in the sun. If you ever find mildew on the wool, thoroughly clean it asap. If you don't want to use wool, try cotton changing pads with an absorbent core and waterproof backing.

By using the right materials to protect your bed, you will not have to worry about nighttime accidents. This will allow you to be relaxed while your baby enjoys sleeping without a diaper. This in turn will make it easier to pee baby in the middle of the night since you won't have to unnecessarily disturb him or spend time removing a diaper. But there is a chance that having a diaperless baby in bed will (at first) keep you on high alert and cause you to lose sleep, in which case you can try the next best thing. If you prefer to use a cloth diaper without a waterproof cover, or if your baby pees through a disposable diaper at night, your bedding and mattress will also be protected by using wool or other absorbent materials.

Some families don't worry about taking baby to pee at night. They figure that if they devote time to pottying during the day, they won't slow down the process by going off duty at night. Many families believe their baby will simply outgrow bedwetting.

If you are not getting up at night and baby pees most nights for a year or longer, it may be wise to reassess the situation and change tactics as a means to help him avoid long-term nocturnal enuresis (bedwetting at night after the age of 3 years). Enuresis is an elimination disorder that can last for years. In fact, adults in their twenties have been found to still be incontinent. There are a number of treatments available, but none are guaranteed to work. If your baby is showing repeated signs of enuresis, it might well be worth the sacrifice to get up at night and take him to pee, as a gentle and natural way to combat the problem before it progresses into a true elimination disorder. It would of course be preferable for your child to learn to stay dry all night at a relatively young age, rather than going through years of the embarrassment and discomfort of bedwetting.

Nighttime regression after staying dry for a month or longer can be caused by emotional factors. "Children's brain patterns change if they are overly tired, stressed, or depressed, preventing the sleeping brain from detecting signals from the bladder and awakening. The problem can be expected to disappear as soon as the child is back on an even keel. . . . Urinary tract infections, sleep apnea, diabetes mellitus, and seizure disorders can also cause sudden bouts of bedwetting. See your pediatrician if your child begins bedwetting after having remained dry for a month."[32]

# chapter  7

# parental attitude

## Be Positive, Never Punitive

A positive, confident and consistent attitude on the part of parents and all others involved cannot be overemphasized. Without the right attitude on your part, you cannot expect to reap all the benefits. It is important to make toilet time a relaxing and enjoyable time for your baby. This can only be accomplished if you practice patience and exude encouragement and confidence.

Infant potty teamwork creates a special feeling of intimacy and closeness between parent and baby. Your infant will enjoy being held in your arms, touching your face, patting your hands and caressing you. You will enjoy cuddling him in your arms as you gaze at each other, directly or via a mirror. All of this enhances bonding and communication.

Together you accomplish an amazing feat. Express your joy and satisfaction in whatever way feels most natural and spontaneous to you. Some mothers display their excitement by clapping, praising or otherwise celebrating, while others prefer to be matter-of-fact and simply remark, "You peed," or "You pooed," without showing much emotion. In any case, it is a pleasure to see your child respond so naturally and happily to toilet training at such a young age. It is a relief to know that your baby doesn't have to spend much time in wet or soiled diapers.

At first you may need to discipline yourself to be available on time for baby whenever reasonably possible. Do not punish him (or yourself!) if you arrive too late. Avoid making him feel like a failure if he wets his pants and/or goes in the wrong place. If he accidentally goes on the floor, furniture, bedspread, etc., don't despair and don't blame him. Just clean up and move on. When he wobbles, stumbles and falls while practicing walking, you will not feel angry or frustrated but will encourage his attempts. The same attitude applies to pottying—it is normal to experience many spills over the months, just as you expect your baby to take many falls while he is learning to walk.

Be open-minded. If your child wets his clothing, try to determine why. It may be due to illness, travel, emotional problems, a change in schedule or a change in baby's natural body rhythms. If the schedule or rhythms have changed, as they will do a number of times over the months as he grows and matures, be alert and flexible enough to change with your child. Mothers who nurse on demand and rely mainly on timing to know when baby needs to pee may at first find it tricky to anticipate when he needs to go. Since he nurses whenever he pleases rather than at fixed intervals, he is likely to pee and poo at irregular intervals. In this situation, strive to learn your baby's body language, vocalizations and other signals. Observe when he evacuates in relation to breastfeeding bouts. Trust and make use of your intuition.

It is also up to you to provide a cozy and peaceful environment. Your baby must never feel under pressure to perform. This means that you cannot be in a rush. If you find you do not have the time to correctly and peacefully potty him on some occasions, do not hesitate to use a diaper at those times. It is far better to do so than to project negative feelings onto your baby. If you're feeling exhausted, take a break and go back to training pants or diapers. It's better to have a pee or a poo in the pants than to get stressed out.

Every one of us occasionally experiences a "bad day." If you are tense or in a bad mood, gain control over your negative emotions so you do not direct them at your child. Babies can instantly sense when you are upset and negative. They detect your mood in things like your behavior, facial expressions, tone of voice, body movements, muscular tension and breathing. Teach yourself to accept the fact that you will make mistakes. If you "miss" several pees or poos and find that baby's elimination is "out of sink" (sync), don't become distraught and don't assign blame. *Infant potty training is not an all-or-nothing endeavor.* It is unrealistic to expect perfection from yourself or your baby until the process is complete. Consider yourselves to be gradually working towards eventual perfection, knowing it will take many months, mishaps, cuddles and laughs to reach that goal. The difference between a good day and a bad day is often not so much the things that happen but your attitude towards them, whether you can laugh about them or not.

Babies also have the occasional "off day." On such occasions, they may not give their usual signal(s), or you might miss their signal. If a baby is ill or if there is a change in his daily routine, this can throw his timing off for a while. No blame or guilt should be assigned. Pay closer attention to your baby and resynchronize with him as soon as possible. This could take a number of days in some situations.

All of the above reflects the fact that it takes a mature and engaged person or team of persons to work with baby. The best candidates are mature, dedicated, gentle and patient parents and caregivers. This method is not something for a typical teenage mother, for example, since a teenage mother is still a child herself and is likely to be somewhat self-centered, without the dedication and patience it takes. Nor is it suitable for those who cannot arrange their priorities to put potty training at or near the top of the list for a minimum of a few toilet sessions a day.

Find a balance between the following:

- The more regularly and faithfully you adhere to the guidelines, the more likely your child will be diaper free at the earliest moment possible.
- It is better to occasionally resort to diapers (and this is not a failure on your part if you do so) than to wear yourself out or direct anger and frustration at your child.

In other words, be as consistent as possible but not to the point of becoming stressed, obsessed, exhausted or frustrated. Sometimes we try too hard and make too big a deal out of toileting. Remember, a relaxed flow is essential. You can't expect to be there for every pee, just as you can't expect to be there for every baby step or every time your baby mispronounces a word.

When your child is old enough to use a potty, he should never be forced to sit on it for long periods of time. A good range is 2–10 minutes, depending on the age and attention span of the child. This does not mean you should let your child avoid potty time altogether. Be firm in your convictions by finding creative ways to encourage him to sit on the pot. When necessary, entertain, distract or fascinate baby to keep him on the potty. Take a break if he doesn't go at the expected time, then come back a while later to try again. Do not use force or other negative emotions. Potty time should be pleasant.

This method is not about control. If you frequently get into a battle of wills, you might as well resort to conventional potty training methods. Strive to remain neutral, nonchalant and nonjudgmental while at the same time letting baby know potty time is a necessary and serious part of life. Some have asked: If my baby isn't signaling, am I choosing/controlling when he has to go? As long as you base toilet visits on *his* timing and as long as you are not "overdoing it" by trying to be too perfect, you are responding to his needs and not exerting your will or control.

## Be Patient and Relaxed

Although the roles of patience and taking a relaxed approach have already been mentioned, their importance in relation to infant pottying cannot be overemphasized. Some parents set out with unrealistic expectations, not realizing that they will be progressing in baby steps along a lengthy and winding path. A good approach is to take things one day at a time. The daily steps you take are like the pieces to a jigsaw puzzle. Some puzzles are easier and faster to assemble than others. Some are more complicated than others. Look for patterns to fit the pieces together. If you are relaxed and good-natured about it, everyone involved will enjoy the process. There will be mistakes, misses and mismatches along the way, but with determination and loving interaction, you will gradually build and complete the big, beautiful picture.

When you first start out, be kind to yourself and don't worry about the opinions of others who aren't familiar with what you are doing. It's hard to relax if you are being judged by people who don't understand. If helpful, be discrete by taking your baby to the bathroom and closing the door for privacy. In many ways, the learning curve for infant pottying can be compared to that for breastfeeding. For example, during the first 6 weeks you might not feel confident or secure about what you're doing and if this is the case, during this time you might want to avoid the scrutiny of your in-laws or other relatives and friends. Take it easy and don't beat up on yourself if things don't go the way you had hoped. You and your baby are learning together and eventually the process will become second nature for both of you.

The mother of a 7-month-old captures the feelings of many in this communication. "Friends and family can't keep quiet. I've got the baby who sits on a pot! Funny, when I started, I couldn't quit talking about it. Now that it's a part of us, I don't think of telling everyone about it like I used to. As we gain ground (success), we're creating a local sensation. In fact, I would like a little less publicity until we finish, mainly because I never seem to have a perfect day. For instance, the day he dazzled my friend and peed in her sink, he turned right around and pooed in his pants an hour later. I had put him on the floor to play and lost my connection with him. I try not to sweat the misses. Each day is a new challenge to get it right. Each nap is another opportunity to watch for him to wake and put him on the pot. When I started this, I often thought too much about those who had graduated. I wanted the whole picture too soon. Now I know that the journey is part of the joy. It's like living in 3-D. I can experience this child to the fullest."[33]

## Customize Your Approach

Different people with different babies need to take different approaches, per the expression "Different strokes for different folks." Capitalize on all your strengths. Combat your weaknesses and convert them into strengths whenever possible. For example, if you are the laid-back and lazy type, your casual, stress-free and relaxed approach is a true asset, but you may need to strive to be more strict and disciplined in responding to baby's cues. Prioritize your day so you are sure to "be there on time" for baby whenever reasonably possible. Make an effort to be more structured and consistent.

If you are a perfectionist, your abilities to be persistent, consistent, punctual, organized and focused will prove to be extremely helpful, but you need to unwind and appreciate yourself and your efforts. Accept the fact that there are bound to be many accidents and misses and that perfection will not be a reality until baby is fully toilet trained. Be objective rather than subjective. Practice reacting to a puddle of pee on the kitchen floor as if it were a puddle of water. Nonchalantly wipe it up in the blink of an eye as if nothing has happened and carry on with whatever you were doing. Do not feel you have failed or let down your baby.

## Evolving with Baby

Just when you think you have it down to a science, your child will change. Evolve and change with your baby. One way to view the various stages is to compare them to progressing through school.

### Kindergarten
These are the first really fun days, when you discover what a joy your newborn is; spent perhaps partly with baby on your belly, in a sling or maybe next to you on a mat in the middle of your living room; learning to read and respond to each other's signals.

### Elementary School
This is the in-arms phase, consisting of many days of standing by the sink or tub; holding, cuddling and coaching; listening, learning and laughing; perfecting the interpretation of each other's signals.

### Junior High School
Moving into the potty phase, this is where it can get a little rough for a while; when identity is everything, with both of you trying to establish who knows best; sampling a taste of rebellion.

### High School
This is the final phase, which often begins around the time of learning to walk, setting out on the road to true independence; at times a battle of wits, but all in all a fun and interesting time where character and personality blossom.

### Graduation
The day of graduation arrives rather suddenly. It is almost unexpected after all your efforts, and looking back, you remark to yourself, "How time flies! It wasn't the easiest thing I've done, but I would not trade this experience for anything."

## Consistency and Confusion

A frequently asked question is: "If I'm not consistent on a regular basis, will this confuse my baby?" As long as you are fairly regular for some potty sessions each day, you will not confuse your child. A typical scenario is to have a fairly regular morning and/or evening routine, but a relatively chaotic afternoon schedule. You may be constant and punctual first thing in the morning and before bedtime at night, but you have a job or other children and must deviate from your desired or ideal scheme in order to attend to other duties. Many mothers keep their babies apprised of the situation, "I can't get you to the potty while we're out driving around (or homeschooling or working in the office—fill in the blank) so you need to use diapers in the afternoon." For more, see Chapter 8, "Part-Time Pottying."

What *is* confusing is to be erratic and irregular, only taking baby to pee when it is convenient for you. Those convenient times will dwindle until they disappear altogether. In addition, once baby senses that you aren't really serious about communicating and working together towards potty training, he will stop signaling you.

## Caveats

- Do not use force with your child.
- Do not be punitive.
- Do not expect too much of yourself or baby.
- Do not be judgmental.
- Do not view this method as a form of competition with others.
- Do not try to prove something to yourself or others.
- Do not try to create a superbaby for others to admire.

## Why All the Fuss?

To the millions upon millions of Asian, African and other families using this simple and natural method, an apology is in order. These families would find it strange to read a book full of advice and caveats on such a natural and normal subject. Parents in many other societies cannot imagine why anyone would even want to discuss this simple topic. Unfortunately, infant toilet training has been maligned and misunderstood by Westerners to such a degree that all this fuss is warranted at the time of publication. Perhaps someday awareness of this gentle method will become more commonplace, Western parents will enjoy spending more time with their babies and the discrimination against infant toilet training will be put to rest.

## Weighing the Options

Toilet training is an essential part of a child's life. It is a very important parental function or duty, yet many parents put it off as long as possible, for one reason or another. Some feel they do not know how to toilet train a child. Others find it inconvenient and too time consuming. Some find it messy and disgusting. Others assume that a child will miraculously train himself when old enough.

If one considers the first 2 to 4 years of raising a child as a whole, infant potty training saves time, spares the environment and is more hygienic than traditional Western methods.

Contrary to what many doctors may tell you, there is not one method of toilet teaching that is ideal for every parent, child, home situation and life-style. You may find yourself in a position to use this method with one child and not with your next, depending on your domestic situation or your frame of mind.

A practicing mother informed me, "I talked to a lady who trained her firstborn, a girl, using this method. It worked wonderfully, and she was toilet trained at 15 months. With her next child, the mother got lazy and didn't use this method. Oh, how she regrets it now! The second child is 2½ years old and has no interest in toilet training and shows no signs of self-training. Her mother is really kicking herself for not using infant toilet training with her second girl."[34]

The main drawback to infant toilet learning is that it is time consuming, but all methods take time in one form or another. Infancy is a logical time to start toilet learning, since a small child requires a lot of time and attention anyway. Why not use that time to also toilet train your baby? It will save you time, money and work in the long run, and your investment will pay off royally for all concerned.

# chapter 8

# part-time pottying

Acommon question is: "Can this be done part time?" Yes, depending on your definition of "part time." If you start late or do it part time on a fairly consistent basis, it can work. This chapter deals with some part-time scenarios and their chances of success. A number of suggestions are given, but parents must always bear in mind that each child is unique. Use, mold and adapt the suggestions to fit your situation and baby's rhythms, habits and tendencies. Part-time pottying is one of the ways this method has been adapted to Western living.

The starting point of this topic is to accept that during the in-arms phase and most of the potty phase, no mother will ever get her infant to go in the toilet place or potty for her on every occasion. Some are successful with all bowel movements, but not with urination. Getting every pee in the pot would be far too time consuming for even the most devoted caregiver, and it would impose far too many restraints on a mother or caregiver. It would also be demanding on baby if she had to be taken to eliminate on every single occasion, in sickness and in health, at night, when transitioning from one particular timing to another, while traveling, when visiting relatives, on shopping sprees and so on. In short, it is unrealistic to expect to get every pee and poo in the potty during the early months. This only becomes possible when baby has completed the process. In the meantime, the amount of "hits" will gradually increase over time. As stated earlier, this is not an all-or-nothing thing, and in this sense, it could be said that everyone does part-time pottying for a while.

But if there are long stretches in the day where baby can't be pottied—if you work outside the home and use a babysitter or daycare, for example—the issue of part-time pottying becomes more of a concern to parents.

## Time Management

Savvy time management is essential. You will need to carefully prioritize child care, work outside the home, housework, mealtimes, social life, leisure time, sleep and all other aspects of daily life. Regular toilet sessions for baby need to be high on the list of priorities, even if potty visits are only possible a few hours, or even just a few times, a day. Obviously, the more regular and diligent you are (without overdoing it), the better. Finding a reasonable and harmonious balance is the key.

If helpful, make a list of priorities and post reminders on the refrigerator or around the house. Using a timer as a reminder to take baby to the bathroom may prove beneficial. And, as always, remain sensitive and responsive to your internal clock. When necessary, elicit the assistance of others. This can include your spouse or partner, relatives, older siblings, friends, a nanny or a babysitter.

## Siblings

Older brothers and sisters can be a great help. In some societies, child nurses are a part of life. Relatively young siblings, friends or child nurses routinely carry and potty babies. It is of course necessary to teach an older child the exact procedures needed to keep baby safe, content, clean and healthy. This in turn can give a mother a welcome and needed break. Siblings helping siblings naturally increases family bonding and closeness.

It is possible to toilet train two or more young children at the same time. There are two scenarios for this. The first involves twins, triplets, etc., of the same age. Infant pottying is used by many families with twins, in large part because the parents are anxious to reduce diaper use asap. Twins develop and progress at their own individual rates, so variation is to be expected. The importance of remaining relaxed is essential since you are in one sense doubling the potential for stress. One mother of twins puts it in perspective: "If you can't potty perfectly, it's no worse than the other imperfections you will encounter in your parenting process."

*John Lamela*

6-month-old twins Tressa and Wyatt with their mother, Julie, who took an interest in infant potty training when Wyatt developed severe diaper rash. At 6 months, Tressa was more receptive to the potty than her brother.

*Shivalila*

An 11 year-old helps toilet train 4-month-old Kanoa

The second scenario involves families who learn about infant potty techniques when one child is already a toddler and on time to use with their newborn or infant. A child 2 to 4 years old who has not yet been potty trained is likely to be encouraged to work on potty learning alongside her baby brother or sister and vice versa. Older children tend to be more enthusiastic about potty learning if they are in the company of someone else going through the same process. They may well feel responsible to set an example for their baby sibling.

## Working and Homeschooling Parents

Mothers and fathers who work can use this method, as long as they establish and maintain a fairly regular daily routine of infant potty activities. This section also applies to parents who have more than one small child and parents who homeschool one or more older children.

The most likely way for part-time pottying to succeed is to be as regular as you can, even if it is for just one or a few potty sessions a day, at the same time each day. The best, most effective and usually most convenient times to implement part-time pottying are:

## First Thing in the Morning

Pee and/or poop baby in the morning, ideally upon waking. If your infant can "hold it" for a while upon waking, you can let her nurse or feed, then take her to go. If she can't hold it throughout the whole feeding, try these three steps:

1. Let her nurse briefly/consume part of her meal.
2. Take a short break to go potty.
3. Resume the feeding.

If it makes baby upset to interrupt a feeding, hold her over a receptacle while feeding her and make the "sssss" sound (or whatever sound or words you prefer to use) when she goes. See Chapters 3 and 4 for photos of pottying baby while nursing. This also works with bottle-feeding. When baby is a little older to the point where she can retain her elimination longer and does not seem to mind interrupting a feeding briefly to visit the toilet place, transition to a new routine of taking her to evacuate before feeding her first thing in the morning.

## After a Nap

If you are at home when baby wakes from a nap, this is another excellent time to take her to the potty or other toilet place. If you find your baby doesn't need to go upon waking, observe and make a note of her timing in relation to waking up from a nap. Does she pee 5 minutes later? Does she pee 15 minutes later? Jot down or make a mental note of the timing and use this information to help you know when to potty her after a nap. Don't forget to watch and listen for her signals, to read her body language (if any) and/or to follow your intuition.

## Before or after a Feeding

Once you get to know your baby's natural rhythms, you'll start to notice a relationship in the timing between eating and elimination. Some parents pick this up straightaway while others need days or weeks to learn elimination patterns. Some parents claim their baby has no regular elimination pattern. These parents can rely on other means (body language, signals from baby or intuition) to know when to take baby to eliminate. Eventually, most children will establish a more or less regular pattern of elimination. The pattern may not be steady throughout the day, but there will be a few things that will become predictable. For example, most babies poo in the morning, either upon waking or soon after their first feeding or breakfast.

*Vanessa Lorentzen*

A break in homeschooling allows Hollis to take his baby brother for a quick pee.

## Before Bed at Night

In an effort to avoid bedwetting, it is good to take baby to eliminate before going to bed. It is possible that she will not need to pee before her last feeding or before going to bed, but a short visit to the toilet place is still a good idea since she will understand that she should at least try to eliminate before bed. Most babies are able to make themselves go if there is a reasonable amount of urine in the bladder, so even if she doesn't have a full bladder, she may empty out the contents, which in turn will help her remain dry at night.

If working parents and homeschooling parents are able to find a trustworthy and reliable caregiver (nanny, babysitter, older sibling or grandparent) who will continue with toileting during the day, this will of course be a bonus and enable baby to advance even faster. Parents should give their caregivers explicit training and detailed instructions. They should require frequent feedback in order to be certain the caregiver has the right attitude and approach. It is important to keep tabs on the caregiver's frame of mind, to be sure she is comfortable with infant pottying and that she does not feel stressed, experience excessive impatience or direct anger at baby. Once they get over their initial surprise at hearing about the concept of infant elimination training, most caregivers are delighted to work with a baby in this capacity.

If you need to send your child to daycare, look for one that is willing to potty your baby at least a few times a day. Many daycare centers have never heard about infant potty techniques, so be prepared to give them a brief introduction and see how they react. Daycare centers usually put toddlers on the potty throughout the day anyway and might be willing and even delighted to do the same with an infant. If you cannot find a daycare that will do this, go for the next best thing, which is to find one that is diligent about quickly changing wet or soiled diapers and pants. Before leaving your baby at the center, tell her what to expect: "The ladies here will potty you," "The people might not know when you need to go, so don't get mad if they are late," "The people here don't use potties but will change you really fast," "We'll get back to the potty after daycare," or whatever else is likely to assure a stress-free experience.

Homeschooling parents can work out a schedule whereby one or more family members take on the pottying responsibility at fixed times each day. A sample schedule follows:

When baby wakes in the morning ............. mother or father

At breakfast or in
relation to first feeding ................................................ mother

Mid-morning ....................................................... older sibling
during break
between lessons

Midday ................................................................ mother or
older sibling
during lunch break

Nap time .................................................................. mother

Afternoon ...................................................... mother or older
sibling during
break between lessons

Evening ...................................................................... father

Bedtime ...................................................... mother or father

## Unexpected Extended Interruptions

Sometimes parents meet with unexpected circumstances and find they must direct their efforts to help a sick relative, sort out financial problems, recover from an illness or injury, etc. Such events take considerable time and energy, resulting in unintended gaps in potty training. The good news is that if you have spent a minimum of a month or two pottying your infant, a reduction or temporary cessation in the time you spend at it does not necessarily mean she will forget all that she has learned. Parents who have had to take a break due to unforeseen circumstances have been pleased to find that their baby still remembers the in-arms potty routine after a break of some days, weeks and even months. There is no formula for knowing how long a baby can remember the stimulus-response conditioning, but some families have reported taking a break of up to a month or longer, only to find their babies anxious to pick up where they left off. For a testimonial to this effect, see Part 2, Chapter 6, "An Online Adventure." Again it must be emphasized that each child is different—some will retain things longer and better than others.

While it is not advisable to take time off, it is comforting to know that all may not be lost should you be forced to take an extended break.

## Traveling Parents

Some practicing parents take their baby with them on most or all business trips and vacations. It's fine to continue with infant pottying while traveling as long as you feel comfortable and relaxed about it. If it proves too difficult, use a diaper on such occasions.

Travel can disrupt baby's regular routine and natural timing, especially if she misses or is awakened from naps. In some situations, travel can throw parents off schedule more than it affects baby's timing. In any case, once you return home, your baby will soon return to her regular routine, unless there is a significant change in her surroundings or unless she is at the point of changing her natural routine anyway. Observe and heed her signals, and you'll soon be back on track.

Some families who travel several times a year with baby report that the travel does not interrupt their pottying at all. Baby adapts to traveling, learns to sleep whenever she is tired, grows accustomed to staying in hotel rooms or elsewhere and does not mind using new and different toilet places. With toddlers, vacation time can sometimes be the catalyst that leads to finalizing toilet training—parents are more relaxed, have more time and patience and might find that it is easier to let baby go bare-bottomed at the beach, lake or river.

If you travel frequently without baby and don't want to interrupt her toilet teaching, look for a relative, nanny or babysitter who is willing and happy to work with her during your absence. You'll need to give thorough training, leave written instructions and do a few "test runs" before entrusting your baby to a new caregiver.

## Erratic Pottying

It is not advisable to use part-time pottying if you are going to do it in a haphazard and erratic fashion. Do not repeatedly start, stop and restart for no apparent reason such as being lazy, irresponsible or a procrastinator. It takes long-term and consistent commitment. Taking an occasional break for illness or if you need a little time off is okay as long as it doesn't happen repeatedly. Remember that the most likely way for part-time pottying to succeed is to be as regular as you can, even if it is for just one or a few potty sessions a day, at the same time each day. If you cannot stick to a fairly regular minimal schedule, it is better not to use this method.

## Multiple Caregivers

Most babies do fine with multiple caregivers. Caregivers can of course include family members, such as siblings, grandparents, aunts and uncles. Having help with pottying will give the principal caregiver a break and a boost. You can divide the day into shifts or else at times when the whole family is present, let everyone be in charge of a particular aspect of the routine (holding baby, removing pants or diapers, cleaning up if there is an accident, dressing baby, etc.), making it a family undertaking or assembly line.

In the early weeks of life, infants have no fear of strangers. If you need to hire a nanny or babysitter and want to teach them to potty baby, it is easiest to begin this before baby develops a fear of strangers or a sense of shyness. This is not to say that you cannot have multiple caregivers once a baby is shy or apprehensive of meeting new people. Many families have no problem introducing an attentive newcomer to care for their child at any age.

If a child proves to be truly upset by being held by a certain person, do not force the issue. Try introducing baby to another caregiver and see if this helps. If not, you'll need to wait until she overcomes her fear of strangers or until she is more open to being held by others. Sometimes a caregiver will be hesitant to potty your child. Baby will sense this hesitancy, and it may cause her to not want to work in this respect with a particular caregiver.

## What to Expect

By using part-time pottying, parents help maintain baby's natural awareness of elimination. She will learn and remember how to release both urine and feces upon receiving your cues. She will be able to take advantage of this process whenever you are available to take her to the toilet place. This will make it easier to complete potty learning when both you and your child are ready and able to devote the amount of time it takes to read and respond to each other's signals.

# chapter 9

# stage by stage

This chapter gives a general description of what to expect of pottying stage by stage. It is mainly intended to serve as a quick reference guide, to consult after having thoroughly read and digested Chapters 3 through 7. The idea is to refer to the particular section that applies to your baby's current age and corresponding stage of development, rather than to read the chapter from start to finish. There is repetition of some tips and other items throughout the chapter since certain things may overlap between stages and also because different babies do different things at different ages.

The stage-by-stage guidelines describe and explain the typical potty progression of a healthy baby after a normal or fairly normal delivery but do not encompass the variations in patterns that may arise out of the uniqueness of each child. Variables in environment, family situation, cultural background and health may also yield somewhat different results. Likewise, it is not possible to include every eventuality that may occur. If your baby responds differently from the behaviors discussed in this chapter, it does not necessarily mean you are doing something wrong. In other words, all babies will not follow all of these general guidelines, but this chapter gives a good indication of what is feasible at different ages and stages.

Beginning infant potty training the first day, week or month is a matter of preference rather than necessity. Families who feel strongly one way or the other should follow their instincts or intellect. You might find it less stressful to wait a few months until baby eliminates less often (once your milk comes in, she may pee every 5 minutes for some weeks!); gains more muscle tone and becomes less wobbly; and is awake for longer periods. You may want to give yourself time to recover from delivery, to gain confidence in holding baby or to sort out any breastfeeding problems.

Always bear in mind that it is unrealistic to expect to be on time for every pee and poo. This will only happen when baby has completed potty training. It is fine if you get your infant to pee on cue just once or twice a day at first, especially if she does not pee often (once every 30 or more minutes). If she pees often (every 15–20 minutes, 3 or more times after a feeding), a good starting goal is 2–4 pees a day, then build from there. Do not be too hard on yourself by expecting too much. Remember, it may take some days to catch your first pee or poo.

If you start the in-arms phase before your baby is 4–5 months old, there is a chance that you will rarely or never have to deal with a poopy diaper again, except in case of illness or upset, especially if your infant's elimination timing is fairly regular and you are diligent. Of course, a responsible caregiver needs to be available to take baby to the toilet place on time.

It is generally easier to anticipate a bowel movement than urination since baby's body language and signals for defecation (reddening face, grunting, squirming, passing gas, etc.) tend to be more obvious than those for urination. It is also easier for a baby to learn to control bowel movements than urination, so a baby will typically learn bowel control before bladder control. But some parents do better with the timing of urine than stools, so don't be alarmed or feel you aren't doing well if you find yourself in this situation.

The combination of signals, body language and timing differs from one infant to the next, so there are no hard-and-fast rules on how often to take her to eliminate or on "what should be happening when." Take it one day at a time. Do the best you can with the time and help you have available. There will be both rewarding and challenging times. Do not set unrealistic goals or you will be disappointed, and this may cause you to give up. Communicate as best you can and adjust to the particular circumstances of each day or phase of development. Enjoy your baby!

If baby pees at night and you are able to work with her in this capacity without undue stress, be as regular about getting up once or twice a night as you can as long as you do not feel exhausted during the day. If it proves too difficult to get up at night, wait until baby is older to implement this phase. Never forget that the key to infant potty training is to remain relaxed, casual and positive.

## First Day of Life

The first day, baby will probably pee just once or twice. A healthy baby will pee at least once in the first 24 hours.[35] Some babies might pass a tarry-looking, greenish-black stool called meconium. The meconium is what's left in her intestines from life in utero. For parents wishing to keep their newborn out of diapers on her first day, there are two scenarios to consider:

**Holding Baby**
Many parents want to hold their newborn as much as possible. Some enjoy skin-to-skin contact, while others prefer to clothe their baby. If she happens to pee or poo while you are holding her, make the "sssss" sound, or whatever basic signal you have selected, while she is peeing. If you are not quick enough to give the cue as she is peeing, give the signal immediately after she pees.

**Laying Baby Down**
Whether she is lying next to you or in her own bed, protect the underlying mattress with a waterproof pad, then cover the pad with a soft, absorbent cloth that can be easily removed. Examples of the soft covering include a flannel sheet, a cloth diaper or a soft towel covered by a sheet. If you notice your newborn eliminating, make the "sssss" sound, or use whatever basic signal sound you have selected, while she is eliminating or immediately thereafter. Gently replace the wet items with clean, dry ones.

If you start pottying baby the first day, you will open up the channels of elimination communication at the earliest possible moment. Parents who have caught the meconium with one baby but not with another report that it is easier to communicate with a baby and read her signals if you start with the meconium. When you notice your newborn beginning to evacuate, raise or pick her up so she does not wet or soil herself. Make the "sssss" sound as she goes or, if you're a few seconds late, immediately afterwards. Replace the wet or soiled cloth with a clean, dry one.

**Pre-pottying Tips . . .**

Many mothers do not want to start with the meconium or urination during the first day(s), which is fine. Many will be recovering from delivery, too tired or adjusting to having a new family member. Consider and weigh your particular circumstances when deciding precisely when to start pottying baby.

If you decide to observe baby's timing but do not yet want to hold her over a receptacle or cloth when she goes, lay her on a waterproof area as discussed above, or else place her on a diaper on your chest and observe her timing that way. Give your signal when she eliminates or just after she eliminates.

Make a note of any sound she makes or body language she exhibits just before peeing or pooing. Watch for these same signals to repeat at future sessions, just before she goes.

The first day involves a lot of resting, gratitude, wonderment, joy and bonding through physical contact and subtle communication. Keep baby with you every possible moment. From birth, infants can control the flow of visual stimuli. Mutual gazing (looking in each other's eyes, also called "mutual visual interaction" and "eye contact") enhances bonding,[36] so be sure to make contact by gazing into her eyes when she looks at you.

Many mothers feel the first day has a sacred quality to it. They feel lucid and alert on the one hand yet relaxed, dreamy and sleepy on the other hand. They experience a slowing of time as if in a different dimension or as if a mysterious force were letting this magical day linger. If you want to begin elimination communication with your newborn on the first day, start gently and go from there. If you prefer to savor the day without dealing with baby's timing, wait until you feel ready to begin pottying. Some mothers may have no choice but to wait if baby is being kept apart from her for medical reasons during part or all of the first day(s). If you are in this situation, don't let it deter you from starting infant elimination training once you and baby can be together throughout the day.

## First Week of Life

A healthy baby should stool by 36 hours and definitely not later than 48 hours after birth.[37] Start or continue watching for elimination timing patterns and jot them down. Hold baby securely and comfortably over a diaper or receptacle when you sense she needs to go, or when she starts to go. Some mothers hold their babies bare-bottomed over a tiny, comfortable receptacle (with soft edges and at room temperature), such as a plastic baking bowl, while they nurse, since newborns often go while suckling. Whenever possible, make the "sssss" sound when baby pees or poos, or immediately afterwards. She will soon begin to associate this cue with elimination.

> **Pre-pottying Tips . . .**
>
> Observe baby's elimination timing patterns and jot them down. Whenever possible, make the "sssss" sound when baby pees or poos, or immediately afterwards.
>
> Make a note of any sound she makes or body language she exhibits just before peeing or pooing. Watch for these same signals to repeat at future sessions, just before she goes.

The first week is a magical time, especially if you are able to rest well and spend considerable time bonding with your newborn. The meconium takes about three days to clear out of baby's system. If you are nursing, the composition of your milk will start to change from colostrum to milk around the 3rd or 4th day. Colostrum is the fluid present before the onset of lactation and contains a lot of proteins, antibodies, lymphocytes and other healthy ingredients.

As your milk comes in, baby will drink more and pee more. In terms of pottying, this means that after the first few days of just a few pees a day, baby will start peeing more often and in greater volume, from 6 to 8 times a day. Some babies pee and/or poo in 2–3 spurts. The stools will become much lighter in color, changing to yellow, yellow-green, tan or green, and she'll probably poo 2–5 times a day. One bowel movement a day is okay if she is peeing a lot and gaining enough weight.

The first weeks can be very intense with a newborn, with near-constant elimination. Even if you just make the "sssss" sound a few times a day when she goes and ease your way into catching a daily pee or poo, this keeps the awareness alive. In other words, don't get discouraged before you even begin! And don't feel badly if it turns out to be better for you to start in a few months.

## First Month of Life

You may start noticing a pattern to baby's timing. It is often easier to find a regular pattern with babies who are fed on a (flexible) schedule than with babies fed on demand. Some babies nursed on demand will have a fairly regular elimination pattern, while others may be more erratic. If your infant's pattern is erratic, strive to relate it to the interval(s) of time after feeding and the quantities of liquid she consumes.

Whenever possible, anticipate when baby will need to go and take her to your preferred toilet place. This may be in your lap with her bare bottom over a comfortable receptacle, or it may be over a diaper, sink or other receptacle, whatever works best for both of you. Be sure to give your signal whenever baby pees or poos so she associates this signal with elimination. If she eliminates unexpectedly, give your signal while she is going or immediately after. Don't forget to praise her, tell her what is going on ("you peed") or react in whatever way seems best and most natural to you.

For nursing babies, the colostrum will continue to gradually decrease from mother's milk for up to the 6th week of life, then will cease altogether. Since the colostrum has laxative properties, as it decreases in quantity, so may the number of stools per day. Taking the extremes, around 6 weeks, some babies will continue to poo after every feeding while others may only poo once a week.

It is common for a baby to pee and poo intermittently during one potty session. This means she may pee, wait for a few seconds up to a minute or more, then pee more, wait a bit, then pee again. This is more typical of boys than girls. She might poo, wait a moment or two and continue pooing. This type of intermittent elimination is normal (as long as there are no medical problems, symptoms of illness or other complications to consider) and is part of her elimination pattern.

As baby consumes more milk, she will pee more often and in greater quantity. As her bladder grows, she will be able to retain more urine between pees. Watch for these two factors to come into play from time to time, and observe how they affect your infant's timing.

The first weeks can be very intense with a newborn, with near-constant elimination. Even if you just make the "sssss" sound a few times a day when she goes and ease your way into catching a daily pee or poo, this keeps the awareness alive. In other words, don't get discouraged before you even begin! And don't feel badly if it turns out to be better for you to start in a few months.

---

**Pre-pottying Tips . . .**

Observe baby's elimination timing patterns and jot them down. Whenever possible, make the "sssss" sound when she pees or poos, or immediately afterwards.

Make a note of any sound she makes or body language she exhibits just before peeing or pooing. Watch for these same signals to repeat later in the day. Next time you hear and/or see these same signals, hold her in position to go and give your signal.

---

## Second and Third Months of Life

These are still excellent and exciting months to begin infant elimination training if you have not already started. A baby is still very open and receptive to elimination communication at this age. She is aware of her elimination functions and will understand the signals you give when it's time for her to go. Be sure to read and follow the guidelines and maintain the attitudes described in Chapters 3 through 7. If your schedule only allows for part-time pottying, see Chapter 8, "Part-Time Pottying," for tips, support and inspiration.

Around the 3rd month, some mothers find that their baby is old enough to not mind interrupting a feeding if she has to evacuate. If you sense that baby needs to go while she is nursing or bottle-feeding and it is not upsetting for her to take a break, carry her to the toilet place, give your signal and let her eliminate. Then resume her feeding. Otherwise, try nursing her over a receptacle while waiting for her to go.

**Pre-pottying Tips . . .**

Observe baby's elimination timing patterns and jot them down. Relate her elimination timing to feedings and waking. Whenever possible, make the "sssss" sound when she pees or poos, or immediately afterwards.

Make a note of any sound she makes or body language she exhibits just before peeing or pooping. Watch for these same signals to repeat later in the day. Next time you hear and/or see these same signals, hold her in position to go and give your signal.

Some babies pee and/or poo in spurts. If this is the case with your baby, hold her in position until she has completed all elimination. If you find the length of time between spurts to be uncomfortably long, take a brief break between spurts.

## Fourth Month and Beyond

Continue with the in-arms phase as long as necessary. If baby can sit but prefers to continue with in-arms pottying rather than using a potty, carry on holding her in-arms.

Watch for changes in her timing patterns and adjust accordingly. If she still pees frequently (approximately once every 20 minutes after feedings), you should be getting her to pee on cue 4–6 or more times a day by now (assuming you started at least a month ago and that you or a caregiver are with her during most or all of the day). If she pees infrequently (once every 30 or more minutes), you should be getting her to pee on cue 2–3 or more times a day on a regular basis (assuming you started at least a month ago and that you or a caregiver are with her during most or all of the day).

Baby's signals for defecation are often blatant and easy to read by the 4th–6th month. Some parents get every poo in the potty or toilet place from this age on, except in cases of illness, emotional upset, travel or other disruptions to the regular routine. Do not be alarmed or discouraged if this is not the case for you and your baby.

New variables will continue to come into play as your infant grows and develops, and these should be taken into consideration in relationship to pottying. When she lies in the prone position and presses up on her arms, creeps, scoots or crawls, the extra pressure on her bladder may cause accidents for a while. When she begins to crawl or walk, use and development of new muscle sets may cause extra accidents. She will be interested in exploring her surroundings more than before, and she may forget to signal you at potty time for a while, or on some occasions, until she adapts to her new routine. Conversely, some babies enjoy crawling to the potty or bathroom and will signal you more than they ever did up to this point. When baby begins to eat solid foods, her elimination timing and patterns are likely to change. If there are significant changes or upsets in your domestic situation, such as moving, relationship problems, serious illness or injury, a death in the family or a natural disaster, these will have an effect on baby's pottying.

## Late-Starters

In general, it is more difficult to start infant potty training after the 4th or 5th month than if you begin earlier. An infant may start to lose her natural awareness of the elimination functions around 6 months, so it may prove harder to communicate with her about this. But this is not the case with every child.

Since each baby develops at her own pace, and since there are many variables in each family situation, it is not possible to establish a definitive cutoff time for beginning infant pottying. Some mothers have maintained open and excellent communication with their infants on other fronts and find it easy to incorporate elimination communication into their routine relatively late.

If you discover this method when your baby is 6 months or older and you have the desire, patience and time to try it, a good approach is to combine infant potty techniques with some conventional toilet training methods See Chapter 10, "Late-Starters," for more.

## Sitting

When baby starts to sit, she may want to use a potty or sit on the toilet. Smaller, less stable sitters will need to be gently and securely held in place. Caregivers can use their hands, arms or body to support and steady her on the potty or toilet. Consider sitting on the toilet with your baby, in order to provide maximum comfort, stability and security.

Some babies will prefer to continue being held in your arms rather than start using a potty. It may be weeks or months before they want to make the change to a potty. Let baby's preference dictate the receptacle you use.

If your baby arches her back while you are holding her on the potty, this is usually a clear signal that she is uncomfortable, impatient or wants to get down. You can either let her off or try distracting or entertaining her in an effort to keep her on the potty a little longer. If she relaxes, let her remain on the potty. If she continues to arch, let her off. If you know she still needs to go, give her a short break, then try putting her back on the potty. If she is ill, she most likely will protest sitting on the potty. In this case, do not insist on keeping her there.

## Creeping and Crawling

When baby starts to move about, she will be using and experimenting with new muscular activity that can inadvertently apply pressure to her bladder and cause accidents. In addition, she will focus more on her immediate surroundings than she did up to this point. In her excitement and enthusiasm, she might forget to signal when she has to go. This can lead to accidents or require extra patience over a number of days or weeks while adjusting things to her newfound mobility. It may require more intensive observation on your part in order to take her to the potty place on time. She may now become so engrossed in objects and play that she will resent being interrupted and taken to the toilet place.

It can take days to find ways to entice a newly mobile baby to the potty or toilet place. On the one hand, you don't want to anger or upset her by interrupting her play and exploration; on the other hand, she needs to understand that pottying is still as important as ever and that it must somehow fit into her day. Find a balance between these two factors.

Some babies enjoy crawling to the potty or bathroom once they are mobile and will signal you at potty time more than they ever did up to this point. If you see your baby crawling towards her potty place, be sure to encourage this behavior. Depending on your situation, you can encourage her by following her to the bathroom, holding her in her preferred in-arms position or helping her on the potty or toilet. This can save you both a lot of time and effort. Once babies start to crawl to the toilet place, they may suddenly become noisy about it by vocalizing to you as they head towards the location.

## Solid Foods

Baby's pattern will change when she starts to eat solid foods. Observe her new timing and make the appropriate adjustments to ensure a smooth transition.

Her stools will change in color, odor, density and frequency. At times, constipation and diarrhea will affect her timing. Caregiver and baby will appreciate the benefits of infant potty training more than ever now that she is eating solid foods, since stools will be more of a mess to clean from diapers and baby is more likely to develop diaper rash.

## Walking

When she first starts walking on her own, she may temporarily stop signaling her elimination needs, due to the excitement of walking. The first steps and first days of walking require a lot of concentration on the part of a child. This can distract her from signaling. It might take some days to get her back to signaling you on time. In addition, developing and fine-tuning the muscular coordination needed to walk may inadvertently squeeze her bladder and open the flood gates.

Some babies will happily toddle to the potty on their own and become (more) vocal in signaling you once they can walk. But during the beginning stages of walking, you will need to spend extra time with her. A mobile baby requires more of your attention to keep an eye on her now that she can move about from room to room faster than before.

If she is wearing training pants or other clothing, you'll need to be vigilant about helping her quickly undress for the potty. Avoid clothing that is complicated and time consuming to remove. Fasteners can cost precious seconds and lead to anticipatory accidents.

## Talking

Some babies have completed potty training by the time they begin to use words that relate to elimination. When they are able to clearly verbalize to you that they need to go, it is an added bonus for everyone involved. This is a time of complex learning and understanding, not only in terms of elimination and speech but also in terms of the cause and effect between the two. Your child is learning to put the concepts of time and timing into words at the right moment.

The concept of elimination involves many things, and it takes time to learn to distinguish the various aspects. This is similar to the way an ASL sign can refer to different aspects of a word or sign depending on context and emphasis. For example, in ASL, the sign for "toilet" can be used in different ways to mean many toilet-related things, ranging from "I need to go," to "Where is the bathroom?" to "Take me there," or even "I went."

Babies who have not yet completed toilet training will experiment with using their vocabulary. They are likely to say "pee pee" (or the equivalent) on different occasions. It is not unusual for them to tell you they need to go just before, during or right after they pee. It may take a while until they regularly tell you in advance that they need to go potty. Babies who like sitting on the potty will sometimes tell you they have to go even though they don't really need to. They do this for different reasons, such as testing the power of speech or as a means of getting attention. They soon find clever ways to manipulate you. Don't be surprised if your child gives a false alarm about needing to pee once you have put her to bed for the night. This is, at first at least, a guaranteed ticket to get her out of bed for a while. On other occasions, she may tell you she needs to go potty as a means of getting you to tell her a story or play a game.

## Total Potty Independence

Some indicators that you are nearing graduation include announcing elimination immediately after the fact and releasing a few drops of pee before telling you she has to go. When these start to happen, it may be only a matter of weeks or a few months until she starts to inform you *before* she has to go.

Total potty independence is achieved when baby stays dry day and night on a regular basis. Most babies achieve daytime dryness before nighttime dryness, although there are exceptions. See Chapter 6, "Nighttime," for information on keeping baby dry at night. Some Western babies achieve total potty independence as early as 12 months. The average age is between 18 and 24 months. If factors such as dressing and wiping are taken into consideration, the time frame is longer—some cannot wipe themselves well until age 3–6 years—but these are not indicators of bowel and bladder control. Instead, dressing and wiping reflect new and different stages of development.

## Setbacks

It is possible for a child to have a short-term lapse after potty graduation—maybe a few wet pants during the day or a few nights of bedwetting. Don't panic and don't overreact to a temporary setback! Your child has not forgotten anything. Just give her a few days or a week to bounce back.

True setbacks in toilet learning can happen to any child who has a traumatic or trying experience, including a physical problem such as a serious illness. Regression can even happen to a child who has already achieved total dryness and potty independence. A setback can result from a onetime experience or a continuing problem in the home. If baby regresses, do not use punishment, control or other negativity to try to change her behavior.

Search for a neutral or fun way around her problem as a means to get her back on track. Try offering some kind of reward or encouragement that she will strive to obtain on other occasions. A well-received reward may help her forget or overcome whatever has upset her progress and routine. Sometimes encouragement or a reward can involve someone from outside the immediate family, such as a peer, playmate or relative.

Consider the possibility that you or another caregiver might be contributing to or encouraging the regression. Babies are very sensitive to feelings and can quickly detect an upset or change in the mood, attitude or demeanor of their caregivers. If a caregiver is experiencing negative emotions such as stress, anger, depression, impatience or disinterest, these can have an adverse effect on baby's behavior. It is better to take a break from pottying than to impose your will and bad feelings on her. Don't feel guilty about taking a break. If you feel so inclined, tell baby that you are taking a break for a day or longer. For more on this topic, see "Potty Pauses and Potty Strikes" in Chapter 4.

Be vigilant about the possibility of dangerous physical conditions, and see your doctor fast if you suspect a problem. A bladder infection can cause loss of bladder control, frequent and/or painful urination, pain just above the pubic area or on the side, fever and lethargy.[38]

# chapter 10

# late-starters
## 6 months & older

This chapter is for parents starting with babies 6 months or older. Research conducted since the first edition of this book has yielded exciting and encouraging information for parents who want to start "late" with infant potty training. By using a slightly modified version of this gentle method, it is possible and it works!

There is no clear cutoff age for starting the infant potty training method. Once babies pass the first window of opportunity around 4–5 months, some still remain receptive for a while. Others close down and then open up again, but there is no way to know when this might happen. And it is possible that some babies remain in a constant state of readiness. Their behavior might be mislabeled as "high needs," "colicky," "fussy" or something else. In the meantime, all they can do is await the day that their mothers finally respond to their toilet needs. It's not uncommon to hear the following, "My baby caught on within a few days!" Perhaps the same could have been said many months or even some years ago.

## Duped and Betrayed

Many families do not even hear about infant potty teaching until their babies have passed the first and most powerful window of opportunity, and they feel duped and betrayed when they eventually find out. "I wish I had known about this months (or years) ago!" is one of the most common reactions.

We Westerners have been frightened into believing that we have no right or business using any form of toilet training before our children initiate it on their own, supposedly somewhere in the range of 2–5 years, and that if we dare attempt toileting before that time, we are being "cruel." If the infant potty technique appeals to you and if you approach it with the right attitude and demeanor (see Chapter 7, "Parental Attitude"), you are not going to harm or "screw up" your baby. Infant potty training is as child-oriented and child-led as self-training—it is merely a matter of preference which way you go. The dirty little secret here is not about soiled diapers, but the fact that there are plenty of children who never self-train. And although many do eventually self-train with no apparent effort, what if yours does not? Parents are devastated to find themselves still diapering children at 4 and 5 years of age. Some daycare programs and schools will not admit kids wearing diapers. And why make babies wear their waste at all?

Chapter 16, "History & Theories," presents writings and research indicating that until the 1950s, most children started toilet training before they were a year old. Many started at birth or by age 3–6 months. Yet today's "experts" harp only on those cases where parents were not gentle and used punishment or coercion (definite no-nos for infant potty training), implying that any and all toileting before self-initiation is "harsh." The result is that many Western parents today have never even heard of infant potty training.

## How to Start Late

If your baby is 6 months or older, you'll need to do two things: (1) Make some simple modifications to the infant potty technique and (2) add some traditional toilet teaching tactics to your approach. Most of the basic principles of infant toileting apply (it may be helpful to review Chapters 3–5), but you will need to find, sculpt and hone the best strategy or "recipe" for your child, family and situation. The following is a list of tips and guidelines, starting out with infant potty techniques, then blending into some mainstream conventional tactics that are often effective with toddlers. Some children catch on quickly while others take longer.

## Parental Attitude

Be relaxed, gentle and patient. Accept and enjoy your child's learning pace. Avoid any and all pressure, anger, punishment and other negative emotions, words, intonation or actions.

## Step 1: Choosing Your Basic Signal

Introduce a sound or word that you and your baby associate with elimination. The "sssss" sound is popular in many cultures, or you may prefer to simply say "pee pee" as your baby goes or when you think he needs to go. If he is in "mid-accident" and you are nearby, make the sound to help him learn the association between eliminating and the actual "stuff" that is coming out of him. You can use the same sound (or two different ones) for pee and poo.

## Step 2: Timing and Elimination Patterns

Study your baby's elimination timing and patterns in relation to meals and awaking from sleep, then offer him chances to go at the most logical and obvious times. For example, most babies at first need to go immediately upon waking in the morning and after naps. Thereafter, they might need to pee, say, every 30–60 minutes two or three more times; then the timing may increase to an hour. On the other hand, some 6–9 month olds still pee at 15–20 minute intervals for a while. If your child is eating solids, he might need to go in the middle of a meal, immediately after the meal or 15–30 minutes after eating. Familiarization with these types of patterns can be helpful.

## Step 3: Selecting a Location and/or Receptacle

If your baby is very small, perhaps in the case of a child born prematurely, you may want to start with in-arms pottying. But most late-starters are ready to sit on a potty or toilet. Where you keep the potty or potties is up to you. You can start out by keeping the potty in one place, although most find that moving it around as baby moves from room to room or else placing potties in different parts of the home allows quicker access and yields fewer accidents. Or you may prefer for your child to use the toilet. You can sit with him on the toilet, let him use a child's adapter seat that fits on the adult seat or simply let him sit independently while you keep an eye on him.

If you want your child to be diaperless between toilet visits, the best locations for this are outdoors in warm weather or else in rooms without carpeting. It is easier to detect and clean up after accidents if no carpets are involved.

## Step 4: Positions

Try different potty positions until you find one that is comfortable and convenient for both you and your child. For smaller babies, you can try some of the in-arms positions that are used to hold infants. For more independent and mobile babies, in-arms positioning might not work. Look for a potty that fits your baby; otherwise, you can use the toilet, as described above. Boys often prefer to stand. Some children like to squat on the toilet seat.

## Step 5: Signals and Cues

Study and learn your child's natural toileting body language. Each child has or learns his own set of signals. Some are extremely subtle and hard to recognize, while others may be obvious.

Try sign language or any hand signal you like. This is especially helpful with preverbal babies as it enables them to communicate their needs before they can speak. Once a baby starts to utter deliberate sounds and words, add verbal communication to your list of signals to notice. And remember that your child may at first use the word "pee" for both pee and poo (or vice versa) and/or announce the need to go "after the fact."

## Step 6: Understanding and Commitment

Once you have a good understanding of how infant pottying works, you are at an important crossroads. If you would like to continue, you'll need to make a further commitment about devoting time to your child's "pot luck." Try it for a few weeks, then assess if you want to continue.

If your baby catches on quickly, it will encourage you to continue. If you get no results after 2–4 weeks, you can either simply carry on or else take a break and try again in 2–4 weeks. Even if your child doesn't appear to know what is going on, it is fine to still potty him as long as you are both happy and comfortable with it. Some toddlers develop considerable sphincter control rather suddenly, within just a few days or weeks, but it's not possible to know beforehand if or when this might happen. Also bear in mind that the more potty practice your toddler gets, the sooner he is likely to gain control of his sphincters and master his toileting skills.

Even if you find it is too much for you and give up at some point, your efforts will not have been in vain. Research has shown that many children retain some potty learning, even if their parents give up at some stage, and that it manifests itself later. Toddler toilet teaching tends to be faster and easier with children who had some experience with infant elimination training.[39]

## Clothing

Try to "dump diapers" altogether or as often as possible to help your child unlearn earlier conditioning. This does not mean that you let your child pee and poo all over your house. Use common sense! Although it is not a requirement for babies to be bare-bottomed, it heightens their awareness of elimination and speeds up the learning process (sometimes dramatically). They instantly experience cause and effect. Find a way to work some diaperless hours into your day, when convenient and the least likely to cause stress. For example, if you are going diaperless at home, to avoid worry, you may want to use diapers as a backup when going out.

If you are using disposables, try switching to cloth diapers at least part time. With cloth diapers and no plastic cover, you know immediately when your baby goes. You can thus start to learn and recognize elimination timing and patterns. At the same time, you can change your baby as soon as he goes and avoid encouraging or teaching him to be comfortable with wetness.

Try a pair of training pants, and if they do the trick, invest in more. They are far easier than diapers to pull up and down. In addition, they soak up minor elimination dribbles and protect your busy baby's bottom and genitals.

If your baby seems ready, try regular undies. Pretty undies might be the catalyst that motivates a girl to stay clean and dry. Boys might be inspired to keep their favorite undies dry.

Use easy-to-remove pants. You can sew your own little shorts and pants, using pajama bottoms or sweat pants with an elastic waist as a basic pattern. These are easy to pull up and down in a hurry. Use any material(s) you like, based on comfort, climatic conditions, budget considerations and any other relevant factors.

Chinese open-crotch clothing might work for you. They enable babies to squat-and-go (or sit-and-go) without wetting or soiling themselves. This reduces the worry about dressing and undressing and cuts down on toileting delays and accidents. In cold weather, Chinese pants can be made of warmer materials.

## Combining Infant & Conventional Techniques

### Tactics . . .

- Make potty time fun time. Read books with your child, including books on potty training. Let him play with a favorite toy.
- If or when your child is old enough to care, take him shopping and let him help select a potty. By being involved this way, he is more likely to want to use the potty.
- Use an open-door policy by letting your baby accompany you, dad (fathers are especially helpful with boys) or siblings to the toilet. Let baby observe you and/or other family member(s) using the toilet and talk to him about using the potty or the toilet with a child seat attached. Learning by example and observation can be helpful for many, but don't make a big deal out of it. If your child is curious, he will observe and learn.
- With boys, try target practice by having your son aim at something floating in the toilet (examples: Cheerios, bits of toilet paper or store-bought targets designed for this purpose) or outdoors at his favorite target (example: a tree or a rock, perhaps with an actual target on them). He can also have fun drawing patterns in the dirt or snow, playing pee games such as seeing who can shoot farther, or crisscrossing streams with dad or a brother.
- Concerning praise, do whatever feels right, normal and natural for you and your little one. If you feel like praising your child, fine. If you don't believe in praise, simply state or explain what is happening when your baby goes for you.
- Use trial and error to find what works for you, always remembering that each child and each family situation varies from the next.
- If your child resists the potty or toilet, try to calm and relax him (example: give him something to drink), then offer again.
- For parents starting with children who are already walking, any time your toddler goes on the floor or in his clothing, tell him matter-of-factly what he did and then tell him that it belongs in the potty. Clean the mess and, together with your toddler, take it

to the potty, toilet, hamper or laundry room. Explain again that it is best for the pee and poo to go in the potty or toilet. Do this each time he has an accident.

- Expect some resistance and fooling around by toddlers. For example, when they go through the phase of saying "no" to everything, their "no" does not always really mean "no." In short, if you ask your toddler if he needs to go potty and are met with a resounding "no," this response may sometimes have little to do with your question. This is all part of learning to understand your child's communication.
- Answer any and all questions your child may have about toileting, even if you've already explained the same thing many times.
- Sometimes offering a choice works well. If your toddler is squirming or holding himself, or you otherwise simply *know* it's time for him to go, ask if he would like to go and use the potty or if you can bring it to him.
- Constantly explain what is going on and what you are doing. Try to engage your child in the conversation by asking questions, "Are you telling me you need to go? Do you need to go? Shall we try the potty?" Or if he is in a no-to-everything stage or mood, adopt a "don't ask, do tell" approach, "I think you have to pee. Let's go read a book together while you try."
- If your child dislikes reminders or talking about toileting, don't say anything at all about pee, poo, the potty or the toilet. Every hour or so comment out loud (so he can hear) that you really need to go to the toilet, and then go there. If he follows you and one day uses his potty, don't comment or praise him unless you feel he will be open to this.
- Consult parenting books and look for more ideas. Read through the *positive* tips and advice offered for conventional training and test some of these approaches to see if they work with your child.

### Siblings . . .

- Siblings can be a great help. They can teach by example, inspire, entertain and assist in many ways. Some siblings are better at "reading" their baby brothers or sisters than adults.
- Many families who learn about this method a little late end up potty training two children at once: twins, a baby and a toddler, or even two toddlers. Parents with two small children can teach both children simultaneously, as long as you are patient; don't

have expectations that could lead to negative feelings or reactions; and respect/accept their individual rates of development.

**Pace . . .**

- There will be good days and bad days, amazing successes and the inevitable setbacks. Expect one step back for every three steps forward. Small children are very busy learning many new skills and achieving milestones, as well as going through some occasional discomfort such as when they are teething or ill. Many things (including travel or guests) can interrupt their potty learning on a temporary basis, but they will get back on track if you hang in there.
- Do not expect immediate or clear-cut results for several months. There is no fixed time scale for learning. Many parents feel frustrated if their baby doesn't seem to care about staying dry, forgetting that they taught him to pee in a diaper in the first place. It takes most babies considerable time to unlearn this. Give yours a while to make the connection and transition.
- Never compare your child's results with another in a competitive or judgmental way.
- Some parents have no trouble getting their baby to pee in the potty but reap no results for quite sometime with poos, or vice versa. Don't worry! This too shall pass.
- Go with the flow of your baby's natural learning process. A common scenario at first is for toddlers to let you know they peed or pooed *after* they have gone in their pants or diaper. This is part of the learning process, and your child will eventually learn to inform you beforehand.

**Attitude . . .**

- Be positive—never negative, punitive or coercive. Do not pressure your child.
- If you feel elimination is "yucky" (a Western sentiment or hangup, stemming in large part from having to come into contact with waste when changing or cleaning diapers), strive to get over this feeling. This is where kids gain control or get stubborn, if they know it bothers you. In non-Western societies, mothers just smile at accidents and clean up, with no negative emotional reaction.
- Listen to the voice within, trust your intuition, have faith in yourself, relax and enjoy.

- Be creative. Adopt the motto "Whatever Works" and proceed with an open mind.

## Hurdles You May Encounter

It is usually (but not always) harder to start with a mobile baby who has been "trained" to go in a diaper or who wears disposables and does not associate the feeling of wetness with elimination. Here is a summary of the main reasons it can be difficult to begin at 6 months and older:

- Baby has been trained to go in a diaper.
- Baby has lost awareness of the elimination functions.
- Parents were not responsive to elimination communication in first sensitive period.
- Baby has developed an ego and a will of his own.
- Baby is mobile and active. When he learns to crawl and/or walk, he will naturally want to explore his surroundings, to play and focus his attention on new and exciting things. If he is not accustomed to spending time at potty sessions and if he is not aware of his "toilet muscles," he is not likely to understand why he is being detained on a potty and is thus not likely to want to remain there.

## It's Your Choice!

Clearly, parents should be able to make a personal and informed decision about their preferred method of toilet teaching, and honest and adequate information should be readily available for these purposes. As stated earlier, no one claims that infant potty training is the right method for all families, but it is definitely the best method for many.

If you prefer to give your baby the option to go in a toilet, potty or other receptacle rather than in his clothing, more power to you. If you like the idea of baby going diaperless part time or even full time and would rather use a diaper on the floor than on your child for the occasional accident, or if you'd rather clean up occasional accidents than struggle over diapering, go for it!

# doctors & other experts

Although infant elimination training is not well known in the USA, there are some doctors and pediatricians who are supportive. They have for the most part traveled abroad and witnessed it firsthand, had personal contact with experienced parents or else are (spouses of) immigrants who grew up in cultures where this method is used.

And fortunately, some medical professionals who have never heard of this approach are surprisingly open and inquisitive when they learn about it. I once gave my physician a copy of my book. He had never heard of infant elimination training and was fascinated. During my next office visit, he announced that he had left the book on the table with other reading matter in the waiting room and that several of his patients had come to him in an elated state, explaining that this is the method used "back home" in their native lands. Some physicians and psychologists first learn about infant potty training via rare mentions or articles in medical journals and are immediately receptive to the concept and possibilities. Although we Western practitioners constitute a small minority and face prejudice, ridicule and even hostility, positive momentum is slowly building. This chapter discusses favorable medical opinions and findings, medical "hurdles" and the basic physiology and anatomy.

## Perspectives from East Africa: Three Studies

Many U.S. studies on child-rearing techniques have been conducted in Africa, but none have focused on infant elimination training. Occasionally, some of the reports dedicate a few words or sentences to the topic. Infant toilet training, it seems, is not of much interest to researchers. Most of those who do write about it seem incredulous and reluctant to admit that it is possible and effective.

Fortunately, there have been some enlightening writings published on the topic. Dr. Marten deVries has studied infant elimination training among some African tribes and found that ". . . by studying the naturally enriched environment of preindustrial communities, we may learn lessons from the savanna on how to best optimize the development of infants and their brains for the benefit of children throughout the world."[40] Three studies conducted in East Africa have yielded interesting and exciting results vis-à-vis infant toilet training. Marten deVries published an entire article on the subject in *Pediatrics* magazine. Mary D. Salter Ainsworth dedicated 11 pages to infant elimination practices and training in her book *Infancy in Uganda*. Marcelle Geber conducted a ground-breaking and fascinating study on Ugandan and other African children and included a short but vividly clear description of infant elimination practices.

All three of these studies are briefly reviewed in this chapter. They are further discussed, along with a multitude of findings on infant elimination training by other researchers, in Part 4.

### Dr. Marten deVries and the Digo Tribe

Marten deVries, MD, found that babies of the Digo tribe in Kenya start elimination training at 2 to 3 weeks of age and attain reasonable night and day dryness by the age of 4 to 6 months. The results of this study contradict and disprove the claim by Western medicine that babies have no control of the sphincters and other muscles needed for elimination until 18 months to 2 or 3 years of age.

There is a stark contrast between the experience of the people of East Africa and the view of Western medicine. One of the most famous child-raising experts of our times, T. Berry Brazelton, bases his child-oriented approach to toilet training in large part on maturational readiness. Brazelton advises parents to be patient and wait until their children take the initiative to start toilet training toward the end of the 2nd year.[41] In Africa, the Digo and many other peoples and tribes place importance on infant toilet training. In their experience, muscular and neurological development as defined or limited by current Western medicine are not an issue. They believe and *know* firsthand that infant elimination training is effective.

Dr. deVries points out that cultural differences in the initiation and method of infant elimination training are related to different expectations of infant capabilities and performance. His article discusses a "cultural blueprint" for child-rearing behavior. "A network of complexly related factors shapes a culture's ideas of what infants are and what they can do. Training behavior is carried out in light of these expectations."[42]

DeVries concludes his *Pediatrics* article by urging pediatricians to be flexible in family guidance. He stresses that child experts should take the overall setting into account, including cultural values and infant needs. "By dogmatically advocating a seemingly scientific approach while ignoring the potential diversity and effect of maternal and family expectation, the clinician may, in fact, thwart the training goals."[43] He suggests that further research into this topic will one day yield valuable therapeutic results.

## Mary Ainsworth on Ugandan Elimination Training

Mary Ainsworth reports that in the past, the Baganda infants of Buganda, Uganda, traditionally began elimination training around 2½–3 months. Training is still begun at or before the age of 4 months, sometimes as early as 1 month old and in most cases is done consistently and conscientiously. Success is dependent upon close interaction with babies; more specifically, it is contingent upon the baby giving recognizable signals and the mother's timely response to them. There were some situations where elimination training took longer than the norms given here, but in such cases, the mother was either not present when needed or failed to pay adequate attention to her baby's signals.

The range of ages at which soiling the bed ceased was from 5–11 months; in addition, mothers whose children were trained before Ainsworth arrived claimed their babies finished this phase at 4–8 months. Bedwetting ceased between 9 and 22 months of age.

Soiling the house generally stopped between 8 and 12 months of age (a few took up to 20–22 months), at which time most of the babies were able to go outside on their own initiative when they needed to defecate. The age for ending urinating indoors was just under 12 months. One 10-month-old child could delay voiding, but if his signals were not heard, he would end up going indoors.

Ainsworth concludes that Baganda elimination training is at least as effective as the training methods used in Western cultures. She writes, "If early and rigid toilet training can be viewed as a misguided effort of civilized societies to socialize the child, the stereotype of the primitive society is one in which natural processes are not subject to social interference."[44]

### Marcelle Geber
### on Ugandan Elimination Training

In her ethno-psychological study of African children, Marcelle Geber observed that Ugandan mothers were attentive to all the needs of their infants, including elimination cleanliness. Although she never had the occasion to concentrate her studies on toilet training per se, she noted that Ugandan mothers carrying their babies on their backs were never urinated or defecated on by their babies and that their babies were always clean in this regard. When babies were old enough to walk, she observed them going outdoors, without prompting, to relieve themselves. Geber reported that Ugandan children completed toilet training between 15 and 24 months.

## Favorable Western Medical Opinions

### 1971 – Report by Thomas Ball

Mrs. Lela Humphries devised her own infant potty learning approach for catching BMs and used it with her three children who were born between 1947 and 1956. She stated that while she was feeding her first son, she noticed that each time he had a bowel movement it was during a feeding. "I could always tell by the facial expression when the movements were going to occur." At 6 weeks of age, she would unpin the left side of his diaper, and the instant he made his facial expression indicating an impending BM, she would pull the diaper to one side (without actually taking it off), place the potty between her legs and place his buttocks on it. She left the diaper draped over his front in case he peed. "His position was the same as if he did not have the pot under him. He did not make any kind of fuss." She reported that her first two sons completed bowel training reasonably well at age 6 months and bladder control around the age of 14 months.

Her third son had Down's syndrome, but this didn't deter her. Although she kept no records ("never once thinking they might prove useful"), she recalled that he would scoot to the bathroom door and whine to be put on the potty before he could walk, and that at 16 months he started walking and would head to the bathroom when he had to go.

Thomas Ball explains that her approach can be interpreted within the framework of operant conditioning as "toilet training by reflex. The baby does not get used to eliminating in his diaper and does not feel comfortable doing so, [and] therefore will fuss to have the potty placed on his buttocks. The same applies to a child that eliminates in a diaper for two or three years [and] does not feel comfortable on the pot, but wants his diaper." This is what makes conventional toilet training difficult for many. Diaper changing involves "physical handling with much tactual stimulation and, in many instances, pleasant social interaction. These consequences to soiling diapers serve to reward incontinence . . . it is no wonder that many children actively resist giving it up."[45]

## 1978 – Comments by Gersch & Ravindranathan, MDs

Two doctors endorsed the deVries Digo study via letters to *Pediatrics*. Marvin Gersch wrote that the merits of the deVries article demonstrate, among other things, that "our previous thoughts of toilet training were incorrect; training can be accomplished and has been accomplished at a much earlier age."[46] S. Ravindranathan also sanctioned the observations and conclusions of deVries when he wrote, "Not only does this bring about closer mother-infant interactions, contact, and communication, but it also eliminates future attempts at unnecessary coercive methods on a reluctant toddler."[47]

## 1985 – Study by Paul Smeets et al.

In this study, three girls and one boy started between the ages of 3–6 months. The parents used part-time toilet learning, spending 3–4.5 hours a day (but not every day of the week). To get the attention of the baby, the parent held or tapped the potty, or else called or touched the child while holding or tapping the potty, in order to be sure the baby looked at the potty before being placed on it. If the baby went within about 3 minutes, the adult displayed pleasure and approval; otherwise, the baby was removed from the potty. This phase of the study was completed when a baby had at least 18 BMs on the potty plus 8 out of 10 consecutive training days without any bowel accidents.

The next phase established a relationship between potty reaching/grabbing and both types of elimination. The potty was located 30 cm from and slightly to the right front of the baby. Upon spontaneously signaling or reaching for the potty or else when the mother knew it was time to go, the baby was guided to grab the potty and then sit on it.

All four babies completed training before they could walk, between the ages of 8.5–10.7 months. However, the endpoints or definition of completion here would not be acceptable to all Western families since "At the end of the program, the babies were not yet required to hold their eliminations longer than a few minutes and still needed assistance on taking the appropriate position and dressing and un-dressing."

The approach used was somewhat aloof when compared to infant potty training. "In essence, the conditions were arranged such that the visual and tactile stimuli of the potty could develop into a natural and functional event between two already chained behavioral links, the state of distension associated with straining (the first link) fol-lowed by stool expulsion associated with physical relief and praise by the mother (second link)."

It is important to note that no negative side effects, such as tan-trums or eliminating immediately when removed from the potty, were reported and that "the potty manipulation, as it was used here, was markedly different from other procedures in which the mother places the child frequently on the potty in accordance with a fixed daily regimen. Although these methods may help to prevent accidents from occurring and eventually be successful, they are prone to shaping the child's passive rather than active participation with the potty following her or her observation of internal cues to eliminate."

The study reaches the conclusion that "the maturational explanation for the success of currently advocated delayed training methods should be reconsidered."[48]

## 1990 – Commentary by Paul Fischer, MD

Fischer debunks the American view that a child must be both "psychologically and physiologically 'mature' before successful toilet training can occur. . . . There has been almost no research to document these theories. They are no doubt nonsensical to much of the world where 'potty training' begins shortly after birth." Concerning the Western approach to toilet training, he continues, "By 2 years of age we expect children to have mastered running, speaking, and a variety of social skills. It is amazing that we continue to feel that such children are often not old enough to control a couple of sphincter muscles!"

Dr. Fischer's Pakistani wife and mother-in-law started infant pottying with their 2-week-old daughter and reported that by age 3 months, she "obviously understood the association of the time, sound, and body position with voiding and defecation. By 1 year of age she was out of diapers both during the day and at night."

He states that people in much of Asia and Africa find the Western version of toilet training to be "primitive and unsanitary." Concerning the premise that infant potty training can lead to psychological problems, he states, "I can only speculate that this stems from attempts to use negative reinforcement with 18-month-old children who have had no prior conditioning. This is certainly not the case for the millions of children around the world who are trained in the first year of life."[49]

## 1997 – Book by Charles E. Schaefer, MD

In his book *Toilet Training without Tears*, Dr. Schaefer discusses various methods of toilet training, including what he calls the "early approach" for babies between 3–15 months of age. He reintroduces the method of toilet training used in the USA in the 1920s and

1930s, noting that this was a conditioning process based on learning by association. In addition, he emphasizes that child development experts and pediatricians of the day coerced parents into adopting the wrong parental attitude and that this is what has given early toilet training a reputation for being harsh, rigid and punitive. Schaefer advocates a positive and unemotional attitude as well as a nonpunitive and non-coercive approach. After years of analytic and cross-cultural studies, "we now know that the age at which a child is trained is not the cause of later emotional and psychological problems; rather, it is the parental attitude that is used during the training period that will determine the long-term effect of toilet training."

Schaefer also gives infants credit for having some ability to control elimination. "Although it is not known exactly when a child can attain this kind of muscular control, studies have shown that some infants between three and six months can learn this skill very successfully, provided their caregiver is observant of the signs that indicate a need to eliminate and then acts promptly to put the child on the potty." He also says that babies are able to gain complete voluntary bladder and bowel control starting around the age of 15 months or later and that it is unrealistic to expect complete control before this time.

The early approach in his book is based in part on the 1985 study by Paul Smeets et al. and includes potty reaching and potty grabbing. It is fairly scientific and technical, as opposed to intuitive and intimate. He states that the goal of elimination conditioning is "to establish a close relationship between your baby's body signals and his defecation on the potty." Conditioning is based on associating the feel of the potty against the buttocks. Mothers base potty visits on baby body signals and elimination timing. For these, Schaefer urges extensive record keeping for weeks. He covers a lot in the 20 pages devoted to the topic, including advantages and disadvantages as well as do's and don'ts of the early approach.[50]

## 2000 – Video by Barbara Gablehouse, MD

In her video *The Potty Project*, board certified pediatrician Barbara Gablehouse states that 85 percent of the world's babies are toilet trained by 1 year of age and stresses that those babies "have the same muscles and the same ability to control those muscles as our [Western] babies. We simply need to give our babies the opportunity to practice this skill." She compares toilet learning with the learning of other important developmental skills such as walking and talking.

A baby needs to incrementally learn a variety of related skills over time, such as balancing, standing, stumbling and taking steps, before he can walk, and if parents help and encourage him, he learns faster and easier. In the same way, a baby needs practice, positive reinforcement and time to gain control of his bladder and bowels. "Like all of your baby's learning, repetition is crucial for successful early toilet learning."[51] Her video is aimed at a mainstream parenting audience and includes footage of babies using a small child's seat on the toilet.

## 2000 – Study by Bakker & Wyndaele

Physiotherapist E. Bakker and urologist Jean-Jacques Wyndaele of University Hospital Antwerpen conducted a study to "evaluate changes in the onset of toilet training, the attitudes of parents and the results of training during the last 60 years in Belgium." Their findings indicate that voiding problems have increased in recent years and suggest that a major change in the way parents now toilet train their children compared with the approach used 60 years ago may contribute to the apparent increase in lower urinary tract dysfunction among children.

"Most authors are convinced that the development of bladder and bowel control is a maturational process which cannot be accelerated by toilet training." But their findings contradict this theory, instead indicating that "the age at which bladder and bowel control were achieved showed the same differences among the groups as the ages at the onset of training."[52]

## 2002 – Commentary by Dr. Linda Sonna

Dr. Linda Sonna, psychologist and author, has written a book that provides much hope for (re)introducing infant potty training to the mainstream. In *The Everything Potty Training Book*, Dr. Sonna describes the currently accepted methods for infants, babies and toddlers, and emphasizes that if parents have the time and energy, it is best to begin during early infancy. Otherwise, she strongly recommends beginning shortly after babies can sit up by themselves. She considers it unfortunate that most parents wait until the toddler years, when children typically resist sitting still due to their mobility and high energy level, and resist following directions as the longing for independence increases and autonomy struggles intensify. While working on her book, she did an extensive review of toilet training literature and determined the following.

"Child development experts in the U.S. continued to push back the recommended age for beginning toilet training since the turn of the 20th century, when the custom was to begin around age two to three months. A dramatic change came with the simultaneous introduction of disposable diapers in the early 1960s and the dissemination of renowned author/pediatrician T. Berry Brazelton's 'later-is-better approach' to toilet training. Brazelton warned that to begin before children had achieved adequate sphincter control was likely to create psychological difficulties that might well translate into a significant delay in skill acquisition, and he attributed chronic problems with bedwetting to premature training efforts." Sonna has not found any evidence to support these claims. "While some children do self-train virtually overnight if nothing is done until close to age three, habits of wetting and soiling are well entrenched by then, and many youngsters require a lot of time and have considerable difficulty. It is no longer unusual for children age four to still be in diapers.

"As a result of all of the warnings about the need for toddler readiness, the myth that younger toddlers (and some older ones) lack sphincter control began winding its way through the pediatric community. In 1996, author Jan Faull echoed the modern pediatric and urological wisdom in her best-selling toilet training book for parents entitled *Mommy, I Have to Go Potty*. Faull declared, 'In order to be toilet trained, these muscles [the bladder and rectal sphincters] must be developed sufficiently to hold in the urine and stool. For infants and toddlers, pee and poop simply come out when the bladder or bowel is full.' (Page 3) Faull went on to state, 'How Grandma claims her children were completely trained at eighteen months or sooner is a mystery today.' (Page 12) Amazingly, the knowledge that infants in fact have sphincter control was lost in two short generations. When American parents are informed that many foreign babies are routinely trained at younger ages, their first response is to deny that such a feat could be possible. Their second is to insist the training methods must be harsh and cruel. They cling to that notion even after hearing descriptions of the actual methods parents use."[53]

## 2002 – Commentary by Dr. Simone Rugolotto, MD

Dr. Rugolotto, pediatrician and neonatologist at the University of Verona, Italy, has personal experience with infant elimination training: He and his wife are raising their son using this method. Dr. Rugolotto states that the fact that early infant toilet training is a common practice in Asia and Africa "shows that toilet training in early infancy is possible and without major side effects. Babies can clearly communicate their needs, and we can help them to eliminate in a gentle way, by bringing them to the bathroom and using a potty, in a more natural and comfortable manner than eliminating in a horizontal position into a diaper. Babies do have control over their bladder and bowel functions; otherwise they would eliminate feces and urine continually, which obviously does not happen. More particularly, the elimination process is an active one, and we can see all the efforts made by infants during this activity. When they are not able to retain feces and urine any longer, they feel discomfort, give signals (e.g., cry), and, if nobody helps them, they let the process happen in their diapers.

"To my knowledge, very few Western mothers help their infants eliminate into a receptacle. Unfortunately, to avoid reactions of skepticism and surprise, those who do so do not usually share this information with other mothers.

"Infant toilet training has many advantages and should be supported by current pediatric knowledge. Some of the advantages are the following: an easier approach to 'voluntary' toilet training during childhood (children will accept the potty more easily than children who have never used it before); less cutaneous rash (due to less contact between feces or urine and skin); and a closer bond and better understanding between mothers and their children (when effective attention is given to a specific need instead of the usual pacifier or bottle). We are not aware of any side effects of early toilet training. No evidence-based medicine is available on this topic. Unfortunately, no randomized controlled studies have been done on early-versus-late toilet training, and I hope that in a few years some will be performed to give a new option to children and parents."[54]

## Interview with a Pediatrician

Dr. Leah Lamb is a pediatrician, currently working as Medical Director of CARES (Child Advocacy Resource and Evaluation Team) at St. Luke's Children's Hospital in Boise, Idaho.[55]

Q: *Have you observed the use of infant potty training firsthand?*
A: I've closely watched many women in India and North Africa and also friends in Europe complete the training.

Q: *As a pediatrician, do you endorse this method?*

A: I think it takes a special kind of mother—the kind of mother who is very interested in bonding and in being receptive to her child's needs. I think the onus is on the mother to want to create a certain kind of closeness with the baby so she can be able to respond to the infant's signals.

Q: *Do you think it's a good method, a safe method?*

A: Without question, but as I mentioned, it takes a special kind of mother to bond closely enough and pay special attention to her baby's signals in order for the training to be successful.

Q: *Some doctors and psychologists think toilet training should not be started in infancy. How do you respond to this?*

A: They are referring to punitive, heavily enforced toilet training where there is a lot of negative pressure put on the child in order to perform. The method in this book is very different. This is a really gentle method, a mother-child dyad, bonded interaction. The parent/caregiver works with the baby, listening to his cues and signals. It's gentle and it's kind. I don't see that it would have any negative effect on an infant at all.

Q: *Do you agree that as long as the parents have the right attitude that there cannot be any psychological harm?*

A: I don't think any psychological harm can result. Basically, the child is responding to behavioral conditioning. The sound that the mother makes, coupled with her being in tune with the baby's signals, will result in the child either urinating or defecating on cue.

Q: *Do you think an infant is aware of its elimination process?*

A: Yes, absolutely. Babies know when they are eliminating. They make certain sounds, become still or their faces turn red.

Q: *If children are aware of the elimination process, why is it so hard to potty train a baby if you start the training later, around 2 years old?*

A: They may be aware of their elimination, but they are also aware of everything else around them. By definition, a toddler is very involved in exploration, and if he is more interested in exploration, a toy or a book, he is going to ignore the physiologic call to evacuate. In terms of interrupting his exploration, he may not pay attention to his physiologic prompts at that point.

Q: *Do you think that perhaps a 2-year-old child has already been trained to use his diapers as a toilet and really isn't concerned with toilet training?*

A: Human beings are the only animals that soil themselves. I think babies don't particularly like wearing diapers. They cry when they are wet or dirty.

Q: *Can you comment on the American medical school of thought that teaches that a child cannot be toilet trained until certain nerves and muscles are developed—not before the age of 2, in general.*

A: If you are looking at the traditional method of potty training, a child isn't considered trained until he can walk to the toilet, pull down his pants and evacuate by himself. That is what we in the West traditionally consider to be potty trained. There is a lot of pressure to be toilet trained, although less now than a generation or two ago, but infant potty training is a whole different thing. It is not the old militant-style toilet training of the West. Instead, it is a method where the mother is responding and tuned into her baby's internal, physiologic schedule, and the child has assistance and an advocate who helps him accomplish going to the bathroom. You're not expecting a child to do it on his own early in the process.

Q: *In your professional opinion, is the information provided in this book medically correct and sound?*

A: Yes. This book explores both sides of the physiologic question. Is the child mature enough at age 9 months in order to urinate and defecate on cue? They do it, but they do it with *help*, and I think that's the main thing that needs to be clarified. This is an interactive process between a mother, or a father, and a baby. The parents have to be involved and bonded enough to the baby in order to correctly pick up and act on his signals.

Q: *Do you think the method is just a matter of "catching" the child at the right moment? Some people claim that it is the parents who are toilet trained and not the child.*

A: The parent and baby are working together as a team. In this sense, you could say that the parent has to be trained, although I hesitate to use the word "trained." If a parent is bonded and closely enough in tune with a child's signals, the parent can pick up when the child has to go to the bathroom. As to "catching" the baby at the right time, you have to "catch" him at the right time. That's the whole point, that you are catching him when he has the urge to evacuate.

Q: *Do you agree that a more accurate description of "catching" baby's elimination in the potty is 'being there for your baby to go potty when he needs you'?*

A: Exactly. Women in underdeveloped countries don't find this surprising. If you ask them, "How do you know your baby has to go?" they just know. They support the baby and help him accomplish his task.

Q: *How do you reconcile traditional medical teachings about neurological development and an infant's responding to cues before that development has been achieved?*

A: Traditionally in Western AMA thinking, a child really doesn't have, as they say, the ability to respond. We physicians are taught that the neural maturation that allows for complete toilet training occurs somewhere around the age of 2 years. However, if the child is tuned in and sensitive to prompts in a nonpunitive way, he will respond. It's behavioral conditioning, and the child will "go" for you.

Q: *A lot of people in the USA don't believe it's possible to toilet train a child in infancy. Even when you give them a live demonstration with a tiny baby, they still don't believe it.*

A: They don't believe it because toilet training in this country implies a toddler bopping off down to the bathroom, pulling down his pants, jumping up on the potty and going. That isn't what this method is about. This method is about a parent and a child interacting and accomplishing a task together. In Western culture, we separate our children from us. We don't sleep in the same room with them, and there is much more emphasis on individuation and privacy. The child is seen as a separate entity. With this infant toilet-training method, you're going back to a more natural state where the mother and child are as one unit, where they are interrelating with each other. This method is for people who are very in tune with their babies and who are looking for a unique connection with their child.

Q: *In this country, we only consider a child to be toilet trained when he is totally independent.*

A: Yes. I think we have to be careful about the definition we use. It's the infant-mother interaction in getting the child to evacuate. I would back away from calling an infant "toilet trained" because the term "toilet trained" implies a certain image in the West. With infant potty training, it's something really different. The mother helps the child, and the child knows what is going on and responds. In India and Africa, most families don't use diapers.

Q: *Have you in your travels seen small children, soon after they learn to walk, independently walk to their 'toilet place'' and use it?*

A: Yes, but the societal and cultural standards are a little different. If you just have to toddle to the edge of the compound to go to the bathroom where it is acceptable to go, that's very different from finding the bathroom, getting onto the toilet and going. It's a different environment. We have to be sensitive to these differences when we use the technique in America. The basic premises are the same, but the environment is different. It requires an adult who is sensitive, and primarily this is the mother in the infant stage.

Q: *Some Westerners who aren't very familiar with infant potty training claim that it is too time consuming for parents.*

A: In terms of time, potty training takes time no matter how you look at it. You're going to take time changing diapers, or you're going to take time interacting with your baby and responding to his signals. So you are going to spend time dealing with the evacuation from your child, one way or the other. This is just a different method. Millions of third world kids can't be wrong. It certainly works, and it's a matter of whether you are interested in something different, something innovative for the baby.

## "The Doctor's Out" . . . *to lunch* <g>

Don't be surprised if your doctor or pediatrician is skeptical of infant potty training. Many are unfamiliar with it and advise against it.

Today's standard clinical wisdom assumes that an infant is not aware of elimination and has absolutely no ability to retain his urine or bowel movements. This does not jibe with the fact that millions of families around the world demonstrate and experience the opposite.

Urination and defecation involve the use of both voluntary and involuntary muscles. As the name suggests, "voluntary" muscles are those over which we have conscious control, while "involuntary" muscles are not under our conscious control.

A child who begins toilet training in infancy can learn to control the voluntary muscles of the urinary bladder and bowels at the earliest moment possible. By the time he gains full control of these muscles, he is thoroughly acquainted with a grown-up toilet routine.

The main muscles involved in going to the toilet are the sphincter muscles. These help control both the bowels and bladder. They are circular muscles that constrict an orifice. In a normal contracted condition, they hold the orifice closed. In order to allow the orifice to open, the sphincter muscles must relax.

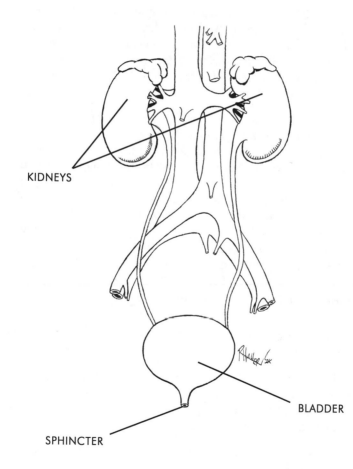

KIDNEYS

BLADDER

SPHINCTER

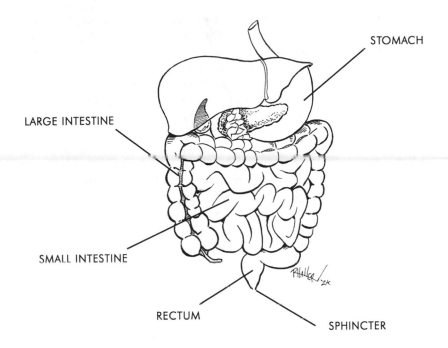

STOMACH

LARGE INTESTINE

SMALL INTESTINE

RECTUM

SPHINCTER

Doctors and medical books in Western countries typically state that the sphincter muscles mature between 20 and 24 months of age. It is mainly on this basis that they dismiss the concept of starting potty training before 1 or even 2 years of age. What they fail to mention, however, is that their 20-to-24-month figure represents the extreme—the longest time it takes for these muscles to fully mature—rather than the average. They do not take into account the many babies whose muscles develop before 20-24 months. They do not consider the fact that infants are able to release urine and bowel movements upon association with a signal to release. Likewise, they fail to consider societal factors such as acculturation, support, parental devotion and lifestyle choices.

A more accurate statement is that with regular practice, the sphincter muscles can complete development between 12 and 24 months of age, with 18 months being the average age at which a baby can be potty trained reasonably well but still needing to be reminded at times, with only occasional accidents. As with everything in life, there are always exceptions to the rule. Some babies gain complete control before 12 months of age, while others may take longer than 24 months.[56]

There is another equally disturbing problem with the current Western medical philosophy of potty training. The premise that a child cannot control urine or bowel movements until a minimum of 20–24 months of age implies that a baby lacks any muscular control of his bowels and bladder before that time. The very first time your infant responds to your cue to pee or poo, you will prove this theory wrong and see that your infant does indeed have some control over his "toilet muscles." Even if it turns out that your child develops complete control over the sphincter muscles at a relatively late age (2½ years or older), infant potty training will still prove a positive and useful experience in many ways. For example, reducing the use of diapers, especially disposables, also reduces the chances of urinary tract infections. Babies are especially vulnerable to urinary tract infections (UTIs) because the fecal matter in their diapers can introduce bacteria into the urethra. Girls are more at risk because their urethras are short and straight, providing an easy means for bacteria to enter the bladder, the ureters, and even the kidneys.

There are babies and parents with challenging medical conditions or disabilities who have had good results with infant potty training, depending on the severity of their condition or illness. These include spina bifida, cerebral palsy, Down's syndrome, deafness, low vision, blindness, partial paralysis, wheelchair confinement (by caregiver) and other conditions that result in delayed development. Although parents should expect toilet training to take longer in most of these situations, it is comforting to know that it can be done gently and at a natural pace.

## Misconceptions

There are many misconceptions about infant elimination training. The two main sources of the misinformation are:

- Association with, or assuming it is the same as, the parent-directed and at times punitive and forceful method generally used in the USA until the 1950s.
- Incorrect conclusions drawn by those who do not understand the method. For example, when I gave a review copy of *Trickle Treat* to a prominent (but now defunct) health food store in Glendale, California, the review committee there reached the erroneous conclusion that infant potty training is (of all things) unhygienic. The committee falsely assumed that infant pottying involves letting babies crawl or run around naked all day long, peeing and pooing at will all over the house! Nothing could be further from the truth.

Whatever the source, the misconceptions are so emotional and deeply ingrained that some adults who were potty trained much earlier than they believe is possible refuse to accept this fact. In short, they are in denial. In December 1999, two pediatricians debated the topic of toilet training on a morning TV chat show. One of them (male) advocated starting training around the age of 15–18 months. The other (female) was opposed to any sort of toilet training at all and advocated letting a child wait and self-train around the age of 3 or 4 years. Her opponent challenged her by stating, "I bet you were toilet trained as an infant." She replied that her mother indeed tells her that she was potty trained at 10 months, then went on to say that she does not believe her mother's claim.

There may be other reasons why Western medicine ignores the fact that babies in other societies gain control over the sphincter muscles before the age of 12–24 months. For starters, most Western doctors and experts are not familiar with the method used in Asia and Africa. They have had no first-hand experience with their own children, no feedback from practicing parents in America and no guidance from textbooks.

Doctors, pediatricians and nurses who visit countries where infant potty training is the norm typically have a favorable opinion of the method if they take the time to meet, observe and speak with practitioners. Curious or skeptical visitors to these areas will be told politely and in no uncertain terms that babies are satisfactorily toilet trained between the ages of 6 and 15 months. Parents will smile or laugh if you try to convince them otherwise.

Some physicians who travel abroad observe families using this method but are convinced that it can only work in foreign cultures and settings. This implies that Westerners are not capable of working closely with their babies and do not want to spend the necessary time with their babies. They are mistaken about this in that there are indeed Western families who want to devote the needed time.

There is also a racial component to consider. Infant toilet training is the heritage of most, if not all, "people of color," yet Western culture denies its merits and ignores its existence. Asian- and African-Americans have the right to at least be informed about the way babies are raised in their ancestral homelands, then to make an informed decision on whether or not they want to adopt these practices and customs. A certain percentage of Westerners, upon learning about this method, discount it by maintaining that it is a primitive method used by backward, poverty-stricken women who don't know any better or who have no choice but to use this "barbaric" method. Instead of recognizing and applauding the beauty, significance and fabulousness of the close relationship and communication between infant and mother, the general take is that these unfortunate women would certainly prefer to use diapers if they had the choice and opportunity.

Some doctors may elect to completely ignore or reject infant potty training simply because the majority of Americans don't or won't embrace it. Doctors may not have the inclination, desire or energy to "go against the grain."

In some cases, the denial may arise from a fear or dislike of being proven wrong. If doctors were to claim that babies can be potty trained around 15–18 months and this did not prove to be true for the population as a whole, they would appear to be wrong.

With the proliferation of lawsuits, whether frivolous or merited, medical professionals might hesitate to give advice that can't be etched in stone as true for nearly every child. They may fear lawsuits from parents who expect too much of their babies and mistreat them as a consequence.

* * * * *

There are a number of ways to change the tide, dispel the myths, end the skepticism and put the doubting doctors and perplexed parents at ease. Individual families can share their experiences, joys and triumphs, but the onus ultimately rests on medical professionals to acknowledge the possibilities and merits of this method. Perhaps this can only happen when members of the medical community observe other cultures where it is prevalent, conduct open studies on the topic and experience infant potty training firsthand. The testimonial of a family physician who has had good results toilet training her own infant daughter can be found in Part 2, Chapter 9, "A Physician Speaks Out," and Part 3, Chapter 2 presents the testimonial by an Australian MD. Medical experts who have no personal interest in this method are nonetheless responsible for letting their patients know about it. As one mother puts it, "I realize that this will probably never be a mainstream way of behaving in the U.S. I just think that people like me who *do* resonate with this idea should have access to the information more easily than we do now."[57]

# chapter 12

# diapers

In this chapter, we will consider the role diapers play in infant potty training and the pros and cons of cloth and disposable diapers. We'll also touch on some ways diaper bulk can delay development.

Parents who start toilet learning in infancy or even early toddlerhood will most likely also use a relatively small quantity of diapers, and for this reason, the arguments for and against cloth and disposable diapers are presented here. Some parents may elect to use both types, depending on their personal set of circumstances.

## Minimal Use of Diapers

Part-time use of diapers is one of the ways infant pottying has been adapted to Western culture. Until relatively recently in human history, diapers or diaper substitutes have played almost no role in child rearing. While the majority of parents in rural Asian and African villages do not use any diapers at all, most practicing parents in Western countries prefer to use diapers on infants on occasions where wetting or soiling can be troublesome, such as on trips or outings, when baby is ill, at night if baby wets the bed on a regular basis or between potty sessions while baby is physically too small to wear training pants.

Infant potty parents drastically reduce the number of diapers used compared to what is required for full-time diapering. Most prefer cloth diapers to disposables, for a number of reasons. They prefer keeping baby in cotton and other natural fibers. They tend to be more vigilant at pottying and changing babes in cloth and find that infants wearing cloth are more aware of elimination too. Some have found that their babies willingly pee in disposable diapers at night but not in underwear or cotton "dipes." Parents are likely to stay at home with baby or arrange one-on-one care in order to have someone reliable available to potty baby—or expeditiously change dirty diapers—and thus do not feel a need for the conveniences of disposable diapers. They also tend to believe that using cloth diapers is better for the environment than using disposables.

It is important to note that infant potty training does not in any way exclude the use of disposable diapers for parents who prefer them. Both types of diaper are compatible with the method. The "bottom line" is to reduce and then eliminate the use of diapers as soon as possible.

Infant potty families should not be too hard on themselves. Although the ideal situation would be to eliminate diapers altogether from birth, this is not practical or realistic for most. It is important to find a balance between infant elimination training and other activities. Don't be so fanatic about it that you lose your perspective. It is better for your baby to pee in a diaper on occasion than to be around an uptight or exhausted parent obsessing about "potty perfection."

## Cloth or Disposable Diapers?

There are convincing arguments on both sides of the cloth-versus-dis-posable-diaper debate. Manufacturers and marketers present compelling cases for the superiority of their respective products and the inferiority of their competitors' diapers. Parents need to consider and weigh the facts in relation to their own particular circumstances and lifestyle, then make an informed decision. There are situations where parents may prefer to use one type of diaper but are forced to use another. Don't worry or feel guilty about not being able to use a particular type of diaper if it jeopardizes the health or well-being of your baby.

Some of the main factors to consider when choosing diapers are cost, health, convenience and environment. The environmental impact of diapers is covered in Chapter 13.

### Pro-Cloth & Anti-Disposable Arguments

- Cotton is natural and soft and lets baby's skin breathe.
- Cotton diapers are far cheaper to purchase than disposable dia-pers since only a few dozen cloth diapers are needed as opposed to thousands of disposables. Your savings increase if the cloth diapers are reused with any future children you may have.
- With cloth diapers, you avoid chemical gels, dyes and other pos-sible synthetic irritants. The super-absorbent polyacrylate (SAP) in disposables absorbs urine and stores it as a gel next to baby's skin. For sensitive babies, this chemical can be toxic. It can also stick to infants' genitals. Some of the other ingredients of dis-posables are heavily treated pulp/cellulose, polyethylene, glues, dyes and synthetic perfumes. The toxic chemical dioxin may also be present in them.[58]
- Good diapering practices (changing and laundering) can make cloth the equal of disposables in terms of staying dry and avoid-ing diaper rash.
- Parents don't need to make frequent trips to the store since they only need a fixed supply of cloth diapers.
- Diaper liners catch stools so you don't have to rinse the entire diaper after each poop.
- The word "disposable" leads parents to believe they can dispose of dirty diapers without any effort or bother, yet baby's skin usu-ally needs cleaning with each change of a diaper, and it takes hundreds of years for disposables to decompose in landfills.

- The chemical dryness of disposables lets parents delay changing diapers under the false pretense, "As long as it feels dry, it's all right for baby."[59]
- The feeling of dryness of disposables delays the learning of cause and effect and can add months or as much as one to two years to toilet training a baby who wears diapers full time.
- A cotton diaper has a multitude of handy and baby-friendly uses, including serving as a washcloth, towel, light cover, cushion, sunshade, bib and toy (peekaboo).

### Pro-Disposable & Anti-Cloth Arguments

- Child-care centers usually require disposables.
- Disposables are more convenient since you can just throw them away and forget about them.
- Using disposables drastically reduces laundry.
- Disposables are adapted to fast-paced living where parents feel "time challenged" due to work or other reasons.
- Baby feels dry due to the absorption of moisture by disposables.
- For some, disposables may be healthier for the skin and reduce or eliminate diaper rash since they keep baby dry.
- Bad smells are less offensive than with cloth diapers.
- Parents can get away with being lazy about changing diapers.
- Babies and parents are less likely to awake in the middle of the night if baby pees in an absorbent disposable diaper.
- With a severe rash such as one caused by a yeast infection, disposables may be the only way to ensure baby stays rash free. Since yeast is resistant to hot water and detergent, cloth diapers can continually reinfect baby.

## How I Made Use of My One Disposable Diaper

When my youngest son was born, I was given a free sample disposable diaper along with a lot of other sample baby products. Since I preferred cotton diapers, I had no use for the disposable diaper . . .

. . . that is, until one day when I was a passenger on an airport shuttle van. My baby and I were stuck in the van longer than expected due to a delay. I knew my son had to go, but he was still too small to use a potty, and there was no "toilet place" for him to use in the van. I whipped out my sample disposable diaper, opened it up, held my infant over it and gave him the signal to go. He pooed on the diaper from a safe distance above, keeping his little bottom nice and clean. When he was finished, I folded up the diaper and disposed of it at the airport. That was the only time I used a disposable diaper.

## Diaper Rash

The term "diaper rash" refers to a variety of rashes that occur in the area of the body covered by a diaper. Genetics and hygiene contribute to the occurrence or lack of diaper rash. The different types of rash have different causes, but all are exacerbated by wet skin. Causes include:

- friction (typically where moist inner thighs rub together or where elastic rubs the wet skin)
- skin bacteria (bacteria begin to form as soon as baby wets or soils a diaper or other underwear)
- irritated skin (typically resulting from skin contact with soaps, detergents or lotions)
- allergic reaction (can affect more than just the diapered area)
- psoriasis (a skin disease that affects more than just the diapered area)
- yeast infections

Most parents have found that diaper rash can be relieved by letting baby be bare-bottomed at times. Exposing skin to air is a natural and gentle way to let it dry and be free of irritants.[60]

Diaper rash can be a blessing in disguise if it leads parents to try infant potty training and gives baby the gift of early emancipation from diapers. Families practicing infant pottying on a fairly regular and consistent basis rarely encounter diaper rash since their babies are rarely in wet or soiled garments.

## Diaper Bulk Blues

Imagine an infant, developmentally ready to turn over for the first time ever, being denied this joy for days or weeks whenever she is wrapped in diaper bulk. Or being deprived of the freedom to simply grab her toes whenever she wants, except during diaper changes. Babies love to do all sorts of things with their feet and will touch, grab, hold, gaze at and play with them constantly, often pulling them in front of their face, if given the chance. This early natural behavior must have a purpose, yet is limited by diaper wearing. How about the joys of wiggling and squirming naked or in a T-shirt, being able to twist and bend as far as your little body, joints and muscles will allow, without restriction. Or feeling, exploring and being touched on that whole sensitive area of your body, from waist to thighs, that is otherwise often "out of bounds."

More sophisticated coordination can be hampered too. Parents who let their babies go diaperless during some or all of the day report that their children scoot, sit, crawl, squat and walk sooner than when swaddled in diapers. "When my baby has a diaper on, it slows her down. Without the diaper, she scoots all over the place, and earlier than any of our other (diapered) children did." "The first time my son pulled himself up onto his knees and into a sitting position, he was not wearing a diaper." "For us, the diaper bulk restriction was most noticeable with sitting. It is *so* hard to sit on a big lumpy diaper!" "Katherine sits more gracefully, instead of just plopping down on a padded bum. Instead, she gently lowers herself down from standing."

By reducing diaper use, you are not only advancing infant toileting and helping the environment. You are also giving your baby a head start in physical development.

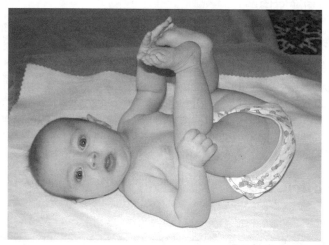

*Friederike Bradfisch*

**4-month-old Jutta, unrestricted by diaper bulk
and free to explore her feet.**

# chapter 13

# environmental
# issues

Perhaps not a day passes without some scary gloom-and-doom environmental statistics being paraded in front of us or forced down our heavily polluted throats. Everything, it seems, is bad for us, bad for our health, bad for the world, bad for the atmosphere and bad for . . . baby!

While the selection of a preferred toilet teaching technique is certainly not a life-and-death issue, there are consequences beyond convenience to consider. Many concerned families are first attracted to infant potty training when they learn how environmentally sound and beneficial it is. These aspects will be covered in this chapter. The important thing to remember here is that "you can make a difference."

Even for those who are "turned off" by environmentalists, bored with apocalyptic predictions, dislike radical environmentalist tactics and resent the erosion of our freedoms and bank accounts via legislation instigated by certain environmental organizations, there is no denying the environmental damage caused by conventional toilet-training methods. Using an environment-friendly means of potty training does not involve donating money or otherwise supporting any particular group, since there is no environmental movement promoting this method. Instead of donating dough, families using early potty training actually save a considerable amount of money on diapers, laundry, water and other costs, on average $1,500–$2,500 per child.

An average baby uses 6,000–8,000 diapers by the time conventional toilet training is completed—and the quantity is increasing among families who delay longer and longer. It is not uncommon to use up to 10,000 diapers per child. Whichever type of diaper is used, tremendous amounts of resources are required to manufacture and clean or dispose of them.

Although it may be more convenient in some respects to use traditional diapering methods for two to four years, the detrimental effects of "full-time diapers" (whether disposable or cloth) on the environment cannot be denied. By reducing or eliminating the use of diapers, you personally can conserve natural resources and reduce pollution.

## Water

Tremendous amounts of water are heated and used to clean the following:

- cloth diapers
- dirty baby bottoms, hands, legs and other body parts
- wet/soiled baby clothes, bedding, towels, mattress covers
- caregiver's hands after changing diapers

Water is polluted by laundering cloth diapers and manufacturing disposable diapers. Flushing disposable diapers down the toilet clogs sewer lines, creates tons of extra sludge each year and wastes large amounts of water.[61]

## Trees

More than one billion trees go into the manufacture of disposable diapers in one year.[62] It takes the pulp from one tree to make 500 to 1,000 disposable diapers.[63] At that rate, you save 10 to 20 trees per child by using the infant potty technique.[64]

Manufacturers of disposable diapers claim that the tree population is actually increasing thanks to them. The fact that tree farming is profitable encourages the planting and careful management of more and more trees as the demand increases. This, they say, results in more trees being planted than are cut down. No rare or endangered trees are used to make disposable diapers.[65]

## Landfills

Nobody thinks twice about making a mountain out of a landfill. And this is what appears to be happening all over the Western world, and in particular, the USA. Although the statistics vary and there is no way to determine exact figures, it must be evident even to the most environmentally disinterested that disposable diapers take a lot of space in landfills. Diapers are the third most dumped consumer product found in American landfills (after fast food containers and newspapers).[66] The number of disposable diapers used in a year in the USA is staggering, somewhere around 20 billion.[67] This translates to more than five million tons buried in landfills each year. The annual cost to taxpayers for disposal of disposable diapers is now near half a billion dollars.

Groundwater can become contaminated by viruses carried in the human feces and urine from disposable diapers. Flies and other insects drawn to the diapers can also spread viruses and bacteria. The most common diseases that are currently spread via diaper waste in landfills in Western countries are:

- enteroviruses (diarrhea and other intestinal diseases)
- rhinoviruses (influenza, common cold, etc.)[68]

In lesser developed lands, the situation becomes more hazardous to the health. More than 100 different intestinal viruses can be excreted in human feces, including hepatitis and—via vaccines passed in urine—polio. Although disposable diapers are used in far greater quantities in Western compared to third world countries, use of disposables is gradually increasing in the larger cities of many nonindustrialized societies. Finally, traces of the toxic industrial contaminant dioxin can be found in disposable diapers. This can be harmful to both baby and the environment.

## Biodegradable?

So-called biodegradable diapers are made of cornstarch-based plastic, biodegradable elastic, wood pulp and rayon, and they are chemical free. However, biodegradable disposable diapers don't solve the landfill problem. They have been shown to decompose in two to five years in a laboratory, but in fact take much longer (up to 500 years) to decompose in a landfill, due to compaction and lack of sunlight, water and oxygen.[69] Although they may decompose faster than standard disposable diapers, they still use the same space in landfills, and the health risks are the same. The only way for biodegradable diapers to be environmentally effective is to have them processed by a sewage treatment plant.

## Diaper Services

Diaper services are not a very environmentally friendly solution to pollution. In some ways, use of a diaper service merely passes the problems on to someone else.

Many of the services use large amounts of toxic chemicals, including chlorine bleach and other polluting agents, to get the diapers as white as possible. The diapers must be collected and delivered, requiring fuel and adding to traffic congestion and air pollution.

For parents who prefer to use a diaper service, here are some positive points to ponder. Less electrical energy is used this way since the diapers are washed collectively.[70] Cloth diapers can be reused, and this spares trees. Plastics and other unnatural materials are not present in cotton diapers. Using a diaper service is cheaper than buying disposable diapers. You don't need to make frequent trips to the shop to buy disposables since you only need a fixed supply of cloth diapers. You will reduce your weekly garbage pile and cut down on waste going into landfills. Last but not least, you can send the laundry out for someone else to do.

## So What?

Despite the statistics cited in this chapter and the fact that a widespread educational campaign could greatly benefit the environment, environmental groups have, for all intents and purposes, remained indifferent to the idea of reducing or eliminating diapers through infant potting. The most any organization has done so far is to publish a brief review of *Trickle Treat*. Infant potty training is not an easy sell. There are no frightening or heart-rending photos that can be used to outrage the population in order to extract large donations or allow the media to sensationalize the topic.

Another disinterested group consists of parenting magazines, even those advocating a natural lifestyle. Both mainstream and alternative parenting magazines find infant pottying too inconvenient to even mention to their readers. In addition, magazines lack the courage to write about it, preferring to remain loyal to lucrative advertising "diaper dollars."

On an individual level, parents may think, "So what? Who cares about these environmental statistics?" One baby's worth of diapers may not seem to matter. But when the diapers of hundreds or thousands of babies are compiled, compacted or cleansed, the toll on the environment and our natural resources is staggering. It is our children and grandchildren who will have to deal with the mess we are making. We, as responsible adults, should cut back on pollution and depletion whenever and wherever reasonably

O brave new world, that has such diapers in 't.

possible. One effective way to do so is to reduce or eliminate the use of diapers by starting toilet teaching in infancy or as soon as you first hear about
it. Since environmental groups have so far not embraced the cause and the
media and parenting magazines don't dare broach the topic, the role of
individual responsibility takes on tremendous importance here.

# chapter 14

# conventional
# training

The current standard method of toilet training in the United States involves using diapers until 2 years or older and beginning training when a child decides he no longer wants to wear diapers. This is considered to be a child-led approach. Several books have been written with the philosophy "baby knows best," i.e., baby will toilet train himself or indicate when he is ready. These books invariably sound the alarm about any kind of toilet teaching before baby is "ready." But in some ways, the current conventional wisdom has turned out to be "conventional unwisdom" for many families, as well as for the environment.

By waiting to toilet train baby until he approaches, reaches or surpasses the "terrible twos," parents unwittingly invite all sorts of power struggles and psychological complications. For the first years of life, it was considered acceptable for baby to go in his diapers. Then suddenly one day, it becomes apparent that even the most well-meaning parents want the routine to be changed. Wetting or soiling the diapers is now considered "naughty," "dirty" or somehow wrong. This change in attitude, or so-called growing up, can be confusing and lead to an array of struggles and difficulties. One important advantage of training in infancy is that an infant is too young to engage in a battle of wills. As long as parents adhere to the correct behavior (see Chapter 7, "Parental Attitude"), no harm can come to baby, and he will benefit from not having to experience the humiliation of dirty diapers.

In parts of Europe, some parents still tend to start earlier than in the States. When baby begins to show a physical and psychological readiness to cooperate, parents start sitting them on the potty, somewhere between the ages of 15–20 months. But even in Europe, parents are being pressured to start later and later.

## Conventional vs. Infant Toilet Training

Conventional late potty training will likely remain the norm, at least for a few more generations, since it is a more convenient method in ways important to fast-paced living. Due to the fact that infant potty training has been so misunderstood and maligned, it is necessary to strongly demonstrate its strengths and advantages over conventional training.

The truth is, there is not one method of toilet training that is ideal for every child and family. Conventional potty training is better for some families, while infant potty training is better for others, depending on the parents' attitude and family situation. Both methods of potty training can be harmful if misused and abused by impatient parents and caregivers. Both methods can be successful if adhered to correctly. The golden rule of both is: Never make an issue of toilet training. Patience and a relaxed, matter-of-fact attitude are keys to healthy toilet training. Aside from age, the main differences between conventional and infant toilet training are in the realms of communication and timing.

Some problems you may incur by starting at a later age include the fact that many toddlers and older children:

- cannot easily understand what a potty is
- have little or no awareness of elimination
- cannot communicate toilet needs
- don't like to be put on the potty or toilet often
- don't like to remain on the potty or toilet
- don't mind if they soil their diapers or pants
- use "potty time" as a means to an end, such as playing "power games" to assert their independence and test their parents
- aren't interested in toilet training
- refuse to go without a bribe or reward

By contrast, infants:

- can understand the concept of a toilet place from birth
- are aware of elimination
- can easily communicate the need to eliminate
- like being held during the in-arms phase
- like to be taken to eliminate when they need to go
- don't like soiling their diapers or pants
- are too young to play "power games" and to test their parents during much of toilet learning
- grow and flow with infant pottying
- don't require a bribe or reward to go

Some of the "games" toddlers and older kids like to play include:

- refusal to use the potty
- retention until they leave the potty
- retention in order to "get attention"
- intentional use of inappropriate places (floor, sofa, etc.) as a toilet
- unnecessary demands to be taken to the toilet

Small infants are too young to engage in these types of manipulative games. Once babies begin to crawl or walk, they are more fascinated by their surroundings and want to explore and play, rather than start learning about toileting, whereas small infants learning this in and from their mothers' loving arms are naturally cooperative. As they grow, they typically transition easily to using a potty and rarely engage in the toddler games mentioned above. They may try some of the games as part of their explorations of life but quickly outgrow them, provided their parents and caregivers do not punish them, use force or impose negative control. As with conventionally trained toddlers, those who began toilet learning as infants may need to be entertained or distracted for short periods of time in order to entice them to remain on the potty. This is not considered to be punishment or reward. And all toddlers, no matter how they learn, can regress in their pottying if they undergo emotional, stressful or other negative events in their family life. If the stressful situation can be cleared up within a matter of weeks, they usually resume pottying at the stage where they left off.

In carrying out traditional potty training, some adults—parents, baby-sitters, daycare workers or others—aggravate the situation by physically or verbally abusing and punishing a child. Some yell and scream at the child or spank him when he has an accident or does not perform as desired. These sad situations can be avoided by using infant potty training, as it expressly forbids the use of all negative behaviors and tactics. It should be noted that many users of traditional potty training also reject negative tactics.

The full-time diapering of traditional Western toilet training typically involves:

- denial (assuming that babies aren't aware of elimination functions)
- delay tactics (delay changing dirty diapers and delay the start of potty training)
- instant gratification at baby's expense (caregivers can get away with not changing dirty diapers until they feel like it)
- diaper wars (battles to change a squirmy baby's dirty diaper and clean a dirty baby bottom)
- ignoring and suppressing baby's signals
- spending less time with baby

By contrast, key characteristics of infant potty training are:

- affirmation (acknowledging that babies are aware of elimination functions)
- propitiousness (working with baby at the easiest time for him to respond to conditioning and to communicate his toilet needs)
- sacrifice for baby's benefit (diligence and responding to baby's signals on time)
- cleanliness and dignity (no one has to be in contact with baby's eliminations which go straight into a receptacle rather than a diaper)
- responding to baby's signals
- spending more time with baby

## Lifelong Trauma?

Pediatrician Amy Plumb, who practices at the University of Wisconsin Children's Hospital and advocates a late-start "toilet teaching" technique, was asked if a particular method of toilet training can scar a child for life. Her response was no. Is this frequent claim of psychological damage by toilet training just a myth? Dr. Plumb's reply:

> "Yes, I think it really is. And there is lots of worry about, 'Oh, well, I potty trained my child wrong, so everything went downhill from there.' And really, it has nothing to do with it. Everybody gets potty trained one way or another, and there have been no studies I know of that show any bad influence long term on whatever method is used."[71]

Difficulties can and do arise, whether purposeful or inadvertent, when using any type of toilet learning. One of the main causes of upset stems from a lack of communication, as illustrated by the following true story.

> The earliest memory that "Linda" (now a mother herself) has of her childhood involves the frustration and trauma of toilet training. When she was 2 years old, her mother and some of her mother's friends took Linda with them to see a movie. During the feature film, little Linda pooped in her diaper. She was extremely uncomfortable and didn't want to sit in the mess. However, her mother and friends were deeply engrossed in the feature film and didn't notice her plight. As she could not speak well enough to explain her desperate situation, she stood up on her seat to get her mother's attention and try to signal to her for help. Upon standing, some of the feces trickled down Linda's legs. This upset her even more. Her frustration with not being able to communicate her predicament was unbearable.

> While standing on the seat, she grabbed some of the poop and reached out to show it to the adults, again attempting to signal her plight. In the dark, her mother mistook the contents for candy and happily announced to the friend sitting next to Linda, "Look, Linda is offering you some of her candy! How sweet."

> The friend reached for the object in Linda's hand and, needless to say, was horrified to discover the little girl was handing her human excrement. Once the friends realized what had happened, they had a good laugh. This made Linda feel embarrassed. In addition, it

seemed like hours before anyone changed her, which made her feel humiliated, helpless and trapped in the mess.

Looking back on the event from adulthood, Linda realizes that from that day on she had trouble expressing her feelings to others, for fear of being humiliated and ridiculed. She became withdrawn and distrustful of others. Throughout her childhood, she suffered from bouts of constipation, but didn't realize it was because she was holding back her bowel movements for fear of reliving the stressful experience.

# chapter 15

# dispelling
# the myths

This chapter presents a compilation of counterarguments to some classic challenges made by disbelievers. Everyone has an opinion about potty training, and these opinions will likely disagree with yours. Friends, relatives and sometimes even strangers will offer advice, much of it unwanted. If they are not familiar with infant potty training, they will probably find it strange or, in the extreme, even accuse you of cruelty or child abuse. These accusations are, of course, completely unfounded.

In some situations, one parent does not receive support from the other. Sometimes only the mother wants baby to be potty trained from infancy, while in other situations the father finds he has no help or encouragement from the mother. This can make the process more difficult, not only because you may end up doing everything on your own but also because baby can usually sense resistance and negativity. Skepticism from family members, friends and neighbors can be tough to handle.

It is nice to discover that you are not alone! There is a growing online community of enthusiastic mothers who will gladly offer you inspiration and share their wisdom and experiences. You can also join or start a local play and support group. You may be able to find support and encouragement from relatives who are familiar with infant toileting. It is surprising how many immigrants and grandparents are acquainted with the method. It is like a breath of fresh air to speak with those who can tell you about their own experiences. But for now, if you are facing negativity and resistance, you may find it helpful to read and reflect on ways myths and rumors can be dispelled.

## "It's about Potty-Trained Parents" . . .

When people first hear of infant potty training, one of the common negative retorts is to exclaim that it is the parents who are potty trained, not the baby, thus implying that baby has nothing to do with the process. The naysayers do not realize that adult and child communicate, work together as a team and thus undergo reciprocal learning and reinforcement. The skeptics do not understand that an infant has some control over urination and defecation and that this improves gradually over the months with the help of an attentive caregiver, until total control is achieved.

Does the fact that a baby cannot feed himself mean we should not feed him? Does the fact that a baby cannot dress himself mean we should not keep him in clean clothing? Does the fact that a baby cannot change a diaper mean we should let him be soiled and wet? The answer to these and similar questions is, of course, no. Then why should a willing parent be criticized for taking care of baby's toilet needs in a loving and different way at a relatively young age?

Newborns and infants cannot be viewed as independent of their caregivers since without them they would not survive. The fact that infant pottying is not necessary for survival does not mean it is without merit.

## "It's Purely a Matter of Catching" . . .

Some may argue that infant pottying is basically about "catching" baby's pee or poo at the right time and that this is merely a matter of luck. This is indeed part of the equation, especially at the start, but certainly not the whole equation. If you start early enough, baby will be and remain aware of this bodily function. For the first few days or weeks as you are learning to communicate with each other about elimination, it might well be a question of "catching" his waste in a receptacle, but once you are familiar with his timing, body language and signals, and once he associates your cues with the function of elimination, it becomes a question of "being there on time" for baby.

## "It's too Inconvenient" . . .

Some Americans lapse into a fast-food mentality when it comes to raising children—and especially when it comes to potty training. They want it fast, they want it now and they want it to be easy; otherwise, they opt to put it off for as long as they can. Now that disposable diapers are more absorbent than ever and, through the use of super absorbent gels, give babies the feeling of being dry the moment they pee, Americans are delaying potty training even longer. Daycare centers abound with children ages 3 and 4 who have not yet begun, and disposables have increased the largest size to size six.

Each time baby poos, and frequently when he pees, something must be done. Parents can do that "something" immediately before the fact or else sometime after the fact. Either way, elimination requires attention, time and energy. It is a matter of preference how a parent decides to take care of the situation.

When Westerners first hear of infant pottying, their reaction is one of disbelief and disapproval. "That's just too inconvenient!" is a common defense. Fortunately, not everyone likes or agrees with the concepts of having babies for convenience and "convenience comes first." Don't let those who elect to delay toilet teaching convince you to delay too.

## "It's for Parents' Convenience" . . .

I had to scratch my head when I read this argument in a letter to the editor in *Mothering* magazine.[72] The reader passionately argued that helping baby avoid wetting or soiling a diaper is a matter of convenience for caregivers and is "Victorian" in its "repressive, antilife aspects." Readers of this book will note that not one of the testimonials refers to infant potty training as a "convenient" method and that this claim is not made anywhere in the book. It has been repeatedly emphasized that it takes dedicated, devoted, patient and diligent caregivers to work closely with baby. Granted, mothers appreciate not having to clean diapers, but this is also beneficial for baby since it is far more hygienic and comfortable not to sit in a soiled diaper. In addition, many babies dislike being held down for diaper changes, and the battles resulting from this tend to increase over time.

The word "repressive" refers to excluding something from the conscious mind. This book repeatedly refers to the stimulation and encouragement of baby's awareness of elimination functions, as well as to the symbiotic relationship of mutual benefit to baby and caregiver that develops. Indispensable elements of this close relationship include bonding, intimacy, communication, caring, patience and respect.

For those who care to see things from a different viewpoint, the convenience argument is reversible—and certainly the way mothers in many other societies view the issue. Diapers are used for parents' convenience. We force babies to wear diapers because it's easier to leave them in diapers than pay attention and quickly respond to their signals. Parents can and often do delay changing a diaper until it is convenient to do so. The washing machine, disposable diapers and diaper services have liberated women a great deal in terms of convenience. Mothers' liberation from cleaning diapers has led to babies' imprisonment in diapers. (This argument is *not* intended to instill guilt in anyone using a different method.)

Finally, as stated in the "It's too Inconvenient" section above, parents using this method do not have babies for their convenience and do not raise children believing that convenience for the parents comes first.

## "Baby Isn't Ready" . . .

Baby *is* ready! Western medicine teaches that children are not physically or psychologically ready to start toilet training until they are 18 months or older (Europe) or 2–3 years old (United States). Both have been disproved by billions of families around the world. In other societies, parental communication, expectations, training and guidance are the keys to readiness and success.

One could make the argument that infants aren't ready for conventional toilet training, and this is true in the sense that an infant can't say "pee" or "poo," cannot walk to the potty or sit down on his own, etc. But these prerequisites are irrelevant where infants are concerned. As one mother put it, "It's like saying a baby is not ready to learn to walk before he can tie his shoes."

## "It's Dangerous" . . .

Those who declare that infant toilet training is harmful have never met or observed a family using it and have no idea what it entails. Instead, they read accounts that refer to the old method of early toilet training. Furthermore, children's psychological problems, if any, usually stem from their overall relationship or a lack of communication with their parents rather than from one particular aspect or phase.

The relatively few Western doctors who have witnessed the method abroad and who have remained skeptical have either not given it serious consideration ("far too primitive for Westerners") or else they believe Western families are incapable of dedicating the time and patience needed. To categorically dismiss infant potty training due to the latter view is tragic and belies the strength, devotion and love of those who want to use this method.

## "It's Impossible" . . .

Upon first hearing about infant potty training, many assume it's fake or just a passing fad. The denial is so strong that some refuse to believe toilet-training accounts coming from their own mothers. When one woman first heard about infant toileting, she wrote, "My grandmother is from Jamaica and says that my father was potty trained by the age of 3 months. My mother always just dismissed this notion, but now it makes perfect sense."[73]

A defeatist attitude guarantees failure. In other societies, families *know* it is possible. The combination of their history and confident attitude go a long way towards making it possible. The testimonials and cross-cultural studies presented in this book demonstrate not only that infant potty training is possible but also that it is prevalent and has been the norm for generations throughout several societies around the world.

## "It Takes Just as Long" . . .

A favorite argument used to discourage families from adopting infant toilet training is to claim that toilet training takes equally as long, or even longer, when you start in infancy. This is generally false if infant potty training is done correctly, especially if the years of diapers and diapering of conventional training are included in the equation. But even more important, infant pottying is not about competition or finishing at a certain age.

## "Wearing Diapers Is Part of Being a Baby" . . .

Some parents feel that wearing diapers is part of being a baby and that infant toilet training is a way to "rush baby to grow up." They want baby to be a baby as long as possible, and this includes using diapers. This is a matter of preference and choice.

There have been, and still are, far more babies in the world raised without diapers than with diapers. Babies are born with the ability to communicate about elimination. The fact that some parents choose to recognize and respond to a baby's elimination communication does not mean their baby is being forced to grow up in a hurry. Any tool that enhances communication between baby and caregiver is valuable. A baby who pees in a receptacle is just as much a baby as a baby who pees in a diaper.

## "It's Unhygienic" . . .

The idea of babies going diaperless leads some to conclude that these babies pee and poo all over the house. While some diaperless babies have occasional accidents indoors, infant pottying does not involve letting children eliminate whenever and wherever they please.

## "It's Obsessing about Bowel Movements" . . .

This is another ridiculous argument that has nothing to do with reality. Again, it is offered out of ignorance, by those who are referring to a different method of toilet training infants or to their own strange hang-ups. There is no obsessing about bowel movements. Instead, caregivers are attentive and watch for signals from baby, in order to know when to take baby to go. There is certainly nothing wrong or obsessive with monitoring and being receptive to baby's signals and natural timing.

## "Freud Says" . . .

Sigmund Freud's famous but outdated postulation that early toilet training leads to the development of the anal character traits of orderliness,
cleanliness and miserliness has never been proven. The theory is good fod-
der for gossip but nothing more. The influence of toilet training on personality is debatable at best, with many psychologists believing that Freud's list
of character traits are the by-product of other child-rearing practices or the
child's upbringing as a whole. In any case, his theory was based on the
harsh method of early toilet training which is not advocated in this book.

# chapter 16

# history & theories

## Toilet Training by Early Man

How was baby's elimination dealt with in the earliest of times? It seems plausible and logical that it was managed from birth rather than delayed. In warmer climates where little or no clothing was needed, it was easy to observe and anticipate elimination timing. Small babies were held and carried at all times since it was too dangerous to leave them on the ground or unattended. This made it easy to notice and immediately act on baby's signals. There were no elaborate home furnishings to worry about and thus no reason for adults to mind if a baby urinated or defecated in a cave, dwelling or other shelter. Likewise there was little concern if a baby peed on anyone since no one wore expensive clothing. All this allowed for a relaxed, casual and natural approach to toileting baby.

It seems likely that the first substantial use of skins, furs or plant material to catch infant elimination would have been with populations migrating to, and living in, cooler climates where babies would have to wear garments for warmth. Putting clothing on an infant makes it more difficult to be attentive to elimination since it is not as easy to notice when baby voids or needs to void. The introduction of crude clothing for warmth thus added another step to toilet training.

## Western Attitudes 1400–1800

In 1472, the first medical book ever published was about the care of children. Author Paolo Bagellardo discussed the problem of bedwetting "not only up to the age of five or six, but sometimes even into puberty"[74] and offered an array of sometimes strange remedies.

Before the 1800s, personal and public hygiene was not an issue. There was no plumbing and no such thing as a bathroom as we know it today. Toilet training was not of much concern to parents since babies were swaddled much of the time, and people believed a dirty child was a healthy child. There are no references to toilet training in child-rearing manuals of the day.[75]

Well-wrapped swaddling clothes served as both a babysitter and a diaper. Babies could be ignored and left alone or bundled in a corner for hours since the swaddling prevented their moving about the room or house. Babies were changed infrequently. Their bottoms were wiped and powdered with the dust of worm-eaten wood (the baby powder of the past) but rarely washed with soap and water. Soiled and wet swaddling cloths were dried by the fire, often without a washing, then reused. At the end of the 17th century, philosopher John Locke recommended putting babies in a "pierced chair" placed over a chamber pot after meals and leaving them there until they urinated and defecated. This was the precursor to the potty chair which appeared in the 1940s in the form of a small armchair in which a baby could be strapped until he finished his business.[76]

## "Early Toilet Training" Method (circa 1840–1950)

In the 19th century, cleanliness became a virtue. Going to the toilet was begun at the age of 3 or 4 months, and babies were held over the chamber pot at set times throughout the day.[77] A method known as "early toilet training" was used in the United States for over a century, until the 1950s, and even longer in Europe. Parents and child experts believed this was the best method available in their day and made good-faith attempts at using it. Most Western medical professionals today are familiar with the method of early toilet training and assume that infant potty training is the same.

Research Specialist Dr. Thomas S. Ball had this to say about the "habit training" aspect of early toilet training: ". . . what has sometimes been called 'habit trained' comes about when the child is routinely placed on the commode according to a set daily schedule. In these circumstances the child defecates when placed on the toilet. While it is sometimes a matter of luck in 'catching' the child at the right time, there are children who do withhold their feces until placed on the toilet. They do not, however, seek out the toilet when 'nature calls' and would soil themselves if taken off the routine, even if a toilet were available." He then emphasizes that habit training is based on the timing imposed by the mother or nurse, ". . . in the habit training procedure placement on the toilet constitutes the first step in what may or may not develop as a chain of behaviors. If being put on the commode does eventually become the first link in a chain leading to evacuation, the whole sequence is cued or set off by something done to the child by someone else."[78]

Americans of family-raising age are surprised to learn that toilet training in infancy was commonly used in the USA and Europe in fairly recent times and for more than a century. At first, this seems like exciting news and in some ways it is, yet in other ways, early toilet training is the bane of infant potty training.

As the names imply, both early and infant toilet training are started in infancy. Although there were some positive elements to early toilet training, such as the fact that experts and parents recognized baby's ability to learn about elimination early in life, the negative aspects have, unfortunately, come to be associated with and attributed to any form or method of toilet training in infancy. Methods advocating an early start are labeled "severe." Since none of the negative aspects are a part of infant potty training, it is helpful to compare the two methods. The following table lists the elements of early toilet training which are not a part of infant potty training.

| Early toilet training | Infant potty training |
|---|---|
| based on the fixed timing of the mother or nurse | based on baby's natural elimination timing |
| little or no attention paid to baby's signals | based on observing and responding to baby's signals |
| sometimes recommended the use of punishment | punishment forbidden |
| advocated use of suppositories and enemas | suppositories and enemas never used |
| method unnatural | method natural |
| method baby-unfriendly | method baby-friendly |
| method inflexible | method flexible |
| method harsh | method gentle |
| method strict and rigid | method casual and relaxed |
| approach negative | approach positive |
| approach one-sided (adult in control) | approach cooperative ("teamwork") |
| baby sometimes treated as an object | baby always treated as a feeling, thinking human being |
| baby sometimes strapped onto potty for long periods of time | baby held in-arms in phase one and sits on potty without restraints in phase two |
| baby sometimes left alone on potty for long periods of time | baby held in-arms in phase one and never left unaccompanied on potty in phase two |

## Relativity of Child-Raising Philosophies

Having compared early and infant toilet training, with an emphasis on the negative aspects of early toilet training, it must now be said that in general parents and experts of all generations strive to do what they believe is best for babies, with respect to the customs, philosophy, attitudes, resources and fashions of their time. It is also important to bear in mind that the teachings of one generation tend to produce a reaction that often results in the opposite trend in the next generation and a pooh-poohing of the child-raising practices of parents and grandparents. It is easier to understand trends and behaviors when viewing them in relation to the mindset of the epoch in question. In trying to understand child-raising techniques of the past, it is necessary to bear in mind that certain words can have very different meanings and connotations from one generation to the next.

In the 17th century, reason was the most admired quality. Westerners believed that correct thinking would free them of the superstition and religious dogma that had controlled them for so long. Self-control was the main means of discipline during this Age of Reason. In keeping with this philosophy of knowledge, English philosopher John Locke advised parents to instill self-control in their infants by means such as leaving babies to cry rather than picking them up every time they cried and requiring them to "stool regularly" everyday after breakfast.[79]

By the late 18th century, the Romantic Movement was in vogue and shifted the emphasis from reason to emotion and feelings (two words with fairly different connotations than they have at the start of the 21st century). The Cult of Childhood was born,[80] although looking back, parents of today might not recognize it as such. It gradually increased over the years, picking up tremendous speed in the 1960s, and is still with us today.

In the early 20th century, behaviorist psychology came into vogue, with an emphasis on controlling children through training rather than fear. John B. Watson taught that children should be raised by following rules and by being subjected to a strict schedule. He taught that "nurture" was of utmost importance. His definition of "nurture" is radically different from the meaning of the word today. He urged parents to never hug or kiss children, never let them sit in your lap and to give them no more than a pat on the head if they have done something extraordinarily good.

Around the 1950s, permissiveness came into fashion as a reaction to Watson's teachings. Pediatrician Benjamin Spock was all the rage. Even though he believed in following rules, he was so much more relaxed about them than his predecessors that he seemed to be championing permissive-ness.[81] By the time he passed away in 1998, society had become much more child-oriented—to the point of child worship in many respects—and Spock's philosophy of the 1950s no longer seemed permissive.

With respect to infant toilet training, most Western pediatricians and psychologists of today label it severe, harsh and bogus. Although these and other accusations reflect the "conventional wisdom" of our times, this does not automatically make them correct and true. Strong counterarguments to these views are presented throughout this book. Indeed, compelling anecdotal evidence and accounts by numerous practitioners, researchers and observers from around the world have attested to the fact that infant elimination training is both gentle and effective.

## Writings on "Early Toilet Training"

The writings on early toilet training are extensive, with a few very different from the method described in this book. Here is a sampling of what some of the experts, authors and publications had to say about it in their day . . .

### 1870
### Tullio Suzzara Verdi
*Maternity, a Popular Treatise for Young Mothers*

As soon as a baby can sit, put him on his chair every morning at the same hour to encourage defecation. "If it is disinclined, a little stick of castile-soap may be introduced into the rectum for a few minutes, which will stimulate it to act."[82]

### 1888
### Pye Henry Chavasse

Chavasse wrote a series of advice books for mothers. He maintained that a baby is ready to be placed on the stool at a regular time each day, starting at the age of 3 months.[83]

### 1894 & 1903
### Luther Emmett Holt
*The Care and Feeding of Children*

A baby is usually ready to start training by the age of 2 months. "A small chamber, about the size of a pint bowl, is placed between the nurse's knees, and upon this the infant is held, its back being against the nurse's chest and its body fully supported. This should be done twice a day, after the morning and afternoon feedings, and always at the same hour. . . . in a surprisingly short time the position is all that is required. With most infants, after a few weeks the bowels will move as soon as the infant is placed on the chamber." Holt claimed that using suppositories would result in success within 2 months.[84]

## 1912
## Roger H. Dennett
### *The Healthy Baby*

At the age of 8 months, the child should be placed on the chamber every hour of the day.[85]

## 1913
## Francis Tweddell
### *How to Take Care of the Baby*

"The training of a child's bowels should begin at about the second month, and can be done in the following manner. A small pot is placed between the nurse's knees, and on this the baby is seated, taking care to support his body firmly, and to brace his back against the nurse's chest . . . if this is kept up with regularity, and the baby is in good health, he can sometimes be trained in this respect as early as the age of three months. . . . The training of the bladder is not so easily accomplished, but a great deal can be done by the practice of holding a child over the pot about a dozen times a day. In many cases, this is so successful that by the end of the first year diapers can be dispensed with entirely during the child's waking hours."[86]

## 1914
## Mrs. Max West
### *Infant Care*

"In order to do away with the need for diapers as early in life as possible, the baby should be taught to use the chamber. This training may be begun by the third month, or even earlier in some cases. It should be carried out with the utmost gentleness, since scolding and punishment will serve only to frighten the child and to destroy the natural impulses, while laughter will tend to relax the muscles and to promote an easy movement. In order to be effective, the chamber must be presented to the baby at the same hour every day, usually just before the morning bath, and it must be presented persistently each day until the habit is formed. Much time and patience will be required on the part of the mother."[87]

## 1919
## C. L. Hull & B. I. Hull
### in *Pedagogical Seminary*

The authors collected data on children ranging from 9–31 months and refer to two distinct processes, "the first the power to relax the sphincters at will initiating micturition; the second the power to inhibit spontaneous tendency to such relaxation while in situations inappropriate for micturition."[88]

## 1921
## Mrs. Max West
### *Infant Care*

This edition advises starting bowel training even earlier than the 1914 edition. Training should start as soon as a mother recovers from delivery and should finish by the end of the first year. The mother should place baby on the chamber at specific times each day, "not varying the time by five minutes." This requires "unlimited patience" on the part of the mother. Gentleness and laughter are no longer included. There is no more warning against scolding and punishment.

"Almost any baby can be so trained that there are no more soiled diapers to wash after he is a year old, and many mothers accomplish the result much earlier than this. . . . The mother should observe the hour at which the baby soils his diaper. At the same hour the next day she should hold him over the chamber, using a soap stick, if necessary, to start the movement, and thus continue day after day, not varying the time by five minutes, until the baby is fixed in this habit." Mothers are advised to stop with the soap stick after the first 3–4 days, or as soon as possible.

No start time is given for bladder training. "The baby should be given the chamber very often, perhaps once an hour, at least." Mothers were discouraged from using diapers. "One device for teaching the baby not to wet is to put him into drawers very young, discarding the diaper much earlier than is usually done. The warm, thick diaper constantly suggests to the baby the idea of wetting and no doubt retards his training in this regard. He will not like the feeling of the wet, cold drawers, and there will be nothing about them to suggest wetting, but rather the reverse."[89]

## 1921
### J. P. Crozer Griffith
*The Care of the Baby: A Manual for Mothers and Nurses*

"[C]ontrol the emptying of the bladder and the bowels. By the time it is 3 months old the baby becomes conscious of these acts, and even before this early age its education may be begun. . . . If the mother will hold it over a receptacle on her lap a little while before either evacuation is expected, the child will very gradually learn to recognize the purpose of the procedure and will act accordingly."[90]

## 1921
### L. Pouliot
*Hygiène de maman et de bébé*

"It is stated that the newborn urinates almost every time he is undressed, a few seconds after making contact with the air. Knowing that he will urinate, place him in a crouching position above a chamber pot and support his buttocks. This position will induce urination. After some days, the newborn will have made a strong association between the two sensations: the flowing of urine and contact with the chamber pot. He will become accustomed to urinating only in his pot—that is, except during his sleep—and you will have made him clean from his earliest weeks."[91]

## 1922
### Roger H. Dennett
*The Healthy Baby*

"When baby reaches the age of four months, if he is strong and well, we begin to train him to have stools at regular intervals. It is surprising how soon the little things learn to use the vessel. At stated times each day (once or twice, according to his previous habits) he is placed upon a small infant's chamber, which is comfortable if it exactly fits the buttocks. This may be held in the lap in order to support his back. He soon learns to grunt and strain whenever he is placed upon it, and the habit is quickly established."[92]

## 1923
### S. Josephine Baker
*Healthy Babies*

"Training the child to use the chamber for bowel movements may be commenced as early as 2 months. The best way is to place the baby on a

small chamber with his back supported against the mother's knees. . . .
Training of the bladder is not as easy as training the bowels, but systematic
attempts may be made at about 3 months of age to train the child by placing him on the chamber four or five times a day, with his back well supported. . . . While some children take a long time to learn the meaning of
this, some learn very quickly."[93]

### 1924
### Richard M. Smith
#### *The Baby's First Two Years*

"A baby can be trained to have a movement regularly each day by putting him on the chamber in the morning at a definite time. Some babies can
be trained from the first few weeks of life, others not until later."[94]

### 1928
### John B. Watson
#### *Psychological Care of Infant and Child*

"It is quite easy to start habits of day-time continence (conditioned responses) when the child is from 3–5 weeks old by putting the chamber to
the child (but at this age never on it) each time it is aroused for feeding. It
is often surprising how quickly the conditioned response is established if
your routine is unremitting and your patience holds out."[95]

### 1929
### Martha May Eliot
#### *Infant Care*

"Almost any baby can be trained so that there are no more soiled diapers to wash after he is six to eight months old."[96] The absolute regularity of
potty visits is required. This is the most rigid or "severe" edition of *Infant
Care*.

### 1930
### Harry R. Litchfield & Leon H. Dembo
#### *Care of the Infant and Child*

"The question of how early an infant should be trained is one that has
resulted in a great divergence of opinion. Many psychologists and behavior-
ists are of the opinion that an infant can be trained at three months. It is
our belief, however, that the reports of infants so trained are somewhat ex-

aggerated. We have not been fortunate in seeing these infant prodigies. It is our opinion that if an infant is trained between the ages of six and nine months its mother is entitled to award herself a blue ribbon."[97]

## 1930
### Marion L. Faegre & John E. Anderson
*Child Care and Training*

"[Bowel] training may begin as early as the sixth week, if the baby is in good physical condition. The mother may hold the infant over a receptacle in her lap, the child's back being toward her, and supported by her arms and body.

"Too rigorous attempts at training should not be made, nor should the length of the training period be protracted. The child should never be made tired or uncomfortable by the procedure."

Concerning "the dry habit," the authors write, "Beginning not later than one year of age, watch the child for several days and note the time it urinates. Place the child on a vessel near the time you have noted and keep a record of the number of times you are successful in anticipating his needs. This routine procedure should take place before and after naps, immediately after meals, before going to bed, either once during the night or just before the parents retire, and directly upon arising."

The authors recommend a casual, relaxed approach and suggest the child be "taught a simple word, gesture, or grunt to indicate his needs, as soon as he realizes the possibility of control, which is usually between the twelfth and nineteenth months.

"Bear in mind that children differ greatly in speed and permanency of learning, hence, though one child achieves control by eighteen months, another may not be completely trained until he is two and one-half years old."[98]

## 1932
### Martha May Eliot
*Infant Care*

Bowel training can be started as early as the end of the first month and should always be begun by the third month. Patience is required, and the result is well worth the effort. "Almost any baby can be so trained that there are no more soiled diapers to wash after he is 6 to 8 months old."

"To begin the training, the mother should notice at what time the baby soils his diaper. The next day at that hour she should hold him over the chamber, using a soap stick, if necessary, to start the movement, and continue this day after day, not varying the time by five minutes, until the baby is fixed in this habit."

Bladder training should be started at 10 months. "Some one simple word should be used each time he is given the chamber so that he may associate the word with the act and learn to use it himself a little later." Daytime control is usually achieved by 2 years. Mothers were urged to immediately change wet clothing to help establish a "dry habit." It was advised to praise a child who keeps dry but not to scold when he has an accident. Nighttime bladder control is not learned until "between the second and third birthdays, after control during the day is well established."[99]

### 1935
### Margaret Evelyn Fries

Fries found that the age to start bowel (and bladder) training ranged from 2–17 months, with the modal age being 4 months and the average age 6 months. The length of time to complete the bowel training process ranged from a few days to 8 months, with 1–2 months sufficing for most infants. No length of time was given for completing bladder training.[100]

### 1938
### May Elizabeth MacIver Law
*Baby Care* (No. 4)

"Many doctors and nurses recommend training the baby to the use of the pot as early as one month or six weeks old, but others are inclined to letting him use his diapers comfortably for at least three months or even until he is at the sitting up stage. . . . In the fourth month, the mother should hold the baby over a pot after his 10 a.m. feed, and after the 6 p.m. feed."[101]

### 1938
### C. Anderson Aldrich & Mary M. Aldrich
*Babies are Human Beings*

"The developmental formula for true training is simple and efficient. After a few weeks of life, automatic evacuations gradually become less frequent so that only one or two occur daily. Their time and number vary in different children but the tendency for them to come at definite periods in each day is steadily more pronounced. As soon as it is possible to discover the exact moment at which the mass movement takes place, it is reasonable to put the baby on a chamber or toilet-seat and relieve his mother of the irksome task of diaper-washing. When he is placed on the toilet-seat at *his* right time, his brain naturally develops the necessary association between the mass movement, the toilet-seat and his own, satisfying effort. Our coöperation in this growth process is merely to observe the baby's own rhythm, in selecting the time of day for a bowel movement. Such synchrony leads to training at a reasonably early date and does not subtract from the baby's innate capabilities. When this is done, real, permanent training becomes a fact."[102]

### 1938
### Ethel C. Dunham & Marian M. Crane
*Infant Care*

Bowel training may be begun "as early as the sixth month or even earlier," requires patience and regularity, and is usually completed by the time the baby is one year old. "To begin the training, the mother should notice at what time the baby usually soils his diaper. She may even observe signs that he is about to have a bowel movement, such as grunting and getting a little red in the face. At that time she should hold him over the chamber for a few minutes." Baby should be put on the chamber "each day for a short period until he establishes the habit of a regular bowel movement."

Bladder training is started at the age of 10 months and follows the same method as bowel training, except it takes longer to complete. Most children should have daytime control of the bladder by 2 years of age. The baby should be changed when he is wet, praised when he remains dry but not scolded if he has an accident.[103]

### 1942 & 1945
### Dorothy V. Whipple, et al.
*Infant Care*

It is good to start bowel training at 8 to10 months when the baby begins to be able to control the muscles of his bowels. "Some babies have a bowel movement at almost exactly the same time every day, so that it is possible for the mother to put the baby on the toilet when she sees he is about to have a bowel movement. This . . . should not be confused with real training. One mother who did this was asked whether her 5-month-old baby was trained. 'No,' she said, 'he is not trained, but I am.' In real training the baby learns to take part in the effort and to try to wait until he is on the toilet before he has the movement. A baby cannot do this until he can control the muscles of his bowels. Usually by the time the baby is 8 to 10 months old he will begin to be able to do this. At this age, however, he will not be able to delay the bowel movement for more than a short time, nor to make a stool come very far ahead of the time it should come of itself." The training will probably be complete in 4 to 6 weeks time, although accidents will still occur from time to time for several years.

Bladder training starts soon after bowel control is fairly well established. Place the baby on the toilet to urinate after each feeding. "Sometimes a little cool water poured over his genital region helps to make him understand what is expected of him." The baby should be changed when he is wet, praised when he remains dry but not scolded if he has an accident. Daytime control of the bladder develops between the ages of 2–3 years, although some learn more quickly than others.[104]

## 1946
### Allison Davis & Robert J. Havighurst

Davis and Havighurst conducted a survey of child-rearing patterns and found that bowel training was started at or before 6 months in 40% of the cases; completion was by 12 months in 28%. Bladder training was begun at or before 6 months in 14% of the cases; completion was at 18 months by 49%.[105]

## 1951
### Marion L. Faegre
#### *Infant Care*

"Many babies are not ready to start learning bowel control by the end of the first year. One and a half or 2 years is a much more common time for them to learn willingly. If a child is not forced, control takes place very quickly when it does come. A few babies have unusual ease in adapting and have few accidents after they are a year old.

"Much of the trouble mothers have in helping their children learn bowel control (and later, bladder control) comes because the babies get the idea this is a battle." The importance of not rushing training and treating baby as an individual is stressed. The baby cannot consciously hold back or push out a bowel movement until his nervous system is sufficiently developed.

"When some neighbor tells you her baby was 'trained' at a very early age, take it with several grains of salt. You can be sure it is really she who 'trained' herself to recognize little signals . . . Or, her baby happened to be one whose bowel movements came at quite regular times."

It is best not to begin bladder control until "well along in the second year, or even later. However, babies differ very much in the time when they are ready for different kinds of learning . . . Just be sure not to put your baby on the toilet more than two or three times a day, and not interrupt him at interesting play."[106]

## 1958
### J. W. B. Douglas & J. M. Blomfield
*Children under Five*

The authors conducted a survey and found that in 1958, 60% of English mothers started to "pot" their infants during the first 2 weeks of life; 25% started between 2 weeks and 6 months; 15% started after 6 months. By the age of 1 year, 47% had completed toilet training; at 18 months, 83% were finished.

"Neurologists generally consider that 6 months is the earliest age at which myelination is sufficiently developed to support voluntary control."[107]

## Infant Toilet Training in Modern Times

Over the centuries, the simple and natural method of infant toilet training has hardly changed at all in nonindustrialized parts of the world. It is still the norm for millions of families in Africa, Asia and South America. Some third world cultures and countries undergoing rapid change and industrialization have only slightly modified their infant toilet training method to coincide with modern living standards, with the result that they have maintained the fundamentals of the original practice. Mothers and caregivers still start in the early months of life. They still hold or carry infants much of the time, making it easy to observe and respond to baby's elimination timing, and they still complete toilet training at a young age, between 8 and 18 months.

In Western countries and affluent areas of third world countries, factors such as fast living, expensive furnishings, fancy clothing, extreme cleanliness, diapers, bundling babies in clothing, baby-strollers, cribs, playpens and mothers working outside the home have greatly complicated, delayed and slowed down the toilet-learning process for many. In the 1950s, some Western physicians concluded that babies cannot control the sphincter muscles before the age of 18 months and in the 1960s, that premature toilet training could cause psychological problems.[108] In the 1970s, disposable diapers gained widespread use, and the diaper industry grew into a huge money-making enterprise. Entrenched and trendy theories about letting baby dictate when to toilet train coupled with instilling fear in those who go against the grain and begin toilet training in infancy have also discouraged many from trying, completing or even learning about infant potty training.

## Sensitive Periods

Maria Montessori brought the concept of sensitive periods to prominence in the 1960s. A sensitive period is a critical period during development, a time when a child is naturally and optimally receptive to learning a specific task and when a particular event has its greatest consequences. In 1997, Swiss author Rita Messmer encouraged parents to be aware of their children's sensitive periods and recognized infancy as a sensitive period for infant potty training.

"Let's consider people in Africa, the Americas and Asia who traditionally carry their babies on their backs in a sling. Although the babies are usually naked in the sling, they do not pee and excrete on their mothers. The mothers are very tuned in to their babies' elimination needs. A baby signals through his behaviour when he has to go. The mother then quickly swings the baby from the sling and holds him out to the side where he takes care of business. After that the baby is put back in the sling on his mother's back, and the mother carries on with her work. If, occasionally, a mother gets wet, the other mothers laugh at her and she is regarded as a bad mother. The advantage for these people is that the child is naked, so a mother is able to develop a much better feeling for her baby's bodily functions. The babies are quickly cleaned with a little water, and there is no real fuss about anything. Moreover, toilet training never reaches the degree of importance and complexity that we give it in the Western world.

"After reading about these experiences in other cultures, I wanted to give it a try with my own children. I found very quickly that the opinions of many psychologists and pediatricians couldn't be right. When my son Stefan was almost three months old, I held him over the toilet and told him to pee. He was still too small for a potty, couldn't sit on his own, so I did what indigenous women do, but instead of aiming him off to the side, I just held him over the toilet. I hardly finished speaking when a little fountain sprinkled from his penis into the toilet. At first I thought this may be a coincidence. But when the same was repeated over and over, I knew it couldn't be sheer coincidence. I also found that every time I removed his diaper, he seemed to be waiting to be held over the toilet.

"It is clear to me that this sensitive period ends sometime around the fifth month. After that, babies want to go on eliminating in the place they learned to do it and are used to. This could mean that, during the sensitive period, they learned to eliminate in a diaper no matter where they are, and they want to go on doing it this way.

"Many child-rearing books insist that a small child can't control his bladder and warn that early training is useless and harmful. In cases where the sensitive period has been missed, I agree with the psychologists. Early toilet training can be problematic, especially if pressure is used against the child's will and imposes parents' unrealistic expectations of cleanliness. Pressure and control are never the way for children to be toilet trained. There is no moral or pediatric reason for children to be toilet trained early. Such ambitions do more harm than good.

"But by being aware of this sensitive period, we can make things easier for ourselves and our babies by letting our babies be in control of their own elimination."[109]

Dr. Thomas S. Ball also made the connection between sensitive periods and infant potty training. In a 1971 article about a "toilet training program devised by Mrs. Lela Humphries" (a woman who used this method with her three children), Ball writes, "With extreme perceptiveness, Mrs. Humphries indicates that the problems frequently associated with toilet training at age two or later stem from the fact that considerable maladaptive learning has already taken place. In a special sense, *by age two the child has long since passed through an important state of readiness for training*. As she points out, ' . . . a child that eliminates in a diaper for two or three years does not feel comfortable on the pot, but wants a diaper.'"[110]

## P.S. . . . Animals Toilet Train from Birth

It is of interest to note that most mammals, with the exception of man and possibly the great apes, lick their young from birth, not so much to clean them but to stimulate organic and behavioral development, including the function of elimination. In his book *Touching: The Human Significance of the Skin*, Ashley Montagu reports that he found a common factor in observations reported by experts and experienced persons who work with animals (veterinarians, animal breeders, zoo staffers, farmers and ranchers), namely that:

"[T]he newborn animal must be licked if it is to survive, that if for some reason it remains unlicked, particularly in the perineal region (the region between the external genitalia and the anus), it is likely to die of a functional failure of the genitourinary system and/or the gastrointestinal system."[111]

In short, he found that most mammals depending on their mother for sustenance during the first days of life have to first be stimulated, then later taught how to eliminate, or they will die. An animal starts the elimination function(s) and training by licking the elimination areas of her newborn at regular intervals, usually in conjunction with nursing, for up to several weeks.

Until this essential function of licking was discovered, many orphaned neonate mammals in captivity could not survive. They can now survive if a caregiver simulates the maternal stimulation of the elimination functions. This can be done by stroking the neonate animal in specific areas or using material such as cotton swabs to elicit elimination at regular intervals in relation to feedings.

N. Blurton-Jones and Ben Shaul compared mammals that nest or cache their babies with those that carry their babies. They found that baby animals that are cached often do not urinate or defecate unless stimulated by their mothers. This is presumably a way to avoid attracting predators to the nest by scent.

Mammals that cache feed their young at widely spaced intervals, produce milk with a high protein and fat content and have high sucking rates. Mammals that carry (including followers) nurse more or less continuously, produce milk with a low fat and protein content and have low sucking rates. Humans and all other higher primates have the milk composition and sucking patterns of carrying species yet behave like nesting animals by not continuously carrying and nursing their young.[112]

Why even mention the topic of toilet training by other mammals? It is interesting to note that many other mother mammals (i.e., cachers) deal with the elimination of their young from birth. In their case, it is a matter of life and death, whereas humans have the choice and option to delay toilet learning for years by using diapers.

# chapter 17

# compatible
# lifestyles &
# philosophies

nfant potty training is compatible with every lifestyle where parents are gentle, nonpunitive and willing to try this method. This includes both urban and country living; mainstream and alternative ways of life; families of faith; medical professionals and academics; and young and older parents. Since the 1970s, there have been important and wonderful breakthroughs in child raising, resulting in the publication of inspiring books and also in the formation of helpful and supportive (play)groups and Internet chatrooms, listservs and websites. This chapter discusses some of these groups and philosophies. Most of the practices have been in use for centuries but have only recently been embraced by Westerners. They are all natural, loving and commonsense behaviors.

## Attachment Parenting

Mary D. Salter Ainsworth was the first to study the development of infant attachment. The study took place in six villages in Buganda, Uganda, where she studied 28 Baganda infants in 1954–1955. Mary Ainsworth had originally set out to study weaning and separation but ended up focusing mainly on the development of attachment. The resulting book, *Infancy in Uganda*, covers her study in detail—and also includes 11 pages of information on infant toilet training in Buganda. According to Ainsworth, Part IV of her book constitutes the work's main contribution to the psychology of infant development, especially her four chapters on the development of attachment and the concluding chapter. Her study laid the foundation for a parenting style which is now called "attachment parenting."

In the early 1980s, pediatrician William Sears coined a new term for the intuitive, high-touch and responsive parenting style he advocated. He called it "attachment parenting" (also called "AP") and defined it as the five baby B's: bonding, breastfeeding, bed-sharing, baby-wearing and belief in baby's cries.[113] These practices have been commonplace in many parts of the world for centuries but have not been in use by Westerners until fairly recent times.

### Bonding

There are two types of bonding: birth bonding (immediately after birth) and long-term bonding. For an hour or more after birth, baby is in a "quiet alert" state[114] and is very receptive. This is a good time, but certainly not the only time, for an intimate exchange and connection with your newborn. Joseph Chilton Pearce defines bonding as "a nonverbal form of psychological communication, an intuitive rapport that operates outside of or beyond ordinary rational, linear ways of thinking and perceiving."[115]

Dr. Bill and Martha Sears stress that while birth bonding is a very important thing, parents must take a balanced approach to it. "The conception of bonding as an absolute critical period or a now-or-never relationship is not true." The over-hyping of bonding in the 1980s caused unnecessary guilt for parents who were unable to spend the first hours or days with their babies for medical or other unavoidable reasons. In these cases, the Sears state that "catchup bonding" is possible.[116]

The other type of bonding is less mysterious. It is a long-term process of spending loving time together for days, weeks, months and years.

## Breastfeeding (or Attentive Bottle-Feeding)

There are three scenarios to consider under this heading.

- The optimum situation for baby includes breastfeeding on demand for as many years as your child wants to nurse. Extended breastfeeding and child-led weaning are ideals which few Western mothers can actually achieve in full, largely due to societal pressure. La Leche League emphasizes that breastfeeding is important for bonding, baby's physical well-being and establishing harmonious long-term parent-child relationships.
- If physical, medical, domestic or other reasons make it impossible to nurse on demand for as long as you desire (some babies self-wean before they are a year old), do not feel guilty or depressed. Be realistic and set a different set of goals for yourself, based on your individual circumstances, so you and baby can savor and enjoy every available moment of breastfeeding.
- Mothers who are not able to breastfeed at all can substitute attentive and loving bottle-feeding whenever possible. Feed baby in a calm and quiet location. While cradling her in your arms, simulate aspects of breastfeeding such as letting her pat and squeeze you or letting her fiddle with your hair like a nursing baby does. Maintain eye-to-eye contact. Hold and cuddle her for as long as she likes.

## Bed-Sharing

This is also called family bed, shared sleeping and co-sleeping. It works well for most but doesn't work for everyone. The important thing to remember is that parents should consider their overall situation when deciding whether or not to sleep with their babies. Basically, there is no right or wrong place for baby to sleep. If sleeping in the same bed proves impossible, let baby sleep in the same room, as close to you as possible.

Some babies and/or parents cannot sleep well in the same bed or room, resulting in a lack of sleep, crankiness and negativity during the day. In most families, however, sleeping with baby guarantees that everyone sleeps through the night.

Co-sleeping usually solves nighttime parenting problems such as getting up to check on baby, nighttime feedings and crying. Baby can nurse whenever she pleases and fall right back to sleep. She feels secure throughout the night. It is very cozy for the whole family to sleep together.

Family sleeping is controversial for three main reasons. Some parents fear it will ruin their sex life while others think they will "never get the child out of our bed." A relatively small number of babies have been suffocated while sleeping in the family bed. Normal and healthy parents who are sober and not high on drugs are instinctively aware of baby's location in the bed. The same mechanism that stops people from falling out of bed at night prevents parents from rolling over onto baby while asleep.

Most babies throughout the world sleep with their parents, which has been the case since the human race came into existence. It is enjoyable and perfectly natural for parents to sleep with baby.

## Baby-Wearing

Baby-wearing refers to carrying your baby with you, as opposed to using a stroller or leaving her in a crib. Wearing your baby enables you to be aware of and responsive to baby's signals and other communications. It increases intimacy and touching, two very positive elements of bonding. Baby-wearing actually allows parents more freedom since they know where baby is at all times and are constantly aware of her condition and needs. Carrying baby can also enhance her social development since she is able to closely observe you interacting with others. Studies in Africa indicate that infants who are carried and experience much physical contact with their mother or another caregiver are often more precocious than Western babies. Their social, muscular and motor skills develop faster, and their level of contentment is higher.

Most advocates of attachment parenting agree that the best type of carrier is a sling, especially for breastfeeding mothers. Other carriers include a front carrier, side carrier or backpack.

## Belief in Baby's Cries

Western parents are afraid they will spoil their baby by holding and soothing her (nearly) every time she cries. Attachment parenting advises parents not to let baby "cry it out." Find a balance, whatever feels right and comfortable, in relation to your baby's crying. It is normal and fine for baby to want to be held and comforted, and this type of attention will not spoil a baby. She will eventually want to explore her surroundings on her own as she becomes mobile.

Attachment parenting is an ideal and is easier for a stay-at-home parent than a working parent. Parents who work can still apply several elements. A part-time mother can use the assistance of a caregiver to help cover the times she is away, then reconnect with baby after work or whatever separates her from baby.

AP is flexible in many ways since it is based on parents' intuition and individual circumstances. It is important to realize that it is not possible for all willing parents to implement all five of the Sears Baby B's. Parents should not feel guilty if they cannot do all they want for their baby. Be careful not to overdo things to the point of exhaustion and burnout.

Interestingly, in societies where AP has been practiced for centuries, infant potty training has also been the norm. In this sense, it can be considered a sixth Baby B (Bladder/Bowel awareness). Here are a few websites for further information and links:

| | |
|---|---|
| Infant Potty Training Web Ring | www.timl.com/ipt |
| Diaper Free Baby (Find playgroups & mentors!) | www.diaperfreebaby.org |
| The Potty Whisperer | www.pottywhisperer.com |
| Elimination Communication Yahoogroup | http://groups.yahoo.com/group/ eliminationcommunication |

## The Continuum Concept

*The Continuum Concept* by Jean Liedloff compares the child-rearing practices of modern Western culture with those of the Yequana Indians living in the Amazon rainforests of Venezuela. The "Stone-Age" Yequana people are confident, happy and live in harmony with each other. Fighting, sibling rivalry and "terrible twos" are unheard of. Yequana babies do not wear diapers.

The continuum concept itself is the idea that babies instinctively expect certain kinds of experiences that were part of human life for millions of years. When these innate expectations are not met, the baby may experience stress or even trauma. Modern mothers and fathers would instinctively fulfill these expectations if not for our high-tech culture's tendency to undermine our instincts, or what Liedloff calls our "continuum sense."

Liedloff emphasizes the importance of the in-arms phase, whereby a mother or other caregiver is in constant physical contact with baby 24 hours a day (accomplished in part by using a baby carrier, preferably a sling), from birth until baby begins to crawl, usually around six months. At this point, the infant can leave and return at will to the caregiver.

From the vantage point of an active, trusted caregiver's arms, a baby feels totally safe and secure, and can learn about life through passive observation of adult activities. Constant contact helps the caregiver tune in to the baby's needs and respond promptly to the baby's signals, including those associated with elimination.

"Continuum babies" are also allowed to sleep with their mothers and are breastfed on demand, day and night—usually for at least two years. Children are not punished but are made to feel welcome and worthy. These behaviors are the most common throughout the world's cultures, and industrialized countries are finally beginning to recover the wisdom of the ages.

Jean Liedloff, who made five expeditions to the South American jungle and spent a total of two and a half years there, maintains that Westerners are taught not to believe in their instinctive feelings, which would support the in-arms phase, sleeping with baby, breastfeeding, etc. We have a natural yearning to be close to our babies but have been taught to ignore our instincts at times. We accept the false notion that our babies will grow up independent and unspoiled if we leave them alone and let them cry. We follow the trendy baby-care expert du jour and turn our backs on what we know in our gut is right. When we as a species act against our nature, we inadvertently create antisocial behavior.

Liedloff barely touches on potty training in her book but does mention that the Yequana are relaxed and loving in the way they deal with it. Mothers quickly aim their babies away from themselves when babies begin to evacuate, then casually clean up any excrement. Urination on a dirt floor is of no consequence. Elimination by a baby is almost a nonevent, except for the gleeful laughter that follows an occasional soaking. Jean Liedloff's book and ideas are discussed in depth at the Liedloff[117] Continuum Network's web site:

www.continuum-concept.org

## Postpartum Honeymoons

In many nonindustrialized parts of the world, mother and baby spend the first days, week(s) or 40 days together in (near) isolation. One or more relatives or friends take care of all the needs of the mother, baby and rest of the family during this time. (Sorry, dads, this "honeymoon" is probably not the kind you had in mind!)

In Senegal, Wolof mothers spend 7 days in seclusion with their newborns. The Falasha of Ethiopia spend 40 days in seclusion in a hut with their newborn boys and 80 days with girls.[118] In China and India, mothers spend 40 days in bed with their babies, bonding, getting to know each other and gaining strength after the delivery. In India, both mother and baby receive a daily massage. A special food called *punjiri* is prepared for the mother to munch on a few times a day in order to increase and improve her milk and also to help her recuperate. *Punjiri* is also eaten throughout much of the pregnancy. Ingredients used to make the Western version of *punjiri* are almonds with peel, pistachio nuts, ginger, cardamon seeds, coconut, raisins, sugar or honey, semolina and clarified butter *(ghee)* or butter. The Indian version is much more elaborate, using exotic ingredients normally only available in specialty Indian or Asian shops.

Often a mother-in-law or other relative will help care for mother and her newborn in American homes. If no relatives or close friends are able to care for you, you can hire a postpartum *doula* or other experienced caregiver to help during the first week to 40 days.

In most European countries, new mothers receive help from nurses or other health workers during the first few days or weeks after birth. Parental leave schemes are in place for working parents.

## Homeschooling

Public education in the USA has been going steadily downhill for more than 50 years, a process now referred to as "the dumbing down of America." Millions of American children, teens and young adults are illiterate. They are also ignorant about history, science, math, government, life outside America, politics . . . basically anything and everything academic. Parents are so disgusted with public education that many have resorted to educating their children at home.

Homeschooling one or more children means a parent is at home full time. Infant potty training can be worked into the daily routine on either a part-time or full-time basis. Siblings who help with the baby will learn both responsibility and punctuality.

part **2**

TESTIMONIALS
–USA

# chapter 1

# a 10-month-old graduate

Lois Baas is a nurse living in Michigan. She has a BSN from Calvin College. Her husband, Craig, has a BA in psychology. Lois gave up her nursing career to be a stay-at-home mom. She made a conscious decision to use cloth diapers instead of disposables, unaware that there was an even better option to consider, until she read a short piece about "potty untraining." It had very little "how-to" advice but enough information to inspire her to give it a try. Her son responded impressively to the devotion of, and close communication with, both of his parents and their attentiveness to his elimination needs. Much to their surprise and delight, Zachary graduated at 10 months of age. At this point, he met the criteria identified by the Asian and African definition of "toilet trained," namely, being basically accident-

*free combined with good communication skills that allowed him to signal his toilet needs to his parents. Their amazing story, submitted in 2002 when their son was 2½ years old, follows. Bear in mind that finishing this young in the West is exceptional, and you should **not** expect the same results. Please do not feel discouraged if your baby takes considerably longer.*

I recall my mother sharing that my siblings and I were all potty trained by 2 years of age. I thought this was a realistic goal to strive for with our first child and figured I would follow traditional potty training, but start earlier than many of my peers who were waiting until closer to 2–3 years of age to begin. However, a brief testimonial in a parenting book inspired me toward a whole different approach than planned. The author wrote of observing infants being trained in a third world country and of successfully using this with her next two babies. Four days later, after reading this account and discussing it with my husband, our 4-month-old son peed for the first time in the toilet. A week later he pooped in the toilet and never soiled another diaper!

## Starting Out

From his birth, I had our son wearing cloth diapers with vinyl covers during the day and a disposable for nights. When I began this method, I did away with the vinyl cover when at home during the day and began using cloth diapers with a vinyl cover at night. This way I could easily identify when he peed, as the cloth diaper was obviously wet. I replaced the diaper in between toilet visits and changed it diligently when any sign of wetness occurred during the day (nights are addressed later). The first time I tried to pee Zachary, he went! This was very encouraging and gave me the incentive to continue to pursue this approach. Zachary already had good back and neck control, and I positioned him on the adult toilet as per my limited reading indicated, supporting him against myself as I straddled the seat, sitting (or standing at times) behind him as we faced away from the tank. I was not about to get peed on if possible! As he went, I would say "pee pee," and it wasn't long before positioning him and giving him this verbal cue was all he needed. Eventually all I had to do was position him and he knew to eliminate. When he voided in this position, he emitted a stream over the seat or between the seat and bowl. Could he shoot far! But I was just so thrilled that he went and was learning that I did not make much of it except to get a wipeable mat to replace the toilet rug surrounding the base. I learned to help him with aiming down and this worked until he was big enough to straddle the seat further back; this new positioning allowed him to shoot into the bowl more efficiently without my assistance for aiming downward, and it also eliminated the "skid marks" from his BMs.

## Bowel Movements

Bowel movements were easy to identify as Zachary's cues were obvious. He would grunt and grimace, and his face would flush. Observing this, I would take him to the toilet and position him as I did with peeing, and as he went, I would give the cue "do do." At home, positioning in response to these overt cues was eventually all that was necessary. On a rare occasion, if he needed redirection or was away from home, the verbal cue came in handy. His movements were not frequent, though he was breastfed exclusively for 6 months and continued breastfeeding until 18 months. I identified a pattern, too, which helped. He would typically go once a day or every other day, after his mid-morning nursing. This pattern shifted to after his morning snack when he was eating finger foods regularly. If Zachary didn't have a BM, the next day he usually had two. Knowing this, I looked for a second one later in the day or before bedtime. It seemed, too, that he could often wait until he was sitting down to pee to have an impending BM at the same time. By 10 months he was signing and giving other cues (mentioned later) for the potty, not differentiating whether it was to pee or poo. At 15 months he was verbally cueing "do do" every time he needed to go and did what I dubbed the "do do dance" as he would prance around and run to the bathroom.

## Peeing

"Catching" pees was elusive. It seemed to be a hit-or-miss phenomenon as Zachary didn't have any obvious cues with these for some time. As I look back, I believe I was gradually tuning in to some sort of timing while I also became aware of his anatomical cues of slight scrotum contraction and penis extension—especially with an *impending* pee. Zachary peed very frequently at first—something you become more aware of when you change a diaper upon each sign of wetness rather than wait until it is saturated. It wasn't uncommon to potty him, put on a fresh, dry diaper, only to have him pee again. Many times he would begin peeing before or just as I got his diaper off and before being positioned on the toilet. This improved as he developed control and when he transitioned to training pants, with easier removal versus diaper pins. If I missed a pee or noticed Zachary in the process, I would give the verbal cue "pee pee," remove his diaper and position him on the toilet to reinforce where to "go." As he gained even more control, he would stop and wait for me to sit him on the toilet before finishing. Initially, running a stream of warm water from a peri-bottle (squeeze bottle) between his legs and/or running the tap would often promote an impending pee, helping him to relax when first learning. Sometimes other types of distraction helped, like a quick visit from his pet dalmatian or Daddy. Often just sitting for a short time was all it took, with Zachary looking up adoringly at me and my returning his gaze with smiles.

I believe he learned to associate his body's response to relaxing to my verbal cue of "relax" as we implemented the above. This wasn't intentional training, but did prove beneficial to the ongoing process. If Zachary ever became fussy or signaled to get off the toilet by arching or stiffening up, I would take him off and leave the bathroom, keeping him in-arms and diaperless. I figured those times he didn't have to go yet, but with his great frequency, I anticipated he would need to go soon and would return within 5–10 minutes to try again, with success. Keeping him in-arms assured me of preventing an accident, as he demonstrated a desire to not "go" when being held. Having the diaper off meant ease at returning him to his position on the toilet without interruption of removing a diaper and pins. Doing this probably helped me discover his timing intervals and helped him learn some control as he "waited" to try again.

After a month of "winging" it with the limited information I had, I read *Trickle Treat*. I attempted to discover Zachary's cues, but confirmed that he did not have any obvious signals nor a regular timing pattern. I relied on his subtle anatomical cues and obvious timing patterns, such as upon awakening or after nursing, and on my developing intuition. I would think to myself, "Zachary hasn't gone in a while," or, "Maybe he has to go." If I trusted myself, he rewarded me with going and keeping dry, but if I doubted myself or was distracted, I would miss.

Between 5–6 months, much to my delight, he began to communicate with grunting. This worked well until he began to use this new form of communicating to signal for other things (i.e., to nurse, for attention or to practice newfound vocal abilities). It was at this time that I became unsure of myself and took my son more frequently than necessary to the bathroom. It is easy to misconceive that all this becomes a perfect routine, rather than a development of communication. I soon found out that other mothers went through the same thing and that the best thing to do was back off and relax. It was around this time, too, that I discovered what I call a "warning pee." I would check my son's diaper when uncertain if he had cued and find a warm, wet spot. This prompted me to take him to the bathroom where he would commence to pee a large amount, after patiently waiting for me to remove his diaper and position him. This was a fascinating development in communication during this phase of second-guessing myself. It also reconfirmed that he truly was developing control at such a young age!

Between 6–7 months, Zachary was rolling onto his tummy more frequently, and although he'd signal with his grunt, it was often too late, as this position would put pressure on his bladder. I got into the routine of giving him full reign on his tummy after a nap when he had emptied his bladder thoroughly—having voided a couple of times. Then I would rely on timing to try to toilet him before an accident could occur. Though this was not foolproof, he could play longer in that position uninterrupted. At just 7 months he awoke after rolling onto his tummy for the first time in his sleep. I toileted him and found that he was still dry. I suspect that the pressure on his bladder woke him up, and he was able to wait until he was on the toilet to pee. He was sitting up more now and learning to crawl, too, thus keeping him off his tummy. Other cues began to emerge. Zachary was cueing visually with a beckoning or imploring look. Upon seeing "the look" and responding/ taking him to the bathroom, he eliminated with success on the toilet. It was so encouraging! After beginning solids at 6 months, I also became aware that when he seemed to lose interest in eating earlier than usual, it often meant he was concentrating on "going" or was about to "go." As I continued with this method, I was becoming more in tune with him and starting to experience subtler forms of communication. It would just "hit" me that he needed to go, and then I began to connect this with what he was or was not doing at the time. I would share these findings with my husband and he, too, would help me focus in on these cues. How connected I felt with my son!

At 6½ months I introduced Zachary to training pants. I first began for short periods when his timing was more predictable, during late afternoon to early evening. After about a week or so, I bit the bullet and went full time with them, as I found these more convenient (easier and quicker to remove) than a standard cloth diaper with pins. At first, while out and about and at night, I used a vinyl covering over the training pants "just in case." By 7 months he seemed to be able to hold it and wait, demonstrating a degree of development of control that he had not shown even a month prior, and by 8 months I was utilizing training pants with him exclusively, without the vinyl covers. As a result, I became even more in tune with Zachary, being "forced" to focus on him and his communication. We would have 0–3 accidents a day and often go several consecutive days without any accidents. I also began to use a timer to help keep aware of when Zachary needed to pee again, based on his timing. This helped me remember when I was caught up doing other things which were distracting and making me lose focus.

*Lois Baas (from video)*

Zachary taking care of business.

At 9 months, he was able to patiently wait to be positioned before "going." In fact, this seemed to happen almost overnight, when the interval between potty sessions increased from 20–45 minutes to up to 2½ hours, just a week into his 9th month.

## Outings

I toileted Zachary upon leaving home and upon reaching our destination. In between, if necessary (depending on the duration of the trip), I relied on timing and cues. Sometimes he would release a tiny trickle of pee when pottied and then not want to go more until we got home. Upon arriving home much later, he would pee a large amount. When he held it this long, I wondered if he sometimes didn't like where I was taking him when we were out. Or maybe it was that when he was not "bursting," he preferred to wait until we got home before peeing. But when he really had to go, it didn't matter where I took him, he would go. I became comfortable pottying Zachary in the great outdoors, if necessary, and became "fluent" in the locations of the local restrooms.

When traveling longer distances, we would pull over to the side of the road. I would position him on my lap straddling my spread thighs, facing away from me out the open passenger doorway of our truck. Upon giving him his verbal cue, he responded just as at home. He first did this at 6½ months. The open door and sitting in the cab provided privacy while he shot a stream away from the vehicle. One time when we were parked at the side of the road for a pee, a police officer pulled up alongside us. My husband explained that we were giving our son a potty break. The officer looked in the vehicle and asked our infant son if he felt better now!

When colder months came, I provided a portable receptacle: a bowl or covered bucket used primarily to pee in as he seemed to do all his BMs at home. When traveling distances versus around town, Zachary typically was lulled to sleep. Then, when he awakened, I would pull over to potty him. As he got older, he often was able to wait until the next exit or rest area. Once he was awake, I would rely on timing, but more often he would signal if he needed to go again.

From 8 months on, the combination of using training pants and the lack of distractions found at home improved my focus on his pottying when we were out. He stayed dry with longer and longer intervals between toileting. Around 9 months, he was consistently dry when away from home and at nights, without accidents, unless I missed or ignored a signal. He was holding it much longer and waiting until I took him to a bathroom or suitable place outdoors.

## Developing Communication

Around 8 months, he started to come to me while saying "ma, ma, ma," and then would tap my leg to go potty or nurse. Then he started crawling to the bathroom when he had to go. There were times where he would drop his toys or interrupt his play to do this. If I was sitting on the floor, he would crawl to me and tap me on the leg or else crawl up onto my knees and into my lap if he had to go. At 9 months, I observed him lean towards the bathroom with his imploring look as he watched his father go there to shave. Another example of this type of signaling happened shortly after he had just peed in the toilet and left the bathroom. A few minutes later, he came and tapped me on the leg. I questioned it at first since he had just nursed and been toileted. Then it dawned on me that he probably had to poo, so we went back to the bathroom and he pooed in the toilet!

At 8½–9 months, he was staying dry with rarely an accident, both day and night, and wearing only training pants under his clothes. His cues proved to be reliable. When he would indicate that he didn't need to go, he stayed dry. When he cued to go, he consistently had to go. Occasionally, he would use the more subtle cue of dropping everything to concentrate, so I still needed to be in tune to this.

Near the end of 9 months, he began crawling to the bathroom and pulling himself up to stand at the toilet. He would even open the lid and pat the seat at times, while waiting to be positioned. Other times, he would hold my hand and we would walk to the bathroom together. Also at the end of 9 months, we began instructing him on the ASL sign for "toilet" by making the sign every time we asked if he needed to go and every time we took him to the bathroom. When he gave indication of his need to go, we again would use the sign as we took him into the bathroom. He caught onto the meaning of the sign before he tried to use it. Next, he practiced making the sign, at first not consistently using it at the right time. Then, all of a sudden, within a week of introducing him to the sign, we all clicked with it. He would even sign "toilet" when he heard someone else flush or when someone uttered the word "toilet." Signing was decidedly helpful in public settings such as church in that it was a subtle communication and only we were aware of why we stepped out of the service for a moment! Here are a few things I wrote about his signing at 10 months:

*Yesterday while nursing, he took himself off and looked at his fist. He appeared to be signaling, so I asked if he needed to go and gave the ASL sign. He looked thoughtful for an instant, then resumed nursing. After a bit, he again unlatched and signaled. I took him to the bathroom where he pooed in the toilet! Also, as we've been teaching the signing, which has only been about a week, he began to look or lean toward, or crawl to, the bathroom. I've been teaching him the whole process, letting him crawl or helping him walk to the toilet where he opens the lid. I help with undressing and positioning him, then he eliminates, I help with dressing, and together we flush (which he loves!), close the lid, turn off the light and leave the room.*

*A few days later, while he was happily playing, I realized it was quite a while since he'd "gone" so I inquired, "Do you have to go potty?" and gave the ASL sign. He looked at my hand, dropped everything, crawled to the toilet and lifted the lid as he waited for me to get him undressed to go. When he is in-arms and I ask both verbally and with the hand signal, he pats the hand I am using to "sign" when he has to go. Otherwise, I see him either stare at the fist he makes or else position his thumb as he waves the fist around (he can't twist his fist yet so can't quite get the sign right). He signals clearly and most certainly knows what it means!*

*He tries to get his thumb positioned between the forefinger and middle finger but doesn't always manage this yet. Then, instead of making the side-*

*ways twisting motion with his fist/wrist, he waves it! When he cuddles up over my shoulder, I feel the movement of his signing. The "waving motion" with his arm makes his cue pretty obvious when I cannot see his hand. And tonight while nursing him, I was sleepy and may have dozed a bit. I suddenly noticed he was off the breast and that he was "waving" over and over, so I took him to the bathroom for a pee.*

*Lois Baas (from video)*

Zachary signing the toilet sign to his grandfather.

At some point, he figured out that if I was closer to the bathroom than he was, he could get a free ride to the bathroom in my arms, and resorted to "the look" when crawling towards me or calling out to me. He was a very resourceful little boy!

He began to say "bah, bah" for "potty" around 10½–11 months, in addition to signing. This was his first verbal communication to eliminate. He began to say "potty", "pee pee," and "do do" around 14–15 months and eventually dropped the signing altogether.

## Nights

I did not address nights initially when I began this training. From birth, Zachary slept in a bassinet in our room and then transitioned to his own room around 3 months. Any time he awoke, we did not automatically assume it was to nurse and checked his diaper and changed it as necessary.

By just over 4 months, almost a week after beginning infant potty training, he was sleeping through the night. Interrupting his nights to potty him had never occurred to me.

When Zachary was about 6½ months old, I had found and read more material on this method and discovered his restlessness at night was a cue for his need to pee. If I ignored his restlessness, he would often go in his sleep. When I responded and toileted him just as I did during the day, he would pee, then return to bed asleep, no longer restless as he had been prior to being toileted.

I now felt challenged to pursue nights in addition to my daytime focus, to meet his toileting needs around the clock. An underlying concern I held was long-term bedwetting, especially since I had a boy. This was something that ran in both sides of the family. Having read that this method tends to prevent this also attracted me to address nights. I had already switched to using cloth diapers with a vinyl covering prior to this time as the disposables made it difficult to determine if he was waking up dry or not at times (such absorbency!). I am sure, too, that wearing cloth diapers helped lead to his awareness of wetting at night.

## Sleep Deprivation

He became fully awake for toileting at times, even regularly for a while, and with this, Zachary also resumed nursing in the night to return to sleep. I felt that this pattern had created a perpetual need for him to awaken again at night, since his bladder would fill again. I found that he would awaken to pee 30–60 minutes after having nursed and fallen asleep at bedtime and then would awaken every 2–3 hours thereafter. But I was determined to meet his needs around the clock and do feel that this diligence led to his being dry at night much sooner than expected.

Admittedly this was exhausting in the beginning, for I responded to every little sound. When he was around 7 months, I had him sleep with me, as I was so tired. I had been running into his room, just across the hall from us, at every noise, checking him frequently throughout the night to be sure he didn't wet in his sleep. The temporary family bed arrangement seemed to stop the accidents at first as I was able to sense his restlessness and respond immediately; sometimes he remained asleep as I toileted him, and occasionally he nursed back to sleep. I absolutely loved this closeness at night, but unfortunately I became sleep deprived. Though at first he was restless every time he needed to go, this pattern changed. He began to awaken to be toileted or as soon as we returned to bed. With my availability, he began to nurse constantly throughout the night, not just to return to sleep after toileting. He also began to have an accident every once in a while; this was probably because I was so tired that I was no longer in tune. This interrupting sleep pattern created perpetual fatigue for me. I believe that I was so tired with trying to be in tune faithfully in the night, along with frequent nursing, that often by morning he was already wet. I believe it also impacted my day progress, too, in that I would have less success and find myself losing patience. This was *never* taken out on my son. But I sure was hard on myself! It warranted evaluating our specific situation to guard my sleep in order to promote a relaxed environment with which to proceed with this.

Sleep deprivation jeopardizes this method! Once I heeded the advice of both husband and friends and relaxed at night, and once Zachary resumed sleeping in his own room around 7½ months, we both slept more at night, and the accidents decreased markedly.

## Overview of Nighttime Approach

Step 1 consisted of responding to Zachary's restlessness in his sleep. Whether he awoke fully or not, I took him to pee. He would often pee (or on a rare occasion, poop) on the toilet in his sleep, leaning against me with his eyes closed while he eliminated and afterwards just sigh. At first when he partially awoke while being toileted, he would start to pee, stiffen and not finish going. I would then do as I did during the day and encourage him to relax, whereby he did and would finish. This assured me of returning him to bed with an empty bladder.

For Step 2, I applied timing in addition to watching for restlessness at night. Timing helped me know when to take him to the toilet on occasions when he was in a deep sleep and didn't stir at night. The transition to training pants also eased our nighttime routine. For a while I would remove his training pants before picking him up to take him to the bathroom, to help communicate that this was why I was coming into his room when he was supposed to be going to sleep. If he was already asleep and I knew it was time to pee, it was convenient to remove the pants en route to the bathroom and replace them when finished. He was sleeping in training pants and pajamas with a super absorbent bed pad over his sheet in case of accidents. The pad was easy to remove and replace when necessary, and Zachary would often sleep through all this undisturbed.

Step 3 happened around 8–9 months when he began to wake more and more on his own to be toileted, as opposed to my responding solely to his restlessness or timing. Upon awakening, I would hear him moving and find him up on his knees, waiting to be taken to the toilet. He seemed to connect that Mommy or Daddy would respond if he awakened to pee at night.

Step 4 happened around 9–10 months when he cried out to us, got up in his bed and waited to be toileted. At first, on a few occasions when he was in a deep sleep, he would begin to pee, awaken, stop peeing and cry out to us. Upon being toileted, he would finish peeing, as evidenced by his voiding a *large* amount. He soon gained even more control and would wake up dry. The absorbent pad was now obsolete.

From this point on, we used a combination of all four steps, and accidents soon became a thing of the past. At 9 months, his pattern was to pee before his bedtime routine, nurse, and then pee again before going to bed awake. I found that if he did not fall asleep right away, relying on timing helped avoid a potential accident. Using a timer proved essential in preventing accidents and meeting his elimination needs when not with him, as it helped remind me to toilet him when I could not observe cues or would become distracted doing other things. The timer was also helpful in confirming his *need* to go versus his desire to stay up longer by using toilet visits as a bedtime delay tactic. To accomplish this, he would cry out (or at 10 months sign), and when we got to the bathroom, he would void just a trickle of pee. Once he learned we would be faithful by taking him when he truly needed to go and that we would not fall for any "mischievous miscommunications," his cues resumed reliability.

At 10 months when he awoke on his own, he would call out to us and then upon our arrival, we'd find him standing or on his knees, making the ASL toilet sign by emphatically waving his little fist.

When he nursed at bedtime only (versus in the night once or early mornings at times) at around 15 months, he consistently slept through the night again, though he was doing this on and off prior to 12 months. I assumed his marked decrease in night frequency was likely related to his bigger bladder, being able to hold it longer and not refilling his tummy each time he was toileted.

After he weaned at 18 months, he did not awaken at night unless he had something to drink prior to bed that made him have to go at night. He continued to be reliable in waking up when he needed to go to the bathroom. Imagine having a young toddler who can drink before bedtime or in the night and still stay dry, awakening on his own to be toileted!

## Relations with Others

Other than my parents, who had given us the book from which we were introduced to this method, we did not initially discuss this outright with anyone. It was in part because we lacked knowledge about it and were "trying it out" and also because we did not want to put pressure on our son as he was learning this with us. I was discreet when in public or at friends and family. Many assumed we used their bathrooms to change a diaper when in reality we were toileting our son.

Though Zachary wore training pants to his 8-month healthy baby checkup, it wasn't until his 10-month visit that a nurse took notice and inquired if we were starting potty training already. Imagine her shocked expression when I explained that we were essentially done! She was flabbergasted but asked several appropriate questions. As I explained, she responded with interest and understanding. By the time he returned for his 12-month visit, it was common knowledge in the doctor's office that Zachary was potty trained. The nurse at that time didn't seem too interested or was just skeptical and said Zachary was "a first" for them and that he would be an "experiment," whatever that meant. The "growth and development brochure" they handed out for 12–18 months states, "Most children are not ready to be toilet trained at this age." When the doctor touched on the subject, he was reminded that we were already done with this, but he never broached for details. At Zachary's 18-month visit, the doctor caught himself as he went through his list of "what to cover" that visit, recalling that we were already done with potty training. It was just "accepted" and never challenged.

We have been fortunate that our inner circle of friends and family were very supportive, especially after they were educated on the method. I was very protective of Zachary, though, maintaining a casual approach and not encouraging an audience, which could create undue pressure to perform.

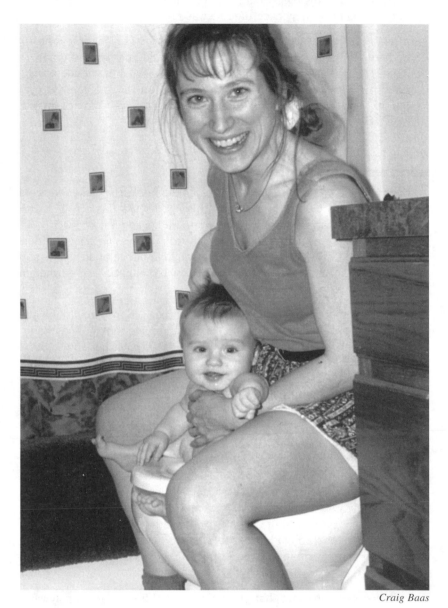

*Craig Baas*

Zachary at 7 months, with mother Lois

This was affirmed by other moms doing this who reported from experience that it could cause a child to "seize up." With the exception of my spouse, it wasn't until a month or so before Zachary "graduated" that I even had others help with toileting him and only then when visiting in our home.

## Reflections

Would I ever do this again if I had the opportunity? You bet! Would I do anything different? Much would remain to be seen. I would definitely relax more, which I imagine would come easier from experience, knowing more of what to expect and having more confidence. I would expect to use my experience as a springboard, adding the nuances of a different personality of another infant. Having a daughter versus a son and starting from birth rather than at 4 months of age would definitely warrant some changes. But I would still be diligent to both day and night training, though starting both from birth.

The pluses far outweigh the challenges. Though early completion of training was a draw to this method, I honestly did not think he would "graduate" before he walked independently, especially as I did not start this with our son until he was already 4 months old. I was hoping to finish between 12–18 months or so, but was prepared for it to take a full 2 years. In the meantime, Zachary was out of diapers and using the potty very early. What a thrill it was to see him respond so well to this! I cannot imagine ever choosing diapers now! I packed away diapers when he was 8 months old, after they had sat around for a month unused, and needless to say, my laundering was cut down significantly. I never hauled the diaper bag with me on short errand trips once he was in training pants, and I packed it away before he was a year old, having only been using it for toys, snacks and a change of clothing which never got used. Zachary never experienced diaper rash nor had a phobia about using an adult toilet or flushing his excrement "down the hole." I was never limited in where I pottied him with this method, so never had to interrupt it. He is not a bedwetter. And the ultimate kudos to this is the incredible endearment to my son! This method compliments the bonding that already is promoted through nursing. I would highly recommend giving this method a try. After all, what have you got to lose . . .? Oh, yeah . . . , all those hundreds of wet, dirty, smelly diapers! Blessings!

# chapter 2

# two 16-month graduates

L aura Diane Moore has two children and has successfully infant potty trained both. She holds a master's degree in advertising from the University of Texas at Austin. Her husband Tom Griggs is a professor of teacher education, and the family resides in Colorado.

Laura first heard about infant potty training when she read an article about it in an environmental newspaper. The article described a means of toilet training that didn't involve many diapers and included a review of the book Trickle Treat. Laura was intrigued. As an environmentalist, she was always looking for ways to "contribute more to solutions than problems." She *read the book and then a few months later, Laura got pregnant. She knew right away that she would try infant potty training and that she would never use disposable diapers.*

*Aside from the environmental benefits, another thing she liked about the method was the idea of not having to change many diapers. She also liked the challenge of trying infant potty training. Laura provided the following information in 2000.*

## Sara

Although Laura went through a difficult labor and a cesarean section with Sara, these didn't deter her from breastfeeding or starting infant potty training from birth. This is reflected in Laura's diary . . .

### Sara

#### First Week

There are no potties small enough for an infant, so I've taken her first potty from a set of plastic mixing bowls I received as a wedding gift. The bowls are the nesting kind and have a smooth edge, a handle and a rubber nonslip rim on the bottom. I figure that as Sara gets bigger, she'll just progress to the next size mixing bowl until she's big enough to sit on an official potty.

The day I tried the method for the first time, I confidently held my tiny Sara over the smallest mixing bowl and presto! behold—a trickle treat! It was amazing.

The potty training has been a little hard these first few days because Sara is breastfeeding (on demand) and peeing and pooping a lot. Also, I'm still recovering from the C-section, but all things considered, we're doing okay with the potty training.

By the end of the first week, I feel I've had quite a bit of success in figuring out Sara's potty patterns and rhythms, especially her nighttime patterns.

I keep her in a cloth diaper when she's not on the potty since I know I won't be getting all her pees in the potty.

## Two Weeks

Sara gets up about every two and a half hours at night. Last night, after sleeping for two and a half hours, she was still dry. I woke up, put her to the breast and held the little mixing bowl under her. She immediately pooped and peed in the pot. This has been a consistent pattern for a number of nights now—waking up three or four times dry, nursing and using the potty successfully at the same time.

Everyday it gets easier and easier to get her to go in the pot. In fact, she usually goes right when I hold her over the pot, or soon thereafter. Sometimes we have to wait for a while. If she doesn't go fairly soon, I take her off the pot. But I know that eventually she'll go, so it's a matter of trying again in five or ten minutes.

She is still nursing on many occasions when I hold her over the potty. I just place the potty in my lap under her bottom while she nurses. I think she is very, very aware of the "potty position," whether she is nursing or not. She doesn't like a wet diaper, so I think she appreciates going in the pot.

Her signs to pee are pretty subtle so far. I haven't quite put my finger on them yet, so it's mostly by timing that we go to the potty.

It's easy to tell when she needs to poop. She gets squirmy or fussy. When she is in the process of peeing or pooping, she relaxes and makes a certain facial expression.

There are three main cues I use to let her know it's potty time.

1. I hold her in position in my arms, the same way every time.

2. I use the potty in the same place in the house.

3. I ask her if she has to go potty. I use a certain intonation or inflection in my voice and ask in a singsong way, "Shall we go potty?" or "Do you want to go pooter in the pot?" It hasn't been necessary for me to make a specific sound related to the function to get her to go. I just hold her in the position and ask her if she wants to go. Sometimes she'll reach down and feel the pot there, and this is another way she knows what's going on.

I put a diaper on her in between feedings because I know I won't be around to take her potty every single time she has to go.

Tom is very supportive. He hasn't had a lot of opportunity to hold Sara over the pot yet because she's just two weeks old and mainly goes while she is nursing, but he looks forward to helping when she's a little bigger.

This method is about being diligent. When you know it's time to go to the potty, you shouldn't blow it off and think, "I'll just let the diaper catch it." I've been disciplining myself to take her to the pot, and it's starting to pay off already. It's frustrating when I don't get her to the potty on time, but I'm never angry at her about it.

## Five Months

Sara has graduated to the medium-sized mixing bowl now, and she likes sitting on it. I sit cross-legged with the potty in my lap, then hold Sara in my arms and on the pot. It's a relaxing position for both of us. When I put her on the potty, she always tries to make herself go, even if it turns out she doesn't have to.

We put her on the potty several times a day. If she wants to get off, she'll start squirming and let me know, and I let her off. Many times she just plays with her toes or we'll chat, and she'll take her time. She'll just remain sitting on the potty until she has to go. Tom helps when he can. I've also had some help from my mother and grandmother when they are around.

I've learned to figure out more of her patterns such as how much she needs to go. She'll have an initial surge of pee or poop. If I take her off the potty right away, it's usually too soon. If we wait, there is usually a second round of elimination.

I can usually tell by the timing (and not by intuition) when she has to pee. Now that she is a little older, she urinates less frequently. Her bladder is larger and stronger, so she is holding it in longer, and we go to the potty less frequently than the first months. It seems like she pees more when she's active than when she's calm.

I still keep cloth diapers on her when she is not on the potty because I'm not totally diligent. I've learned that if I miss a few pees, it doesn't matter. I don't beat myself up for using diapers in between potty sessions. I'm using far fewer diapers than if I were not doing infant potty training.

She has never had diaper rash since she is rarely wet or soiled. When I don't have the potty with me, I find it a real nuisance, so I invent potties. I'll hold her over a sink in a public bathroom, and she'll go.

She still squirms or gets fussy when she needs to poop, so we've had great success getting her to poop in the pot. Another cue from her happens in the mornings—she will pass gas and I know she'll soon be needing to poop. I get 90 percent of her poops in the potty now. It's a rare day that she poops in her panties and for me, from the standpoint of hygiene alone, it's worth doing this.

She is still nursing all she wants, so the poops are still loose. This is another advantage of this method. If you're breastfeeding your baby, the poops are a real mess. If she ever goes in her diaper, it's very messy to clean the diaper and her bottom. The mess ruins the diaper covers, and I have to wash them right away. It's so convenient to have her go in the potty instead. I wipe her bottom with toilet paper, then we fill up the potty with water and rinse it down the toilet—finished, done, I don't have to deal with it anymore. She stays very clean using the potty, even when she has diarrhea.

It really feels good, like I really accomplished something when she does a big poop in the potty in the morning. Now that we have been doing this for five months, I can't imagine not using a potty with her. It makes sense for hygienic reasons and also for convenience. Often when I lay her down to take off her diaper, if I don't put her on the potty, she'll end up peeing anyway, on the diaper. She associates my taking off her diaper with potty time. So I just pick her up, put the potty under her, and she goes in the potty instead of on the diaper.

She is sleeping more through the night, from 11 p.m. until 5 a.m. She'll wake up dry, and as soon as she wakes up, I put her on the potty and she pees a lot. She signals me when she is through or if she wants to get off the potty.

It often seems like she purposefully waits until she is on the potty before she goes. I think it's the positioning. Once I get her in this position, she knows to go. Maybe she wouldn't have gone in her pants at that very moment, but as soon as she is on the potty, she goes.

We like this method of toilet training. I feel it's good for us. I have a closer relationship with my daughter because of it. We communicate and are close throughout the day. I'm more aware of her rhythms. We're doing something together that we wouldn't otherwise be doing together if we were using diapers all the time. It helps the environment. I don't feel like I'm wasting a lot of water or trees.

## Six Months

She is so used to the method that all I have to do is hold her a certain way without her diaper and if she needs to go, she goes right away for me. I don't have to say anything anymore. She doesn't need verbal cues at all.

Once she gets in the position, even if she wasn't going to go right then, she goes unless there is absolutely nothing to eliminate. I don't keep her very long on the potty now that she is more active. She is good at letting me know if she doesn't need to go or when she wants to get off the potty.

We're doing really well, getting almost every poop and many pees in the pot. Using this method helps keep us bonded. Since I'm spending all this time with her anyway, breastfeeding her and not going out to work, trickle treat is just a logical extension of my lifestyle. It makes sense to potty train her now. I'll be finished when most parents are just starting.

I still need to pay attention to her timing and body language, which helps my awareness of her rhythms remain strong. Her pattern of a big surge followed in a few moments by going a little bit more continues, so I just keep her on the potty a little longer after she initially goes. Her other clues, such as passing gas before she poops, are the same. She poops four or five times a day, mostly in the pot.

She has the routine down really well. Sometimes I encourage her, remind her exactly what we're doing. If I'm late getting her to the potty, I try not to let it upset me. I used to get frustrated because I feel so responsible, but now I'm more relaxed about it. At first I thought it might confuse her or make it more difficult to potty train her if I don't get her to the potty all the time, but this is not the case.

There are times where she doesn't appreciate going on the potty, like when she is playing. I'm sensitive to situations where I know it's time for her to go on the potty but she is busy playing. I don't force the issue. I don't interrupt her play a lot, because I respect her as a person. I respect her boundaries.

### Eight Months

Since she sits so well now, I decided to stop holding her over the potty. She has graduated from using the mixing bowls in my lap to sitting on a regular freestanding portable potty. When I sat her down on her new potty for the first time, she pooped right away for me. No problem with the transition to a regular potty. I carry the potty with me everywhere, even room to room. We take it in the car and on trips. I have video footage of her sitting on her potty along California Highway One near Big Sur while we watch the sea otters frolicking in the ocean.

If I am ever without the potty, I find a makeshift substitute. One time I held her over a plastic bag in a park when she had to poop. Other times she'd poop in the grass or wherever we were and I'd scoop it up with a plastic bag like I do for my dog. Anything so I don't have to clean poopy diapers!

### Nine Months

From a health and hygiene standpoint, this is the best method. It can't be beat! She hasn't had a bowel movement in her pants for months. We're up to about 99 percent success rate with the poops. She has still never had diaper rash.

When we travel, if I don't have a potty handy, I hold her over a diaper and she goes for me. Even though there is no potty under her, she knows it's time to pee or poop when I hold her in the potty position.

I still keep a diaper on her. When she's active, she pees every 30 to 45 minutes. If I get interrupted or involved in something and don't take her to the potty on time, she'll pee in her diaper. In other words, I'm pretty diligent but not fanatical.

If she's in the vicinity of having to go and I place her over the potty, she'll go. She can make herself go. I don't have to hold her and wait for a certain moment. This tells me she has pretty good control over her potty muscles.

When friends ask me to tell them about this method and I tell them my daughter hasn't had a poop in her pants for months, they don't believe it.

Some of the books you read advise against infant potty training, but they aren't referring to the trickle treat method at all. They say starting early can have traumatic results, but this only happens if the parents are forcing things on the baby. You have to be sensitive to the child, and if the child resists, you can't force the issue. If any "damage" can occur, that's where it would occur, with forcing.

The method gives my daughter a sense of self-respect. After my experience with infant potty training, I would never consider delaying the start of potty training until she is 1 or 2 or older.

I now work in my home and have child-care people come into the home to help me with Sara. At first, they tried to take her to the potty, but she wouldn't let them. So I just told them not to even try doing the method with her. They still help though. They know when Sara has to go and let me know, "Sara looks like she needs to go to the bathroom. Do you want to come in and hold her over the potty?" Then I hold her over the potty and sure enough, she goes.

It's true this method takes time, but in most cases potty training takes time regardless of when you start it.

**One Year**

She does most of her business in the potty. She has excellent control of the elimination functions.

We've been in some unstable situations, moving, house-sitting in unfamiliar environments, but it doesn't disrupt her potty training. She's relaxed about it wherever we are.

**Sixteen Months**

She can now verbally communicate her need to eliminate, so I have stopped putting diapers on her altogether. As soon as I stopped with the diapers, she was able to go to the potty on her own. I don't have to be very diligent anymore. She has had a few "accidents" (pee) during the day, but never fails to poop in the potty. I'm so glad to have her completely out of diapers.

Since she is still sleeping with us at night, I was a little nervous that she might have some nighttime "accidents," but my fears were unfounded. To this day, Sara has *never* wet the bed.

### Looking Back . . .

Looking back, it's obvious that all my diligence has paid off. Sara was completely out of diapers before 18 months and potty trained way before any of her friends. Most people who saw me taking her potty as an infant were curious but skeptical. They would say, "Nice for her, but never for me," or make comments like, "It's easier with girls." But every once in a while I'd meet someone who was more open-minded, and some of these moms have successfully potty trained their own babies.

Sara is 7 years old now. An amusing leftover from her early potty training is that she still always announces when she has to go to the bathroom. She still has some memories of her infant potty training, partly because we sometimes talk about it and have videos and photos of her first few years, including some potty scenes, and partly because her baby brother is using the method. Beausoleil was born a year ago, and Sara has been helping me potty train him since he was born. Needless to say, she's an expert on the topic. She is mature for her age, and we're still very close.

## Beausoleil

After the success she had using infant potty training with her daughter Sara, there was no doubt in Laura's mind that she would potty train her second child from birth too. At the time of publication, Beau was 17 months old.

## Beau

### First Week

I started potty training Beau when he was 4 days old. The very next day I was reminded (after several years' break between babies) of how important it is for me to be available on time for his elimination. Timing is everything with this method. As with Sara, I nurse Beau while holding him over the baking-bowl potty since he eats and "goes" at the same time a lot. Beau pees more often than Sara did, so it's pretty hectic and intense at the moment.

I'm using the same small plastic mixing bowl that I used with Sara. As with Sara, I'm keeping a diaper on him in between potty visits. Since he pees so much more than Sara, I'm using a diaper service to get through this phase. Another reason to keep the diaper service is that we plan to move soon, and I don't have as much time as I need to devote to Beau's pottying.

### One Month

Beau is 4 weeks old, and we have moved into our new home. Because he was born 3 weeks "early" (before the due date) I hadn't finished all the packing before giving birth. As a result, I had to do a lot of packing and other things to get ready for the move during the first 4 weeks of his life. Therefore, I haven't been totally focused on doing the method. Now that we have moved and are settled, I have started using the method in earnest.

### Three Months

He's starting to settle down to a more predictable routine. I am able to catch more and more poops, although still using the diaper service and going through 140 diapers a week. Since he sleeps in the bed with us, I keep a diaper on him at night, just in case. He's a great nighttime sleeper and often wakes us with a dry diaper. I hold him over the potty bowl when he wakes up in the morning, and he makes a BIG pee and sometimes a poop.

### Four Months

I'm having continued success with the method. One day he went 12 hours using the same dry diaper since I was able to respond to his needs to eliminate in time. I'm having much more success now that he is holding his head up better and having more predictable bowel movements.

He's sleeping 6½ hours straight at night. Until now, I was getting up at night and putting him on the potty when he squirmed at night. I've decided we both need more sleep, so I'm letting him fall back to sleep instead of putting him on the potty. He has been dry in the morning, and I get a BIG pee in the pot, sometimes even a poop, when he wakes up.

## Five Months

We're down to 90 diapers a week. He's sleeping longer at night (8 hours) and still waking up dry.  He really has the hang of using the potty bowl and is quite content with it.

## Six Months

If he doesn't need to pee and I set him on the potty bowl, he will arch and stand himself up. If his penis is at all stiff, I know he'll need to pee soon, so I wait a moment, then put him back on the potty and he cooperates—stays on the potty and pees. As with Sara, pees are trickier to get 100% since babies pee so often.

His first tooth appeared, and I've introduced solid food (mostly banana). These two things have combined to impact his digestion. His poops are more solid and predictable. I now realize he signals his need to eliminate using body posturing and distinct breathing.

I canceled the diaper service. We own 30 diapers and three diaper covers. I wash a load of diapers only once every three days.

## Seven Months

Since he can sit up well on his own now, I bought him a BabyBjörn® potty. He has adapted to it well.

## Eight Months

I get quite a few pees a day.

Since his top teeth came in and he gets more solids in addition to nursing, the consistency and timing of his bowels varies. There has been a transition period with his bowels since starting the solids. I missed his poops for a few days—what a drag! He now goes a day or sometimes two between poops, but not always, so I'm doing better with the poops.

I have begun to use sign language for simple, everyday communications with Beau since he cannot speak yet. The sign for "poop" is a clenched fist. I have signs to use when I ask him things like: Finished? More? Food? Pee? My theory is that he will be able to communicate with sign sooner than words, and this might enable me to finish with diapers even sooner.

**Ten Months**

He has a bad case of diarrhea but is willing to let me hold him over the potty. Fortunately, he is doing all his diarrhea poops in the potty. Needless to say, I feel very committed to this method since it has kept him so clean and eliminated so many messes for me to clean.

**Eleven Months**

He has diarrhea again, and even though his signals sometimes get out of sync, it's still well worth using the potty. It takes me 10–15 minutes to do the whole procedure—undress him, potty him, wipe him off and dress him. When I consider the amount of time it takes to clean all aspects of a diarrhea mess (diapers, clothing, baby, my hands, etc.), I much prefer spending time cuddling him on the potty and getting him to poop there instead of in a diaper. I also feel it's a matter of dignity for him not to poop in a diaper.

**Twelve Months**

We no longer use nighttime diapers since he always wakes up dry.

Beau now gives the sign for poop while he's pooping. I'm using his BabyBjörn® potty less and less since he doesn't like it. He protests if I put him on it, so I either hold him over the original mixing bowl or, if he needs to pee only, the sink. If he has to poop, I hold him over the toilet. He lets me know if he doesn't need to go or if he doesn't feel like being held. Sometimes I give him a toy or something to distract him and then he'll calm right down and pee. There's some intuitive analysis going on when he protests at the exact time when I sense he really needs to pee. Sometimes I let him go back to what he was doing, then I'll try again a few minutes later and he'll happily pee. I respect his communication and don't force the issue at all.

## Thirteen Months

Beau is walking more and more, and my goal is to have him out of diapers by the time he's walking full time. The success goes back and forth. If I keep him out of diapers, I really have to keep him in sight. He will sometimes give me the sign for poop before he goes, but just by seconds, and I have to immediately respond or he poops on the floor. More and more often, he comes to me and I intuitively know he's telling me he needs to go. There's no overt sign, just his being there and my instinct. It's quite an effort, this training, but one great thing is that he is absolutely clear about what the potty is for, and he can make himself pee. Once, he has actually walked up to his little potty (when his diaper was off), sat down and peed. I was so excited! I'm ready for more successes like that!

## Fourteen Months

He was doing well, then went on potty strike. He has had several accidents with his diapers off, so I've had to resort to diapers again. He has been wearing them off and on for a few weeks. He hates being held down while I put on his diaper. I haven't figured out why he is on strike, but we'll weather the storm.

## Fifteen Months

His potty strike lasted about one month in total and has now ended. It was frustrating for him to be held down while I put a diaper on him during that time.

One day I just looked at him and said, "You're ready." I put him on the potty, and he was happy to start using it again.

The other day he sat on the potty by himself and pooped. Then he moved the potty over to his toys, sat on the potty again and pooped more. He signals me with body language and gestures. If I ask him, "Do you need to poop?" and the answer is yes, he grabs his crotch to let me know. If he has an accident, he comes to me and grabs his crotch to let me know.

## Sixteen Months

Beau is now toilet trained day and night! He wears pants without a diaper or underpants. This makes it easy to pull down his pants in a hurry when he has to go. Although preverbal, he has no problem letting me know when he has to go. He will often come and find me, take my hand and lead me to the throne.

A recent bout of diarrhea caused me to be on extra alert for subtle signals and timing. I continued with my resolve to not diaper him. We made it through the illness without an accident, thanks to both our efforts. We are triumphant! No more diaper wars! All at the tender age of 16 months!

*Tom Griggs*

Laura Diane and Beau (at 16 months)

# chapter 3

# kamala's
# 9 successes

Vivian Kumjian ("Kamala") has toilet trained nine children from infancy—the first baby starting at 5 months of age, and all the rest starting with the meconium at birth. Seven of these are her own children, two girls and five boys. All the babies she worked with were toilet trained by the time they walked, anywhere from 10–14 months of age, depending on the child. Kamala didn't notice any difference in the degree of difficulty in toilet training boys and girls. Her story, from 2000, is mainly one of communication on various levels.

My first baby, Naya, was born in 1974 in Virginia. We spent much of his infancy in Mexico. When he was 5 months old, I made an interesting discov-

ery. He was lying on a blanket when he seemed to be trying to tell me something. He made a slightly distressful vocal sound while looking me in the eye
and waving his arms and legs around. For some reason, I picked up on the
idea that he might have to pee. I squatted down and took him in my arms,
leaning him against my chest while holding him by his legs. This seemed a
natural and comfortable position for us both. As soon as I held him in position, he peed. Of course, I was thrilled that my son had responded to my
cue. I had never heard about infant toilet training before, although I had a
sense that a mother has the ability to be in tune with her baby's elimination.

From that day on, the toilet scenario with Naya became like a game of
responding to sound and body language. It was touch and go for a while in
that he wouldn't pee every time I thought he had to. I had to try different
solutions. When I say it's like a game, I don't mean that you are doing something to your baby. It is something that you do together. When I say it's like
a game, I don't mean that you are training your baby. It's more a matter of
training yourself than training your baby. It's a question of training yourself
to listen, pay attention, be aware and respond. It is just as natural to respond to toilet needs as it is to respond to a baby being hungry or tired.
Your baby tells you when he wants to eat, when he wants to sleep, when he
wants to go for a walk, when he wants to play, when he is angry, and he also
tells you when he has to pee or poop.

You have to really want to participate in the play, in the game. You have
to bond with your baby and learn each other's sounds, timing and body language. For me, responding to Naya's cues to pee or poop was part of a
whole, not a separate thing or task that had to be done.

I worked on getting us into a symbiotic relationship, in tune with each
other's timing and communication. The fact that I carried Naya around in a
*rebozo* (sling) everywhere I went made it easier to constantly be aware of all
his needs, including his elimination timing. He would make a sound or cry
when he wanted something, and I gradually learned to figure out exactly
what he needed. If I felt it was time for him to eliminate, I'd hold him out.

I was very interested in learning to communicate with Naya on a psychic
level. I believe in telepathy and that most of us haven't learned how to use
it. I had to untrain myself in some ways in order to be able to listen to Naya.
I had to learn to listen to the voices inside me and respond to my son. It's
like hearing a thought in your head and another person remarks, "I was just
thinking the same thing." This happens a lot, but we don't always pay attention to it. The same sort of thing happened with elimination communication
with Naya (and later my other babies). I heard the thought and had the feel-

ing that he had to go, acknowledged that thought/feeling, and he responded by peeing for me.

Since Naya signaled to me vocally, I listened carefully to his vocalizations and took the time to learn their meaning. The sounds he used were not the same every time. He'd make a noise to call to me, like someone trying to grab my attention. Of course, he couldn't yet say anything like "hey," but he created his own sounds to get my attention. I responded to his elimination cues by picking him up and holding him in position to pee or poop. I made a "shh shh" sound or else just said "pee" when I was holding him in position. Using the sound reinforced the communication between us. From the moment I understood that he always yelled or cried when he had to go, I never again needed to depend on timing to tell me when to take him to eliminate. Once I learned his language of vocalizations, he was always the initiator of the communication.

Of course there were times when I wasn't available for him. It's not possible for any mother to be present for every single pee! If I wasn't around when he signaled me and it got to the point where he couldn't hold it any longer, he'd just pee in my absence. I'd say, "You had to pee, and I didn't catch it." I never made a fuss or a big deal about it, and I certainly never felt or expressed anger.

When he was 10 months old, we moved to the wilderness, among the sequoias in Southern California. Living in a natural environment made it easy to continue since not putting diapers on a baby makes toilet training much easier. By the time a baby can walk, it's just a matter of his knowing where he has to walk to pee. Another advantage of living in the country is that it involves a different sort of timing. You're more relaxed, and it's easier to be in tune with your kids. You're not worried about your house, carpets and belongings. I'm not saying that it's necessary to live in the wilderness to do this, but for those who have the opportunity to live in a more natural environment, it can make it easier.

The experience with my second baby, Ituri, was different. I held him out right after birth to empty out his meconium. We were in a very lucid time and space immediately after the birth, and holding him out established a unique form of communication between us from the very beginning of his life. I learned from Ituri that babies are aware of elimination at and from birth. This proved to be the case with the rest of my kids too. In the minutes, hours and days after you give birth, you are very lucid. This is when communication is the most open between you. Things happen at a very slow pace and seem very clear. You are in a different dimension. After the first week or two, the communication starts getting more difficult because that "clear space" starts getting more cloudy. You have a lot of things you have to do, there is a lot of activity around you, a lot of distractions so it's more difficult to tune into your baby. It becomes more of a challenge to stay in close communication with baby, but it is possible.

In addition to the close bond established at birth, the same pattern of communication and attention-getting that I had experienced with Naya happened with Ituri—and in fact, with all seven of my kids and two other babies I worked with. At 6 months, Ituri got to the point where he would hold his pee and yell until I got the message. I'd hold him out, he'd pee and then he'd sigh with relief.

I was living a communal lifestyle when I was in my twenties. We spent three years in the wilderness. I gave birth to Ituri and my third child, a daughter named Sodasi, there. There were two other babies from different families born there too. We adults were all training ourselves to open up to be in communication with the babies. This was our focus. All the babies in the commune were toilet trained from birth. All the adults came together to help each other with this. Sometimes I had to be the interpreter of babies' signals since some adults couldn't figure out why a baby was crying. We strove to change our conditioning in order to identify, bond and communicate with all the babies. It was like living in an extended family where all family members spend time raising the children.

I have read books stating that babies can't control their bowels or bladders, but this hasn't been my experience at all—not with my own seven infants and not with other babies I have worked with. All my babies learned to control their bowels and wait for me to pick them up and hold them out. They would get really mad at me if I wasn't paying enough attention to hear their calls. It was like they said, "Come on! Wake up! I have to pee!" Ituri was the first of my kids to use such clear communication. Naya had been more mellow about it, probably because I had started later in life (5 months) with him. It was less important for Naya in that he didn't mind as much if I didn't make it on time for him. But Ituri demanded it—and he demanded it loud and clear!

The sound and quality of communication shapes a baby's mind from birth. The best part of toilet training for me was the quality of communication. It was a real thrill. It wasn't a matter of me training my baby. It was more like changing or enhancing a relationship through natural communication. It opens you up to a whole new quality of communication with your baby. Communication about elimination is not a separate thing, just part of the whole repertoire of communication and caring. All my kids communicated vocally with me most of the time, but there were also times where I picked up on their need before they communicated. It was a give-and-take communication, a symbiotic relationship. I was pleased but didn't reward or praise my kids when they peed for me. I considered it a natural thing, just like eating, something that didn't need praise or special recognition.

We are all born with natural instincts, and mothers have a natural ability or instinct to be in tune with baby's body language, timing, communication, play, feedings, etc. In the industrialized world, many mothers don't follow or identify with their instincts. They have adapted to civilization and industrialization and try to make their children adapt quickly. Everyone wants to train their kids to fit in society, and they miss a lot this way. Everyone is always busy, in a hurry and operates with a linear mind, which is not how a child's mind works. This is why I visit third world countries as often as I can. People there live at a different pace and have a sense of respect for children.

Following our natural instincts is similar to the way an animal is in tune with her babies. Animal maternal instinct overrides (nearly) every other instinct. And speaking of animals, one of our dogs had nine puppies. She died, and we had to raise the pups. We put them in our tent at night. In the morning, they would all file out together, waddle out into the woods and take care of business there. Everyone knows that it's harder and messier if you delay house training a puppy. If you were to wait for a puppy to self-house-train, it would never happen. Why do we expect puppies to be toilet trained when they are babies, yet think our own babies aren't capable of what puppies can do?

My babies were never alone. When they were tiny, I carried them around with me in a *rebozo*. Once they could sit up, they didn't like the *rebozo* anymore and didn't want to sit in a backpack. At that stage, I carried them on top of my shoulders or with their legs wrapped around me like a monkey. At night, they slept with us. I'd use a pad or a towel with a diaper on top to protect the bed. I didn't put a diaper on my babies at night. I tried to get up based on timing, but this was difficult, so I wasn't very diligent about this aspect.

When a baby starts crawling, the situation changes a lot. They get involved with their surroundings, forget to signal and go on the floor. You need to pick them up, tell them it's the wrong place to go, carry them to the right place and tell them that's the right place. They eventually catch on. By the time my kids walked, there was no problem at all. They graduated from (a) crawling to (b) knowing where to eliminate to (c) walking and being finished with toilet training.

All my kids were finished with toilet training when they started walking, any-where from 10–14 months. This included nighttime too.

We moved to the countryside in New York in 1990. My youngest girl, Roshi, was 13 months old. Living in New York was the first time I experi-enced any reservations from people about infant potty training, but most people ended up reacting positively after seeing how well adjusted my kids are. They are very social, communicative and centered, and they aren't whiners. Their behavior makes people stop, think and realize that the scare tactics about infant potty training are false.

I find it sad that American doctors and pediatricians don't recognize in-fant toilet training as a positive and wonderful method. It's awful seeing 2-year-olds and 3-years-olds in Pampers. Doctors and other professionals learn what they know from books and not from experience. In one sense, it's like alternative medicine versus allopathic medicine. Many doctors won't recognize natural herbal remedies. Look at all the children wearing diapers in daycare these days. I had a friend visit me with her 3-year-old boy in dia-pers. He totally refuses to communicate with her about going to the bath-room. Her doctor had told her it's okay to wait, "Let the child lead," and all that, but it wasn't getting any better as he got older. It was getting worse. Doctors and teachers claim a baby is not capable of understanding going to the potty. They say it takes time and that a child should be the one to ini-tiate potty training. Nowadays they say a 3-year-old doesn't have the intel-ligence to go to the potty if he isn't "ready."

This brings us back to intelligence. I think a lot of parents have trouble potty training their kids because they cannot acknowledge the intelligence of their babies. Parents use baby talk and treat their babies like cute objects or pets. When there is respect for a child and acknowledgment that he knows what he's doing, it makes a difference. If you talk to 3-year-olds more as adults than as babies, they will acknowledge it. At age 3, all my kids and all the 3-year-olds in our group communicated well. They could understand and articulate their thoughts and desires. I have found that 3-year-olds in diapers refuse to learn to communicate. This is, in part at least, because of the way they are (or aren't) communicated with.

I think the fact that my kids vocally called to me when they needed to pee or poop is due to my acknowledging their communication on all lev-els—vocal sounds, body language and psychic communications. Respond-ing to a baby's communications without putting up barriers in the form of questions and doubts is crucial. For example, if a baby could verbalize his request to pee, my response should be to take him to pee, rather than responding by repeating his question or request. If a baby could say, "I have to pee," I should not respond by repeating his question and double checking, "Do you have to pee?" or showing doubt, "Are you sure you have to pee?" I should just hold him out to pee and give a direct response that way. It's a spontaneous response.

I was 42 and still living in New York when I had my last baby, Osel. He's 5 now. I hadn't had a baby for a while and was more mature. From the beginning, I had total communication with Osel. The moment he was born, we were in sync. He would hold his elimination until I or one of his brothers or sisters could take him and hold him over a pot. He was never alone since I carried him almost everywhere and also because he had four brothers and two sisters to hold him and take him to pee if I couldn't. There is a communication of love among brothers and sisters, and a baby senses that. A baby knows when he is being cared for with love rather than someone just doing a babysitting job.

Osel would make sounds or grunt until we'd pick him up and hold him to pee. My experience has been that babies will wait for a reasonable amount of time to be taken to the bathroom. In this sense, they have some control from birth. Osel confirmed that what I had to do was let him initiate the communication, let him tell me if he had to go. I didn't have to anticipate it or wait very long while holding him to pee.

I went on a trip to Europe with Osel when he was 18 months old. Even though he had been potty trained since he started walking at 10 months, I was apprehensive of dealing with the airplane lavatory on such a long flight, so I put a diaper on him. That was a real mistake. I kept telling him, "Just pee in your diaper," but he wouldn't. There was no way he was going to pee in a diaper! He cried in protest until I took him to the lavatory, removed the diaper and held him out to pee. I never tried putting a diaper on him again!

# chapter 4

# elimination timing teacher

L inda Penn ("Natec") has authored her own book on the topic of infant
  potty training. She calls the process "elimination timing." She began
  elimination timing with her son at birth, weathered a two-month communication strike with him at age 14 months and gave away any remaining
diapers at 20 months. Linda has worked with many infants and taught their
mothers and caregivers elimination timing techniques. Her report is dated
2000.

Elimination timing is oriented towards getting parents to realize that
they need to learn and work with baby's natural timing, rather than forcing
baby to comply to the timing of adults. It's not a question of training, so the

term isn't "elimination training." Elimination timing involves looking for baby's elimination patterns and timing.

I learned the term "elimination timing" from my teacher, who realized it through travels in Asia and Latin America. When he returned to the States in 1976, he told a friend of mine about it, and she immediately began elimination timing with her infant son. She showed me the technique.

I advise parents to start with the meconium. To catch the meconium, cradle the newborn in your arms while holding his rear end over a disposable pad or a receptacle. A "chuckie" (blue waterproof pad used in home births) is ideal for this. To avoid using diapers, use a waterproof pad with a diaper or towel on top. The reason I recommend beginning elimination timing as early as possible is that it's easy to see elimination signals in infants. It's really obvious when they are so small.

The first week, continue having the baby go on something disposable. After that, use a pot, bucket, sink or other receptacle. Some mothers hold a receptacle under their infant's bottom while nursing so they don't have to interrupt a feeding. In warmer climates, peeing baby outdoors is another option.

Each baby has its own pace of developing neck and back strength. When baby's neck gains strength, squat and hold the infant under his buttocks and upper thighs, spread his legs a little and lean his back against your stomach. In this way, you support the baby's neck and back.

New mothers are flooded with information about all sorts of things. Once you settle down, you'll see that, in general, a baby makes some kind of movement before pooping. Then you'll see patterns. When babies wake from a nap, they usually pee. There will also be a pattern related to feedings. Some babies pee or poop during a feeding while others go after they eat. Each baby is different, but a pattern is there. Some patterns are regular while others are not so regular. The combination of the pattern and noticing any particular movements or other signals tells you when to take the baby to pee or poop. Hold the baby in position, make the "pssss" sound and talk to him. You can ask questions like, "Do you have to pee?" If baby has already peed, confirm this by saying, "All right, you peed." It's not so much a process of the caregiver doing it to the child as much as it is the child and the caregiver working together.

If you carry your baby, he will usually wiggle, squirm or fuss right before it's time to pee. When baby squirms, you can ask, "Do you have to pee?"

Then hold him out to pee. If he has to pee, he will. If he doesn't have to pee, he won't, and that's that.

What starts getting this established is the communication back and forth between baby and caregiver. Your baby will then tell you he has to pee in one way or another. It might be by vocally signaling you or else you can look for a psychic communication. It depends on the baby.

On one level, babies are aware of elimination from the start. If an adult caregiver gives a symbol to this, the concept becomes concrete, and this is how a child keeps that awareness. My experience is that babies communicate consciously about elimination with a caregiver by the age of 3 months. At 3 months, babies can also hold their bladders. Doctors in industrialized countries say that children can't, shouldn't and couldn't hold their bladders until 18 months or older. This has never been my experience since my introduction to elimination timing in 1976.

Babies respond well to your verbal cues. Be careful not to cue a baby before you have him in position or he'll go in the wrong place. There have been times where I said to babies who are 5–6 months old, "Oh, you have to pee," then I'd have to immediately say, "Wait, wait, wait, not here, wait!" They hold it until I get them in position and tell them, "Okay, now." Then they pee.

One of the easiest times to get a baby to go for you is when they wake up in the morning or from a nap. Most babies have to pee when they wake up. If you take them to pee as soon as they wake up, they start associating this with a pattern that goes like this, "I just got up, and she's taking me to pee. This is when and where I pee."

You have to be prepared for a lot of elimination accidents with infants. Many babies don't have a regular pattern to peeing. That's why it's so nice to take them after they sleep because you're fairly certain to get them to pee for you then.

Some babies I've worked with give vocal signals before they need to go. Of course it's easier to know when to take baby to go if he gives a vocal signal. Some babies chirp before they have to go. I remember a 5-month-old who would scream in bed at night until someone took him to pee. He refused to pee in the bed. A 13-month-old girl made a unique sound, a creaking inhalation sound, when she had to eliminate.

Perhaps the hardest signals to pick up are the psychic signals. Those are tricky. You have to pick them up by feeling and intuition. It's like the feeling we all get from time to time, "The phone is going to ring and it's going to be

Susie." It's a symbiotic, intuitive, telepathic hookup between mother and child. There are generations of people in tune like that. They get a feeling, an intuitive flash that tells them what is going to happen. We tend to test these intuitive flashes by ignoring them. Then when they come true, we say, "I knew that was going to happen. I knew he had to pee. Why didn't I listen to myself?" This is a typical reaction after you get peed on. It's a matter of getting in tune with your baby and in sync with his elimination patterns.

New mothers get really excited about communicating with their baby in such a productive way. They praise the baby. This is fine. I did it with my son. If you have another baby or work with other kids, it's not as exciting and you don't tend to be as exuberant. If you have more than one child and do this with them, like everything else you do with them, it gets easier, you get more confident and it's not such a big deal. The important thing is to let the child know that you know he has responded and done the right thing. Your reaction can vary from matter-of-factly stating "you peed" to being very excited, clapping, jumping up and down. It doesn't matter which way you behave, the baby will understand. When a baby feels the caregiver feeling happy, that's a reward.

There are significant psychological benefits to elimination timing for all concerned. Fathers who might feel left out in the beginning stages of child rearing can now have another essential role through elimination timing. My experience has been that all parents feel empowered and thankful to learn a compassionate communication skill with their children.

Siblings and kids in general are really good helpers with elimination timing. They are in tune with babies and are great about telling you if a baby has to pee.

People often ask if girls learn elimination timing faster than boys. I don't think there is any difference. I think girls are more work because you have to wipe between the folds to clean and dry them.

After you've done this for a while, it becomes second nature. It's totally natural, in the flow and no big deal anymore. It takes a commitment to do this. There are some mothers who give up and go back to diapers for one reason or another, and that is okay. This is not an achievement test for parents, so there are no failures. For everyone who does try elimination timing, remember that the key to this whole thing is to just relax.

When my son Kawa (now 12) was born, we caught the meconium and continued elimination timing with good results for the next 14 months. I had a lot of help from his father and a group of friends we were living with. My

*Photographer unknown*

Kawa and "Natec"

friends called me "Natec," which means "heart of the date palm," and some friends still call me by that name.

It was easy to tell when Kawa had to poop. He would get a red face and grunt. His pooping pattern was very regular, so it was easy to have him poop for me. Peeing was fairly regular in some ways but not in others. Five minutes after he began nursing, he'd pee. Sometimes I'd interrupt the nursing to take him to pee after the first five minutes, but if I felt he didn't want to stop nursing, I'd hold a receptacle under him. It was a flexible arrangement between us. After that very predictable pee, there was no regular pattern to his peeing, and he did not give any obviously consistent signals.

He was nearly done with my supervision at 14 months. Then his life and environment changed drastically. His father and I separated, and at the same time, I moved away from the group of friends we had been living with—the caregivers who had also raised Kawa. I moved to Hawaii alone with my son, and he stopped signaling to me when he had to eliminate. This was a big problem. I had to put my son in diapers for the first time at age 14 months! Two months later, he remained dry at night but still did not signal me. He was out of diapers, though, because he would go outside to pee. Since we were living in a rural area and a warm climate, this was no problem. When he was 20 months old, he spent the night at the home of his uncle. When Kawa went outside to poop, the uncle told him in no uncertain terms that pooping outdoors was not allowed at his place. After that night, Kawa started using the toilet.

Most kids don't go through problems like this. They go straight to the potty as soon as they can sit and don't go on strike, but occasionally you get a child who will test you or have emotional upsets and use elimination as a means of protest. Looking back, I realize Kawa went on strike because his environment and social surroundings had changed so drastically.

Hawaii is a great place to work with elimination timing since the climate is so mild, and babies can be minimally dressed most of the time. There are lots of people with alternative lifestyles living in Pahoa. People learn about me by word of mouth. There have been so many elimination timing babies in this area that in 1999, the local health food shop posted a sign that requested: *"Please no babies without diapers in shop."*

*You can read more about Linda Penn ("Natec"), her philosophy and teachings, in her booklet Infant Communication: Raising Babies without Diapers . . . and More. The book is 28 pages, $6.00 including shipping, and can be ordered by writing to:*

Natec,
HCR2 Box 6838
Kea'au, HI 96749

(e-mail: natec@interpac.net)

# chapter 5

# dentist mom

L iz Reiter is a dentist in the San Francisco Bay Area. Her husband Holger is a Ph.D. in neuroscience, a businessman and a researcher who works from home. They have a son Nicholas who is 4 and a daughter Erika who is 2½. Liz did not learn about infant potty training in time to try it with her first child. Her testimonial is dated 2000.

I was introduced to this kind of potty training by another mother. She gave me the book *Trickle Treat* and told me how she had used it with her daughter. It sounded interesting to me. I thought it was a good idea. It made sense to me, with my background in science, to potty train my daughter from birth. It reminded me of Pavlov's dogs and similar behavioral theories.

My husband read the book and was positive about the idea. I had a nanny working for me at the time since I was working three days a week. My nanny read the book, found the idea interesting and said she'd be happy to help me with the potty training. We started with Erika when she was 7 weeks old.

I was very diligent with the potty training and so was my nanny. My husband helped out when he could and was thrilled with the results. I hired a second woman to help around the house a few hours a morning for a while. She read the book, was positive about it and helped us with potty training too. Erika had no problem when people other than myself took her to the potty.

I did not find it overly time consuming to use infant potty training. I didn't have any real problems other than it seemed to go a little slow during the first month or two, meaning we didn't succeed in getting Erika to pee for us on a regular basis at first. I would hold her over the potty for about 30 seconds, and if she didn't have to go, I'd stop and try later. We decided that if we could get her to pee twice in the potty in the morning and twice in the afternoon, that we were having a great day. We called them "catches," and if we got four catches in an entire day we were very happy. Even if we only got a few pees or poops a day at first, it was apparent that she knew why I was holding her over the potty. The interval between when I started to hold her and when she would pee got shorter and shorter, so I knew the association with my signals was working. After about two months, it seemed to just start clicking: I knew her cycle better, and we didn't have to hold her as long to get her to go.

As for pooping, she used to wake up around 4:30 in the morning when she was tiny. I'd hold her over the potty and she'd immediately poop. It was really easy to know when Erika had to poop. She would make faces and grunt and then I'd quickly take her diaper off, hold her over the potty and catch it. When she got a little bigger, I'd take her into the bathroom and she'd poop for me there. I hardly ever had to clean a poopy diaper after she got the hang of it. That was great, especially after changing dirty diapers for almost three years with my son.

The potty I used for Erika was a little white potty bowl insert from a blue older-style potty chair that my neighbor had used with her kids. The potty insert was just the right size to hold under Erika's little bottom. I just held her over it, like the pictures in this book show. In the beginning, I always took her to the potty in the bathroom, in front of a mirror, and I always made a "sssshh" sound to cue her to pee.

When Erika was about 6 or 8 months, I started using the potty in other places besides the bathroom. I took the potty with me everywhere I went. I would also often stand or walk around the house with Erika on the potty (See Chapter 3, "The In-Arms Phase," in Part 1 for a photo of this). My nanny put Erika on the potty in many different places at home, sitting or standing. We did this more as Erika got older.

I continued my dentistry work until Erika was 10 months old then sold my practice in order to stay home with the kids full time. My nanny continued to work part time with me after I stopped working. She worked mornings almost every day until just recently. My mother, grandmother and everyone in my family have been supportive of Erika's infant potty training, but most of my friends (except the one who introduced me to the idea) think it is strange. They couldn't understand what I was doing, even when I gave them the book to read.

When Erika was nearly 13 months old and walking, we put the potty insert bowl back into the blue potty chair, and by 14 months she'd walk to the potty chair on her own. I would say, "Let's go potty," and she would just run in there and sit down. Occasionally she used the potty with no prompting at all. But she wouldn't use the bigger regular toilet until she was almost 2 years old. When I went out, I'd have to hold her over a diaper to go since she wouldn't sit on a regular adult toilet until 20 months. I didn't push the "big potty" issue, then one day she told me she wanted to use the bigger potty. After that, she'd sit on any potty.

I haven't done much about night training since Erika only occasionally wets at night. I have always put a cloth diaper on her at night. When she was smaller and used to wake up for feedings at night, I would hold her over the potty and keep her clean and dry this way. Ever since she started sleeping all night, I have just let her sleep through the night and put her on the potty before bedtime and when she wakes up in the morning.

When Nicholas was about 2½, we started potty training him the traditional way. Erika was already being put on the potty all the time when Nicholas started, so he knew what the potty was and this helped him. It was one of the benefits of having the children close together and of learning about infant potty training in time for Erika. Since I was doing it with her already, Nicholas just naturally knew what was going on and tried to do it as well. He was interested but not as easy to convince to use the potty. We tried various things and eventually got him to pee on it and then poop. He was harder to get to use it to poop. We knew when he was pooping, but he refused to use the potty chair until we tried giving a reward when he used it (a small gift from Santa—it was Christmas time).

It got to the point where I had to have two potties in the bathroom. When Erika had to go, Nicholas wanted to go. And when Nicholas had to go, Erika wanted to go too. The encouragement was great for both of them.

I found it frustrating to introduce traditional potty training to Nicholas when he was 2½. At that age, kids want to be independent and play. They aren't interested in sitting on a potty if they never have before, whereas my daughter was used to using the potty from a very young age, so there was no transition at all for her. It was just gradual learning until she could go on her own, and by the time she reached that stage of independence, she could be truly independent since she had already finished with potty training.

At 2½, she knows when to go. I don't have to prompt her at all. She doesn't have accidents anymore either, whereas my son who is 4 still has some accidents. It took me over a year to get to the point where I didn't have to prompt him anymore by asking, "Do you have to go?" He quickly mastered pooping but took over a year to really learn to not have peeing accidents. Erika is already completely out of diapers. I hadn't even started with my son when he was Erika's age, yet I'm completely finished with her. I think it's much better for a child. It's great not to have to wear diapers all the time.

It does take diligence, but the reward is that your child will be out of diapers early and completely independent around 2, whereas nowadays most parents don't even start until 2 or later. It's much messier to wait. And Erika never had diaper rash because she was always dry.

I would certainly use infant potty training again if I had another child. When anyone asks me about it, I tell them it's the greatest potty training I ever learned. I thought it was fantastic. I don't have anything negative to say except it would be nice if people were more supportive of it. I think one reason people are negative is that they are thinking of the old way early toilet training was done in this country in the past. It's not the same method at all.

When I told my grandmother I was using infant potty training, she said, "Oh, I did that with your mom. I sat her on a potty with a little tray and left her there until she went." I told her what I'm doing is different, that you don't make the child sit there until she goes. When my grandmother used to tell me that my mom would poop in the potty at age one, I didn't believe her. This was when my son was a little older than one, and I thought there was no way he could have pooped on the potty at age one. But when I did it with Erika, I could see what my grandmother was talking about. It's a totally different mindset when you've never done it.

Every mainstream parenting book I have read, like books by Penelope Leach and Dr. Brazelton, all say to delay potty training until your child is "ready," and they sternly warn parents not to use early toilet training. I read in many books that you should wait until your child gives you signs that he is ready to be potty trained, and this was very confusing to me. They tell you to wait until your baby goes two or three hours between pees, wait until your baby wakes up dry from naps and all that, but with my son, these things never happened! When he was 2½, I thought, "This is getting ridiculous." I started potty training him and it was fine. Another problem with the mainstream books is that they all made me very fearful of starting potty training "too young." They teach that if you start young, you will scar your baby, your baby will be emotionally disturbed if you potty train him too young or that it won't work. What I don't like about those books is that they don't even recognize that there are other possibilities available.

When infant potty training is done in a totally positive, loving, nurturing way, when it's never forced on a child, it works. You just hold the child over the potty, and if they don't go, you take them off, and there is no negative connotation involved. I didn't have any trouble with Erika. I was happy to use this method. Everyone who helped me was excited too.

If I mention my success with Erika to a pediatrician or people with a background in science, they say, "Well, you just trained yourself. You didn't train your daughter." That was true in the beginning. I was training myself to recognize the signals Erika was giving to tell me when she needed to go, and I was timing things to see how long until she would "go" after a feeding. But at the same time, she was learning to associate my cues (holding her a certain way in a certain place, making the ssshh sound, etc.) with going in the potty instead of in a diaper. One thing I always noticed was if I put a diaper on my son or daughter, they would use it. If I took them out of diapers and told them to try to stay dry, they would make more of an effort not to go in their pants. It's so simple and logical.

Erika was out of daytime diapers when she was 18 months. People still are surprised and impressed at her and ask me how she can be out of diapers so young, at 2½. But I have also started hearing comments like, "My friend had a 2½-year-old, and he was trained in just two weeks. So why did you go through all that work when you could have waited until Erika was 2 and then done it fast?" Well, there is no guarantee that a child is going to be one of the few who learn potty training so easily. I have met many other

children who are 3 and sometimes 4 years old and still use pull-ups or diapers. Why take the chance? Why use so many diapers? Why put up with
messy diapers for years? If you use infant potty training, you know your
child will be out of diapers at a young age. It makes kids happy about being
in control of their bodily functions so young. They like to be in control of everything, and this is one more thing for them to feel good about doing
themselves.

*Jeanne Reiter*

The Reiters with their children at the beach.
(left, Nicholas age 4; right, Erica age 2½)

# chapter 6

# an online adventure

Jennine discovered and began infant potty training with her sixth child, Elly Joy Johnson, when Elly was 10 weeks old. Jennine keeps an internet diary of Elly's progress. Her diary is reproduced here up to the age of 15 months. After that time, Jennine gave birth to another child and began infant potty training with her new baby. At some point, the family encountered health complications and Jennine wasn't able to dedicate as much time to toilet training as she would have liked. Nevertheless, her story is included here. Since some readers are bound to run into difficulties for health or other reasons, Jennine's story is of interest. For updates, visit her web diary at: http://www.users.uswest.net/~ptlfhb/journal.html.

## Elly Joy Johnson's Experience
### in Potty Training

### February 3rd, 1999

Today Elly (10 weeks) showed progress in our training experiment. I say experiment because this is my first attempt to train an infant to void on cue. I caught Elly before her bowel movement, which usually isn't very regular. She was sitting in an infant seat on the floor next to me when I heard her make grunting sounds. I needed to be quick or I was going to miss my chance to get her over the bathroom sink before she started pushing. I praised her by saying "That's great Elly. You're pooping!" I took off her clothing from the waist down and held her over the sink, with her back to my chest and my hands holding her legs up, in a squatting position. I made "our sound" which sounds like "sssss" and she began to grunt again. In one rather explosive sound, she pooped and was done. This took about three minutes in all. Because I was moving my children's bedroom arrangements around, I put Elly in a diaper. She did wet in it because I missed her cues. I am remaining flexible as I have five other children to care for and cannot always be so observant. My goal is to train (her and myself) every day as best I can . . . praying all the way.

### February 4th, 1999

I would like to explain a few things about the post from yesterday. First of all, Elly is breastfed exclusively and because of that, her bowel movements are very small and loose. When I say that she pooped in the sink, I never thought that some people might think that is gross. To me, it is no big deal. I just rinse it down the drain and wash the sink with a cleaner. It is up to you to choose the container you would like to use. I also use a little plastic bucket when we go out or at night when I do not feel like getting up. I rinse that with a mild cleaner after each use. Today is going well. Elly remains dry and our routine is being formed. It seems that Elly wets within ten minutes of her feedings and then again in a half an hour. She has never peed while sleeping. I love that I feel more in tune with Elly because of our attempt to potty train. I feel I know her better than I did with my other children. I pay more attention to her needs because I am more aware of her signals and her attempts to communicate them to me. I'm feeling really positive about this, and this has affected our relationship in a good way.

## February 7th, 1999

This weekend has been very busy. We have been out a lot and busy while at home. Our training has gone fairly well considering our schedule. I am trying to train my 10-year-old daughter, Kaitlyn, to learn Elly's signals so that I can get some extra hands involved. It will be a blessing to have her help. Elly is going through a growth spurt right now. She is nursing a lot more than normal, therefore she is eliminating a lot more. I have noticed that our normal times for peeing are off because of it. I plan on spending some of my afternoon tomorrow getting back on track by observing her, making our sound ("sssss") while she pees and recording it on paper so that I can get into a rhythm again. It really does seem to "go like clockwork." Just as she seems to be hungry at certain, regular times, she also eliminates regularly. I plan on including Kaitlyn in our afternoon's observation time.

## February 20th, 1999

I am finding it difficult to get time to enter my journal on the computer, as you can obviously tell. Our days are just flying by, and I cannot believe that it is the middle of February already. Elly is 3 months now. Her training continues and we are having new success. I took a suggestion of a friend (Marie, thank you!) and started setting a timer to remind me to get Elly to the potty. This has helped me tremendously. Now I can get my things done knowing that I will not forget when the last time I took Elly to the toilet. Elly has more control of her neck muscles now and can hold her head up nicely. It seems to make her happy, and we find that she picks her head up slightly when she has a bowel movement as if she is finding a better position to push in. She responds well to our signal to her that it is time to pee ("sssss") and she even knows that when we hold her in our position (her back to our chest with our hands under her knees, drawing her knees to her chest) that it is time to go. I am finding that our verbal signals are becoming less important, although I still use them.

## April 19th, 1999

We are in the midst of selling and buying a house. Due to the lack of time on my part, I am afraid that my efforts in potty training Elly have gone by the wayside. I have NOT given up hope. Once things settle down, I expect to hit it with full force again. One thing I have noticed is that Elly cannot stand to have a wet or soiled diaper. She fusses at once if I do not change her, which indicates to me that she IS aware of her diaper being wet. She still responds to the "sssss" cue and that will help me when I can get back to our training. This experience has been wonderful. I LOVE the closeness that I have shared with Elly through potty training as an infant. I loved getting to know her cues so early in life. I will continue to update this page once we are in our new house. God Bless!

## September 9th, 1999

We have moved into our new home and life is returning to normal once again. Elly will be 10 months in three days and I cannot believe that time has passed so quickly. I had completely stopped my efforts to train Elly to use the potty because our life was so very unsettled for several months. Around the middle of August, I decided to try Elly on the toilet again. I was expecting her to have forgotten everything we had begun, but she DIDN'T! I put her on the toilet and made our "sssss" sound. She started grunting immediately and within a few moments, she had a bowel movement. Keep in mind, I had not been working with her at all since before April! I had not received any of her signals that she used to use to indicate that she was going to move her bowels. She just simply responded to something deep within her. At first I thought it was a lucky break. I tried later on in the day when I was changing her diaper. I set her up on the toilet and she pushed instantly. The result was another bowel movement!! I called all the children in to watch, and they could not believe their eyes! We broke out in giggles and a round of applause for our little Elly. This is amazing to me. We started off using a technique that I was very skeptical about, and now I am seeing incredible results after months of postponing our training! It is my prediction that Elly will start using a small potty chair within a few months. Once she can walk, I expect that she will sit on the chair by herself when she feels the need to go potty. I am so excited to think that our babies can retain this kind of memory and it reemphasizes to me how crucial these first few years are to our children. Elly may not remember being placed on the toilet, but she remembers what to do when she is set on one. She may not remember all the hugs and kisses she has received, but she knows how valuable she is to God and to us! I love to see Elly smile and giggle when she knows she has pooped in the toilet. She KNOWS!! Babies are amazing! God bless and we will keep you posted! I do plan on continuing until Elly is completely trained. I cannot imagine stopping at this point, after seeing how she has retained what she learned in the beginning of her life. My friends are astonished when they see Elly go on the toilet. I video taped her this weekend, just for "proof"!

I'm pregnant again and can't wait to use trickle treat with the new baby. The benefits are so wonderful. I plan to completely document everything this time.

### December 10th, 1999

Elly is continuing to use the toilet with great results. If I put her on, say after a nap, and she does NOT need to go, she makes it very known to me by pushing her body forward in protest. I imagine her thinking, "Hey! I didn't tell you that I need to go!" I am learning to trust her to communicate the need to go, rather than assuming it is time. This is the time where I am truly seeing the fruits of this method. I am so glad that I will not face toilet training during her "twos" and "threes." In the past I have waited until this time, only to be faced with my children's temper tantrums and defiance when they would rather go in their diaper than to do something I wanted them to do. This milestone in Elly's life will pass with only joy! She has grown up thinking that this is how we do it. She knows nothing else.

One of the criticisms I have received recently after sharing Elly's training was this:

"Children aren't animals that need to be trained like dogs. With my children, we didn't even mentioned potty training until they were over 2 years old, and then they understood what was going on and were ready for it. It was simple."

This was from an older mom who felt it was rushing childhood to potty train from infancy. I couldn't disagree with her more! I explained that this experience was not one of rushing through babyhood. (Anyone who knows me would know better than that!) Rather, this experience left me feeling very bonded and close to Elly. I must say that I feel a bit of pride about knowing Elly so well.

This same mother went on to say: "The same with teaching our kids to read, they read when they were ready. My son wasn't ready until he was 9, but when he finally started to grasp reading he learned very fast." While I applaud this mom for not pushing her child, I pointed out to her that she still exposed this child to books and the alphabet song, knowing that the reading would follow. This is what I have done with Elly. I have exposed her to the toilet from infancy. Soon she will be using it completely on her own.

I encourage mothers to ignore negativity regarding infant potty training. The rewards are priceless.

### January 7th, 2000

Elly's progress has been hampered by a very long bout of pneumonia through much of December. We have been using disposable diapers since she has been too miserable to bother with being placed on the toilet. She is recovering now but is out of the habit of using the toilet. I'm trying to reestablish our routine, but she seems to have lost interest in it.

### February 16th, 2000

Elly is now 15 months old and is communicating very well. Her potty training was not going so great UNTIL we started training our two year old, Isaiah, to go on the potty. Suddenly Elly's interest has peaked again, and we are finding that she is wanting to be placed on the toilet. Now she is going to the bathroom door and knocking on it to let us know that she has to go. When she does this, I ask her "Elly, do you need to go potty?" She shakes her head "no," which is her backwards way of saying "yes." She still has "accidents" when she is busy playing, but so does my three year old. I expect this.

Our large family thrives on routines. We have a certain time for breakfast, lunch and dinner. We have quiet time, running time, reading time and lego time, to name a few examples. I have found it very easy to include potty time into our day. This has somewhat formed Elly's elimination habits as her body is accustomed to going at certain times of the day. I know that she usually has a bowel movement around 9:30 am and then again after her nap at 3:00 pm. This helps me watch her carefully in case she forgets. My goal is to have my two year old trained before the new baby arrives in May. I could possibly have had three in diapers had I not used this method of training with Elly. Instead, I will have more time to spend with my new little one, and you can bet we will use the trickle treat method with him or her.

# chapter 7

# elimination communication

Rosie Wilde lives in Seattle. She discovered infant potty training when her first son Dakota was 3 months old. Dakota finished at 22 months. Rosie started at birth with her second son Ian, who was 14 months old at the time this interview was updated in 2002. Rosie has a web site dedicated to the topic of what she calls elimination communication ("ec") and has introduced many families to this method via her website, hard work and enthusiasm.

# First Son

My first son was 3 months old when I stumbled upon this method. I was surfing around on the Internet and found an article on elimination training in infancy. I read part of it but was so upset by it that I turned off the computer. My upset was due to skepticism about being able to do this within the confines of our culture. My curiosity got the better of me, and I switched the computer back on and continued reading. Before reaching the end of the article, I stood up, went to Dakota's changing table, took his diaper off and said, "We're going to try something different. If you need to pee or poop, try and let me know. I'll try to understand you. If I don't seem to get it, try telling me another way. We're both going to make mistakes. We'll do this for one hour and see how it feels." I returned to the computer to read the rest of the article. Before I had finished, he wiggled, squirmed and grunted a bit. I took him to the bathroom, and he pooped for me. We continued doing it from that first day until he was finished with toilet training at 22 months.

In that first hour of trying the method, he pooped once and peed a few times. Then it was time for us to go to bed. I thought to myself that I had been lucky for that first hour but that I'd need to find out more about it the next day. That night I didn't put a diaper on him when we went to bed. When I woke up in the morning, I said to myself, "This is silly. It worked so I'm not going to *not* do it, now that we can do it."

For about the first month, I carried him around with a flannel under his bottom, until I learned his signals. Up to 4 months of age, I kept a little bucket in the room with us, but then he started letting me know far enough in advance that I could take him to the bathroom. He preferred going in the bathroom where he saw us use the toilet and soon refused to use the bucket anymore.

We had varying degrees of success over the months, depending on his mood. He was a pretty high-needs child. At times he was involved in teething or learning a skill and didn't pay attention. There were a few difficult days where we missed nearly every pee or poop. No matter what happened, it was always a cooperative effort between us, and I learned not to fear making mistakes. Some days we "hit the pot" 90% of the time; on other days just 75%. Either way, we were connecting all the time, and I loved it.

With my son, the communication was often by psychic means. This meant I had to be tuned in to him. It might sound strange, but I often heard the word "pee" in my mind when he had to pee or poop. It was very clear. Whenever I received that communication, I took him to the bathroom and he'd go. I don't communicate telepathically in other ways, so it was very hard for me to trust it.

My husband had the same experience with hearing "pee" in his mind. When Dakota got older, a very good friend of mine named Alice started co-parenting with us, and she had the same experience too. She would suddenly hear the word "pee" in her head, take him to pee and he'd go for her. For people who wonder whether or not babies are telepathic, we have anecdotal evidence that they are!

The communication with my son was not only psychic in terms of hearing a word, but I eventually realized that I was also *feeling* it in my body. I actually felt what his body was telling me I needed to do. It took a while to figure out what was happening because this feeling was not a feeling in my bladder. The level where his bladder was in relation to my body is where I felt it. For example, I felt a full bladder at my sternum when he was small. It took me a while to realize that he was communicating the impression of "This is what my body feels like, Mom. Can you help me do something about this?" As he got taller, the feeling moved down in my body. That's when I started to understand the feeling. When it got low enough to be felt in my abdomen, it felt like I needed to pee, but I knew I didn't need to. Then I'd hear him say "pee" in my head, and I understood that he was letting me know what his body felt like. I once read about an anthropologist who asked an African mother how she knew when her baby needed to go. The mother replied, "How do you know when you need to go?" I think this may be the origin of that quote, from the mother actually feeling her baby's full bladder.

Dakota signaled me in a number of other ways. I had the best results reading his signals when he was in the sling and when I was relaxed about the whole thing. I made the "pss pss" noise in an attempt to get him to vocally signal to me ahead of time. He started making this noise around 7 months, but only when we were out in public. He would also holler ("Mama, Mama!"), cry (usually only when waking up with a full bladder), crawl to the bathroom door or crawl to me and look at me. The times I missed getting him to the bathroom were when I was not focused—talking to someone, reading or otherwise not tuned in to Dakota. I know many other online mothers whose babies vocalize in some way to get their mothers' attention before they can speak.

Sometimes Dakota signaled and I took him to the sink where he would try to go but nothing happened. If I turned on the water, the sound usually helped him pee. If that didn't work, I kept his pants off, walked around for a minute or two, then returned to the sink and asked if he wanted to try again. I think this is a more relaxed approach than spending a lot of time waiting at the sink, which could create performance anxiety.

My husband helped with toilet training. When he wanted to focus on tuning in to Dakota, he was 75–80% able to know when Dakota needed to go. My husband doesn't like the type of deep, intimate communication needed for this, so the first few months he had a lot of wet T-shirts and sometimes used diapers. It challenged his emotional intimacy issues. It is much more emotionally intimate to be in communication with a baby than to just stick a diaper on him. I think that is another reason why people resist this so intensely. Diapering is a lot of work, yet most people prefer to do that than be in tune with their children. It makes me think that we have an entire culture that is invested in being dissociated.

Once my husband got over that, he was glad to help. He griped about it occasionally, but what let me know that he liked it was that he told his friends about it and was proud that we weren't diapering our baby. When I say "proud," I mean proud that we were listening to and meeting our son's needs.

The position we used was to hold him under the thighs, behind the knees in front of the bathroom sink. When he got old enough that his poops didn't easily go down the bathroom sink, we held him the same way over the toilet. In fact, that became so familiar to him that he still usually climbs on the toilet facing the back of the toilet.

When he started scooting and crawling, things got a little confusing. He peed on the floor a lot without giving any cues. We figured out that the pressure on his tummy and bladder made it difficult to control his bladder. We placed him on a mat during this phase. In the same vein, sometimes he would be playing on his belly, ask to pee but when we got to the bathroom, nothing happened. I think that when we picked him up, the pressure on his belly was reduced, and he no longer felt the urge to pee.

In general, the only time I diapered him was to take him shopping. I always asked him to let me know if he had to pee and assured him that I'd take him to a nearby place, remove the diaper and let him go. When we got home half an hour later, his diaper would be dry. This was a baby who normally peed every 10 minutes. This told me right away that he had an ability to hold it if he wanted, at least up to a certain point. Once we saw that he was holding his pee in an effort to avoid going in an unfamiliar setting, we constantly encouraged him, "Don't hold it if you really have to go."

As for travel, we cloth-diapered him and gave him the option of letting us know when he needed to go. He stays dry when he naps. This has always been the case, so we scheduled traveling around his naps. Whenever we got to a rest stop, we took him to pee. Very rarely would we arrive somewhere and find he had a wet diaper. This concerned us, and I kept telling him that if he needed to go in the diaper, he should go. We didn't take a potty along with us. He was familiar with peeing in sinks and public bathrooms. I've also peed him into shrubbery outside shops. If people don't feel odd having their dog pee on an area of decorative landscaping, I let my son pee there.

By the age of 7 months, he had reasonable control. We didn't have to diaper him anymore to take him on a 30-minute trip to the grocery store. By 9½ months, he always told me if he had to go, unless he was teething, preoccupied or in a resistant phase of saying no to everything. At 11 months, he only peed about once an hour, and if we were outside or driving in the car, he was great about signaling me verbally. By 14 months, he took care of all his own pooping. Of course, I had to wipe his bottom, but he walked to the potty and sat down on his own. Sometimes he said "poop" to call me to come and sit next to him.

We had a small, low potty that he could get on and off by himself. He felt secure on it. He hated the traditional larger potties. They were very unstable and scary for him. We got him a BabyBjörn® low plastic molded potty, and he loved it.

We took a casual approach to nighttime. If I didn't care about him wetting the bed, I didn't wake up. Until he was 6½ months, I kept a little bucket by the bed for when he needed to pee at night. After that, I took him to the bathroom sink. Sometimes he didn't wake up fully, and I didn't disturb his slumber. He just peed in the sink and fell right back to sleep. I hardly woke up either and certainly never felt sleep deprived. By 12 months, he was capable of communicating his nighttime needs to me and holding it until I woke up and got him to the bathroom. He did well at this most of the time before he was a year old, but by 12 months, we didn't have a wet bed unless I was sleeping really heavily. I have found that babies don't go in their sleep unless they are extremely relaxed or in a very deep sleep. I discovered early on that when Dakota woke up, it was because he needed to pee, not because he wanted to nurse or was ready to wake up. I've cross-checked this with many mothers online and they all agree that what seems to wake a baby up at night is a full bladder. The baby will fall back to sleep if you nurse him back to sleep.

Around the age of 11 months, Dakota went through a really intense potty strike for 6 weeks. He stopped signaling, and when we took him to the sink to pee, he arched his back and yelled. During that time, we diapered him. That was the only time he wore diapers throughout the day. He didn't like it at all. He preferred going bare-bottomed or wearing pants because they were less restrictive than a cloth diaper.

I found that babies only go on strike if there is an emotional issue involved. It is your job to figure out what is bothering your baby. Since babies cannot speak or physically do much, they sometimes communicate by *not* doing something—like a nursing strike to let you know that erupting teeth are painful.

When he started his potty strike, I tried using positive reinforcement, but soon found that it caused an intensification of any resistance he was having. I'm sure I prolonged his strike by 3 weeks by praising and rewarding him. On the rare occasions, about once a day, where he communicated and we got to the sink on time, I got excited and told him it was great that he had communicated and that I really appreciated it. That was followed by a day of running away from me and peeing on the rug or in his diaper. I posted this dilemma online and got a reply that said that maybe he was perceiving my praise as pressure. We soon learned that Dakota felt manipulated by praise unless he initiated it. This applied to all aspects of his life. If he wanted to celebrate the accomplishment of something, he ran to us clapping and we clapped with him.

I finally found the cause of his strike. He wanted to use the big toilet instead of a potty. Once I figured it out, he started signaling again. He liked the adult toilet so much that at first he often signed when he hardly had any pee in his bladder.

My good friend Alice was living with us when Dakota was born. She didn't have a chance to help with toileting until he was about 14 months old. This was when they were bonded and close enough that I could go out for an hour and leave Dakota with her. It clicked for them immediately, and Alice never got peed on. When we were both in a room together, we both heard "pee" in our heads when Dakota needed to go!

He didn't start taking over his own peeing until about 20 months. I think it irritated him that he had to pee so frequently. He was very busy and didn't like stopping what he was doing. We moved to Seattle when he was 22 months old. We gave him free reign of one of the bathrooms where he used the adult toilet. He has been potty trained ever since.

## Second Son

I started at birth with my second son Ian. I'm much more relaxed this time. It's the same with other things you experience with your first and second child. You are more relaxed with everything, like nursing or when they fall down. I literally had never held a baby before I had Dakota. I assume tribal people don't go through this because they are around children all the time, but our culture isolates adults from children.

Starting with a newborn gave my second son more confidence in me than my first. Dakota went through 3 months of me not having a clue. One day, when Ian was 3 or 4 days old and nursing, I looked down at him and said, "You need to pee, don't you?" He unlatched and looked at me. Then he latched again, then unlatched. He decided he wasn't willing to interrupt nursing to pee, so he just peed on my leg, and he knew I didn't mind.

It felt like a cooperative arrangement with Ian right from the beginning, instead of me saying at 3 months, "I'm sorry. I completely missed the boat. Can you help me figure out how to do this?" This is why Dakota had to "yell in my head" to get my attention. With Ian, I right away felt like "We are doing this together, and if we have off days, we're having off days together." I'd have days where I just couldn't deal with it and I'd tell him, and we'd take a break.

If Ian is teething and peeing on me, I just think, "Oh, you're teething." When he was smaller, I'd just put a flannel under him and knew we'd be back to it again the next day. It was the same when he went through his learning-to-crawl phase. It took him a long time to learn to crawl. It took about 2 months, and during that time, his message was, "Do not bug me about elimination communication!" And it didn't bother me. "Okay, fine. I know we'll just pick this up again in a month." And right now, he's learning to walk and we're doing the same thing again. If he's in-arms, he never pees on me unless he is sick or if I just consumed dairy products. If I pick him up and he doesn't want to go, he isn't as intense as Dakota. Ian doesn't scream; he just stretches his legs out to tell me "no" and I put him down. I know that in another few months, we'll be 99 percent potty trained.

People often say, "It's your second baby. You must not have any messes now since you're so good at it." I tell them that, on the contrary, because I'm not sitting around stressing over it and because I've made up my mind that if we were living in an indigenous environment with dirt floors, babies on the floor wouldn't have any need to signal—and that's why they don't like to signal when they are on the floor or learning how to walk—I just don't worry about the times he pees when he's down crawling or learning to walk. I pay a lot of attention to him when he's in-arms or we're in bed, and I trust that in the next few months, he'll start coming to me more and more when he's on the floor.

People striving for perfection might want to rethink things. A more experienced mother is actually more relaxed about elimination communication and trusts that the process is going to work. I have a slogan: "Even ec done imperfectly works."

With Ian, I don't hear the word "pee" in my mind when he needs to go. The same goes for my husband, Alice and another family member who have helped pee Ian. We've all just had a sense that "it's time for Ian to go." I tell them that if they think he needs to go, that's him saying he needs to go. "If the thought suddenly occurs to you, that's his message, and it's not actually coming from you." In this way, they have been able to get him to pee when they have been tuned in.

The sensation of having a bladder in my chest is gone with Ian too. With Dakota, any communication I got from him was strong, "Dakota to Mom. This is communication," whether it was the sensation in my chest or hearing "pee" in my mind. This makes sense because Dakota's intensity is turned up much higher than Ian's. It makes sense that Dakota's message would make a huge impression. With Ian, the communication has always been much softer and subtler.

I think the fact that the communication is different is due to me. My first baby had to work really hard to train me. The second baby knew the receptors were already working, "Mom has already got this figured out. I don't need to work as hard."

## Elimination Communication

I found this method very easy, far superior to any of the alternatives. It was easier than the mechanical work of diapering and washing diapers. I much preferred spending time focusing on my sons and reading their cues to dealing with diapers and laundry. In addition, it was good for the environment, cost free and perfectly compatible with our lifestyle. It promoted all the positive aspects of attached child rearing that I wanted to include. It went along with breastfeeding, meeting my children's needs, carrying them in a sling and not leaving them alone with another caregiver in infancy.

My general approach is to do anything I can for my sons to take us in a direction of how we evolved. I believe that the more I can do to make their development closer to what their genetic blueprint is, the better chance they have at being fulfilled in life. I believe a child is born with a set of instincts based on where we were thousands of years ago before we started developing culture. The instincts have not had a chance to catch up. Infant toilet training is one of those instinctual behaviors. It's not a matter of survival, but this doesn't mean it's not important. A child communicates elimination needs from birth. The fact that a child communicates this from birth tells me it is important, that the communication happens for a reason. Babies communicate their need to eat from birth. They communicate their need to be held from the moment they arrive. They also communicate their need to pee and poop from the moment they arrive. If you leave a need unmet or unacknowledged, you cause a person to shut down in that area. This can happen at any age, but especially with a very emotionally defenseless infant. It's no wonder that children conventionally diapered and potty trained have a terrible time toilet training because they have had to literally shut down the part of their brain that communicates their need to eliminate.

This is a topic that you can't freely discuss with strangers on most Internet forums. People don't understand the method so you tend to really get beat up on most public forums. When I posted a message saying I wasn't diapering my 4-month-old son, people posted some very negative and strange replies. They said I was punitively teaching my son to go on command or follow a time schedule. This is the only way most people can see it. They don't have any other frame of reference. They are told by their pediatricians that children don't have the neural pathways or muscular control to hold their bladder until at least 2½. If you buy that, then you have to assume that people who are doing this are abusing their children. I think this is part of the resistance to this method. Another argument against it is that some think it's just a fad.

Even after you tell people this is baby-led, many still think it is something artificial you are forcing on the baby. They can't understand that it is part of an infant's needs set, along with being warm. They say, "This isn't really learning. This is the infant training the parent," which is not such a bad thing. Babies train us when to feed them and train us when to hold them. What's wrong with letting them train us when to take them to pee?

In my first son's early infancy, I was very careful about not deliberately reading a lot of things on infant care. I knew I would disagree with the mainstream. When I started reflecting on diapers, I thought, "What if this were my partner and he suddenly couldn't move his arms and legs and couldn't speak. Would I make him sit in a diaper until I felt like changing him?" No! Just like I wouldn't force him to be fed on a schedule. Obviously that would be inhumane and disrespectful. I agree that it is very much a matter of training the parent since a baby can't get up and take care of elimination needs by himself. As parents, we are supposed to get up and do this for our babies.

Almost everyone I know personally has been supportive, especially after they get a little education and realize I've never forced my sons to do something they would not otherwise do. The only difference is that we communicate and they peed somewhere other than in a diaper. Most people do not believe this kind of thing is possible, and then they see it happen. Everyone I know has soon come to think of it as normal. Friends who aren't parents and who had never given child rearing much thought hear about this method, and it clicks. In the past, they had always thought diapers were fine. Now they see a baby and think it's awful that a baby has to sit in its own mess.

Of course, when you think it would be fun to show it off, you get peed on. It's useless to try and have babies do potty tricks because they will pee in your lap if you do. It must be an unwritten rule to always pee in mom's lap when she is trying to impress her mother-in-law.

On my web site, I advocate elimination communication as part of evolutionary behavior. I've had mostly positive feedback on the site, but one lady was upset at this idea. I think it is because if you believe in evolution, you have to work hard to justify not using this method.

There is also a lot of advice offered on the web site. For example, if anyone comes to me with an ec problem that can't be resolved by taking their baby to a different location or using a different position, especially if the problem started right around the time the baby started eating solid foods, I recommend they try eliminating dairy and wheat from their diet for a month to see if it helps. A lady on the ec list was doing well for 7 months and then suddenly her baby was no longer responsive, so she went back to full-time diaper for 6 months. If she tried to pee him holding him under the thighs, which flexes the pelvis, he would scream. It was very painful for him. Having had irritable bowel and irritable bladder from dairy allergies, I can totally relate to this. When he was 13 months old, I convinced her to change her diet. Within 48 hours, her son was peeing and pooping exactly as he had been at age 7 months. It was astonishing. There are a lot of kids who are allergic to wheat and dairy, but it goes mostly undiagnosed

On the e-mail list, we discuss elimination communication topics and share our joys and insight. It's helpful to learn things such as fresh baby pee is basically sterile. With strictly breastfed babies, pee has no bacteria as it comes out of the body, unless you're sick. It's full of discarded nutrients. The moment it hits the air, it starts growing bacteria, which is why it starts to stink and is also why wool is such a lovely substance to waterproof your bed with. It's also helpful to use wool pants over a diaper with no cover. It won't allow bacteria or fungus to grow, so it doesn't smell once the urine is dry.

I've inspired hundreds of mothers to use elimination communication, if not full time, at least part time. They have all found it easy.  Many found out about it after their babies were born. Some started relatively late, one at 9 months and another at 11 months, and they did fine. I think it's okay to start this late if you are gentle, neutral and relaxed. I think the chances of success for late-starters depend a lot on how much their babies' communication has already been respected, as well as how the babies have handled not having that need met earlier. One little boy who started at 9 months had days where he would take a diaper to his mother and want to be diapered. The other days, he did not want to be diapered at all. His mother paid attention to his cues and followed his lead. He's 2 now and toilet trained.

Use this link to visit Rosie's website and "elimination communication" yahoogroups e-mail list: http://seafish.freeyellow.com/index.html or if it becomes outdated, use an Internet search engine to find these websites.

# chapter 8

# a mom &
# two nannies

S herri Tomlin is a chiropractor living in San Jose, California. Her husband
Robert Martines is also a chiropractor. They have their own practices.
Sherri first heard about infant potty training when their son Lucas was
7 months old. Here's what Sherri had to say in 2000:

I was in an attachment parenting playgroup and one day one of the
mothers started talking about infant potty training. The first thing I thought
was that the woman was crazy. She demonstrated how the method worked
with her little boy, and I found it interesting. I went home and thought of all
the reasons why it wouldn't work for me: because I work, because I use

babysitters, because my husband might object, etc. I had lots of doubts, but this is the way I always process things, by working through my doubts.

Several days later, I woke up, went into the kitchen and got a bowl to see how it would fit Lucas. I wondered if he would accept or reject it. He was seven and a half months old. I had been told that six months was the maximum age that I should start this, but I also had understood that it needs to be done before babies disconnect from their sense of elimination. Being a chiropractor, I understand how the nerves and the nervous system work and that it's extremely different from individual to individual, no matter what the books say or what other people's experiences are. There are always exceptions or unusual circumstances. The way I started potty training Lucas was to just test a bowl to see how it would work. The bowl was from a set of nesting plastic bowls from the kitchen. I sat him on the middle-sized bowl in my lap since that was the way my friend had held her baby and also because the bowl wasn't stable on its own. Lucas didn't object, and we just went from there.

At first, I tried to get all his pees and poos in the bowl, even at night. I wasn't sure if he was "too old" to start infant potty training and wanted to communicate by my actions that I was doing everything I could to help him stay connected with this natural ability.

Before we had started the potty training, Lucas used to cry frequently during the night. When I started getting up and putting him on the potty, it quieted him down. I realized his crying was his way of letting me know he didn't like to be wet, and in this way, I knew for sure that he was still connected with the sensation that he needed to go potty even though he was over the recommended threshold to begin infant potty training. He confirmed that I wasn't too late to use this method with him.

I got up at night with him for a month or two, then decided I didn't want him to wake up crying, so I started using a disposable diaper at night since it suppresses the feeling of wetness and could last through his wettest nights.

I still tried to get the pees and poos during the day for a while and even now I still get quite a few. I know if I put more time into it that we'd get more pees in the potty, but lately we're mainly concentrating on the poos. He's 12½ months old now and usually goes when he gets up in the morning, once in mid-morning and then again in the afternoon.

Lucas has two caregivers or babysitters. The caregivers happened to already be good friends of each other when I first met them. They even live on the same street. One of them is a nanny and the other is a school teacher, so they are both very experienced in working with children. One of them takes Lucas three mornings and the other takes him two afternoons, for a total of five half days a week. When I first met them, I told them about infant potty training, but they were reluctant to try it.

I knew I could do infant toilet training with or without the help of the caregivers. I understand that even tiny babies know the difference between individuals and will test different individuals in different ways. They'll do one thing with Grandma that they won't do with Mom. If the babysitters wouldn't use the method, I planned to tell Lucas, "When you're not with Mommy, just go in the diaper." Then when he was with me again, I'd say, "Tell Mommy when you need to go." I verbalize with him because that's how I communicate best, even if he's picking it up on a different level—from my tone of voice or body language.

I got the book *Trickle Treat* and immediately gave it to the caregivers— I hadn't even read the book yet! At first, they didn't want to commit to it. After some days, one of them came to me and confessed that they had been doing it for three days. They talk to each other every evening. They had been discussing it with each other and had decided to give it a try.

Lucas works well with the caregivers. In fact, sometimes he is easier with them than with me. I found out that their original hesitation was that they feared they wouldn't do it right. They wanted to do it perfectly. They feared they would make a mistake or somehow harm the child. They discussed it with each other and decided that either they would both do it or neither of them would do it. They thought it would be wrong for one of them to do it and not the other. They thought it would be okay if I did it and they didn't, but they saw each other as a unit. I advised them to do their best, have fun with it and above all to have no "judgment" about it.

They are very proud of their success. They keep a notebook for me. Everyday I get a page of detailed notes of what went on the during the day, and this includes the potty progress. They write if he peed or pooed in the potty or if they missed getting him to the potty on time.

We used the little plastic bowl until one day someone dropped it and cracked it. Then I bought a potty. Since it had a stable base, I could let Lucas sit on the potty on the floor instead of in my lap. He had no trouble sitting on it. I kept my arms around him at first. It was like I was the one who needed to go through the infant process instead of him.

I've noticed that sometimes he'll pee three times within five minutes. He doesn't always release everything the first time he pees. Sometimes he shivers when he's peeing on the potty. When he shivers while he's nursing, I realize he just peed. I've talked with other mothers who have noticed that their babies shiver when they pee too, but it's too late to get them on the potty at that point.

I have had troubles here and there, as do most parents using any type of toilet training. At each new stage, there is something for me and Lucas to work out, or for my caregivers to work out. Above all, I listen to Lucas, and not other people, about what's going to work with him. I figure things out and go with the process without any judgment about it. We live day to day and don't use percentages or anything like that. Sometimes we have several perfect days in a row, and some days it is difficult. On difficult days I try to focus on not getting frustrated. I strive to just accept the frustration and feel it fully so I can let it go and move on.

Some say that this method is too inconvenient for Americans. My response is that I didn't have a child for my convenience. I'm not potty training Lucas for my convenience. When I started doing this and telling people about it, there seemed to be more doubt from other people. The more I gained certainty about it, the less I would hear negative things from other people. I explain that it's something that third world countries do and that we used to do a long time ago. They drop their jaw, open their eyes and say, "Yeah, I see."

I was raised with a lot of wilderness camping, so I've used some of that with taking care of Lucas in that I'll take the potty anywhere. I wish I had trained him earlier to go over a toilet in a public bathroom because he won't, so I take his potty with me and use it in the back of our sport utility vehicle. I open up the back and say, "Okay, Lucas, we're going camping now." And I put him on the potty in the back of the car. At first it bothered me when people looked but now it doesn't.

One time we were at a restaurant and Lucas was grunting so I took him out to the car in the middle of the dinner and left my husband at the table. Lucas pooed in the potty, then I took him back and was feeding him in the restaurant when he started to grunt again. I took him back out to the potty in the car again. I started wondering if I should be interrupting my dinner and leaving my husband alone in the restaurant for long stretches. I wondered what others were thinking. Out in the car, we had success with the potty. Later I heard my husband talking to other people and telling them that we were doing this method and that he didn't care if he was in a traffic jam in the middle of the San Francisco Bay Area, he would pull over on the side of the road where everyone could see what he was doing, but he was going to take care of his son and do what was right for him. I understood then that he didn't feel inconvenienced by me leaving the dinner table at the restaurant. Interruptions like this don't happen very often but when they do, I don't mind.

Lucas started to crawl relatively late, around 10½ months. Since then, he has been more interested in everything in his environment, in exploring things, and it has become more difficult to keep him on the pot. Sometimes I put him in a diaper, then set a timer for five minutes and put him back on.

Sometimes when he won't sit on the potty I take him outside and let him wander around naked. That seems to give him a little space, time to deal with things and then he goes back to the potty. It's really a dance—a pushing and pulling. Sometimes it's a struggle. Sometimes when we're dancing we step on each other's feet, but most of the time we're having fun with it.

One thing that helps him stay on the potty recently is lots of snuggles and hugs. I kneel down and play with him, do pat-a-cake and hug him a lot.

His cues for pooing are (1) he grunts, (2) he cries, (3) he's quiet and trancelike or (4) he crawls behind furniture. Rather than going to someone, he goes away from us and gets very quiet, which is unusual for him since he's usually very vocal. The babysitter says he's hiding from her. I think he just wants to be alone for a minute while he poos.

I think Lucas has fairly good control over his muscles at this point because sometimes he'll sit on the potty and wait for me to put his diaper on, then immediately go in the diaper. He only does it for one elimination, then we're fine for a while. When he does this, I don't feel like it's something he is doing to me. He is experimenting. When I hear the term "testing," some people think the child is doing something in order to see what you'll do in response to it. Well yes, that happens because I'm part of the environment, but he's testing loads of things besides me. He is testing his nerves, his muscles, his sensations of what it's like to not go in the potty and to go in the diaper. Then he makes a decision and frankly if he decides to go in the diaper for the next month, that's his decision. If it's because I'm not paying attention, then I'll work harder but if it's because of something he's choosing, then I'm fine with it.

I don't praise him a lot when he goes potty. I try not to praise him about much. My husband praises him, but I don't. I just simply state fact. When he started crawling, I didn't clap and say, "Yay, good boy! You're so wonderful." I just stated, "You're crawling," and he gets from my tone of voice that I'm excited about it. I'm not a robot about it. When he falls, I don't make a big thing out of it. I look at him and say, "Oh, you fell down." He hardly cries when he falls down, compared to other kids I've seen. When he goes in the potty, I state fact, "You went pee pee in the potty," or "You went poo in the potty," or if he does a big poo, I'll say so, "Oh, you did a big poo."

My mother-in-law is a pediatric RN and thinks this is wonderful. She is very open-minded in many ways. My mother also thinks infant potty training is interesting. She says that my grandmother would be proud of me. When I started doing this, my mother said, "Oh, my goodness, this is what my mother tried to do with my children." So I found out that my grandmother, whose mother was German, had put me on the potty whenever I visited her when I was an infant, but it only happened occasionally because she lived in another town. My grandmother didn't see it as a special method, so she couldn't explain it to my mother. Even though my mother likes the method, she is hesitant to put Lucas on the potty. If he has to go, she brings him to me and I put him on. This is helpful. The only time she'll put him on the potty is when I am not around.

We travel to a lot of seminars with Lucas, and of course I take the potty with us. Our flights are usually short, just an hour. The seminars are in the hotel, so he's with me there. I find potty training easy in the hotel.

Unfortunately, people have been told you get Freudian results if you potty train a baby too early. My reply is that it's me who is being trained, and I'm doing something that is still being used in the majority of the world. In this country, even the most conservative people have an understanding of going back to what we used to do before technology took over.

I feel wonderful about this method. I'm really happy we're doing it. It fits in with the lifestyle we chose before we even knew about Attachment Parenting or infant potty training. We were already doing the family bed and carrying him a lot instead of putting him in a stroller. Since he spends about four hours a day with a babysitter, I feel it's important for me to hold him a lot when I'm with him. I know from my chiropractic training about the nervous system that brain development is enhanced when babies are held and moved about. I think the most important aspect of the potty training is the spiritual side.

There are three main ways that I know he needs to go potty. First, timing. A lot of it is based on timing, putting him on the potty just after a meal or when we get up in the morning. Second, communication. He signals me in different ways like grunting, crying or crawling over to get me, although

*Robert Martines*

Lucas takes a pee . . . in the family SUV

sometimes he crawls to me right after he has peed in his pants; I take this to mean he is uncomfortable and wants to be changed. The third element I use is my intuition. For example, one day I was leaving the office. It was late in the day and I was just pulling out when I had a thought, "I wonder if Lucas needs to go poo? When was the last time I pooed him?" I almost did something that is typical of me, which is to say to myself, "Oh, he's fine. I'll do it when I get home." I almost drove out the driveway. That was the moment I realized, "Wait a minute. That's the little voice in me, talking to me." The more I listen to that little voice, the clearer it becomes. I backed up into the parking lot, nursed Lucas, then put him on the potty in the back of the truck, and he went. I had a successful outcome from listening to that little voice.

I think listening to that voice is important. The times that I have missed getting him to the potty on time and I feel frustrated with myself are times when I'm on the telephone, doing the laundry or driving somewhere. In other words, something is distracting me, and I'm not listening to that little voice. I have to listen to that little voice about many things, not just elimination. That voice really connects you with what you need to do in life. This is what I love about this method and from being with my playgroup. They have helped me be more certain about what I'm doing, and I don't need to defend myself when I'm with the group. It's like an island of peace. It's not that society attacks us for doing unusual things, but people are curious and question me, and I always have to explain things. In the playgroup, I don't have to explain myself, so I feel a lot of support in that way.

When a new idea comes along, people go through four phases. Christopher Columbus went through this. First he said the world was round and that he could travel around the world. People said he was crazy. After a while, they looked at his information and said, "That's interesting. I wonder if it will work for him?" They funded Columbus and said, "Go ahead." They saw him sail around the world and thought, "I wonder if that will work for me?" Then some of them got on a ship and tried it. Eventually society said, "I'm glad we thought of this." This is how a new idea becomes accepted. It goes from "You're nuts" to "I see it works for you" to "I wonder if it will work for me?" to being accepted as normal.

I understand this firsthand as a chiropractor. Society and individuals are going through those phases now in regards to what I do every day for people in my office. I went through that process in a matter of days with this elimination method. I thought my friend was nuts when she first told me about infant potty training. Now I think of her as a genius.

This method isn't for everyone, but people should at least know it's a viable option. If it sounds right for them, they will try it. In trying, they will succeed or fail. If they succeed, great! If they fail . . . no harm done, but it's certainly worth a try!

# chapter 9

# a physician speaks out

*Dr. Lauri Nandyal graduated from medical school in Cincinnati in 1989 and completed her family practice residency in 1992. She worked in rural Ohio for 4 years until 1996, doing full-scope family practice including obstetrics and, consequently, a lot of pediatrics. Lauri has three girls of her own, ages 8 years, 5 years and 1 year old. Since her third child was born, she has reduced her clinical work in order to stay home with her family. Here is what the doctor had to report in 2000.*

I didn't learn about this method of toilet training in time to use with my first two girls. It was merely by chance that I learned about it when my third child was about 2 weeks old. I was chatting with my neighbor, who happens to be from India, and she told me that she had toilet trained her children from early infancy. I was completely flabbergasted to hear this. As a physician, I had never even given this type of thing a moment's consideration. Even in my many travels before motherhood, I was oblivious to the practice of infant toileting. It's just one of those things that doesn't enter your consciousness until you're a parent. Plus, in medical school we're taught that it's physically impossible to toilet train an infant, and this is what we tell our patients. So the concept really took me by surprise. Needless to say, I set to work right away and was thrilled to learn that my baby could hold her bowel movements and later her urine.

My neighbor told me how she had toilet trained her children. Her first two were born and raised in India where she was under the wing of her mother, sisters and sisters-in-law and had their help and guidance. Her third child was born in the United States where she was on her own with toilet training. Her method involved holding her baby on her feet. After a feeding, she would sit on the floor or the bed and prop her baby on her feet over a newspaper or a diaper, and in response, he would "perform." She further mentioned that in India, at least in more traditional families, mothers carry or hold their babies much of the time, and babies don't wear diapers. One way mothers stay dry is to take their babies to the toilet every 45–60 minutes and prompt them to go. They may squat the babies in a corner in the bathroom or outside and make a "sssss" noise to cue them to go.

My neighbor in Ohio used the same sound with her children. I haven't had a great deal of success with my baby responding to any particular sound for urination. Also, I don't have the energy to undress my baby from several layers of clothes, socks, etc., and put her on the toilet that often. I feel good if I manage to take her every hour and a half. Aside from the initial explanation by my neighbor, my learning process consisted mainly of on-the-job training. I didn't find any books about this until my baby was about 9 months old. At that time, I read a chapter in a book on toilet training which mentioned "other methods" and gave some credence to early toilet training but did not really encourage it. That was the extent of the literature I found until Laurie Boucke's *Trickle Treat*.

Since I really didn't feel comfortable with the actual method my neighbor described and since I figured that the procedure would eventually lead to using a toilet anyway, I decided to start there—that is, using the toilet—from the beginning. The position I use with my daughter involves me squatting in front of the toilet or else sitting on a small stool placed at the front of it. I prop my elbows on my knees and hold her securely with a hand under each armpit. In this way I was able to support her head until she had good head control. She is in a squatting position over the toilet, facing me, with her bottom hanging over the toilet bowl. This position is all she has ever known, and she has never seemed frightened, as some might expect. I always have two hands on her and have always provided adequate, comfortable and secure support. One word of warning: Little girls can "shoot" when they urinate. If my baby is not aimed downward, she'll pee on me and the toilet seat. I have to lean her a little forward to pee straight down. If she doesn't really need to go, she may resist me positioning her. I've come to trust her knowing when she's done too. She'll straighten out her legs and stand upright. Occasionally, I've hurried her off before this signal, only to be sorry later. Also, in this way, I don't have additional dirty diapers, apart from the ones she wears between toilet visits. We use diapers between potty sessions, mainly because I can't find any training pants that are small enough to fit her. (The smallest are size two. I guess they figure no one here buys size one, but they must be selling them somewhere!) At night we use a diaper, to spare the bed from accidents. She may awaken during the night indicating she needs to go, but I can't arouse her enough for her to happily use the potty, so the diaper is there just in case. When she goes in the toilet, I usually say "good girl" or give her a kiss. I don't jump up and down with excitement. I did at first because I was so surprised, but now I'm a bit more matter of fact, just smile and say "good job" or something like that.

I started by concentrating on bowel movements rather than urination. I don't recall her ever soiling a diaper at night. Early on it was a part of her routine to stay clean at night, perhaps because we started this practice so early. This encouraged me to take her to the toilet for her daytime bowel movements. I waited a while after a feeding, anywhere from 10 to 30 minutes, then held her over the toilet. I was amazed the first time it worked. In fact, I didn't even realize she had gone because BM is so liquidy at that age. I suppose I was expecting more straining to accompany it. Her timing at first was pretty unpredictable since I breastfeed her. I take her to the toilet at least five or six times a day, usually after a feeding. At first, we had success about one out of three times. We eventually got her BM routine down really well. Since about 6 weeks of age, she has rarely soiled a diaper even while awake.

When she was about 6 months old, I realized I could also TIAN (toilet in advance of need) to try and get her to urinate in the toilet. She had started being dry upon awakening from naps. So Mommy became trained to take baby to the potty after naps and by keeping an eye on the clock. I rely on a sense of how long it has been since her last elimination, and sometimes

I have the presence of mind to pay attention to her signals. Her signals aren't terribly blatant yet. She doesn't make a specific sound or noise that I've been able to discern as a signal to me about her need to pee. With bowel movements, she "toots" or passes a little gas, and this lets me know she has to go. About 90% of the time, a BM is preceded by a toot of some kind, but not all toots are followed by a bowel movement so it gets a little tricky. If she toots and hasn't had a bowel movement, I try to get her to the toilet. If she has more than one a day, I may neglect to act on that signal. Fussiness may be another one of the ways she signals, but fussiness can mean a number of things, so again it can be tricky.

The point is that even though her signals aren't always obvious, I do feel she tries to signal me. I suspect that some of the cries and discomfort expressed by my older two girls were ways they were trying to let me know they needed to go. I was in another world with regard to toilet training then and didn't pay attention to their cues. We think that when a baby cries it is because she is already wet or dirty. But maybe it's because she doesn't want to wet herself and she is trying to signal us to do something about it.

As for our prompting the baby to go, we grunt or make a bearing-down noise to cue bowel movements. We also have been trying some baby sign language. We may hold, pinch or wrinkle our nose, as a sort of "stinky" or smelly sign, to ask her if she has to go. For urinating, we make a water-flowing sound. Lately, she sounds like she's trying to say "go" and sometimes pats her diaper to let me know.

Parents who define toileting readiness by verbal cues or signs from their babies announcing that they need to go may be disappointed at first. The way my baby communicates is too rudimentary for this. There are times where we miss—I'm too distracted and don't listen to her signals, or we are out and can't get her to the toilet. Other times I misread her, take her to the toilet but she doesn't have to go. It also depends on whether I have the time to take her first thing in the morning and what solids she has eaten previously. They change her pattern somewhat. If she drinks apple juice, she has more frequent bowel movements. To do this, you just have to learn your child's biological time-clock and practice patience.

When our daughter was 9 months old, we spent 3 weeks in India. My husband is from Andhra Pradesh, India. While there, I interviewed my sisters-in-law about infant toilet training. My husband was unaware of how he had been toilet trained in infancy. He was the last of 10 children and since this isn't something that most fathers do with their babies anyway, he was not familiar with this method. Early one morning, my baby seemed to be very uncomfortable. Her diaper was totally dry, so I figured she might be signaling to let me know she needed to go to the toilet. I raced her to the bathroom and just barely got her there on time. She really let loose as soon as I held her in position. Up until that point, I hadn't given her credit for being consciously continent. She had been dry during the day for several days, and I now realized she was indeed aware and trying to communicate. I don't know if there was a consciousness that awoke in her sooner than that or if it was my projecting on her what I was hoping she could consciously do. The pattern of displaying discomfort before needing to go has happened more frequently since our trip abroad, and as soon as I get her on the toilet, she usually goes. I definitely feel that my daughter has some control, or else she would just go in her diaper without first signaling her discomfort.

Here in America we have certain societal norms that are more restrictive than in many other societies. For example, regarding breastfeeding in public, only lately can American women feel relatively at ease about nursing in public. If we were as liberal about public toileting as they are in many parts of the world, we'd really get ourselves in trouble. However, I think that public sanitation is a very good thing and is to be thanked for most of our public health advances in the West. A downside of the Western lifestyle with respect to practicing infant toileting is that we raise our children pretty much in isolation. In India and many other places, at least before industrialization, they raised their babies in a community setting, and mothers had help. It makes a big difference. It gets lonely here, and it isn't easy to toilet train an infant, and run a house, cook, chauffeur and supervise older siblings and do all the other things we'd like to do, but if you believe in it, it's a great thing to do for baby, parent and mother earth.

Sure, this method seems inconvenient. Some days I dedicate an hour to the potty if you add it all up. It's just another thing to think about, and our society is too busy, too distracted with so many things to do. My reasoning is that we have to deal with our babies' bottoms one way or another, and we can do it right from the beginning or postpone the process and have to re-educate the child later when it may be a bigger hassle. We can't change this pattern unless we really have the will to change. It's a mother's individual decision. I don't feel badly if someone honestly admits she is too busy to do this. I think, though, if more people really understood the impact on the environment and the potential harm it can do to children sitting around in wet diapers or by exposing children to chemicals like dioxin for so long, parents might be more motivated to try this. As a physician, if I see a mother whose baby has diaper rash, I'm able to prod her a little and recommend the child be in cloth or "flapping in the breeze" or that something

"new and different" be done like infant pottying. There has to be a motiva-
tion to change behavior. Our society doesn't make it easy. Paper diapers are
just too darn convenient . . . at quite a price.

I pooh-pooh the stories about psychological damage resulting from infant toileting. I have read the comments of Freudian psychologists and think
the concern about trauma has only to do with the coercive way early toilet
training was practiced in the early 1900s. Back then, folks were encouraged
to tie their kids to potty chairs and got angry at them if they didn't perform.
Of course, that was a warped approach. Spending time with your child and
playing with her cannot be harmful even if it's on a potty. Obviously, I never
leave my baby alone on the potty at this age. If my daughter is tired of sitting on the toilet, I quit. I never force it on her. My baby enjoys spending
time with me wherever we are. I strongly feel that this method cannot harm
my baby any more, and likely much less, than the customary Western way
that I used with my older two whom I began retraining around the age of 2
years. I'm sure they sensed the frustration I tried so hard to hide when they
had toileting accidents or wet the bed. Now I realize that I was asking them
to follow a new set of rules after I had miseducated them from infancy
about where bodily waste belongs. I dared to blame them when I was the
one who decided to change the rules, as one must do when using conventional toilet training. I regret missing the opportunity to educate them properly from the beginning.

Western medicine teaches that it is not possible neurologically for babies to be toilet trained in infancy. I don't know where that idea came from.
It appears to be "medlore," simply something that somebody passed on
from their own experience. It's not coming from an in-depth study on the
topic that I've ever found. What the layperson doesn't realize is how much
of medicine is just hearsay. We don't have "randomized, double-blind, pla-
cebo-controlled" studies backing up more than about 30% of what we do.
Much of medicine is an art or approach that has been passed along. Our
present advice on postponing toilet training until 15 months or later due to
"neurologic immaturity" is obviously ignorant, given the wealth of evidence
to the contrary in cross-cultural reports. Who should you believe, millions of
babies dry by age 6–9 months or the so-called experts?

The medical community may play a word game with you and say that an
infant isn't consciously continent, or isn't holding it, but just letting go in a
timely fashion or due to conditioned reflexes. You can rename it whatever
you want, but the fact is, my child can stay dry longer than it takes for her
bladder to fill up. She can hold it. There is no question, if you wait until 1 or
1½ years to start introducing babies to the toilet, it will take them a while to

unlearn what you taught them and accept the new rules. But if they start with a continence program at birth, they will know that there is more to life than just sitting in a diaper. Although my personal experience with infant toilet training is limited to one child, I know that the rest of the world doesn't toilet train the Western way. My sisters-in-law have children who stayed dry day and night at the age of 6 months, so I know our babies have more control than we think they do.

Other "experts" may say that mom is the one who is trained. Whomever! The point is, waste goes where waste belongs, and a baby can learn from the beginning that sitting in a wet diaper is not necessary or welcome. Yes, the mothers are integral in initiating the process, but their babies can sleep through the night, wake up dry and wait to go to the toilet after sleeping 8-10 hours. Babies abroad aren't any smarter than ours, but maybe their parents are!

There's a new field of ethnopediatrics—the study of child-care practices around the world. *Our Babies, Ourselves*, a book by anthropologist Meredith Small, is wonderful and clarifies how relative our child-rearing practices are. It also underscores the point that our babies are capable of much more than we realize. We even underestimate their abilities regarding something as basic as communication. For example, they have the ability to learn expressive sign language before one year of age, yet few parents attempt to communicate with their preverbal babies in this way. (There are some good books on this topic.) We probably haven't tapped the surface of what they can do.

Another factor in suppressing this technique of infant toileting education in the United States is commercialism. Too often, doctors are unwittingly fronts for a particular marketeer—whether it be a pharmaceutical, baby formula or diaper company. I am very aware of how much of my education about prescription drugs came from pharmaceutical representatives who had a product to sell. Manufacturers of disposable diapers have everything to lose from doctors encouraging the infant toileting method or the use of cloth diapers. From the start, hospitals provide paper diapers, which they say are more sanitary than cloth diapers, but all doctors know it is the caregiver's hands that are the real culprits in the spread of germs and that the type of diaper has little to do with it. It's very difficult to get into the ivory towers of medicine. It is a real challenge to change the way doctors get their information. Now that about one third of doctors in the USA are women and many of them are mothers, these issues may be more open to dialogue and reeducation.

I think Western medicine will slowly accept the principles of infant toilet training. Minds are opening because patients are demanding more alternative approaches. Given a little more time and publicity about this issue, I think it will become more welcome in the West. It's a slow process until we "die off" some of the older ways of doing things. I hope we don't have to wait until we suffer more consequences from the environmental impact of our "conveniences." As cultures rub against other cultures and patients begin to pressure their doctors for new information, doctors will become more receptive. It's a revolution that needs to happen.

Dr. Nandyal invites questions and comments on the subject of infant potty training. Interested readers can contact her by e-mail at this address: lnandyal@yahoo.com.

# chapter **10**

# no greater joy

Michael and Debi Pearl discovered infant potty training, or "potty untraining" as they call it, while they were doing missionary work in Belize in 1983. They learned it in time to use with their fourth child. The method worked so well that they also used it with their fifth and last child and continue to be advocates of the method. Accounts of their experiences with infant potty training are included in two of their books: *To Train up a Child* and *No Greater Joy*.

"No Greater Joy" is also the name of the ministry of Michael and Debi Pearl, under the auspices of The Church At Cane Creek in Tennessee. Michael has been a pastor, missionary and evangelist for 35 years. The

*Pearl's five children were all homeschooled and are now missionaries and church leaders.*

*Debi Pearl explains how she modified and used the method with her children, after seeing it used in Belize.*

On a missionary trip to Central America, we were amazed by the practice of the primitive Maya Indians in not diapering their babies prior to stuffing them into a carrying pouch. The infants are all potty trained. After experimenting on our own and after further observation, we discovered that an infant is born with an aversion to going in their "nests." The parents "untrain" them by forcing them to become accustomed to going in their pants. It is instinctive in a child to protest a bowel movement. He kicks, stiffens and complains.

When my next child was born, I put a cloth diaper on her and laid her on my tummy. In this position, during those first few days of recovery, when I felt the diaper getting warm, I gave the action a name. My newborn came to associate the word I spoke with the release of her muscles. For the first few months, I put her on the seat in front of me so she would feel secure and relaxed. By waiting until I judged her bladder to be full, when I spoke the appropriate word she just released her muscles and repeated the action she had come to associate with the word.

In the early stage, I dribbled cold water down her tummy to stimulate her to "pee-pee." All the external stimuli worked together to provoke a response—the cold seat against her warm legs, the position of her body, the words I spoke, the dribbled water, and her full bladder. My two older children helped, and sometimes even Daddy. It was a ritual about every two or three hours. When we failed to perceive her need and discovered a bowel movement or pee-pee in progress, we still rushed her to the pot, saying the appropriate word to reinforce the association. She caught on quickly, and by the time she was three months old, she would fuss when she needed to go. Until she was about one year old, anytime we were out in public for any length of time, I put a diaper on her just in case of an accident.

I have often wondered if I would have had the same success if I had tried this on my first child. She had many bowel movements each day—often while nursing. Since I only trained the two younger girls, I don't know how it would work with boys. In our child training seminars, we have met other mothers who boast of success with their babies. We have the moms stand and take a bow while we all applaud. Having older children to assist you is a great advantage.

It was never, NEVER a discipline matter. If you wait until the child is three or four months old to attempt training, it may be more difficult because you are working against a learned habit.[1]

*Here is what Michael Pearl wrote about infant potty training in To Train up a Child:*

Being sensitive to the warning signs (after having changed 17,316 diapers with the first three), my wife tried it on our new arrivals. When she sensed that the child was about to "go," she would go to the toilet and place the bare infant against her bare legs in a spread leg sitting position. At first, a little stream of warm water would provoke the start of an impending "tinkle." As the child began urinating, she would say, "Pee Pee." On other occasions, if she missed the signs and a bowel movement was in progress, she would rush the child to the bathroom to finish on the toilet, while occasionally saying, "Do Do." Even if the child was through with his elimination, she still set him on the pot in order to reinforce the training. He came to identify the sound with the muscle function. They become so well trained to the voice command that you must be careful not to say the words at the wrong time.

Now, some disbelieving mothers have said, "You are the one who is potty trained, not the baby." Just as a mother knows her baby is hungry or sleepy, she can tell if he wants to go potty. A three-week-old baby is doing all he can to communicate.

My mother-in-law was equally skeptical until the day my wife said to her, "Stop at the next station, the baby wants to go potty." In a minute, when Deb came out with a thoroughly relieved three-month-old, my mother-in-law was convinced.

For a while, our bathroom became the end of a pilgrimage for those seeking faith in infant potty training. Many a time our red-faced infant girls looked up to see a great cloud of amazed witnesses expectantly hovering in our large bathroom.

Understand, the child is not made to sit for long periods of time waiting to potty. There is no discomfort for the child. An infant soon becomes accustomed to being regulated to about every two hours, or according to sleeping and eating intervals. Many others have also been successful in training their infants.[2]

The Pearls' books can be ordered by contacting the Church At Cane Creek, 1000 Pearl Road, Pleasantville, TN 37033, Internet website address: http://NoGreaterJoy.org/

Caveat from the publisher:

Since first publishing this book in 2000, it has been brought to our attention that some of the Pearls' other child-rearing practices (aside from "potty untraining") involve punishment. In this regard, we would like to reiterate that infant potty training strictly forbids any form of punishment, pressure or coercion. The testimonial by the Pearls indicates that they do not use any punishment or force in their potty untraining approach, and this is why it has been included here. We do not condone any form of violence against children.

# chapter 11

# author's narrative

I raised my first two sons using traditional potty training, starting at the ages of 18 months and 15 months, and finished daytime training at 3 years 3 months and 3½ years, respectively. Both continued to wet their beds for several years. I did not want to go through another round of full-time diapering with my third child and started searching for alternative methods.

Rob was 3 months old when I started infant toilet training with him. At that time, Bibiji, a lady from India, was visiting us with her two children, ages 9 and 11. Bibiji had successfully potty trained her children from birth. I asked her to teach me the method since I had had unfavorable experiences with conventional toilet training, and she was delighted to help. I expected her to take several hours, but she just smiled and said, "It is very simple. It will only take a few moments." I looked at her in disbelief and said, "Can you really get my baby to pee for you?" Another smile lit her face. I was skeptical and asked, "How will you know when he has to pee?" She took him gently and confidently in her arms and said *karega*, which is Punjabi for, "He will go." And he did.

I was amazed . . . and proud at the way this woman, basically a stranger to my son, had somehow communicated with him. I was still a little skeptical, thinking her success  might have been a fluke, and asked her if she could get him to go again. She said, "When it is time." Then about 15 minutes later, she picked him up again and made a "sssss" sound. He immediately peed for her again.

She then explained that part of the trick was a matter of timing. "When you know the baby needs to go to the toilet, then you take him in your arms and give him your signal."

It seemed far too simple, natural and logical. She showed me positions commonly used in India. A few were geared towards outdoor or village living and involved sitting the baby on the mother's feet. Two other positions seemed more suitable for life in the West, and I adopted these for Rob. They both involved holding Rob in squatting position in my arms. I made a comfy cradle of my arms which supported his back, neck and head while I held his thighs with his legs slightly spread apart. He was held in this position over a potty place or receptacle. A variation on this position is to hold baby in the same fashion but for the caregiver to squat down over a potty place or receptacle.

Then Bibiji told me it was my turn to pee Rob. This was about 15 minutes after she had peed him. I carefully and securely held him over the plastic basin we were using, signaled to him and was amazed to see him respond so quickly.

On that very first day, I gained confidence in the method (When I asked Bibiji if there was a word or name for it, she laughed and said, "No, it's just the way we do it."), Rob's ability to respond and my ability to carry out the whole procedure. Bibiji showed me that it was simply a matter of responding to his timing and/or body language and transporting him to the toilet on time. Each time I did this, I signaled for him to go, using the watery sound "sssss" for urination and a grunting "hmmm" sound for defecation.

The body language I first noticed as a signal from Rob was something I had often observed in the past few months but had not comprehended and thus had not responded to. About midway through his early morning feeding, Rob would begin to twist and grunt a little, with a slightly contorted facial expression. I had assumed it was just gas but now realized that this was also his body language telling me he needed to go. At that time, he was still nursing six times a day. I nursed him on a fairly regular schedule rather than on demand. Feeding on demand was not in vogue when my son was an infant. In my opinion, feeding on a regular but flexible schedule makes infant pottying easier in that the timing of elimination is easier to predict and anticipate. This applies to a mother who cannot intuitively detect elimination signals or whose infant does not vocally signal her, which was the case in my situation.

I did not have an abundance of milk, which meant my son would first drink from one breast, then the other. I had noticed that he would twist and grunt a bit when he had finished with the first breast and that he usually pooed about the time I swapped breasts. I was able to put this pattern to good use by holding him over a receptacle to eliminate during the break between breasts.

The fact that Rob had responded was very encouraging. He did not demonstrate any clear warning signs for urination, but by following the intervals of his natural timing, I managed to be effective in that department too.

Within a few days, he understood what my signals meant. I soon found that I was able to use just one sound ("sssss") for both functions.

I kept a journal of development, medical records, significant events, experiences and my thoughts on being a mother for all three of my sons. At the time I learned and used infant pottying with Rob, I had no idea I would one day write a book on the topic, so I did not keep detailed notes about our experiences. There are entries on his potty progression from time to time, and some of them are included here.

Since I didn't know of any official term for "infant potty training," I referred to it as "Indian-style toilet training" in my journal. Back then, the term "toilet training" was used more often than "potty training." The first journal entry on this topic reads, "I started toilet training him Indian style, and it works well. He responds well to it."

His pee pattern consisted of (a) peeing when he first woke up in the morning, (b) peeing every 20 minutes after a feeding, on three or four occasions and then (c) peeing about once every 45–60 minutes up until his next feeding. This was intensive at first, and I did not get him to the sink or basin for every pee. That would have worn me out, but I did get him to the potty place on time several times a day. His pattern was fairly consistent, which helped a lot.

About three weeks into it, we went on holiday in France. I didn't let travel deter me and took advantage of our host country's special plumbing fixture called the bidet. A bidet is an excellent toilet place to use with infant pottying because the size, shape and plumbing are perfect. This little discovery inspired me to be creative, to seek and improvise unique potty places and receptacles whenever necessary and wherever we went.

Intervals between pees gradually increased over time, making it less intense for me. Within a few months, I no longer needed to give the audible signal at all. Whenever I held him over a receptacle in a certain position, he understood why he was there and responded. Each time he went, he was praised. It was a natural, spontaneous and sincere form of praise, a sort of celebration since I was thrilled. We continued to grow closer and improve our communication on a regular basis.

Rob started crawling at 6 months and sitting around 8 months. When he was 9 months old, my journal reads, "He doesn't let me hold him in my arms very long anymore for toileting. I started putting him on the potty instead." We bought him a very small, transparent potty. I highly recommend a transparent potty since it allows you to see exactly when your baby goes. The instant I saw Rob "go," I would praise him and let him off the potty. A few weeks later, my notes read, "He does very well on the pot. It is a joy to see him consciously go in the pot at such a young age. He pees less often now."

At 9 months, there were occasions where he refused to pee in the potty and instead went as soon as I put his training pants back on. I knew this was just a phase and fairly common behavior, so I didn't let it bother me. My notes read, "He is quite good at the toilet training, but sometimes he won't pee when I try to have him pee, and then when I put on his diaper or underwear, he pees in it." It was evident that he clearly knew what he was doing. I considered his awareness and this type of game playing to be an indication of impending success as long as it didn't last too long. Besides, there were days where I was less diligent than others, where I was tired or busy, occasions where I didn't get him to the potty on time and caused him to wet his pants, so how could I complain if there were days when I had to change him?

Sometimes I would feel like I had let him down. I'd feel guilty and/or frustrated if I didn't get him to the potty on time. I felt very responsible and knew he was dependent on me to make things work. After a while, I learned not to be too hard on myself. It took a while to realize and accept that being uptight and angry at myself was a disservice to Rob. Once I understood the consequences, I modified my behavior by disciplining myself to remain positive and relaxed.

At 14 months, my notes read, "He touches his penis and makes himself pee when I put him on the pot." This was further evidence that he knew exactly what the potty was for and that he could consciously make himself go. He'd pee and then either look at a book, play with a toy or leave the potty for some other activity.

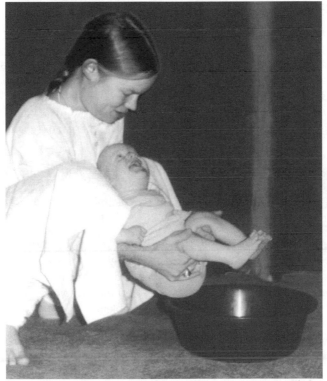

*Khalsa*

Rob at 9 months, just prior to graduating to the potty

The communication between us coupled with his ability to stay clean and dry at the age of 14 months was so effective and inspiring that I wrote an article on the topic. This was in 1980, and the article was entitled "Conscious Toilet Training," with an emphasis on the intelligence, consciousness (awareness) and sensitivity of babies. The information in this article formed the basis of *Trickle Treat* (published 11 years later).

I was fairly consistent with infant pottying and did not relent when we traveled or visited friends and relatives. Since we were still living in Holland, we traveled home to California at least once a year. We also frequently traveled through various European countries and made some visits to India. Wherever we went, I took the potty and used it. This included airplane trips, airports, airport shuttles, rest areas along the roads, camping, hiking, restaurants, just about any place you can imagine. Whenever necessary, I would improvise a potty place.

I remember visiting Lisa, my former roommate and surfing buddy from our university days. When Rob and I visited Lisa, she was staying on her parents' ranch. Her parents employed a woman named Ceska as nanny and housekeeper. Lisa, Ceska, Rob and I were walking along a ranch road when I sensed it was time for Rob to pee. I whipped down his pants and held him in my arms, whereupon he immediately peed along the roadside. Lisa didn't have a clue what was going on, but Ceska grew excited and exclaimed, "This is what we do back in my country of Czechoslovakia!"

I found that wherever we went and had the occasion to improvise a toilet place—whether traveling or doing errands—we encountered curious and puzzled onlookers. Sometimes we even met people (mainly immigrants) who were familiar with the method.

There were occasions from the very start when I traveled without Rob and left him with caregivers. Some of the caregivers were willing to pee and poo him while others didn't take the time and put him in diapers. In short, there were times where I was away for a few days or weeks when no one pottied him. Upon my return, we had no problem picking up where we had left off. It did not jeopardize his progress to stop for a few days or weeks. While I would not recommend anyone purposefully stopping for no particular reason, it is good to know that a break does not automatically spell doom.

At 15 months, Rob started to walk and had developed a small vocabulary. A few of my journal entries around this time read, "Sometimes he cries or whines when he needs to pee," and, "He refuses to sit on the potty when he doesn't need to go."

At 17 months, I wrote, "He sings and talks to himself while walking. His walking improved so much that we have to be careful he doesn't slip away from us. The toilet training is going well. He sometimes walks to the potty on his own."

When he was 25 months old, my notes happily announce, "He's 100% toilet trained, including nighttime! He tells me every time he has to go."

Looking back on the toilet teaching of all three of my sons, it took both my first son and Rob 21 months to complete daytime potty training, while my second son took 27 months. Since my first two sons didn't begin until they were over a year old, they didn't finish until they were over 3 years old, which meant my first two sons and I had to deal with a lot of dirty diapers. By contrast, Rob started at 3 months and finished around 2 years of age, which meant that neither Rob nor I had to deal with poopy diapers for more than a few months. In addition, my first two sons wet their beds at night for many more years after staying dry during the day, whereas Rob never wet his bed at night (except for one time when he was ill) from the day we started. There is no doubt in my mind that infant potty training is well worth the effort for caregiver(s), baby and the environment.

# chapter 1

# africa

## South Africa

*The following four reports were furnished by the Department of Health Services and Welfare, Pretoria, South Africa, in 1988:*

### Lady of European origin, registered nurse, Pretoria

The practice outlined below is the usual one and is taught by the nurse in the health clinic for her community.

The traditional method was to begin toilet training at about 3 months of age, to achieve success at about 6–9 months, all going well.

The baby was supported over a tiny potty, at first once a day after bath and feeding time in the morning. Later, with some success, the mother would try at other times in the day, if possible before the baby was found to be wet, e.g., upon waking in the morning and before going to sleep at night.

Sometimes, I woke the babies who were staying at the clinic at night until they remained dry. Some mothers tried to catch the bowel action first.

The method of early training was not stressful. The mothers would show pleasure in "success" but no displeasure in "failure" if there were accidents.

With regard to three of the children in question, one girl was trained (day and night) at 9 months; one girl and one boy were trained at one year. It was easier to train girls than boys and, in general, girls finished the training sooner.

The method was unsuccessful for only one child at the clinic.

## Indian lady, Asian origin, Pretoria

*NOTE: This communication was paraphrased by the Department of Health Services and Welfare.*

Training from infancy is commonly used in her area. Her parents and many of her friends used it. She felt that there is no difference in training time for boys and girls. Reassurance is very important. Everyone she knows who used the method found it to be satisfying. No one found it to be inconvenient or frustrating. Her feeling was that it all depends on the reaction of the parents—if they are anxious or upset, they will find it frustrating.

## Lady of the Xhosa tribe, registered nurse

1. Among Xhosas, toilet training starts from between 5 and 6 months of age. In the olden days, huts were smeared with cow dung.[1] The mothers used to take dry mashed cow dung and put it on the floor. First thing in the morning (at about 6 a.m.), the baby is held in the squatting position on this cow dung until he urinates or defecates, and then the cow dung is removed. This method is repeated after about every hour until the end of the day.

As time goes on, the child will show signs of restlessness and crying as a sign of wanting to pass urine or defecate. Toilet training is usually completed by about 7 to 8 months. It takes about one month, at the most 2 months.

2. This method has been in use for centuries. Nowadays, some people with economic means use potties and diapers.

3. There is basically one main system, training from infancy, but not from birth.

4. I learnt this system from my own mother.

5. The method is common.

6. Every female member in the family must cooperate and helps if the mother is busy.

7. The babies are woken at night, but not as frequently as in daytime—roughly about twice per night.

8. They are successfully trained around 7–8 months of age.

9. The method used was the same with all the children in my family.

10. It is successful if family members are cooperative and do the same even if the mother is away.

11. The method is satisfying.

12. This method is time consuming. It needs a lot of patience. If the baby takes too long, you must even make the sound of urine coming out, by saying "pssssss."

## Lady of the Tswana tribe, registered nurse

1. Toilet training with Blacks starts very early. They have no nappy to catch the stool for sometime. To have the problem over and done with, outdoor methods are used. Thus the infant learns at an early stage.

As time goes on, the mother learns to notice how the strict routine mealtime regulates the bowel motion times as well.

Babies are encouraged to pass water and stools as the first thing at bedtime and first thing in the morning.

2.  This method has been in use for a long time. The material used is soft grass, dry dung, leaves and water.

    Mother sits with her legs stretched out slightly apart. Baby is then put just below the knees with a little dry dung underneath that would serve as baby's toilet.

3.  A similar type of training involves squatting outside on the soil for the infants who are old enough to already understand.

4.  Mothers usually start training from 4 to 5 months of age.

5.  I learned this from my own mother and culture.

6.  The method is commonly used.

7.  A family member helped me with the toilet training.

8.  Early on, I woke the baby at night. Later, the baby would wake up dry in the morning.

9.  My children completed their training at about 20–24 months.

10. Girls were easier to train than boys.

11. The method was satisfying.

12. The method was time consuming, but otherwise not frustrating.

## Uganda

Stella Sabiiti was a political refugee, residing in the Netherlands when she gave her report in 1989. She is the mother of three children who were born in Uganda.

In Ugandan villages, children are toilet trained at a very early age, while they are still babies. Just like with everything else, children in villages develop faster than children in cities or in the Western world. We start by the 3rd month and finish before one year of age.

In Africa, children are always in the company of other people, grownups or bigger children, who are always ready to help them with everything, including toilet training. Because of this, the mother does not feel a lot of pressure for time or help with the training. Others take pleasure in helping.

This way of training is satisfying and enjoyable. It is part of life. It is our duty, and we do it with patience and love.

Everyone in the village knows the way to train the infants. The knowledge is passed from generation to generation.

# chapter 2

# australia

S arah Buckley is trained as a family MD and lives in Brisbane, Australia, where she is currently a full-time mother and part-time writer on pregnancy and birth issues. Together with her partner Nicholas, also an MD, they have four children, all born at home. It is her faith and interest in the natural processes of birth and mothering that lead Sarah to choose infant potty training with her fourth baby Maia, and she has found it a lot of fun, with unexpected rewards: Maia has been out of nappies from 13 months, and their family laundry is unbelievably easy. (This testimonial was given in 2002.)

I heard about infant potty training, or elimination communication as I call it, when my fourth baby Maia Rose was 3 months old. I was very excited about it, and the timing was perfect, as I had read a few years earlier that African women cue their babies to wee and poo with a "psss" sound, and I had begun to do this with Maia from birth. It made sense to me because it felt closer to our genetic imprint, and I was drawn to the idea of a deeper physical and psychic connection with my baby. The first time I tried it, I held Maia (aged 3 months) over the laundry tub and made the "psss" noise. To my delight, she weed straight away, and we have been doing it ever since.

For our family, doing this has been more fun and rewarding than I could have imagined. It has given us more skin-to-skin contact, less washing, no nappy rash, and, best of all for me, a deeper respect for Maia's abilities and knowledge of her body, and a finer attunement to her rhythms. As well as these advantages, there is obviously less waste and a better time for Mother Earth. And it's fun! Having had three babies in nappies, I have been constantly delighted at Maia's ability to communicate her needs—and to keep telling me until I get it.

Elimination communication also makes a beautiful contribution to my experience of mindfulness in my mothering. Like breastfeeding, it keeps me close to my baby, physically and psychologically, and provides very immediate feedback when I am not tuned in.

As a GP (family MD), the physiology is interesting to me and is totally counter to what I was taught at medical school, where it is asserted that babies do not have sphincter control until close to the second birthday. Obviously the paediatricians didn't consult the global majority of mothers and babies, for whom knowing their baby's elimination needs is as simple as knowing their own.

From the start, I've had a lot of support from Emma (11), Zoe (8) and Jacob (6), who tell me how much they disliked sitting in wet or soiled diapers as babies. Some believe that we set up our society for sexual problems by encouraging our babies to dissociate, or switch off from their genital areas because of the unpleasant sensation of wearing what some have called a "walking toilet." My partner Nicholas wondered about the extra effort that I went to in the first year, but has been very happy to reap the benefits of a nappy-free toddler.

Reflecting on my experiences with babies in and out of nappies, I've come to the conclusion that probably ALL babies signal their elimination needs from an early age, but because we're not listening out for it, we misinterpret it as tiredness, needing to feed, or just crankiness, especially if our baby is in a nappy and we don't observe the connection with eliminating.

In the first few months, I learnt Maia's signals by observing her closely. This was fairly easy, as she was very much "in arms" for her first six months. I discovered that she would squirm and become unsettled, sometimes with a bit of crying, especially if it took me a while to "get it." At other times, it was more psychic, and I found myself heading for the laundry tub, where we usually eliminated, without really thinking. When I was distracted, or delayed acting on my hunch, I usually got peed on. (However, she very seldom peed on me when I carried her in a sling.) Her signal for poop was usually a few farts, or sometimes she'd even pull off the breast as a means of signalling that she needed to go. She didn't want to sit in her own poop!

Learning Maia's daily pattern was also useful. She usually pooped first thing in the morning, and, as a baby, tended to pee frequently (about every 10 minutes) in the first few hours after arising. (My husband found this really tricky when he was "on duty" in the morning.) I noticed that she would also pee about 10 minutes after breastfeeding or drinking. She still almost always pees on awaking; I think it is the need to eliminate that actually awakens her.

In her first year, we used the laundry tub by preference. I'd hold her upright by her thighs, with her back resting on my belly. I also used a small sandpit-type bucket, with a conveniently lipped top, which came into its own at night later on (see below). As she got older and heavier, I found that sitting her on the toilet in front of me worked well—sometimes we'd have a "double wee," which was always successful if nothing else worked!

Along with the position, I cued her with my "psss" noise, and sometimes, when I thought she had a need but was slow to start, I'd turn on the tap as well. After three months or so of doing this, I became more sure of my interpretation and I sometimes gently persisted even where she was initially reluctant, and usually she'd go in half a minute or so. However, for me, it's a fine line, and I think it's vital to have cooperation, and not a battle of wills, which can sometimes develop around "toileting." It's more a dance of togetherness that develops, as with breastfeeding, from love and respect for each other.

On a practical level, I used nappies when we were out and about, and peed her as much as I could, but I didn't expect to be perfect in these, or any, circumstances. We used toilets or took the bucket in the car. When we missed a pee, my reaction was just, "Oh well, missed that one." On hot days, I just lay a nappy on the car seat. If it wasn't convenient to stop, I'd say to her, "Oh, Maia, you'll have to pee in the nappy, and I'll change it as soon as we stop."

Maia didn't like to be disturbed at night in the early months, so I'd lie her on a bunny rug and just let her pee. I changed this whenever I woke up. Or I'd wrap a cloth nappy loosely around her bum and change it when wet. I found that, as with naps, she usually peed on awaking and then nursed.

Around 6 to 7 months, Maia went "on strike," coinciding with teething and beginning to crawl. She stopped signaling clearly and at times actively resisted being "peed." I took it gently, offering opportunities to eliminate when it felt right and not getting upset when, after refusing to go in the laundry tub, she went on the floor. Even on "bad days," though, we still had most poops in a bowl, bucket or the toilet. At nearly 10 months, we were back on track. I noticed that as she became more independent and engrossed in her activity, she was not keen to be removed to eliminate, so I started to bring a receptacle to her. She preferred a bowl or bucket on my lap, and later we began to use a potty: I initially held her while she used it.

At nighttime, I started sitting her on a bucket (and on the breast at the same time, tricky to lie down afterwards and not spill the bucket!). When I was less alert, she peed on a nappy between her legs and/or the bunny rug underneath her.

There was a marked shift in things soon after she began walking at 12 months. At 14 months, to my amazement, Maia was out of nappies completely. She was now able to communicate her needs very clearly, both verbally and non-verbally, and her ability to "hold on" was also enhanced. When she needed to eliminate, she said "wee" and/or headed for the potty—we had several around the house. Nicholas, her dad, was so delighted when she first did this that he clapped her, and so she would stand up and applaud herself afterwards. She began to be very interested in the fate of her body products, and joined me as we tipped it onto the garden or into the toilet. (Now she wants to empty the potty herself.) She even began to get a cloth and wipe up after herself!

With this change, I stopped using nappies altogether and switched to trainer pants—the Bright Bots are great and come in small sizes—for going out. Dresses are great too, for outings with bare-bottomed girls in our warm summer months.

Now, at 19 months, Maia is totally autonomous in her daytime elimination. She tells us her needs and/or goes to the potty herself. Although I take a change of pants when we go out, it is very rare to need them—compared to my other children, she is about the 3-year-old stage with her toiletting.

Nighttimes continue to be busy for us, with lots of feeding and weeing, but unless she is unwell or I am very tired, we have very few "misses." Sitting up at night to pee her seems to me a small effort in return for the benefits we currently reap. It seems, from other stories I've heard, that many babies stop peeing at night even in the first year, or have a predictable pattern, and no doubt Maia will do this in the next year or so.

Reflecting on my experiences, it interests me that babies learn to release before they learn to hold on. This makes it very convenient because, when cooperative, a baby can empty even a small amount of pee from the bladder. (This means, for example, I can know that we are starting a car trip with minimal chance of Maia needing to wee for at least half an hour or so.) In contrast, conventional toilet training is built around the child's ability to "hold on" to their pee and poop, until they can release it in a socially acceptable place.

I wonder, then, about the mind-body implications of this subtle but important difference. Aren't we a society where we tend to "hold on" to our "stuff," often needing the help of others (e.g., therapists) to encourage us to "let it out." One of my friends commented on Maia's relaxed mouth, and this made me wonder if the process might relax the whole digestive tract. I can also feel, in my mothering, the beauty of supporting her healthy eliminative functions, which many of us feel shameful about and would prefer to deny—hence nappies, which hide the eliminating act itself.

Furthermore, the "toilet training stage" is, in Erik Erikson's psychological stages, centred on the issue of "autonomy vs shame and doubt," and it seems to me that Maia has mastered these issues already—she is incredibly autonomous, not to say bossy at times! I wonder if this might be in part due to being an early mistress of her elimination.

For me, the beauty of elimination communication has been in the process, not in the outcome, however remarkable or convenient. Yes, it's great to do less than a full load of washing each day for a family of six, but much more significant is the learning that mothers and babies are connected very deeply—at a "gut level"—and that babies (and mothers) are much more capable and smarter than our society credits. As a mother and as an MD, I highly recommend this very satisfying practice.

chapter **3**

# brazil

M r. Valdir Rocha, a lawyer living in Rio de Janeiro, practiced infant toilet training. In 1988, he explained the following:

Some families train their babies from infancy, but not from birth. The method is a common one.

We learned about the method in talking to relatives, reading books and taking a course for pregnant women sponsored by Globo TV in Rio.

My wife and I trained our son, but we did not wake him up at night, even though he sometimes wet his bed. He was about 22 months when he was completely trained, day and night. If we compare our baby with those of friends who used a different method, his training was very successful.

We were satisfied with the method. We did not find it to be inconvenient, frustrating or too time consuming.

# chapter 4

# canada

ngrid Bauer is a freelance writer, editor, workshop facilitator and full-time parent. She writes and speaks regularly about alternative parenting, compassionate communication, gardening and natural living practices. To respond to her baby's needs for consistent skin-to-skin contact and comfortable, hygienic elimination, Ingrid decided to raise her second child without diapers. She was amazed to discover that she could learn to distinguish intuitively when he needed to go. She then wrote a book about her experiences and research on raising babies "diaper-free." Her third child (and second diaper-free baby) was born in spring 2001. Ingrid Bauer lives with her children and partner on an island in British Columbia, Canada and submitted the following in 2002.

In the fall of 1996, when I was expecting my second child, my partner and I reexamined the diaper issue from a completely different perspective. The question we asked ourselves, as we prepared for our baby's birth, was not "single use or cloth?" It was: "Is it possible to minimize, or even eliminate altogether, the need for diapers?"

Neither my partner nor I had any desire to rush our child in his growing process, nor were we repulsed by body functions. We definitely wanted our baby to relieve himself whenever he needed to. Diapers felt like an impediment to the awareness of these needs. Eliminating diapers, by tuning in to our baby's rhythms, seemed like a natural extension of our parenting philosophy, which is to try to understand, to value and to respond to all our child's needs.

We didn't relish the thought of our baby lying or sitting around in a soggy or poopy diaper, even for a short while. Waste was meant to be eliminated from the body, not plastered to it! We couldn't imagine anyone choosing to spend 24 hours a day with a restrictive bulk between their legs. We wanted our baby to be free to enjoy as much skin-to-skin contact as possible. What kind of message were we sending if we isolated the diaper area from being touched? We were perfectly willing to change diapers, if need be; but at this point, we were wondering if it was really necessary or beneficial.

On our journeys in India, we had seen diaperless babies everywhere. I had also heard about baby-wearing cultures, where mothers were so in tune that they knew exactly when their infants were going to pee or poop and just held them away from their bodies at the right moment. For these women, being peed on was almost unthinkable. How I longed to be this connected to my baby! How did they do it? Was it possible in our culture? Even if I managed to attain this closeness, I couldn't just hold my baby away from me and let him pee on the floor! A friend, who had also traveled in India, gave me a clue. She spoke of naked babies whose mothers just took them off the bus at each longer stop and "peed" them on bus trips that lasted several hours. Based on this tidbit, and convinced that this intimate communication was natural and possible, I set out to rediscover what, for millions of people worldwide, is common knowledge. I learned through observing my son's patterns, by following his cues and my intuition and from the occasional anecdote of someone else's experience.

With no plans or models to follow, things evolved in their own natural way. Early one January morning, after an intense and blissful two-hour labor, our son was born into his parents' hands. The thought of dressing or diapering him never even entered our minds. Outside winter raged; inside the wood stove was stoked, and baby and I lay skin-to-skin, and absorbed each other's presence. Forget about the prescribed hour of bonding! We indulged sensually for weeks on end! Visitors speculated on how old our baby would be before he wore his first clothing. Even the softest diaper seemed too rough for that silk-skinned gentle being.

In fact, he was about 3 weeks old when we first dressed him to go for a longer outing. Until that time, and for much of the following weeks, he was carried naked against us or lay on our bed with flannel pads beneath him, to protect our clothing and the bedding. These I changed the moment they were wet or soiled during the day and several times at night. Gently lifting him to replace the padding was much easier than changing a diaper in the middle of the night. A soft flannel blanket over him prevented the fountain effect, for which little boys are famous.

I started exploring natural infant hygiene with him from birth by making sounds and holding him in position but didn't take him to a toilet place till he was about 4 months. When he pooped, I held him in an upright squatting position by supporting him under his knees, over a change pad, cloths or a diaper. In an improvised approach to my friend's account of the Indian babies, I simply repeated a "cueing sound" two or three times during his efforts. Because we are a bilingual family, I chose *caca*, which is the French equivalent of "poop." (For pee, we used the French word *pipi*.) Sometimes I imitated his soft grunting sounds. Later, I was to learn that mothers in traditional cultures, from Korea to New Guinea, also do this to stimulate a bowel movement.

By 4 months, our son clearly understood our cueing words. He would bear down slightly when I said *caca*. I asked myself whether he really still needed to poop in a diaper, which he was now wearing more regularly. On a whim one morning, I removed his diaper, held him in position and said *caca*. He responded by having his first diaperless bowel movement! I figured it was lucky timing. In fact, it signaled a total end to the washing of soiled diapers. Except for once, in the car, he never pooped in a diaper again.

Tuning in to our baby's need to pee was a longer, subtler process that required deep listening. It started with the "technique" of cueing him and watching for his signals. Gradually, the linear concept of cause and effect gave way to a more synergetic way of being together, and I became as aware of his need to eliminate as I was of my own.

We used various receptacles and locations. Indoors, it was mostly the toilet (always for poops), sometimes the laundry sink (for pee only), occasionally another sink, a bowl or a bucket. In the summer, I took him outside a lot and fertilized the bushes. I always carried him to the bathroom until he chose to begin using the potty on his own, which occurred naturally and gradually over time, between about 14 to 20 months.

At night, although he stirred and partly awoke when he needed to pee, he often really disliked being removed from the bed to the bathroom (I think using a potty by the bed might have worked, but I didn't try). So I tried to pee him before nursing him to sleep, and I used a cloth diaper. He would awaken when he wet it, after which I would remove it immediately (we have a family bed), and he would be naked and dry the rest of the night. He was usually dry through the night, though not consistently, when he 12–18 months.

Sometimes I'm asked at what age my son completed toilet learning. Like weaning from the breast, I don't see natural infant hygiene as a linear process with a specific end point. He first began using the toilet independently at about 12–14 months, but still wanted me to take him to pee many times. Even when, at 2, he rarely needed me, he still wanted me to "pee" him in public rest rooms, when he was sick and in a few other situations.

By the time my daughter was born, I had done lots of research, interviewed dozens of people and written my book about this whole process. Whereas with my son I'd never talked to anyone who'd done it when I started, I had now talked to hundreds of experienced mothers. I am so grateful for the support, the companionship and the opportunity to share the joy of this special communication. With my daughter, I again spent the first precious weeks in retreat, enjoying skin-to-skin contact and getting to know her rhythms. I held her in-arms to go until she was about 7 months when she began to prefer sitting on a little potty. She has slept diaperless from birth—we use a bedside potty quite successfully most nights. I use a cloth diaper for back-up occasionally on outings, especially with cold weather outerwear, to minimize stress.  Otherwise she enjoys diaper-free comfort. This time around I have felt so much more relaxed about the whole thing. Rather than focussing intently on her elimination needs, it has become simply a part of what we do, like nursing or sleeping. I rely even more on intuition and think about the process less, yet misses are much rarer. And I'm far less concerned about misses if they do happen. I accept that it can be hard to get to a toilet place during outings and that the back-up diaper sometimes gets wet. At a two-day workshop recently, she even wore a diaper all day for the first time, though I did bring a potty and try to pee her as much as possible. I guess that during this process, I've learned to be more compassionate with myself too!

She started walking the day she turned 9 months, and three weeks later, just days ago, she used her potty without assistance for the first time. Her brother saw and announced it with delight! Sometimes she puts things in her potty or looks at me and calls to tell me she has to go, or she struggles out of my arms when I'm holding her. Other times, she doesn't signal at all and I rely on intuition, cueing or timing. Sometimes, we still miss. I anticipate that I will be helping her for a while still and I cherish the thought. Having a teen who is growing into manhood really drives home how short that precious baby-time, when my children need me intensely, really is. I want to be grateful for and relish every moment.

What I have chosen to call "natural infant hygiene" (I first called it elimination communication) is far more than a practical method for keeping babies clean, dry and happy without diapers. It offers an opportunity for a deepened intimacy between parent and child and a loving way to communicate with your baby and respond to his or her needs. Our babies are so utterly dependent on us to care for them. Natural infant hygiene offers us a beautiful opportunity to understand and respond compassionately to our baby's needs. It serves to strengthen our own intuition and our intimate connection with both our child and ourselves. With natural infant hygiene, as with breast-nurturing, I appreciate the possibility for a respectful and loving two-way interchange, long before that first word is spoken.

You can read more about Ingrid Bauer, her philosophy and teachings, in her book *Diaper Free! The Gentle Wisdom of Natural Infant Hygiene*. Ingrid describes four integrated approaches to tuning in to your child's natural elimination needs: timing, signals, intuition and cueing. With an emphasis on strengthening the bond between parent and child, the book promises many practical tips as well as insights into the parenting journey. For further details, contact Ingrid at:

Natural Wisdom Press
115 Forest Ridge Road
Saltspring Island, BC
Canada V8K 1W4
www.natural-wisdom.com

# chapter 5

# china

C hina is fairly well-known for its use of infant elimination training. This chapter is especially interesting in that it contains reports concerning three generations of the same family—the parents in China and their daughter and grandson who live in a Western society. The first report is by Sun Mengjia and Li Minqian, retired physics professors from Shanxi University in Taiyuan, Shanxi. The second report comes from their daughter Min Sun, who holds a Ph.D. in Nutrition Sciences from the University of Alabama, resides in Italy and is married to an Italian pediatrician. Both reports were filed in 2002.

# Sun Mengjia and Li Minqian (China)

In China, parents usually begin toilet training around the age of one month or as late as four months. Sometimes they base it on starting after the first 100 days of life since the first 100 days are important in Chinese culture. Babies are considered to be very fragile for the first 100 days. But many diligent mothers and grandmothers start training within the first month with the expectation that, according to a Chinese proverb, they "get twice the result with half the effort."

The reason for starting toilet training in infancy is to help infants build good habits. Many Chinese books on infant rearing advocate early training and include summaries of thousands of cases. There are now also some authors who follow Western beliefs and advise to begin training at age 18 months. But most parents feel that if training starts at this late time, it is very difficult because you have to correct bad habits which have already been formed.

We raised two children and helped take care of (and toilet train) the babies of some relatives on a short-term basis. We toilet trained our two children according to Chinese tradition. A fundamental principle is: Eating and elimination are two coexisting aspects that should be considered equally important.

We learned the timing and regularity of our babies' eliminations, based on their feeding schedule. At the most likely time for the babies to eliminate, we held them in a specific position and guided them with sounds. For the infant elimination position, the baby rests his back against the mother's chest and the mother holds the baby's legs in her hands. In Chinese, to *ba* a baby means to help a baby eliminate (*ba* is a verb in the third tone). A typical sound for voiding is *xu* and for defecation *eng* is often used. These are used to help the infant develop the ability to control elimination, by building a healthy conditioned reflex.

Infants should not be looked down upon—most of them are very smart. Chinese books on child rearing state that babies can recognize the *ba* position with sounds as early as 20–30 days old; this combination can help them accomplish early training. In China, we are proud when our children are trained early. Toilet training is usually completed between 4–12 months.

Receptacles are used, for example a potty or a bottle. But some parents take the baby to the bathroom instead. In villages, an infant sometimes goes on the floor or in the yard, and then the mess is cleaned.

Parents have help with toilet training. Usually the grandparents assist, but if not, a full-time babysitter or helper (who sometimes stays with the family) is hired to follow the mother's instructions.

In China, infants sleep next to their parents, so babies feel safe. In this way, an attentive mother can feel or observe the movements of her baby. During the night, if a baby moves or wakes up for elimination needs, the mother will *ba* her baby to urinate. If the baby does not stir at night, he should generally not be awakened.

Diapers (both cloth and disposable) and open pants are used. In the past, parents used soft pieces of cloth as diapers. Cloth diapers are affixed by using wide elastic bands around the baby's waist and on top of the diapers. If not too tight, the elastic bands won't cause discomfort. When the babies are about 10 to 12 months old, many no longer require diapers. They are mainly used as tools before babies develop language skills. In more recent times, many families are using disposable diapers made from highly absorbent materials, but these are generally used only as a supplementary tool for easier cleaning and to avoid accidents. Open pants are used for convenience and timeliness of elimination, before good control is gained.

Infant toilet training is the main method of both the past and the present in China. It is used nationwide, in villages and cities, and in all levels of society. Income is not a determining factor. Attitude and tradition are what lead a family to use this method. But because there are now books that provide different outlooks and onset times—many of these books include Western opinions and approaches—there is now some confusion among some parents in cities.

The limit on having just one child has not affected toilet training. Having only one child does not necessarily mean a mother spends time toilet training. It is not a matter of time or income, but a matter of concept, personal attitude, and understanding the importance of toilet training.

We have seen some mothers avoid toilet training by using disposable diapers, in order to save themselves the effort. It is believed that this causes weak functional sphincter muscles and a lack of control. Only lazy mothers rely solely on disposable diapers. Their children aren't toilet trained before two or three years of age, which is late in China.

Although we reside in the north of China, this information is applicable to much of the republic. We are constantly in touch with friends at the university. Many are from different provinces in China. We also have relatives who live in other cities and who share their experiences with us.

# Sun Min (Italy)

I think that infant toilet training is a learning process for me as a mother but not a training process for my baby because I am not training him but only learning the timing and communications for his elimination needs. I am helping him build a healthy habit from early infancy. When our son was born, my parents sent information from China on the importance and how-tos of infant toilet training. My first reaction was rejection. I thought, if everybody here (in the USA and in Italy) uses diapers, it will be fine if I do what they do here. In China, babies wear open pants. I can't use them here; otherwise my baby would be considered uncivilized.

But I continued to think about it and talked with my husband frequently, even sometimes at the dinner table where this topic may not be suitable! He, as an Italian pediatrician and neonatologist, had never heard about this. Initially he was surprised, but eventually he told me that I could try anything with our baby. So I started toilet training with a way that suited our lifestyle in Italy—I started early, did not use Chinese open pants but used disposable diapers for a while.

When our baby was one month old, I thought, if I know my baby is going to make stools, why don't I take him to the bathroom instead of watching him make it in the diaper—it's better to bring him to the bathroom and wash him in the same position. The process began with a thought as easy as this.

I actually learned about the in-arms washing position from an Italian friend who is a nurse in newborn care. It was the exact position I used to help my baby eliminate before he could sit. I have learned that my baby gives signals for his elimination needs and that it is also possible to learn his natural elimination schedule.

By four months of age, I was able to help him defecate in the bathroom. By seven months, he stayed dry during day naps. Now he is nine months old and jumps up and down in front of the potty! He always wears a diaper. Occasionally I used traditional cloth diapers but later I gave them up. Sometimes when I am sure he won't void, I have him wear little underpants.

When he goes for me in the bathroom, I praise him and give him a little kiss. When accidents occur, I blame myself for not being able to pay enough attention to catch his signals. Now that he is nine months old, I don't need to observe him so closely anymore. I simply take him to the bathroom when I feel it is the right time. I do think he has learned to cooperate with me in that he sometimes waits by holding it before I take him to the bathroom.

Most of the leading books on child rearing in China state that toilet training starts at one month of age, according to tradition. Today some young parents use diapers until three years of age before toilet training, like is done in the USA or other Western countries.

Here in Italy, some Chinese mothers bring infant open pants to the hospital when they go in for delivery. The Italian nurses don't understand the function of the pants, so they first put a disposable diaper on the newborn, then put the Chinese open pants over the diaper!

Many Chinese mothers who live in Italy also use diapers, maybe because their grandparents are not here to teach them. But we have continued to chat with friends on this topic. Many are interested in it, but not pediatricians. I have heard that some Italian mothers take their babies to the bathroom as early as five months of age. When they tell others about this, the reaction they receive is usually: "Are you crazy? It is dangerous for your baby." When we told some pediatricians about our experience with our son, the first response was that it would damage his neurological development.

A lot of people, whether they are mothers or not, can tell when a baby needs to go, but they have never considered taking the baby to the bathroom for this. Perhaps this is because they have been warned by doctors not to do so, or maybe they just haven't been informed of the whole story.

My philosophy is that everything has to be moderate, and we should not abuse our resources. Diapers can be used before baby gains full control, but learning how our babies communicate their needs is also important and particularly interesting. If they cry due to hunger, feeling ignored or being sleepy or tired, it makes sense that they also cry for other reasons, which include their elimination needs. Babies communicate with us before they can speak. If we don't understand, it is because we don't listen with attentive hearts. If we help our babies eat, dress and wash before they can do these things by themselves, why can't we bring them to the bathroom before they can do this by themselves? Parents should be educated to help children build healthy elimination habits starting at birth, then teach them independent toileting later. This is a civilized and educated way to bring up our babies. We should inform all parents about this possibility, so they can choose whether to start early or at two years of age.

Min Sun, Ph.D.
Department of Mother and Child and of Biology-Genetics
Pediatrics Section
University of Verona

*Valdin/Photononstop*

An Ouighour baby in split pants.
Grandfather and grandson "hanging out" together.
(Xinjiang, China)

# chapter 6

# germany

F riederike ("Freddy") Bradfisch lives in Southern Germany. She was a
  practicing lawyer for about five years and then became a full-time
  mom. She discovered IPT when her first child Wolfgang was 2
months old. Since that time, she has had exciting results with both her
children. At 19 months, her daughter Jutta is on the verge of completion
(2004). Freddy was so inspired by her experiences that she created a
German website and e-mail list where members discuss IPT.

Before our son Wolfgang was born, I didn't even consider cloth diapers.
I thought they would be too much of a hassle. Little did I expect to be doing something far more unusual in our Western world. After using dispos-

ables for two months, I came across a German book on child rearing, *Ihr Baby kann's* by Rita Messmer. In the chapter on toilet training, the author refers to the many women around the world carrying their diaperless babies and "just knowing" when they have to eliminate. This inspired her to give it a try with her own son. She held him over the toilet, and it worked. Although there was not much information to go by, it sounded logical to me, so I placed a little bucket by our changing table. The next time I was changing Wolfgang, I held him over the bucket in a squat and said *Pinkelpause!* (pee-pee break), and he peed and pooed!

From then on, I offered the bucket every time I changed him and also when he signaled that he had to go, or else when he had been dry for a very long time. This worked especially well for poops, and we got quite a few pees, too. He was very good at showing his need to go when carried in the sling. He'd squirm and get restless in a very specific way. I also discovered that he could wait a little bit between signaling and going. He almost never wet his diaper while I was undressing him. A nice side effect was that I was never again peed on while at the changing table (this had happened quite a lot before).

After starting with infant pottying, we also slowly switched to cloth diapers. I wanted to know whether a diaper was wet or not. With IPT, cloth diapering was not half as much work as I had expected. I usually only had to wash diapers once a week and they didn't even fill the washer.

Sometimes I felt rather lonely in my choice to use IPT. I didn't know anybody trying the same thing. All I had was this single chapter in one book! I was really happy when I came across an English parenting page that mentioned something called "infant potty training." Following the links, I found several more sites and an e-mail list. I was not on my own after all! Wolfgang was 8 months old then, and we had been at it for half a year already.

My mails to the elimination communication list became our IPT diary, and I've condensed some of them here.

*"Wet diapers are quite common, but although Wolfgang poops about 3–5 times a day, I only get a soiled diaper about once or twice a week."*

I usually just put him in disposables when going out, as I felt a bit awkward about taking Wolfgang to the toilet when we were not at home. I was also thinking that I wouldn't be able to respond to him very well when out. But reading about others going completely diaperless all the time gave me the courage to try to let him do his business without diapers, even when out. And guess what? It worked BETTER when we were out than at home!

At 8½ months, we started using a potty. I bought the Baby Björn "Little Potty" and continued holding him like I had on the bucket, so it was a smooth and gradual transition. We also started to use the toilet.

Every year we take a bicycle trip in the summer, staying at a different place each night. Nine-month-old Wolfgang came along in his bike trailer and really seemed to like it. Of course we stopped to offer him to go. He did a lot of "tree watering," which he always loves, and I enjoyed not having to take along as many diapers as I otherwise would have. We were away for a week. I used two cloth diapers till they got wet and then continued with disposables (about 2½ a day on average). I washed the cloth diapers at the hotel in the evening and they dried during the night, so I could start over again with them in the morning. Near the end of the trip, Wolfgang obviously had had enough of staying in a different place every evening, and told us through his toilet behavior by refusing to pee or poop on cue.

Fortunately our communication and success rate improved soon after returning home. But not long after, at the age of 10–11 months, we started having quite a few misses due to crawling, teething, a cold, etc. I had been really spoiled up until then because we rarely missed any poops since starting at age 2 months. Here are some diary entries about this phase.

"I suppose it's the pressure on his bladder while creeping on his tummy. If I pick him up to toilet him, he is all indignation and absolutely sure he doesn't have to go. I put him down again and it takes less than 5 minutes for him to pee in his diaper or on the floor. The only way to avoid it is to carry him in the sling until he has to go. He pees a lot, and then there is a break of about 30–45 minutes where he can lie on his belly without peeing."

"At the moment, we are having a poo problem. In the last 2 weeks, I missed one out of two or three poops almost every day. Wolfgang has begun to pull himself up on his knees and into a sitting position, and somehow by doing this he goes without giving a sign. He protests the dirty diaper, though!"

I kept things in perspective with the thought that, were I using full-time diapers, EVERY poo would be going into the diaper at that age. And of course, things improved after a while.

"We are getting much better at this now that I realize he can hold it much longer. In the afternoon and also when we are away from home, he doesn't have to pee for one or two hours.

"I'm so exited! Wolfgang just did some great communicating! I was sitting at the computer while he was playing quietly nearby. Suddenly he started talking angrily, crawled over to his potty and sat down next to it. I took off his pants (no dipes) and put him on it and—peeeee!"

We gradually used diapers less and less.

"Still no misses! Wolfgang seems to have developed some incredible control almost overnight.

"Yesterday afternoon I visited a friend. When we had been there for about an hour, I asked if Wolfgang could use the toilet. 'You can use the changing table.' 'No, thanks, we need the toilet. He's got to pee.' 'If you need a fresh diaper . . .' 'No, actually he's not wearing one. :-)' 'You mean he's TOILET TRAINED????' 'Well, a bit' 'You're kidding!'

"Wolfgang is 13 months old now and hasn't been wearing daytime diapers for weeks. He wears undies and pants instead."

His starting to walk at 14 months threw us off track again a bit, but I was expecting this from what I had read, so I didn't worry. We did not go back to using diapers.

"Wolfgang is too busy taking his first steps to care for anything else. (He is able to walk up to 7 steps without holding himself anywhere!) And aside from peeing in his pants without warning quite often (well, two or three times a day—we're just spoiled, so it seems often), Wolfgang also did some great communicating. The best was the following episode: He crawled out of the room and started banging the wooden block he was holding against something. I yelled: NEIN! (no!) because I thought he was hitting the mirror. As I went to have a look, he was standing in front of the bathroom and banging at the door! When we sat down on the toilet, he pooed. :-)"

Things got a lot easier when at 15 months, he started signing and using a word for his need to go.

"Yesterday after peeing twice and not going to sleep while nursing and also not going to sleep in my arms, I finally put him in his bed. He sat up, waved his hand, said 'dede' (his word for Toilette) and then his diaper was wet. I hadn't thought that the need to pee was keeping him awake since he had peed twice shortly before. After changing him, he went right to sleep."

After many ups and downs concerning nighttime, we stopped using diapers at night at 16 months. I wrote this about nights:

"There is one word for how we are doing, and that is 'fabulously!' When doing laundry today, I realized that Wolfgang has been consistently dry at night for at least a week, as there was not a single diaper in the load!"

At 18 months, we were nearing "graduation."

*"Accidents are VERY rare. Wolfgang consistently announces his need to go by saying 'dede' and waving his hand in that special way. I don't really have to keep track of his timing anymore. Of course, he cannot pull down his pants yet. This is not elimination control but 'dressing and undressing,' and that's another chapter."*

I considered Wolfgang finished with toilet training at 20 months:

*"Now I don't even have to think about when Wolfgang went the toilet the last time, I can trust him to tell me. I even stopped asking him after four or more hours elapsed. When he has to go, he tells me. And if he doesn't ask, he doesn't have to go. We still have an occasional accident when Wolfgang is very distracted and tired, but who cares! We've even had our first 100 % accident-free week (actually even 8 days) a week ago."*

When pregnant with our second child I was already looking forward to using IPT again. Can you imagine someone looking forward to toilet training? Well, I was. And after the birth, we started right away while still in hospital:

*"On the first day, I stayed in bed bonding with Jutta. The next day I did the diapering. They have a room for it, with several changing tables and a sink. The nurses advised to use the sink to rinse baby's bottom after a poo, so I didn't hesitate to let Jutta use that sink as a toilet. I talked to her about how nice it was to be clean and took my time at the changing table, making sure she was diaperless for quite some time. I also held her in a squat in my arms over the sink for about half a minute and made the 'sssss' sound. Nothing happened. I didn't expect it to. I just wanted her to get used to the procedure. On the third day, I left her bare-bottomed on the changing table for some time, and then: Hooray! A pee on the changing table! A few hours later, she peed for me again! 'Sssss.' I didn't put a diaper back on, and after a short time she started to poo. I lifted her gently, held her over the sink and she pooed again! In the afternoon when I held her over the sink and made the 'sssss' sound, nothing happened. Then I tightened my abdominal muscles (she could feel it) and grunted. She responded immediately and pooed in the sink. Wow!"*

At 4 weeks I wrote:

*"After using \*a lot\* of diapers in the beginning, due to constantly changing them, we definitely saved diapers today: Jutta wore the same cloth diaper for more than 12 hours!"*

And at around 7 weeks we started to slowly, slowly go diaperfree:

*"Sometimes Jutta goes diaperless now in the morning. I put her in undies and pants until they get wet, then diapers again."*

We started nighttime right from the beginning as well. At first it would take me about 45 minutes to nurse her, then I'd take her to the bathroom where she would pee and poo in the sink in several spurts. We soon got the hang of it and only needed 15 minutes for nursing and bathroom.

*"Jutta (6 months) is not wearing diapers about half of the nights right now and staying dry half of the nights, too, mainly depending on how tired and committed I am."*

We completely stopped using diapers with Jutta at 7 months—day and night, at home and out.

*"What do we need diapers for? You can do without them, and a 'miss' is not more of a mess than other things, like spitting up and leaking diapers, that always happen with a baby anyway. Still, diapers are so ingrained in our perception of babies that it took me 12 months to get rid of them with Wolfgang (daytime!) and 7 months with Jutta."*

At 13 months she started to use the potty by herself:

*"She is getting better and better at doing this and the last few days when Jutta had to go, I'd just take her pants off and place the potty nearby. She now handles the rest by herself."*

We went on one of our bicycle trips again, travelling with a 3 ½ year old and a 13 month old without taking a single diaper! Jutta only had one or two accidents a day, and we would just wash her pants and dry them on our trailer.

Now at 19 months we are still having around 1–2 accidents a day (some days none!). I am partly using timing and intuition, and Jutta signals by making a farting sound with her lips. She can pull her pants and undies down by herself and only needs help to get them up again. She is close to taking full responsibility for her elimination needs. And I am happy to confirm that IPT was as much fun the second time around as it was the first!

Freddy's German web page is at:
http://www.continuum-concept.de/windellos.htm
Her German-language TopfFit e-mail list can be found at:
http://de.groups.yahoo.com/group/TopfFit

# chapter 7

# india

N eelam and Raj Mehta raised two children in Gujarat, India, using infant potty training. Their daughter Sheil started at four months and
completed potty training at 13 months while their son Yash took
about two months longer to train than his sister. Here is what Neelam had to
say in 2000 on the topic of toilet training her children in the state of Gujarat.

My husband Raj helped me quite a bit with toilet training. We lived with
our extended family so I also had a lot of help from my relatives in the
home. In India, we nurse our babies, then get a feel for how long after a
feeding baby needs to go to the bathroom. Mothers intuitively know when
it is time to take baby to the bathroom. It doesn't take long to learn this.

The feeling is based in part on timing but not on watching a clock. It is a matter of realizing it is time. Poor people, lower class people in my country don't wear watches. These mothers feel and know when their babies need to eliminate.

The closest thing to a diaper that we use is a little cotton garment called a *balotu*. It resembles a G-string or skimpy underwear. This infant underwear is more comfortable and functional than a bulky towel between the legs, which is how Western diapers appear to us. Our infant underwear is made of cotton and ties onto the baby at the top of the thighs. You can buy these little garments ready-made in shops. We wash them and use them over and over. We use these on infants before we start toilet training and also in the beginning stages of training, in between visits to the bathroom. Once our babies head to the bathroom on their own, we let them wear regular children's underpants.

Bathrooms in India are simple and small. Ours was smaller than four feet by four feet. Indian bathrooms typically consist of a tile or cement floor. We don't have plumbing fixtures like a tub, sink or toilet. Instead, we just squat down and go on the floor. There is always a bucket full of water and a bar of soap in the bathroom. We rinse the floor and clean ourselves. This may sound unhygienic to people in the West, but our bathrooms are very clean.

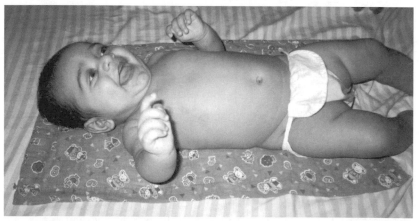

*Neelam Mehta*

A 3-month-old boy, in comfy cotton Indian infant underwear

When we want an infant to pee, we start by making the sound "sssss," which sounds like water. After a while, we just tell them to "go pee pee." We don't make a special noise for them to poop.

We do not have a term for "toilet training" or "potty training." In fact, we do not use a potty when we train our children. When babies are really small, there are two things we do to keep them clean. One is to have them lying on a blanket or soft cloth on a cot (bed). When it's time to poop, we gently grasp and raise the baby's ankles in order to lift his buttocks off the blanket while he is pooping. This way he doesn't get soiled. We replace the cloth under him with a clean one, then lay him down again. Another way we take small babies to poop is by cradling or holding them in our arms while they eliminate. When our children are old enough to stand and squat, we show them how to squat in the bathroom.

I started toilet training my daughter Sheil when she was 4 months old. There were times where Sheil peed in her underwear at first, but I paid attention to the timing between her pees and learned when to take her to the

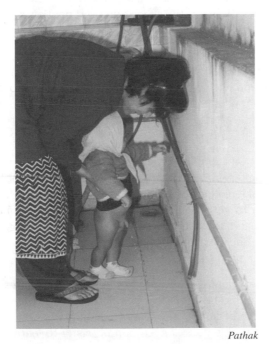

*Pathak*

Mother supports 12-month-old as he pees
in typical Indian bathroom (Gujarat, India)

toilet on time. I would nurse Sheil, then take her to pee about an hour later and then take her at regular intervals after that. I would take her to the bathroom, remove her underwear, make the "sssss" sound and remain in the bathroom with her until she went. I held her in my arms, supported her head and squatted or sat while I waited for her to go. Within a few weeks, the time between pees increased, so I would take her every hour and a half. Then it increased to every two hours. When she went for me, I would praise her, smile and hug her so she would understand she did something good.

At 4 months, I noticed that Sheil would poop three times a day. I wrote down the times she would poop in the morning, afternoon and evening and take her to the bathroom when I knew she needed to poop.

At 6 months, Sheil stopped pooping three times a day and only pooped once a day, in the morning. She was almost finished with bowel training at 6 months. She understood that when I took her to the bathroom and removed her infant underwear, it meant she should poop or pee. Around 6 months, I believe Sheil really understood toilet training. She sensed why I took her to the bathroom and what she should do there. I stopped using infant underwear with her at this stage and used panties instead.

Sheil also started crawling around 6 months. She would crawl to the bathroom door, remain there, look at me and make sounds to get my attention. I think she was trying to say "Ma" or "Mommy." I understood that she was calling me and letting me know she had to go to the bathroom. She would remain by the bathroom door until I arrived to take her to the toilet. As soon as I took her in the bathroom and removed her panties, she would pee.

Sheil took her first steps at 7½ months. At 9 months she walked well on her own and would say "Mommy bathroom, Mommy bathroom" when she had to go. I considered her toilet trained at 9 months, even though she still needed my help to get into the bathroom and pull down her panties. I taught her to squat in the bathroom and showed her how to go without getting herself wet. She was completely toilet trained, able to do everything independently, at age 13 months.

I started toilet training my son Yash when he was 3 months old. From the age of 3 months, he never wet the bed at night, whereas his sister sometimes wet the bed until the age of 4½ months. But for the rest of the potty process, it took my son longer than his sister to learn.

He started to crawl around 4 months but didn't head for the bathroom door on his own until a few months later. I used Indian infant underwear on my son until he was 6½ months. It was harder for me to know when he had to pee than it was with his sister. He would pee more often, so it took more time than I spent working with his sister to keep him dry. He pooped once or twice a day, always in the morning and sometimes in the afternoon.

Around 8 months, he understood what the bathroom was for. At 8 months, he started crawling to the bathroom door when he had to go. At this point, he started wearing underpants. He walked and had good control over elimination at 12 months. In fact, he would always hold it until I arrived to take him in the bathroom. He didn't start talking for another half year, so instead he would use his own sign language to tell me things. He had ways to sign to me if he wanted to pee or poop. I considered him toilet trained at 12 months of age, but he still needed help with his clothing at that age.

Yash was 1½ years old when we left India for the United States. He was almost finished with toilet training at that time so I never used a diaper on him in this country.

Children learn things at an early age in India. This is partly due to living with an extended family where there are always at least eight people living in a house. Children are never alone. There are always two or more people with them. They hear people talking all the time. We talk to our children a lot, and they learn very quickly this way. In my home, if I was not around, my sister, grandmother, mother-in-law or husband would be there for my children. I had a lot of help. I was the coordinator of the potty training. I would be sure someone was always available to take the babies to the bathroom on time.

We sleep with our children in India. In most situations, they sleep in the same bed with the parents for as long as they want. In cases where a baby cannot sleep well in the same bed with someone else, the baby sleeps in its own little bed in the same room as the parents.

In the past, this method of toilet training from birth was used throughout India. Nowadays, I'd say it is used in about 85% of the country. This is because many women now have jobs. In cities, up to 50% of women work and don't have time to raise their kids like we traditionally raise them. The women in cities like to be modern and use the Western-style toilet training with diapers. Families in our cities are living more like Western families. They don't live with the extended family anymore. This is partly because a wife often cannot get along with her mother-in-law. Married couples don't want to have to deal with the rest of the extended family. This means mothers in cities don't have help from the extended family and are using diapers to delay potty training. In villages, families still live together and use the tradi-tional and natural means of toilet training.

In my culture, until recently we didn't think about diapers much. It's becoming fashionable now to use diapers, but when I raised my kids, they weren't used much. Toilet training is just one of many things or routines a mother and family does for a baby, such as feed the baby, dress the baby or walk the baby. We aren't embarrassed about breastfeeding or toilet training. When we visit friends, we use their bathroom to take our babies to pee on time. Our friends do not mind at all. Toilet training doesn't stress or frus-trate people in India. We don't view it as time consuming or a chore like Westerners do. It's just a natural thing, something you do for your baby, part of your duties to raise a child. As a nation, we love children very much and enjoy raising them.

If I had another child while living in the United States, I would still start toilet training in infancy, the same as I did for my other two children. I could not do it on my own since my husband and I own and operate a shop. I would send for my extended family and bring them over from India to be with me and the baby.

# chapter 8

# iraq

Although the traditional method of training in Iraq is now to use diapers until 6 or 8 months old and then to teach the baby to sit on the pot, Basma Baker (of Baghdad) reported the following in 1989:

Some mothers try training even smaller babies (i.e., 2–3 months old) by holding them over the toilet or pot. A mother of six children tells me that she has been using this method since her first baby (her mother taught her) and that it was very successful and that since 4–5 months old, her children started to stay dry and they cry or make some noises to let her know that they need to go to the toilet.

This mother had no one to help her. She did not wake her children at night, but tried to make them pee last thing before bed. Her children were toilet trained at 7–8 months. The method was very successful. It was easier with girls.

Since I heard of this method, I tried to use it with my first baby, but I was not successful. Maybe I don't have enough patience. My friend with the six children says that the method was not frustrating. Maybe her babies were too good.

# chapter 9

# japan

J apanese mother *Ai Nozawa brought up five children using her own version of infant potty training. She has one son, four daughters and fourteen grandchildren. She was 65 years old when this report was filed in 1988 by one of her relatives, Kumiko Iwamoto. Kumiko explained, "My mother's cousin, Ms. Nozawa, lives alone. She is very busy and sometimes disappears because she often visits her children."*

I have heard from her that she began the training from birth with all her children. She opened the diapers at the right moment and called to her children, *shii shii* (which means "pee pee") while the children were urinating, and as a result she completed the training before her children were one year old. She was satisfied with this method.

She began the training from the 7th day after birth. She spread paper (for example, newspaper) on the floor (the passage which is usually boarded in Japan) and put a diaper on the paper. She made her baby sit on that diaper and called to it *shii shii*. She did this and observed the intervals of urination of the baby.

After her baby became 6 months old, she held it on a stool in a toilet. She devised a way to make the atmosphere in the toilet joyful; for example, she decorated the toilet with flowers.

Her husband and her husband's mother assisted her with the training. She did not wake the babies at night. The method was time consuming.

She later helped her children with toilet training of her grandchildren. The method was successful for all her grandchildren. All of them completed the training when they were about one year old. The mothers enjoyed it and found it a good method.

It was easier with the girls than the boys, because generally boys are less sensitive than girls and also because the intervals of urination of girls are longer than those of boys. The intervals of urination for boys were 20 or 30 minutes at the beginning.

This method is not widespread in Japan, as the use of diapers is more convenient. Japanese mothers usually begin toilet training in warm seasons (spring or summer) after their children turn one year old.

In Japan, people generally spread thick rush-woven matting called *tatami* on the floor in houses. In the winter season, the matting is hard to get dry if the children have a toilet accident. Therefore, mothers shift the beginning time by what season their children become one year old.

The traditional Japanese method is to sit a child on a stool in a toilet or a pot called *omaru* at the right moment, when the diaper has been dry for a long time, and say to the child, *shii shii*, etc. The infant word for "urine" is *shii shii*, *shikko* or *chikko*. And the mother gives the highest praise to the child when the child has succeeded in making water in a toilet.

# chapter 10

# malaysia

*S* *aw Har relayed information via e-mails in 2002 on the topic of potty training in Malaysia. She admires the patience, encouragement and time that mothers dedicate to their babies during toilet training.*

Some Malaysian babies start potty training as early as 2 or 3 months old. The baby is held over his potty until he is able to sit on his own. The mother makes a "pissing" sound until her baby responds and urinates. Defecation is usually encouraged in the morning. The mother makes a more forceful sound like "mmm, mmm, mmm" until her baby responds. Potty training works well, and babies learn very fast!

I've heard from some mothers that their babies are so well trained that they only need to change nappies once or twice a day. Babies are taught to do their "business" regularly and happily. Mothers are happy too, knowing that their babies are clean and healthy.

It is surprising for Malaysians to hear that American toddlers are toilet trained after 2–3 years of age. Wouldn't it be harder to get them to sit on the potty, as they would have grown very active by then?

Let's hope that more women will try potty training their infants and experience the joy of finding out that their infants can understand and respond to what is being taught to them and to know that babies are truly wonderful little beings.

# chapter 11

# myanmar
# (burma)

D r. Nyo Nyo Any Mrcog, consultant obstetrician and gynecologist from Ottwe, responded to my inquiries by providing information "based on my own experience and also by inquiring of other mothers" in 1988.

The traditional method of toilet training in the villages of my country is to make the child sit on the feet of his mother, whose feet would be about 6 inches apart, while she is sitting on a low stool, either knees flexed or knees stretched.

This type of training is started by the age of 6 months and completed when the child is able to communicate and picks up the habit; i.e., about the age of 18 months. This method has been passed on for generations after generations. No research work has been done in this field to say how many centuries it has been used.

Some mothers do begin the training at birth, at about 2 weeks of age. The mother holds the infant's feet while it is lying on a diaper. Then the mother makes sounds like *inn-enn*. In fact, I used this method with my babies. Whenever they wanted to pee or pass a stool, they became restless and at that time, I made the sound and the baby started passing.

# chapter 12

# philippines

E ric Dedace interviewed several mothers and grandmothers in the countryside near Sariaya. He photographed them toilet training their infants and small children and filed this report in 2002.

In rural Philippines, especially areas of low-income families, toilet training is casual and relaxed and is begun when a child is old enough to sit and hold its head upright. Babies are considered too young to start before this. Small children are generally taken outdoors to eliminate. In traditional houses with slotted bamboo floors (these consist of bamboo strips with spaces in between and raised a few feet from the ground to facilitate added ventilation), babies and small children are allowed to urinate on the bamboo floor. The urine falls directly to the ground and seeps into the dry soil.

One way to determine if a boy is ready to pee is to see if his penis is hard and if so, the mother gently shakes the organ while saying "sssss" or "shh-shh-shh" to encourage urination. A Filipino father reported that if his infant sons were asleep, he could ascertain when they needed to pee by lifting their diapers and determining if the testicles were closer to the groin area, rather than limply hanging downwards. He would then hold a potty in position and make the "shh-shh-shh" sound.

Cloth diapers, often hand-me-downs, are used. TV ads encourage parents to use disposable diapers, but these are too expensive for many. (Families who don't have a TV watch programs at the homes of friends or relatives.) Toddlers use underpants (also often hand-me-downs). Babies and children from the poorest families go naked.

Before defecation, the mother fills the potty with just enough water to cover the bottom and prevent the waste matter from sticking, to facilitate cleaning the receptacle. Those who do not have a potty simply let their babies defecate on a piece of paper which is then thrown away in a ditch with running water or else into a makeshift toilet dug in the ground and surrounded by coconut palms arranged for privacy. Cues for defecation include "oo, oo, oo" and "mmmm." Mothers know when their babies have to go, based on instinct, timing and body language, especially facial expressions.

Toilet paper is not used. Instead, soap and water are used to wash the buttocks area after defecation. A child is able to do this around 4–5 years old, sometimes as old as 6 years.

In poorer areas, there is sometimes less attention paid to toilet training due to the large number of children in a family and the short spacing between births. A poverty-stricken housewife not only has her children and household chores but also may be forced to work at menial jobs outside the home, in which case siblings end up caring for babies. Sometimes extended family members can help, but often they too are overburdened with their own work.

When I asked some mothers if they ever get angry over accidents, they looked at each other and laughed, amused at the question. They said, "How can you get angry if there is an accident, much less get angry at a child who still doesn't understand how to communicate fully?" Filipinos are very patient, relaxed and laid-back with small children, especially helpless infants. We are less disciplined and organized than some cultures, but we have more

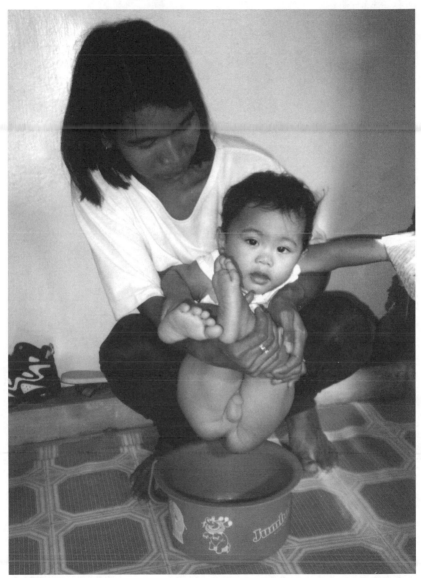

*Eric Dedace*

11-month-old in bowel training position
(Lutucan Malabag, Philippines)

fun and are more inclined to smile a lot. We also have the ability to cope well with stress.

If the notion of a baby being properly toilet trained means being able to communicate so there won't be any mess, then this happens around the age of 2–3 years. At this time, babies can imitate the cue sounds their mothers make and advise in advance that they need to go.

# chapter 13

# taiwan

## Henry Chen, Jr., (Attorney in Taipei, 1988)

1. We usually use diapers with infants between 1–3 months of age. This is because infants are not so reactive to outside circumstances at that stage.

   After the 3rd or 4th month, diapers are still used, but parents will untie the diaper every 3 or 4 hours and hold the baby in front of a spittoon (pot, close-stool) or a flush-toilet (no matter if the baby is asleep or awake) and then whistle a special single tone (a sound like "hsu") for about 2–3 seconds and repeat the whistle till excretion. If not successful, we'll wait 5–10 minutes to do the same action again.

After 4–6 months training, most of the babies grow used to it and excrete on time.

2. I believe this method has been in use by the majority of Chinese families (over 80%) over hundreds of years. Equipment used is the same except flush-toilet.

3. The "whistle" system is the main system. As far as we know, some of the parents (less than 10%) let their baby listen to music instead of a whistle sound when they use the method.

4. We learned the method from our family. As a matter of fact, my two daughters were trained by their grandmother since their 1st month of life.

5. The method is common.

6. Generally, grandma will help with toilet training the children.

7. Toilet training is completed at about 10–14 months of age, depending on the patience of the parents when they train the baby.

8. There is no difference in training girls and boys.

9. I questioned three couples and was told that all of them use this method and were all very successful.

10. We were satisfied with the method.

11. The method was very convenient, but at night it is annoying, since parents have to get up at night.

## Mrs. C. S. Chen (Magazine Editor, Taipei, 1988)

*Mrs. Chen was kind enough to include some of my questions in a poll she conducted for Woman-ABC magazine.*

*What are the primary methods of training used in China?*
- Train the child to utter sounds when he (she) feels like evacuating.

- Whistle or hiss to provoke the child's desire of evacuation.

- Say "hmmm" when holding the child on the toilet.

- Train by calculation based on feeding time.

- Turn on the faucet.

- When the child can sit, use a small potty.

- Have the child sit on the potty at the proper time of day.

*What kind of device did the ancient Chinese mothers use?*
- any available place
- squatting style toilet
- grass toilet paper
- spittoon
- washing basin
- bottle (for boys)
- small round basin
- open-crotch pants (split pants)
- no device at all

*What method did mothers then use for training their babies?*
Lay the child on its back. Unfasten the diaper. Hold and slightly raise up the baby's legs. Make hissing or "hmmm" sounds to prompt the baby to urinate or defecate.

## The Whistling Sound in Adulthood

If the whistling sound is used for many months into toddlerhood, adults who grew up eliminating upon this cue sometimes still react to the conditioning in adulthood. (The same applies to babies who hear the "sssss" sound for a long time.) Here are comments made in 2000 by three people who speak from experience.

1. My husband is furious about me making the "shhhh" sound for our baby because he feels when our son hears the sound later in life that he will need to go to the bathroom. This happens to my husband every so often and he doesn't like it.[1]

2. In Taiwan, many people use a particular whistle. To this day, when I hear it, I feel like going. When we started toilet training our girl, most of the time I ended up going before she did! I hear a lot of people joke about having the same response, but more like suddenly realizing that it may be a good idea to go to the restroom.[2]

3. An American friend of ours who was teaching a class to Chinese students would occasionally whistle absentmindedly out of habit. He noticed some of the students started squirming and then they asked him to please not whistle, as it made them afraid that they were going to pee.[3]

# chapter **14**

# turkey

T he following two reports from Turkey were written in 1988. The mother submitting the first one remained anonymous. When asked if she found it easier to toilet train her son or daughter, she replied, "I think it was easier with my boy because I could offer him a jar."

## Turkish Mother, Istanbul

I know some people toilet train their infant children by holding them to the toilet sink very frequently during the day. I also know mothers who toilet train their children in infancy by holding them to the sink and running water from the tap to imitate the sound of urination. I know many people who have told me that they have succeeded by this method.

## Seyma Dogramaci, Psychologist, Istanbul

I have been in the field for 10 years. I work with children and families on different issues, including bedwetting problems. I am therefore pretty much acquainted with the toilet training methods of urban parents. My answers to your questions are based on the knowledge I gathered from my clients, my relatives and, being the mother of a 10-month-old son, direct from my own personal experience.

Mothers tend to toilet train babies as early as they can. They mainly want to accomplish this before the baby is a year old. The usual way of toilet training is to put the baby in lukewarm water after he is washed and whisper "shhh" in the ear of the baby, which will hopefully motivate urination. If this is done repeatedly at the appropriate intervals, the baby acquires a rhythm. What I mean by "appropriate intervals" is the frequency of the baby's urination, which is mostly determined by keeping him nude in the summer months to see how often he urinates. Once his frequency is obtained, the mother will have to invite the baby for urination at slightly shorter intervals.

It is often the case that daytime toilet training is completed before nighttime training. Mothers leave the diapers off in the day, but keep them on at night for some time more. Most children I have worked with have been reported to have their toilet training complete between the ages of 1 and 2.

As the baby grows older, potties are introduced around 8–9 months. Mothers and grandmothers are the ones to initiate the training. I do not think there is a significant difference between boys and girls in being toilet trained.

The method is usually learned from the elders of the family. Babies are not awakened at night for training purposes, but it is advised to do so when bedwetting is an issue at older ages.

# chapter 15

# vietnam

R andy Mont-Reynaud raised three children using infant potty training from birth. She holds a Ph.D. in Developmental Psychology from Harvard University. She studied with Jerome Kagan and conducted research for her dissertation on emotional and cognitive development among Vietnamese infants in the second year of life. She is currently at Stanford University.

Dr. Mont-Reynaud went to Vietnam in 1967 to study child development. She lived in Saigon for six months, attained a modest level of competence in speaking Vietnamese, then returned to the United States and obtained her master's degree in anthropology. In 1972 she returned to Vietnam and spent two years studying child development and religious beliefs in a village setting. She took up residence in the village of My Duc, some miles from the Cambodian border, in the province of Chau Doc. She adopted her first child while residing in the village—and thus learned about child rearing firsthand. Her son was rarely in diapers in Vietnam and comfortably (i.e., without stress) made the transition to proper toilet behavior by the age of 18 months when he accompanied Dr. Mont-Reynaud back to the USA.

Dr. Mont-Reynaud raised two more children, a son and a daughter, in the USA. Like their older brother, they were kept out of diapers as much as possible and comfortably transitioned to standard toilet behavior. Her report was written in 2000.

I think it is a misnomer to call this process "potty training" since this term implies teaching, or coercing something on, a child, which is not the case. "Potty training" also implies that a potty is used from the start, and this is not necessarily the case in a traditional village setting, such as Vietnam or anywhere else for that matter. In Vietnam, where I learned about infant care and toileting, infants and toddlers are held off the porch or at arm's distance of a lap or taken outside to "go." I call the process "mother training" or "caregiver training" because what it really relies on is the mother or caregiver being responsive to the infant's cues and getting the child to the proper place/location. Adult "toilets" in Vietnam may be shanty structures over a fishpond or river—not an appropriate place for babies! "Misses," in the form of caregivers failing to carry babies to the proper place at the right time, are occasions for laughter . . . and that's all.

The process starts with a newborn. First, you observe when your infant pees or poos and make a little whispering noise at that instant—or soon after. It appears that infants quickly recognize that when they relieve themselves this way, they also hear the whispering noise. Second, make the whispering noise when you know your baby is about to pee or poop. The baby will respond to your cue and "go" for you. It's Skinnerian, basic behaviorist psychology. It is undergirded by the simple fact that newborns pee and poop all the time. It all boils down to training children to respond to stimuli. It's hard to miss, especially if babies are not diapered and you are holding them. Then soon whenever they hear the noise, they will respond if they need to eliminate. The important thing to remember is that it works if they need to go—"if" being the operative word here. Obviously, if you don't have to go, you don't have to go. Newborns go very frequently; that is, they nurse, they poop and that's it!

It doesn't take long before an infant (around 1 month old) understands what you are doing. I say "understand," because you're not sitting down and explaining to the baby, "Whenever I do this, this is what you'll do." It's an association of feeling states. The baby is first feeling a sensation, feeling that he is peeing or pooing, then hearing your cue. Within a week, you can make the little whispering noise and the baby will pee or poo on demand (providing s/he needs to eliminate at that time).

If you don't have any help, the process is fairly labor intensive in the beginning. After labor and delivery, you may not feel like paying attention to this all the time. Sometimes you'll be too tired, busy or breastfeeding. At times it is hit or miss. If you make a good effort, it won't harm a child if you aren't there for every pee or poo. Babies still get it. You can't do it round the clock every single day. If you sometimes don't get to do it or forget, it's not crucial. The important thing to note here is that in the village, folks are not establishing correct toilet behavior as a goal at this stage (or later). This is just how they handle the situation until the child understands and is physically able to walk to the proper place.

Underlying all of this is the expectation that all children will "catch on," sooner or later. Villagers count on the child's natural growing awareness to take over. The early "mother training" seems designed to "coach" the right behavior. The villagers do not see themselves as "teaching potty training," anymore than they would be "teaching breastfeeding" to their babies.

Don't fasten a diaper around a tiny infant. It's better to place the infant on a diaper, but don't enclose the baby in the diaper in the traditional fashion. When you're nursing your baby, if the child is wrapped loosely in a towel or diaper, you'll know instantly when your child pees or poops.

How do you know when your baby needs to go? I asked this question in the Vietnamese village. The women looked at me and said, "Well, how do you know when you need to go?" This tipped me off to understanding the connection between toilet learning and the mother-child bond or the caregiver-infant bond. They are a very close unit. You come to know when your baby has to pee/relieve himself (same as we "know"—or think we know—when a child is hungry or tired. You just "know"!). Most mothers/caregivers (this could be a grandmother, sister or aunt) who are involved, in tune and bonded with their baby know when a baby is hungry or tired. Parents attribute some feeling state to a crying baby. The attribution may or may not be correct at first, but eventually over a short period of time it becomes correct as you get to know your baby.

It helps if you can keep your child bare-bottomed. Of course this is easier in warm climates like in California or Hawaii, but you can do it elsewhere if you want. This method eliminates the diaper rash problem, and it's about keeping a baby clean. The bottom line for potty training is this: If you do not want your child to poop in a diaper, take the diaper off!

You have to spend time with your baby or have a reliable caregiver in order for this to work. Siblings do this in Vietnamese villages for younger siblings. The caregiver needs to be responsive and know your child's needs—but isn't that what parenting is about?

When babies start crawling or walking, keep a little potty where they can see it. It's amazing, they just go there and do it. By the time babies can walk, they get where they need to go if they have observed that behavior. Around 15 months or so, kids begin to understand there is a standard. They understand they are supposed to be somewhere to go potty, that there is a place (i.e., potty) to pee and the rest of the world is not where you pee.

The Vietnamese regard mother training as a natural process. They don't expect children to have difficulties with it—and babies don't. The Vietnamese don't expect it to be problematic for the mother, and it isn't, although there are occasional "slipups." Mother training is something everyone accepts and expects, like breathing. No one teaches us to breathe, but we all do it. Mother training is not something that is learned. It is just something babies do from the moment they are born. They conform to a behavior. By comparison, people in Western cultures have made potty training into an unnatural act and an ordeal.

It is the mother who is primarily responsible for what Westerners call potty training. You might think that the mother never gets a break, but in Vietnam, the baby may be passed around to a whole cadre of siblings and extended relatives or just other folks.

In the villages, mothers don't use a potty, and traditionally there are no diapers. They sometimes wrap a towel around the baby on their lap. If the baby needs to pee, the women just hold the infant facing away from them, either on their lap or at the edge of the porch. The baby quickly comprehends, "I move through space to do this elsewhere."

There are usually no toilets in Vietnamese villages. In the rare situations where there is a toilet, it's a Turkish toilet that you squat to use. Obviously an infant can't squat. The mother goes to the area, squats down, holds the baby with legs spread apart and the baby goes. So you bring the child to a part of the house, or a place outside the house, where it is to go. It's not very far to take the baby.

The Vietnamese don't use a backpack or infant carrier. Babies are held. You don't put a child down because there aren't many places to put a baby down in the village. The floors are dirt or cold ceramic tile, so small children are almost always physically held by somebody. Babies are never left alone. They sleep with their parents, grandparents or older siblings. As a rule, no one sleeps alone; most say they don't like to sleep alone.

Of course this is not a perfect system, and accidents do happen. The Vietnamese attitude towards accidents is very casual—elimination is just a normal thing, this is what babies do and when necessary, you clean it up. If a baby is starting to pee and he's on your lap, you just hold him over the porch to go, or you mop up the spill from the tile floor. If it's a dirt floor, you don't have to worry about it. In our culture there are other things to worry about like carpets and expensive clothing.

In Vietnam, it is a significant rite of passage to become a mother. We only pay lip service to this in our culture. Motherhood is not a rite of passage in America. It's a brief interlude on the way to something else, like waitressing your way through college.

When I lived in Vietnam, disposable diapers were fairly new, and some U.S. agencies were airlifting them into the villages. Laundering was one of the few paid occupations that poor uneducated village women could get, and the USA was airlifting in disposable diapers. People had no means of disposing of them—you can imagine the pollution problem. They were regarded as unsanitary anyway, which of course they are. The Vietnamese found a lot of creative uses for things we airlifted to them. Disposable diapers could be used as bandages, for example. We used to send them baby food in jars, and they thought that it was absolutely disgusting. They were living in a nation of banana trees, and we were sending Gerber's bananas in a jar! When they saw banana in a jar, they wondered how old it was and thought it was rotten. They'd throw out the baby food, rinse out the jars and use them as containers, candleholders, jars for fish sauces or incense burners. I imagine someday an archaeologist will find thousands of Gerber baby food jars in Vietnam and wonder how they got there.

I adopted my first child in Vietnam when he was 4 months old and began mother training immediately. The Vietnamese taught me a simple form of body language that baby boys exhibit when they have to pee. You know a boy needs to pee when you see his penis wiggle. This of course assumes someone is watching a baby boy's penis, which in our culture is a no-no. We don't look at genitals here, but in Vietnam, they do so without impunity. They know that a penis wiggles just before a baby boy has to pee. I'll bet mothers in this country don't know this because we have been bundling babies and toddlers up all these years.

By the time my baby was able to sit up, I could place him on a pot if I had one nearby. When he started walking at 10 months, he had a regular, once-a-day routine for poop. By age 1 year, he was regular like a clock. By around 10 months to a year, many babies are getting regular, and not peeing and pooing constantly, maybe just pooing once a day and hopefully in the morning. You put them on the pot, they do their business and that's it. The rest of the time it's just a matter of getting them to the pot to pee, which is trivial compared to pooing; that is, if you miss, it's less of a problem to clean. This is certainly accomplished during the first year of life. By the time children walk, they know what the elimination standard is and where they are supposed to be with it.

I took my son to an American hotel with a swimming pool when he was 10 months. In true Vietnamese fashion, he was bare-bottomed and wearing a T-shirt to protect him from the sun. Some American women came along and said it was too hot for him to wear a T-shirt and that he should be in a diaper. I put him in a diaper and took off the shirt. Then some Vietnamese women came along and were appalled that he was in a hot, plastic diaper that retained fluids and filth. They asked me how I could have him in the sun without a shirt. I took off the diaper and put the T-shirt back on. This is a clear-cut example of different cultural values and interpretations.

Since potty training is seen as a natural part of life, there is no official term for it in Vietnamese. If you ask them about it, they'll just giggle. They call it *di dai* which means "go pee-pee." The French say *fais pipi* and use a similar method. The French are notorious for early experiences in this domain. Traditionally, they used to try to have their kids potty trained by 6–8 months of age when they could sit up. When a baby sits up around 6 months, French mothers place their babies on a little disposable plastic potty with a handle. If you think about it, what did we do here 100 years ago? We didn't have washing machines or disposable diapers. I think women just subtly communicated with their babies at a lot earlier age, "This is how you do it. This is where you do it." We have forgotten that. There is no literature on it. Nobody considered writing it down! Women were too busy doing it to write about it, and men were not involved.

After spending a year in the village, we moved to Israel where we spent six months, then we moved to Vermont. I later had two birth children, a boy and a girl. It was a lot of fun trying to implement mother training with them from birth. I was 35 and living in California when my son was born. It might have been easier if I was younger. Between nursing and caring for an older child, an 18-hour labor and experiencing my first birth, it was a lot to handle. It seemed to me that newborns pee or poo at least every 20 minutes. I persevered. During the day when I was nursing him, I'd place him on top of a diaper on my lap. I'd make the "sssss" noise when I thought he had to pee and he'd go, or else I'd observe it after the fact and make the noise as soon as I noticed. After three days of this, I took him to the sink, held him over the sink, made the noise and he would pee or poo for me when he had to go.

There was a huge wall-to-wall mirror over the bathroom sink in our home. When I held him over the sink, he could see himself in the mirror and could see me holding him. When he peed or pooed, of course I was happy and would smile. (In Vietnam they don't smile and don't praise a child for peeing. Why should they?) I was thrilled to see him respond to my cue. He could see in the mirror that I was happy with his behavior. Then he would smile and see his reflection in the mirror, and that would reward him even more. I realized there is a cognitive aspect to this, but no one has put this in the context of toilet training. It is cognitively stimulating, making the association between external stimuli and a physical response; then on top of this, the baby is rewarded. In this context, it's by the reflection in the mirror, the smile on the mother's face.

I coupled mother training with some other customs and practices I brought back from Vietnam and thought were useful, namely using a low-lying hammock. I had a huge hammock and placed a beach mat under it, so if he peed it went on the beach mat. The hammock was low so if he fell, he would fall on the floor, which was carpeted. I added some padding in the form of pillows at either end. I would rock him to sleep during the day for a nap.

The noontime siesta is another useful custom I copied from the Vietnamese villagers. Years after my research, back in California, my son would nap in the hammock for two or three hours at noon and would take a second nap later in the day. He kept on taking his noontime nap until he was in first grade. Later on, when he was playing in chess tournaments at the age of 6 and 7 and we were traveling, he could rest in between rounds. There would typically be two rounds a day, and he would sleep between rounds.

The notion in Vietnam is that people and children *will* sleep and *like* to sleep at noon. You don't have to be tired to sleep. In this culture, we feel you have to knock yourself out before you can sleep or that children have to run around until they are exhausted before they will sleep and that in general they don't want to go to sleep. The Vietnamese do not make this attribution. They put a child down next to them, and the child goes to sleep. In our culture, we want to be out doing. We think children need stimulation, and our children fulfill our expectation.

In this country, we use strollers and infant carriers extensively, and babies are dressed or wrapped and bundled. Parents distance their children in this way. In Vietnam, babies and small children are always held. I continued the practice of holding my baby as much as possible, and he slept with us at night. He eventually slept in his older brother's room. His brother and father also helped with potty access when they were around.

When my son was 3 months old, it was time for his checkup. I took him to the local medical clinic. The doctor was about to examine him and asked me not to take the diaper off in case my son might pee. I told the doctor I'd deal with it, took my son to the sink, held him over the sink and made the noise. He peed in the sink. The physician said, "My goodness! That's the first time I've ever seen a 3-month-old potty trained." Of course he wasn't totally potty trained. I was the one who was "trained." I knew he had to go and knew what to do to make him go. The doctor was totally flabbergasted.

The way I proceeded with my children was to take them to go whenever practicable. They easily acquired the sense that these functions were to be espoused in specially defined places and not indiscriminately all over the house.

The second child I gave birth to was a daughter. I started mother training her at birth. I was living in California and used a hammock with her.

Her little brother was 26 months when she was born. She observed him using a potty and seemed to want to imitate him. This is another thing I had studied at Harvard—imitation and modeling. Children want to be like the model. If they see a model doing something, they want to do it too. Monkey see, monkey do. In our culture, children don't commonly see adults on the toilet. We close the bathroom door. A lot of mothers won't even let their children in the bathroom with them, and this is one reason why traditional toilet training takes so long.

My daughter was able to sit on a pot by 6 months. When children need to go, they see the potty and take care of business. Both these children could do this sometime between 6 and 8 months. They would crawl towards the potty on the carpeted floor in the living room. I would see them making their way across the room and sit them on the potty. If you expose children to the stimulus-response behavior in infancy and let them know what the expectation is, it's amazing how fast they catch on. By 6 months, babies understand that a potty is where they have to go. At 18 months, all my children were able to get to a potty by themselves and could therefore be without diapers. They were actually able to be without diapers much younger than 18 months, but there were no mistakes or accidents after 18 months. Needless to say, you have to be pretty attentive, as a parent, to facilitate this in a Western non-village setting—with carpets, no less!

In this country, potty training typically doesn't start until a child is 18 months or older, and by that age, it's something you have to teach. The child has been taught to poop in a diaper and now must unlearn this. By the time some children are 3 or 4, they are afraid to take off their diapers! Training involves a new apparatus, the potty, or a toilet two feet high off the floor, which may be scary for some children. It also involves getting the child's clothes off. In addition, a mother usually doesn't know when her child needs to go because he has been in a diaper all day. It gets to be a pretty high-pressure situation, and if the child fails to meet expectations, it becomes even a more high-pressured situation. In fact, it becomes such a pressured situation that many families don't begin until the child is 3 or 4 years old. This has been made possible by using disposable diapers. The disposable diaper industry encourages this behavior and capitalizes on the reluctance of parents—particularly new and/or young parents—to deal with potty training.

If a child is in a daycare context with one adult per six children, it is difficult to do mother training. It would be a lot easier if the children didn't have to wear diapers, but in our culture it would be hard. In a daycare situation, the owners would probably lose their license for sanitation reasons. Even worse, tongues would wag about child nudity, pedophilia and molestation.

We hold certain beliefs most dear to us in the United States, and in our belief system, children belong in diapers. If you challenge this notion, you run the risk of being ridiculed. To parents and so-called experts who object to raising babies without diapers: If you don't want to do it, don't do it. Save your carpets!

In Vietnam and other village cultures, toddlers see the consequences of their actions in regard to toilet behavior. It's time to look at what we left

*Randy Mont-Reynaud*

Dr. Mont-Reynaud's daughter (6 months)
and son (32 months)

behind when we left village life, look at what other cultures have to offer
and, without preconceived notions, glean the gems from other cultures. We
can't adopt all their customs or import them like soy sauce or tofu, but
many customs are worthy of reflection.

part **4**

# CROSS-CULTURAL
# STUDIES

# chapter 1

# cross-cultural comparisons

Part 4 of this book offers a selection of information and writings on infant elimination training gleaned from various reports and field studies around the world. This chapter begins with a description and discussion of the main methods of infant elimination training, then describes cultural differences between industrialized and nonindustrialized societies vis-à-vis basic infant care practices. Chapters 2–4 consist of excerpts and summaries of published material on the practice of infant elimination training by non-Western and/or nonindustrialized societies. The final chapter pays tribute to Western practitioners and looks to the future for a proper and honest campaign to increase awareness of the method.

## Methods of Elimination Training

There appear to be two main methods of elimination training in nonindustrialized societies, with a third possibility being a hybrid of the two in the form of progressing from one to the other. Diapers are generally not a part of these methods. Nurturant care is the norm.

### Method 1 – Mother-Baby Training

Method 1 is the basis of the method described in this book, whereby the mother or caregiver becomes familiar with baby's cues, timing and patterns; anticipates when to take baby to evacuate; holds baby in a particular position; and encourages elimination with a vocal cue such as "sssss." Baby quickly learns to associate the position and sound with elimination and responds to these stimuli by eliminating on cue. Mother and baby synchronize and blend their behavior, and baby soon begins to signal the need to eliminate in advance. With Method 1, the mother is attentive; communication, intuition and responsiveness play important roles; and mother and infant function as a symbiotic unit. The word "training" applies to the mother-infant dyad in that both undergo a reciprocal learning process, teaching and learning from each other.

### Method 2 – Baby Aiming

This method has two phases. At first, the mother or caregiver is not concerned with elimination training per se when the baby is small, since in some societies, tradition has it that a baby is too young developmentally to understand or do anything about elimination. When baby starts to eliminate, the caregiver aims the child away from herself and, whenever possible, in a favorable direction in terms of keeping the living quarters and herself clean. If baby eliminates inside a dwelling, the mother nonchalantly cleans up any mess or puddle (cleaning urine is not important in certain types of dwellings and in most outdoors locations) and carries on with her activities, almost as if nothing has happened.

Sometimes diaper substitutes made from natural, absorbent and easily accessible materials are used, such as moss, lichen, bark, yak hair, rabbit skin, leather strips or finely powdered dung. In Afghanistan where infants are swaddled, a baby's legs are wrapped around a little wooden or rubber tube that collects the urine and drains it into a bowl placed beneath a hole in the bottom of the cradle.[1]

When the baby reaches toddlerhood, he learns by observing and imitating older children and adults, and by gentle encouragement from his mother. With Method 2, the mother doesn't pay attention to elimination timing but merely cleans up after the fact, when necessary. This method is akin to the Western method of full-time diapering, minus the diapers, emotion and squeamishness about excreta. Babies are bare-bottomed or wear light underwear, so they are more in touch with their bodies and elimination functions.

### Method 3 – Combination of Aiming and Training

The mother starts by aiming baby away from her to eliminate (per Method 2) then eventually begins mutual training with baby (per Method 1) when she feels her baby is old enough to understand. In other words, baby aiming transitions or evolves into mother-baby training. There is no set age for the switchover, but it can occur as early as 2 months.

The research I have conducted thus far indicates that infant elimination training (Method 1) is prevalent in Asia, Africa and parts of non-tribal South America, although Method 2 is used in a few African and Asian societies. Infant elimination aiming (Method 2) is used by South American Indians, Australian Aboriginals and various societies in Oceania, and was used by American Indians in the past. Method 3 is used in parts of Asia and by some African tribes.

## Cross-Cultural Child-Rearing Practices

This section compares basic American (and to some extent, European) child-rearing practices with those prevalent in the developing regions of the world, including parts of rural Africa, Asia and South America. The majority of parents—no matter their nationality, race or culture—defer to the traditions, values, beliefs, knowledge, economics and feelings of their society, in an effort to do the best job they can in raising their children. Environment, technology, religion, morality and social trends also shape the child-rearing techniques of different peoples. It is misleading to think that child care in far-off countries has an archaic simplicity versus the complexity of the West or that the only difference between nonindustrial and industrial countries is a natural style of child rearing in developing countries that is in contrast with an artificial style in Western countries.[2]

There is not one child-care philosophy system that is superior to all others, nor is there one inferior to all others. Every system has its pros and cons. Through cross-cultural studies and research, parents are able to se-lect or reject individual practices and thereby customize and hone their own child-rearing style, calling on wisdom from history and from around the world. Parents should be free to study and adopt the customs and practices they believe are the best for their babies. In this regard, a quote from Margaret Mead's book *From the South Seas* comes to mind: "Lest one good custom should corrupt the world."[3] The fear of doing something different should not hinder parents from doing what they believe is right. In addition, parents who make an honest, intelligent and sincere effort to do what they believe is best for a child should not feel guilty if they later learn of a better way to have behaved or handled certain situations.

The biggest difference between Western child-rearing practices and those of many other parts of the world is the amount of close, physical contact between mother and baby. In rural areas of most developing countries, infants are:

- born at home (sometimes in a clinic) via natural childbirth and immediately held by mother or caregiver
- closely bonded with their mothers during a postpartum honeymoon ("babymoon"), often in seclusion, lasting from 7 to 80 days
- in constant and close physical contact with their mother or caregiver(s) until they walk
- held or carried throughout most of the day
- kept in bed, or on a mat or cot, beside their mother all night
- nursed on demand for 1–4 years, sometimes longer
- immediately soothed and never left to cry
- never alone
- rarely disciplined or punished
- generally not diapered (except in some affluent families or when using natural materials)
- not pressured to be toilet trained

A caretaking model along these lines was coined the "continuous care and contact model" (CCC) by Edward Tronick et al. in 1985. One person, usually the mother, is the primary caretaker, responsible for providing continuous care, constant contact and frequent, short periods of nursing.[4] An example of the CCC model can be found in Melvin Konner's work with the !Kung San (Bushmen) in Botswana where the !Kung infants he observed remained in physical contact with their mothers 70–80% of the time and were nursed four to five times per hour for short bouts. These observations were made during 20 months between 1969 and 1971.[5]

Anthropologist Robert LeVine theorizes that the attentive infant care practices of Africans and others are a cultural adaptation to high infant mortality rates in the countries and societies using them. He refers to this type of maternal behavior as a "folk pattern of preventative medicine in infancy" and a "constant medical alert, a chronic emergency mobilization to save the child at risk." By being held or kept close to a caregiver at all times, a baby is kept out of harm's way and closely monitored for illness. A quick response to crying provides immediate feedback about baby's condition. Minimizing crying from other causes heightens the value of crying as a signal of more serious problems such as disease. Continual breastfeeding assures that baby's fluid level is always sufficient, thus alleviating dehydration from diarrhea, which is one of the main causes of infant death in the tropics.[6]

Different societies have different ideas about what constitutes essential care and what is considered indulgent. LeVine and others postulate that certain behaviors by Western parents, such as a desire for intimacy in social relationships, seem indulgent to parents of lesser-developed areas. In the West, parents lavish their babies with physical and verbal affection, often in public. They believe verbal stimulation will encourage learning and cognition. They spend considerable time smiling at their babies. They make eye-to-eye contact, kiss, cuddle, sing, chat (high pitched or baby talk) and coo a lot, whereas mothers in other cultures typically do not and find these types of behavior indulgent. Westerners feel that mothers in some other societies are aloof in that they do not kiss and cuddle their babies. Gusii mothers do not speak to their babies, considering it a waste of time. Instead, they soothe and nurse.[7]

Most American and European parents believe that behaviors such as maintaining constant physical contact, "nursing on demand" and quickly responding to crying will spoil a child. In Western countries, much importance is placed upon rearing independent children. It is believed that this goal can be accomplished by instilling separateness, self-sufficiency and self-confidence in the child, starting at birth.[8] This same philosophy is seen in the disapproval and suppression of natural instincts, such as (extended) breastfeeding. Nursing a baby in public is often met with embarrassment or hostility. Breastfeeding beyond the age of 6–12 months or waiting for a child to self-wean at ages 2–4 years or older are shocking and repugnant to many.

The American emphasis on isolation starts in the hospital when a newborn is taken from its mother, or at home when the baby is placed in its own bed in a separate room. Compared with Africans, American babies undergo a sharp distinction between situations where they are left alone and those where they are in the company of others. In addition to never being left alone, African infants "are often present as nonparticipants in situations dominated by adult interaction, while the American infant is often kept in solitary confinement when he is not at the center of adult attention."[9] American babies are typically left in a crib, stroller, pram, bed or room on their own for an hour or more at a time, whereas most village African, Asian and South American babies are in continual physical contact with their mothers, carried in a sling or held in their mother's arms or lap. Constantly carried babies are in a position to develop social skills from a very young age by observing their mothers' activities and interactions and conversations with others. "Close physical contact also affords the infant considerable visual and auditory stimulation as he travels about with his mother. Contrast this with leaving a child in his crib for much of the day (even mobiles can get boring!)."[10]

Studies of institutions where children are deprived of a cozy home environment and a loving parent's care demonstrate that these children's social needs and skills suffer from a lack of personal attention. Institutionalized babies are often fed, diapered, played with and otherwise attended to on a schedule rather than in response to their signals. The lack of response to their signals results in apathy and progressive withdrawal.[11]

Whether carrying on conversations or performing labor or other tasks, a typical baby-wearing African, South American, Asian or Eskimo mother is always aware of the needs and state of her infant. It is never necessary to "go look and listen" the way American mothers do when the baby is at a distance or in another room.[12] All of this is true whether a baby is raised only by its mother or by multiple caregivers. Cultures using multiple caregivers include the Balinese (Bali), Gusii (Kenya) and Efe Pygmies (Zaire). The Efe method of multiple care starts at birth and lasts at least the first 18 weeks of life. During naturalistic observations of the Efe, it was found that each infant was cared for by 5–24 different assistants and that several mothers, whether lactating or not, suckled the babies. The system of multiple caretaking appears to be a solution to the problems and circumstances of the Efe foragers.[13]

Another component of nurturant cultures is the casual and relaxed attitude towards infant elimination and toilet training. Although the odor of feces can be unpleasant, there are no hysterically negative feelings about excreta. By way of comparison, Westerners often feel that dealing with elimination is disgusting and "yucky." Some resent or punish infants for making a mess. In extreme situations, these negative feelings lead to abuse and even murder.

Perhaps the reason we are so uptight about feces and urine is linked to our standard of living. Our standards of cleanliness, hygiene and sanitation are the highest in the world. We rarely see or come into contact with the waste products of other people. Rural villagers in lesser developed areas have at best open-gutter plumbing or else no plumbing at all. They use latrines, outhouses placed over water or garbage heaps as a toilet. Instead of toilet paper, they use leaves or their hand to wipe. Perhaps their living in relatively unsanitary and unhygienic conditions is the reason they are not squeamish about excreta.

Western babies are typically surrounded by toys and other possessions—another example of indulgence in the eyes of third world peoples. Most of the toys are for entertainment or learning purposes. Many also serve as a substitute for attentive care. A Western child quickly becomes bored and is at a loss without his toys and electronic gadgets and games, whereas children in many other societies are entertained without these things. I once proudly presented the latest American toys and gadgets to some small children in rural India, but they preferred to play in the fields or to collect rocks and pieces of kite string laying in the village streets. Their mothers ended up putting the shiny new toys in a display cupboard since the kids, including babies, had no interest in them.

Since the late 20th century, more and more Western families have been adopting a number of the nurturant practices discussed in this book—practices such as baby-wearing, family sleeping, quick response to crying and nursing on demand. At the same time, a number of families in third world countries are abandoning traditional ways and swapping some of their customs for Western ones, such as bottle-feeding, early weaning, diapers and leaving baby alone in a crib or other location—mainly in the case of affluent or well-educated families, but there are exceptions. A case in point involves aboriginal women who traditionally carried their babies into the fields in slings but who are now being encouraged to parent like Westerners.[14] In all countries, more and more mothers are working outside the home, and single-parent families are on the rise. Urbanization and commercialization lead to replacing traditional practices with ones considered to be more modern and convenient. Some societies have gone full circle. In Papua New Guinea, government promotion of breastfeeding is a response to increasing modernization and Western influence.[15] And concerning toilet training specifically, letting children run around diaperless is viewed as lower class by the upper class in some third world countries. In an effort to avoid the stigma, some poorer families are abandoning infant toilet training and using diapers.

## Precocity vs. Cultural Factors

Marcelle Geber spent considerable time studying African infants, especially Ugandans, in 1954–55 and concluded in a 1958 report that Ugandan
babies are precocious in some aspects when compared with Western babies. She was amazed to find that Ugandan babies smile and sit months
ahead of their Western counterparts. Geber attributed this precocity to several factors, including the placidity, greater physical activity and positive
view of motherhood of Ugandan women during pregnancy as well as the
quality of mothering in infancy. She also suggested that Ugandan babies
may be predisposed to develop faster than Caucasian babies. Both earlier
and ensuing observations and studies by others found that African babies
develop faster and are more precocious than the children of European
races.[16] The current consensus, which includes Geber, is that: (a) Genetics
is not the cause of African precocity[17] and (b) The cause of faster development of sensorimotor behaviors in African infants during the early weeks of
life is predominantly due to socioenvironmental factors. African babies receive far more physical and social stimulation than Western babies.[18]

Another way to consider the precocity issue is to view the development
of African babies as normal and that of Caucasians as slow. By not focusing
enough time and attentive care on our babies, or by being too protective
and cautious in certain ways we handle them, do we delay their development? Whatever the case, in the long run, it does not seem to make much
difference in North America and Europe whether a baby learns to sit at 2
months or 6 months of age.

When considering the early period of infant development, it is necessary
to view the newborn in a social (parenting or caregiving) context since without it they would die. Caregiving attitudes and behavior can often serve to
speed up the development of infants. As parental expectations, training and
handling of infants interact and feed off one another, they can contribute to
improving muscle tone and motor control in developing infants.

### Parental and Cultural Expectations

Every society has some sort of guidelines for how to handle a newborn, what precautions to take and when to expect what from baby.
Different people around the world have different expectations, training methods and time frames. The age at which a mother and a society expect her baby to learn certain skills can influence the way she
interacts with the baby. For example, most Baganda mothers believe

a baby does not hear sounds until the age of 3 months. As a result, these Baganda mothers do not begin singing to their babies until they are 3 months or older.[19]

In his study of the Digo tribe in Kenya, Marten deVries reported that cultural expectations and attitudes lead the Digo to view their babies as relatively hardy beings and active participants in life. Digo babies do not need special protection from many of the physical elements that Westerners guard against with their infants. The Digo are expected to accomplish certain things at a much younger age than Americans.[20] Where toilet training is concerned, the Digo are close to their infants and use a series of reciprocal cue-and-rule learning starting around the age of 2 months.[21] The tribe believes and *knows* their babies are capable of toilet conditioning in infancy. They therefore *expect* to watch for, learn and respond to elimination signals from their infants, then reciprocate with their own cues, in turn expecting baby to respond, effectively creating a snowballing of give-and-take between mother and infant.

In a later report, deVries compares the Digo with another tribe in Kenya, the Kikuyu, and writes, "This capacity for early training is based on the Digo idea that the child can learn from birth. The impact of the Digo values is further evident when we compare the Digo with the genetically similar Bantu group, the Kikuyu, who live north of Nairobi in the highland area of Kenya. For example, the child may not be carried on the back immediately as babies are in other African societies. Among Kikuyu, although they are relatively more active infant trainers than Western cultures, the concept that a child can learn from birth is less dominant than it is among the Digo. The Kikuyu view the infant as quite vulnerable at birth. Training is thought not immediately possible and must await a developmental growth in competence. We thus have a natural experiment; the Digo mothers are training their babies early and their counterparts among the Kikuyu are training relatively later with measurable consequence."[22]

Cultural attitudes and mores concerning modesty, shame and embarrassment also influence the time scale and method of teaching toilet training. Some peoples are fairly laid back and immodest in their attitudes while others are extremely shy and prudish. In many of the societies portrayed in Part 4, local tribes base their toilet behavior in part on fears related to witches, evil spirits and magic.

## Parental Handling

Another contrast between Western-style parenting and that of many developing countries is in the way babies are handled. Surprisingly, parents in societies more attentive to baby are generally rougher in their handling of babies. In India, mothers and caregivers give daily massages and tend to an infant's needs with quick and abrupt movements. In a study in Karnataka state in India, infants received a rough and vigorous daily massage and other forms of motoric stimulation with the result that at 3 months of age they were above U.S. standards for motor development (Bayley Scales), including 2–3 months ahead of U.S. norms where certain head-control items were involved. For example, 1-month-old infants demonstrated good head control during a pull-to-sit exercise.[23]

The Gusii of Kenya and many others toss their infants in the air or between adults. Babies are handled with much more forcefulness than is tolerated with American infants, "without gasps of 'watch her head, you'll hurt her neck' from grandparents and other protective adults. . . . After handling only a few of these infants with our previously learned cautiousness, we found ourselves becoming much more vigorous. These infants invited such handling. We were drawn in by their vigor and sturdiness and adapted our own behavior to it."[24]

By the age of 3 months, Gusii infants are lifted by one arm and swung onto their mothers' back, without loss of head or trunk control.[25] Mary Ainsworth reported that Baganda mothers do not support the heads of newborn babies. A mother hurries along and takes no notice of the fact that her infant's head is bobbing about.[26] The fact that Baganda babies are carried in a sling may reinforce the infant's ability to hold his head firmly since he learns to compensate for his mother's movements.[27] Baganda mothers typically pick up their babies by grabbing hold of an arm near the shoulder and swinging the baby up onto their back, taking no precautions to support the head. Ainsworth comments that some of the precautions we take in our society to support an infant's head may be unnecessary, overprotective and a cause for delayed control of head and trunk muscles.[28] Crossing into the realm of toilet training with this theory in mind, perhaps the precautions we take in our society are a cause for our relatively late completion of toilet training. Evidence from abroad indicates that by encouraging, working with and training a baby to control his sphincter muscles from the early months of life, we may be able to advance the age at which a child gains control of the muscles and at which the nervous system matures for this activity. This may happen in the same way African babies are encouraged, trained and taught to sit months ahead of Western babies.

## Parental Training

Many African babies receive training in certain skills at a relatively young age. !Kung parents believe that certain parts of motor development, such as sitting, crawling, standing and walking, will not take place without training. They routinely begin early training in these areas, with the result that !Kung babies learn these skills at a younger age than Western babies.[29]

In 1973, Charles Super tested 20 Kipsigis infants in Kenya during the first year of life and found these infants were advanced in skills which were either specifically trained or encouraged by caregivers. These skills included sitting, head control, grasping, and strength and coordination of the legs.[30] Skills such as crawling and rolling from the back to the stomach, for which the Kipsigis infants were not specifically trained, did not show advancement on the Bayley Scale of Infant Motor Development used in the tests. Similarly, Baganda infants proved to be precocious in smiling and sitting, two skills the parents consider to be important and which parents teach from early life.[31]

In a study comparing the sitting skills of Baganda and Samia infants in Africa, both received intensive and prolonged training to sit in infancy. The Baganda trained their infants to sit around the age of 2 to 3 months, purely for social reasons. Samia infants were even more advanced, perhaps because there was more urgency for them to learn to sit early. Samia mothers needed to be free to work in the fields and were able to do so once their babies could sit nearby.[32]

In some societies, including the Peruvians, the Pygmies in Cameroon[33] and the !Kung in Botswana, mothers seat their infants in a little hole in the floor or ground, with a wall of sand or other material around their buttocks to support them.[34] This props them up and helps them develop the strength and coordination to sit at a young age. Babies are sometimes placed in a small, round plastic basin where they are able to grasp the sides for support. In other situations, parents wrap clothes around a baby to support him while sitting.[35]

Expectations, training and handling of infants set the tone and pace for learning. Marten deVries sums this up nicely. "Infant capacity, cultural goals, the physical and social environment as well as maternal behaviour and experience all fit in a web related to neurodevelopment, maturation and outcome measures." He stresses that neurodevelopment follows on a blueprint of both genes and culture. "Every culture and every social niche provides its own signature to the maturation and development of its offspring." He refers to "mechanisms that push or retard the rate of development and train for specific tasks as well as particular psychological characteristics, that have historically provided a survival advantage. Much research in infant development has shown that the neonate is ready and capable for these early learning transactions. . . . The naturally enriched environment of African infant care thus optimizes developmental possibility."[36]

## Scant Research

The topic of infant elimination training has received very little attention by American academia, especially in recent times (since the 1940s and 1950s). No U.S. study has been conducted on this topic. It has been consistently ignored despite the fact that toilet training is at best an emotional ordeal in Western society. I believe the reasons that academia and Western medicine have avoided this subject are cultural. The attitude seems to be that infant elimination training is considered:

- impossible by Western medicine
- dangerous by Western medicine
- too time consuming for Westerners
- too inconvenient for Westerners
- an uneventful process in many non-Western societies where it is rarely a problem for parents
- a female issue of little or no interest to men

This book is a good-faith attempt to present what I believe is a correct rendition of a behavior and practice that has remained obscure in the West. The book does not claim to present scientific data or results. The information in the next three chapters is general and consists mainly of personal accounts. Since no scientific or academic scales or other means of measurement and testing exist, there is no way to reach a scientifically sound conclusion, but this does not mean that a general conclusion and impression about the efficacy of the method cannot be reached. The practices, preferences, cultural tendencies and claims of a number of peoples described in this book all lead to the conclusion that infant elimination training is not only possible and practiced in many societies, but it is also gentle and effective.

## Field Studies in Anthropology

Generally speaking, anthropology has been more helpful to the cause of infant toilet training than has medicine. Field studies and research in anthropology provide interesting material on infant elimination training, not so much because anthropologists or journalists expressly seek this type of information but because it has long been an integral and undeniable part of life in many parts of the world. Field studies would be incomplete without including toilet training, and professionals are required to publish accurate and objective reports. Many of the pieces in Part 4 come from anthropologists or journalists. Here, author Judith Goldsmith compares toilet training in Western and traditional cultures:

"In Western society, toilet training is usually delayed until after a child can walk and talk, much later than in traditional cultures. This leads to further frustrations in child raising, greater dependence on consumer products, and sometimes traumatic attempts at pattern altering. Traditional mothers end their time of cleaning up after their child much sooner, in a much gentler way. Here is yet another area of the childbirth-child nurturing process in which new investigations into old ways would be greatly welcomed.

"As we can see, just as with childbirth, we have often made child nurturing a more complicated process than it needs be. As Dr. H.M.I. Liley has noted, in tracing the development of a child from fetus to toddler: 'From the apparently eternal form of human pregnancy we can deduce that the first children born to early man over a million years ago had precisely the same in utero experience as children born today. However, the ex utero environment has altered. Proto-hominid's (proman's) child was born into an environment so similar to the one that he had just left that he did not need clothing, diapers, playpens, toilet training, spoon feeding, cribs, or any of the other paraphernalia we associate with infant care today. . . . There would be no bottom rashes or routines or formulas and very little crying. . . .This shows that many of the problems we have with our babies have been created by ourselves.'

"When American actress Jane Fonda visited Vietnam in 1974, she left her two-year-old son with a Vietnamese woman doctor while making a tour of the country. During the two weeks of travel, she received reports of what he had eaten, how he had slept, how much weight he had gained. However, a big surprise awaited her on her return. She writes, 'It was only when we got back that we discovered that he'd been toilet trained. Dr. Huong would hold him over a pot at regular intervals, making a hissing sound like running water and sure enough, nine times out of ten, it would work. It still does. It occurred to us that all the talk about how early toilet training creates psychological problems may be just a myth to protect the diaper industry. Vietnamese kids are toilet trained by the time they can sit and they don't seem to have problems.'

"This training of a child to respond to a particular sound was practiced throughout much of the traditional world, with great success, and often from a very early age (much earlier than the one to two years at which toilet training is commonly begun in modern Western societies). For example, in Korea, the child was placed on a jar early in the morning. The mother would say 'shhh . . . ' and touch the genitals to suggest urination, or say 'ung-ga' to encourage defecation. In Japan, at about three months, the mother started training the child by whistling low and monotonously as a signal. In Sikkim, again at three months, the Lepcha baby was taken out on the balcony to eliminate at regular intervals and soon learned to cry when it wanted to be taken out; by crawling time, it simply crawled out by itself. In Busama, New Guinea, also from the third month, the mother would hold the infant over the earth floor as soon as it awoke in the morning, while she grunted and strained to indicate elimination.

"Asia was not the only area in which this technique was used. In Peru, toilet training began when the infant's diet was supplemented with food other than milk (about six months). There, too, the child was held over the floor, at a set time each day. The Gros Ventres of Montana, who began toilet training between the sixth and twelfth month, estimated the times of elimination, opened the baby's cradle sack, and held the baby out, supporting it under its knees and thighs; according to reports, the child would usually respond to this, but if there was a delay, the adults would talk to it and make a hissing noise. Similarly, the Eskimo mother of Alaska held her child on a pot on her lap, and cued it by blowing gently on its head; Eskimo children were toilet trained before their first birthday.

"These practices must have been very common, for there are similar accounts from Africa. At first, the Kgatla mother of Botswana simply cleaned her back after the child eliminated. Before the child was returned to her back she held it and said 'sss, sss, sss,' until it relieved itself. She would take the child down from time to time and repeat this procedure, until the baby had learned to cry when the need arose. When a mother among the Bafut of the Cameroons wanted her baby to urinate, she jiggled it up and down; if she wanted it to defecate, she held it steadily on the floor.

"It seems, then, that 'diapers' were not necessary for as long a time in traditional cultures as they are today; nor was the process of toilet training as complicated as it sometimes is for us."[37]

## Ethnopediatrics

Ethnopediatrics is a relatively new branch of research, dating from 1995 when anthropologist Carol Worthman of Emory University proposed a broader, more-encompassing cross-cultural approach to studying children. The science focuses on the study of parenting practices used in different cultures and the effects of these practices on the health, well-being and survival of infants. The major contributors are pediatricians, anthropologists and child development researchers. Culture and biology are linked and in-terrelated, with an emphasis on evolution, environment and heredity.[38]

Anthropologist Meredith Small of Cornell University discusses ethnope-diatrics in her book *Our Babies, Ourselves* stating, "The name of the field easily explains its goal—*ethno* for culture and *pediatrics* for child health." She starts with the premise that an infant is a perfectly designed organism, knowing when to sleep, when to eat and how to signal its needs by crying. Although most parents instinctively know how they should respond to a baby in need, they don't always follow their instincts. Parents carry personal and cultural baggage that determines how they parent. "Our ideas about child rearing are an amalgam of personal experience from watching our own parents parent, thoughts about how things might be improved upon from the past, and culturally driven directives that guide acceptable behavior in a particular culture."[39]

The ethnopediatrician can provide valuable information and reassurance to parents who are uncertain of their parenting skills. Descriptions and ex-planations of different parenting practices are made available to those searching for answers and improvements for their families. For example, most Westerners have been taught that baby's crying at night is bad and should be ignored. We think crying is something to "break baby of" rather than something that might "break baby." The latter is the way members of most other cultures view an unattended wailing baby. They cannot fathom the idea of ignoring a baby's cries. They are aware and accepting of the fact that all babies awake at night. "Waking up several times a night is not strange—this is what babies are designed to do. Constantly demanding interaction and attention is not the sign of a hyperactive infant—this is what babies need as social animals. And if you, as a parent, feel the urge to sleep with your baby or breast-feed her until she is two, that's okay, because for millions of years people have been doing exactly that."[40]

The big question at this point is whether or not ethnopediatrics will embrace and encourage infant elimination training practices. I believe it is imperative for this aspect of infant care to be included. In this regard, perhaps ethnopediatrics will one day lead to the sanctioning of an official study in order to finally give this method a fair assessment.

In the meantime, since there has not been much academic attention paid to infant elimination training, and since there is such a stigma against it in Western countries, it is hoped that the testimonials in Parts 2 and 3 of this book along with the excerpts and research information provided in Part 4 will inspire Western families interested in this method to give it a try.

# chapter 2

# africa

## Botswana – the !Kung (Konner)

Until recent times, the !Kung of the Kalahari desert in Botswana were primarily a hunting and gathering people. They were called "Bushmen" for 300 years, but since this term is used as a racial slur in southern Africa, it has been dropped from scholarly use.[41] The !Kung are also referred to as San or !Kung San.[42]

In 1972, Melvin Konner reported that among the !Kung of northwestern Botswana, "Elimination has no social consequences for Zhun/twa infants (though it does for problem 'bedwetters' in later childhood). Before he can crawl easily the infant routinely urinates and defecates in someone's lap.

Usually he is not even moved until it is finished, and it is cleaned up with no comment whatever. Gradually, as he acquires control and mobility, he is told to leave the house and, after he is walking well, to leave the village. In many observed episodes, no infant or child has ever been in the least upset in connection with elimination (except infants in the first two or three months upset by the change in position required for cleaning), nor, for that matter, has any adult. . . . Since infants are unclothed and soiling attended to immediately, wetness is never a cause of crying."[43]

Joseph Chilton Pearce presents a slightly different rendition. "Konner, in his studies of the Zhun/Twasi, an African hunting-gathering culture, found the infants carried in the Ugandan fashion. These mothers always knew when the infant was going to urinate or defecate and removed the child to the bushes ahead of time. The mother sensed the general state of the infant and anticipated the infant's every need."[44]

Melvin Konner has confirmed that both of these descriptions agree with his observations. "I would say the mother's response might be either to anticipate and hold the baby away from her; or if she missed the cue, to hold the baby away from her after the baby begins urinating or defecating." If she misses the chance completely, she cleans up afterwards. "In any case, the nonchalance is what impressed me, coming from a culture where we are anything but nonchalant!"[45]

## Botswana – the !Kung (Marshall)

"Babies are naked and, since there are no floors but the desert sand, not much is made of their urinating wherever they are. When they defecate, they are wiped with grass and the fecal matter is cleaned up at once by some older child or adult and carried off. As soon as children can walk fairly well, they are led by the hand and encouraged to go out of the werf for their toilet needs, at first for the sake of cleanliness and, as they grow older, for the sake of modesty as well."[46]

## Kenya – the Digo

In 1974, Marten deVries, M.D., conducted research that included infant elimination training as used by the Digo tribe inhabiting the coastal plain along the Indian Ocean from Mombasa, Kenya, into Tanzania. DeVries reported that 30 of 34 mothers in a random sample of families stated that they started bowel and bladder training at 2 to 3 weeks of age and had succeeded with all aspects reasonably well by the age of 4 to 6 months. The possibility of such a feat is rejected by Western medicine. DeVries attributes the Digo's early effectuation of elimination training to specialized cultural programming. "Other cross-cultural studies have suggested that many seemingly biological properties such as temporal patterning of behavior and developmental sequence are, in fact, culturally programmed.[47] This implies that development follows a peculiarly cultural course based as much on the group's notions of 'what a baby is' and how he or she 'should' develop as on maturational forces."[48]

Since Digo mothers spend most of their time with their babies during the early months of life, it is a logical and ideal time to toilet train their babies. "The mother takes a teaching role and assumes all responsibility in the initial phase of the training process. She places the infant in a special training position outside the house, at first at times when she senses that the infant needs to eliminate (after feeding, when waking from naps, etc.), with the idea that he will soon learn to let her know more independently. . . . For voiding, the mother sits on the ground outside, with her legs straight out in front of her. The infant is placed between the mother's legs, facing away from her, in a sitting position, supported by the mother's body. The mother then makes a 'shuus' noise that the infant learns to associate with voiding. This is done many times during the day and at night."[49]

The infant is rewarded if he voids upon hearing the "shuus" sound. He gradually learns to signal his elimination needs and then to climb into the elimination position just before he needs to void.

A different position is used for bowel movements. The mother sits on the floor or ground with her legs in front of her bent at the knees, heels touching ground, toes touching each other and pointing up. The infant faces her and sits astride her ankles. The area beneath her ankles serves as a little potty. Instead of using a vocal cue, the position serves as the stimulus to encourage the baby to defecate. If the baby evacuates, he is rewarded. If he does not, he is matter-of-factly returned to his previous position or activity, and the session ends.

After a month or two of training, young girls aged 5 to 12 years help with the process. Throughout the first year, occasional accidents are expected and handled casually. The mother or caregiver clean up excrement immediately. Around the age of 1 year when the child can walk independently, he is expected to eliminate away from the living area. If he eliminates in the house, he is given a warning. If he repeats the behavior, he is physically punished.

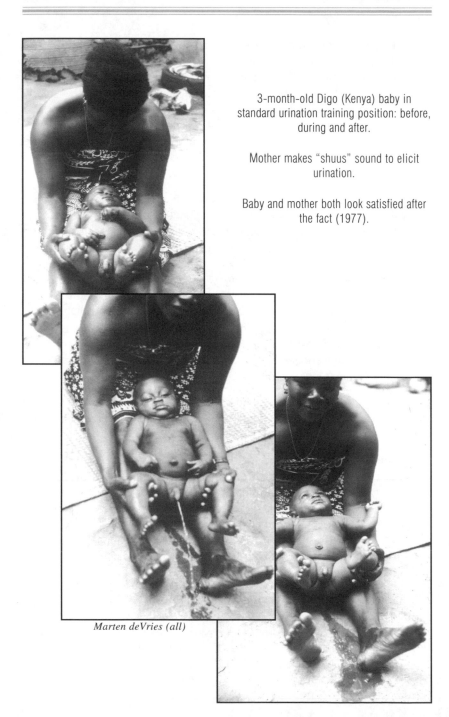

3-month-old Digo (Kenya) baby in standard urination training position: before, during and after.

Mother makes "shuus" sound to elicit urination.

Baby and mother both look satisfied after the fact (1977).

*Marten deVries (all)*

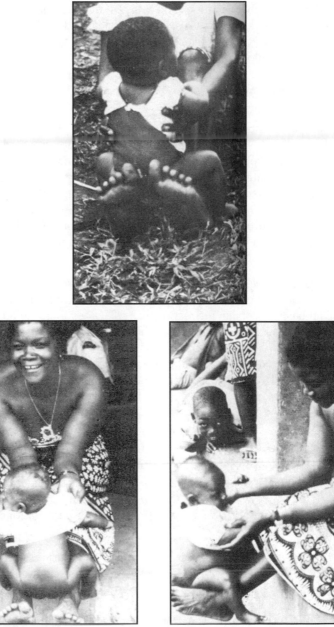

*Marten deVries (all)*

Examples of Digo bowel training position (1977).

DeVries found that variations and delays in training were due to negative caretaking attitudes or illnesses such as diarrhea, and in a few cases due to a child's individual characteristics. He was not able to study the long-term results of elimination training.

## Kenya – the Gusii

Robert and Barbara LeVine wrote a piece on the Gusii in the 1960s and had this to say about toilet training. "Feces and urine are wiped away with soft fuzzy leaves collected by the mother for that purpose, but the mother does not try to anticipate the child's excretion. Most mothers are very casual about it and show no sign of disturbance when their infants soil the cloth and the mother's person as well. Sometimes their response is not immediate, but eventually they wipe up the excrement with the leaves, cleaning the infant, cloth, and themselves. No attempt is made to effect sphincter control during infancy."

Training in sphincter control usually begins shortly after the birth of a younger sibling, the median age being 25 months. When the mother feels her child has had enough instruction, she will cane him for infractions. Another form of punishment is to make the child sweep out the feces himself while the mother tells him what he has done wrong. "The amount of time mothers reported for this training ranged from a week to a year, with the majority around a month. Some mothers who trained quickly attributed it to the fact that they were 'serious' about it and punished severely for infractions."[50]

## Kenya – the Tiriki

Anthropologist Walter Sangree conducted field research among the Bantu Tiriki of Kenya from 1954 to 1956. He has published several articles and a book on the Tiriki and made the following observations on toilet training.

"Toilet training is permissive and gradual; in Tiriki huts, which mostly have floors of pounded earth smeared with dung, accidental soiling by a baby does not pose much of a cleanup problem. Babies are not diapered, and the adult or the child nurse is quick to hold the infant away from her body at the first sign of evacuation. Babies astride their nurses' hips are conditioned to going outdoors to a secluded spot, such as the banana patch, to defecate even before they can walk, and after they are walking they soon learn to head for the out-of-doors on their own through being verbally reminded or, if necessary, picked up and carried to the door. When they are a bit older children learn through the example and admonitions of their elders."[51]

## Madagascar – the Tanala

Anthropologist Ralph Linton visited the Tanala ("people of the forest") in 1926-28. The term "Tanala" applied to all the inhabitants of a certain area, irrespective of their origins and political affiliations. In this sense, there has never been a Tanala tribe. Moreover, the composition of the Tanala is constantly changing, with membership being based mainly on length of residence in the territory. Any group living in the area for more than three or four generations is counted as Tanala. At that time, Tanala culture was archaic in many respects, and the people had only been slightly influenced by European contact.

The island of Madagascar lies off the southeast coast of Africa and is the third largest island in the world. Linton reported that small children were carried in-arms almost constantly by mothers, fathers and siblings. From the age of about 4 months, a baby was carried in the back of his mother's dress, sitting with his legs on either side of her body. He remained on her back except at night or when he was being nursed.

"No clothing is worn under the age of about three years. Even when carried on the back, there is no equivalent for the European diaper. As soon as the child begins to be carried in the mother's dress, it is slapped for befouling her and it learns to control its functions at a surprisingly early age. This was the only offense for which I ever saw a Tanala child punished. [52]

"Diapers are not used, with the result that the child is constantly soiling its mother, and since the clothes that the mother wears are difficult to replace, we have here an incentive for premature sphincter discipline. In fact, anal training is begun at the age of two or three months, and the child is expected to be continent at the age of six months. If after this time the child soils its mother, it is severely punished. In other words, the child is taught to be continent while on its mother's back. The child is however, permitted at intervals to leave the mother's back. It may be interesting to note that the woman is expected to be sexually abstinent for six months after the birth of her child. Thus the period of anal training of the child and the mother's sexual abstinence after the birth of the child coincide."[53]

## Mali – the Dogon

Nadine Wanono has worked among the Dogon on a part-time basis for over 20 years. Her first visit was in 1977. She returns to Mali on a regular basis, for 2–3 months every one or two years. She is an ethnologist, film-maker and researcher at the National Center for Scientific Research in Paris, France. She expressed concern at supplying research information of a general nature since observations often reflect the tendencies of specific local areas. "We have to be careful since there is diversity among the Dogon, and the customs of each region can change when they come under outside influences."

Nadine Wanono worked in the region of Sangha where she made the following observations. "A child is carried on his mother's back for approximately the first 3 years of life. Around the age of 6 months, the mother sits her baby between her legs and encourages him to defecate either on the ground or into a little pot. Some mothers make little noises to encourage the elimination. These vocalizations are more systematic among the Bambara, who comprise the ethnic majority of Mali. Dogon mothers never scold their babies about elimination. A mother sometimes receives assistance from her older daughter(s), sisters and aunts but generally not from her brothers or other men.

"I believe Dogon babies finish toilet training around 18 months, depending on their position in the sibling hierarchy and also on the mother's desires. Dogon women have very heavy workloads, and the time they have to dedicate to their babies depends on the degree of maternal fatigue and also on how much time they have available after work. Their available free time can also vary with the seasons and the time of day in question."[54]

## Nigeria – the Dahomeans

Melville Herskovits and his wife conducted field research on the topic of native life in Dahomey, during a period of five months in 1931. Dahomey was selected in part because it represented a West African civilization more or less in a natural state, one that had hardly been affected by the circumstances of European control. The topic of child raising is included in the Herskovits' colorful account.

"Returning now to a consideration of the development of the normal child, it is to be observed that very young children are carried most of the time on the backs of their mothers or, in rare instances, of nurses. Unless prevented by special circumstances, a mother takes her baby with her wherever she goes, and women may be seen selling in the market, carrying burdens on the road, working in the fields, or dancing in ceremonial dances with their infants straddling their backs. A child is trained by the mother who, as she carries it about, senses when it is restless, so that every time it must perform its excretory functions, the mother puts it on the ground. Thus in time, usually two years, the training process is completed. If a child does not respond to this training, and manifests enuresis at the age of four or five, soiling the mat on which it sleeps, then, at first, it is beaten. If this does not correct the habit, ashes are put in water and the mixture is poured over the head of the offending boy or girl who is driven into the street where all the other children clap their hands and run after the child singing, *Adida go ya ya ya* ("Urine everywhere.")

"In Whydah, the child is taken to the lagoon and washed, this being repeated a second time if necessary. If the habit is then not stopped, a live frog is attached to the child's waist, which so frightens the offender that a cure is usually effected. In Abomey, however, beating is the customary punishment.[55]

## Nigeria – the Kanuri

Anthropologist Ronald Cohen conducted fieldwork in the 1960s among the Kanuri, a tribe residing in the northeastern corner of Nigeria. Cohen published papers on aspects of Kanuri society and history. His book on the Kanuri includes a short piece on toilet training.

As a first step, the mother tries to learn when her baby is likely to urinate. "At first the child is merely wiped clean by the mother, but as soon as it can sit up, it is placed astride her ankles with its back resting on her upturned feet. A little hole is dug in the sandy soil between the ankles and the infant then has a simple and comforting toilet ready made for it by the mother. Afterwards its loins are washed and the hole covered up with sand.[56]

## Senegal & Central African Republic

Alain Epelboin is a medical anthropologist and researcher at the National Center for Scientific Research in Paris, France. He conducts fieldwork in Senegal, the Central African Republic and among children of African immigrants in the region of Paris. His research focuses on the anthropology of sickness and healing, with an emphasis on the effects of (the lack of) sanitation. In March 2000, he replied to my request for information about infant elimination training in Africa.

"In my experience, sphincter-control training begins as soon as a mother comes out of seclusion with her infant—in general, around the age of 1 week. At this time, the infant transitions from lying alone on its mother's bed (covered with cloths which serve as a sort of incubator) to being constantly carried, taken outdoors and passed from person to person—in short, he transitions to being socialized.

"I would say that in the beginning, there is an attentive observation of the infant by the mother, which gradually enables her to coincide the spontaneous voiding of her baby with auditory stimuli, visual interactions and traditional positioning—all stemming from the mother's society and family culture. Later, the mechanism of stimulus-response comes into play (I don't like comparing this to the Pavlovian model, as it is too restrictive and simplistic.)

"In my observations in West Africa, a favorite position involves sitting the infant on the mother's ankles. In corresponding urban areas of Africa and France, the same position is used, but the mother sits her baby on a plastic (chamber) pot which she holds in position between her feet.

"The Aka Pygmies hold their infants in a standing position on their armpits, with the babies' knees slightly bent. Here the emphasis on toilet training is not as great as it is among the peoples of West Africa.

"In some other societies, a regular daily enema is given (via the mother's mouth or a device) for hygienic, therapeutic and preventative purposes. Once the cleansing liquid has been injected, the mother sits on a stool and seats the baby on her thighs above a receptacle.

"As in all societies, African mothers express their satisfaction with their babies. This is sometimes done in a different fashion than elsewhere, in that it is not always apparent to outsiders. In public, the mother is very reserved and adopts a mask of impassivity which conceals her satisfaction. This is done out of fear that too much praise of her baby will attract the attention of malicious and other jealous evil spirits. In contrast, the entourage of siblings and female relatives and neighbors never misses a chance to loudly acknowledge each new "performance" of the baby. Praise and approval are thus always present, though not necessarily displayed by the mother. "Mommies," "aunties," grandmothers or the entourage (especially women and children) play a preponderant role in teaching everyday social conven-

*Epelboin/CNRS*

18-month-old Senegalese in her communal home. For now, privacy is not an issue.
(Malicka, Senegal, 2001)

tions. In this respect too, traditional roles fluctuate, delegating roles of authority to some and roles of tenderness to others.

"As for the role of the father, situations vary greatly, depending largely on
his personality and on the status of the baby (first born, last born, boy, girl).
There are societies where a father takes no part in the daily care of his babies and others, such as the Pygmies or the Bassari of Senegal or in Asia,
where the presence of men in their babies' lives is ubiquitous.

*Epelboin/CNRS*

*Epelboin/CNRS*

A mother in Senegal using classic toilet training position.
Child sits on mother's upturned feet while waiting to go.

*Epelboin/CNRS*

After peeing, baby girl inspects to see where the water went.
(Ibel, Senegal, 1990)

"In Africa, toilet training is completed at as young an age as possible. When ascertaining the age of completion, it is necessary to distinguish between bowel and bladder training, as well as between normal bowel movements and diarrhea (unfortunately fairly frequent in these regions).

"In general, whether it be toilet training or its corollaries (for example, many cultures restrict wiping to the use of the left hand), African cultures are very precocious in this regard, with remarkable results. The early accomplishment of sphincter control corresponds to the rapid psychomotor development of babies up to 12–18 months and has been emphasized by experts on infancy. It is my opinion that this precocity is related to the incessant social stimulation to which infants are subjected, not only by their mothers until weaning/separation but also by the many other people involved."[57]

## Senegal – the Wolof

Jacqueline Rabain is a researcher at the National Center for Scientific Research in Paris, France. Her background is in anthropology and psychology, and one of her specialities is child anthro-pology. She has done fieldwork among the Wolof in Senegal, starting with a visit in 1965–66 and followed by visits in 1994 and December 1998–January 1999.

Jacqueline Rabain told me that starting at the age of 2 months, a mother sits her infant on her ankles. She holds her ankles spread apart to make a place for the child to urinate or defecate. A baby can hold its head up straight at 2 months. The mother supports him in position on her ankles by holding his arms steady. She encourages the child to eliminate by making a whistling "sssss" noise. A mother does not compliment her baby when he has eliminated for her. She often passes the time chatting with other women during the potty process. This behavior was observed in 1965–66.

A child is not expected to be toilet trained before he can walk. Rabain states that she never saw children under 3 years of age being scolded for urinating on the ground. There is a lot of emphasis for the child to learn to defecate "in the bush" behind the home. This is learned mainly by imitating adults and older children; the baby is trained by their example.

"I made a field trip to the same villages and the same families in January–February 1994 and December 1998–January 1999. At that time, I observed that small plastic potties had been introduced and were available from the local street markets. They are fairly common now. I do not know if the pot is used as early as sitting on the mother's ankles but saw it used by children from 18 months to 2 years of age."[58]

## Sudan – the Batahein

Writings published in 1970 about a sampling of Sudanese Arab children belonging to the former nomadic tribe, Batahein, reveal that elimination training was started at the age of 6 to 8 weeks in 60 percent of the families surveyed. Diapers were not used, and training was mild. The baby was held between the mother's knees and learned to make a smacking noise to indicate that it needed assistance. No formal training was used in 33 percent of the cases; these children learned spontaneously to imitate their older siblings. Enuresis nocturna was fairly common but not related to toilet training. The fact that infection of the urinary tract was common seems to explain part of the high frequency of enuresis.[59]

## Tanzania – the Chaga

German scholar Otto Raum, whose father was a missionary among the Chaga near Mount Kilimanjaro for nearly 40 years, included the topic of infant elimination training in his 1940 book *Chaga Childhood*. He found an "obvious slackness in training" or overall relaxed approach, except in some situations of long-term enuresis. "As in the case of weaning, no evidence could be found for the traumatic suddenness which psychoanalysts would fain impute to it, so does the interest in excreta lack the morbid glamour ascribed to it by those theorists."

"The control of urination and defecation forms part of the child's learning. That it be done successfully is a constant concern of the mother. Indeed, the marriage ceremonies foreshadow this." Men are discouraged from making disparaging comments about a mother's duty of toilet training her young and are taught to be patient with their wives should they find their clothes soiled by a child.

"A timed habit, absent in the case of feeding, one would expect to be inculcated only by women who have come under European influence. Some of these begin to train their children one or two months after birth to defecate at a fixed time every morning. In the majority of cases, however, regularity is not insisted upon. The child lies on a piece of leather. Any excreta have to be wiped away with dry grass as soon as possible to prevent the rotting of the hide and a bad smell. As long as the child is carried about, the mother closely observes it and develops an almost uncanny knack of guessing its needs. Whenever it wakens, becomes restless, or, in the case of a boy, has an erection of the penis, it is held out. . . . As the child grows up and learns to walk, it is taught to retire into the [banana] grove.

"Enuresis calls forth a variety of measures. The steps taken with smaller children are magical. When a baby is about nine months old, its mother collects drops of rain in the hoof of a goat or the involutions of a colocasia leaf. This she gives to the child as a medicine, saying, 'Take and drink this drug. It will keep you from wetting the bed.' A bigger child is shown the puddle and scolded. . . . Some children never learn to control urination, though they are scorned for their deficiency and told that this will be an obstacle to their marriage. (Enuresis is a ground for divorce.) In such cases a boy prefers to sleep with the hens in a corner of the hut, where he can pass water with impunity."

As in many other societies, Chaga boys have a sense of humor where urine is concerned. "It serves as an ever-ready lubricant when boys make models out of clay, and occasionally they will urinate on each other for fun."[60]

## Togo

In their 1998 exquisite work entitled *Babies Celebrated (Bébés du monde)* , a book rich in photos which are described by anthropologists and other researchers, Béatrice Fontanel and Claire D'Harcourt take us on a tour of mothers and babies around the world. Here is a sample selection that touches first on Africa in general, then on Togo in specific.

In Africa, it is rare to see a woman soiled by her baby. Africans "seem able to detect the slightest signals of their children's toilet needs. At the most subtle movement or change of breath, they understand the message and take them off their backs and put them onto their ankles in an instant. If an accident happens, the mother is ashamed and embarrassed.

"Some ethnologists qualify the commonly held belief that in Africa babies' bowel movements do not provoke revulsion. Nadine Wanono points out that long deodorant necklaces of cloves are worn by the mothers of young children, and Suzanne Lallemand reminds us that in many traditional rural societies men complain about these smells. In central Togo, there is even a song with the refrain, 'To smell as bad as a woman who has a baby.'"[61]

## Uganda – the Baganda (Ainsworth)

Mary Ainsworth dedicated 11 pages of her book, *Infancy in Uganda*, to the topic of infant elimination training. She studied 28 Baganda infants and their mothers in 1954–55. This took place in six villages about 15 miles from Kampala, in the former kingdom of Buganda (now simply a geographical region of Uganda rather than an administrative unit). Throughout most of her book, she uses the term "Ganda" to refer to the Baganda.

"The method of training consists in holding the baby down in a squatting position, his feet on the ground, with the mother's arm passing across the baby's back, supporting it, and holding him under the arm farthest away from her. The mother's other hand usually was on the baby's body also, but it was not clear to my eye whether it was used to provide support or pressure. The baby is 'held down' immediately after he wakes from sleep and immediately after feeding. Indeed, as one of our old informants told us, the mother might interrupt feeding, if she sensed that he was about to have a bowel movement, and thus avoid soiling."[62]

The Luganda word for holding the child in this position is *okusimba*, a synonym for the verb "to plant." An alternative position observed by Dr. Hebe Welbourn and described as "holding out" refers to holding the baby under the armpits in a standing position, with his feet touching the ground.

The child eventually builds up an association between being held down (or out) and elimination. "Most mothers implied quite clearly that the practice of 'holding down' was designed to catch the child at an opportune time when he was ready to excrete but had not yet done so. They all placed stress on the need for vigilance if the child was to be caught. They attached importance to the convenience of avoiding soiled or wet beds by undertaking this practice, but at the same time they believe it to be a method of training."[63]

The mothers displayed much patience throughout the period of training. Babies were never scolded or punished for accidents; instead, lapses of control were treated in a matter-of-fact manner without fuss.

Ainsworth concludes that "Ganda training in elimination control is at least as effective as the training methods used in our culture. It rests for its effectiveness not so much upon a schedule of holding down but upon the child's own indications of need. Before he can actually signal his needs the mother gears her practices to what she has observed of the child's rhythms, and holds him down at times when he is most likely to defecate or urinate. Soon he is able to signal his needs with special sounds that she recognizes even before he can verbalize. The extent to which control is something accepted by the child rather than imposed upon him is shown by his tendency to take the initiative himself in finding the appropriate place to excrete waste when he is old enough to get there under his own steam. All of this is contingent upon the mother's (or some other adult's or responsible child's) omnipresence and responsiveness which ensure that the baby's signals will not go unheeded."[64]

Mary Ainsworth's book contains a table which details the age at which elimination training was begun by each baby in the study. The ages range from 1 to 6 months. Details of completion of the following landmarks, in order of occurrence among the Ganda, are also provided for each baby:

- nighttime ("bed") bowel control
- daytime ("house") bowel control
- nighttime ("bed") urinary control
- daytime ("house") urinary control

Ainsworth theorizes that "it may well be that the task of learning first of all that the bed is a place *not* to be wet or soiled is an easier one than learning that elimination can take place only in one place—on a potty or toilet. Having grasped this notion it is perhaps easier to take the next step of delaying until the proper place is reached than it would be to learn that all at once without intermediate objectives."[65]

## Uganda – the Baganda (Kilbride)

In 1990, Philip and Janet Kilbride published a book about family life in East Africa. In a chapter entitled "Children of Value," the authors attribute the precocity of Baganda and Samia infants mainly to cultural factors—a topic introduced in Chapter 1 of this section. Infant toilet training practices of the Baganda are discussed as part of the early learning of infants.

"'Toilet training' occurs gradually and casually, although it may be begun as early as two or three months of age. Whenever a mother senses that her infant is about to urinate, she will 'hold him out' in the air and or with his feet touching the ground. This is not supposed to be done quickly or suddenly and, often, if the infant has already begun to urinate, he will be left seated on the lap. He is held in a squatting position with his feet touching the ground in order to defecate. Children are usually not taught to excrete outside the house until they are old enough to understand (i.e., when they can speak). Until then, the child's excretia [sic] is wiped up with a banana leaf and deposited in his latrine. Most children are 'toilet trained' and use their own latrine by the time they are three years old. Many urban mothers use diapers, but because they are expensive, they have few of them; therefore, they are likely to remove the diaper and squat the child if they anticipate an elimination."[66]

## Uganda (Geber)

In her study of African children, Marcelle Geber observed that Ugandan mothers were attentive to all the needs of their infants, including elimination. She noted that Ugandan babies never leave their mother. At night, they sleep on the same mat, skin-to-skin with their mother. During the day they are carried on her back wherever she goes, without urinating or defecating upon her.

The Ugandan mother "never misreads the needs of her infant, whether he wants to suckle, urinate, defecate. In a quick and tender movement, she rolls him from her back onto her hip, then holds him against her chest with her wide hand; or she slides him to her side and holds him out by his arm so he doesn't get her wet; or else she takes him out of the cloth sling and holds him seated between her two hands so he doesn't soil himself and doesn't soil her."

A Ugandan mother is so intimately connected with her infant that she senses and responds to "the slightest movement, the tiniest whimper and the most subtle gesture" which communicate the child's needs. The same is true on occasions where she is not carrying him but has, in accordance with tradition and duty, offered him as a sign of welcome to a visitor to hold.[67]

When the babies were old enough to walk, Geber observed them going outdoors, without prompting, to relieve themselves. She reported that Ugandan children completed toilet training between 15 and 24 months.

## Uganda (Pearce)

In his book *Magical Child*, Joseph Chilton Pearce writes, "Jean MacKellar told me of her years in Uganda, where her husband practiced medicine. Local mothers brought their infants to see the doctor, often standing patiently in line for hours. The women carried the tiny infants in a sling, next to their bare breasts. Older infants were carried on the back, papoose style. The infants were never swaddled, nor were diapers used. Yet none of them were soiled when finally examined by the doctor. Puzzled by this, Jean finally asked some of the women how they managed to keep their babies so clean without diapers and such. 'Oh,' the women answered, 'we just go to the bushes.' Well, Jean countered, how did they know when the infant needed to go to the bushes? The women were astonished at her question. 'How do *you* know when *you* have to go?' they exclaimed."[68]

## West Africa

Hélène Elisabeth Stork is a professor of clinical and anthropological psychology at the Institut de Psychologie de l'Université René Descartes in Paris, France. She conducts research on the comparison of child-raising techniques and early interactions between the family and infant in different cultures. She is the author of several books, ethnopsychological films and scientific articles.

In her 1999 book *Introduction à la psychologie anthropologique* , Hélène Stork describes the method of toilet training used in West Africa. Sphincter training is ". . . very permissive. Adults never force anything that would sur-pass an infant's level of sphincter maturation. An infant gradually learns toilet behavior by imitating siblings and adults. No timetable or device such as a Western potty is used. The young baby wears no diapers, yet his mother, who carries him everywhere with her, is never wet. Being in constant contact with her baby teaches a mother to sense, through empathy, the meaning of the slightest whimper or movement made by her child. She knows precisely when and how to respond, and has the ability to distin-guish, for example, between her baby's desire for the breast and his need to defecate. To stimulate this function, the African mother, in similar fashion to the Indian mother (Stork, 1986), sits on the ground and installs the infant on her ankles, spreading them at precisely the opportune moment. Her use of onomatopoeia, which evokes the sounds of evacuation, encourages the baby to go. A mother never expresses any disgust when picking up feces and throwing it out of the area where daily life takes place. Toilet training is not an occasion where a child confronts an adult, as is often the case in the West. Self-soiling is not the goal of any punitive attitude and thus never manifests itself as a means of protest by the child."[69]

# chapter

# asia

## French Polynesia – the Marquesans (Linton)

In 1920–21, anthropologist Ralph Linton spent nearly a year in the Marquesas, a series of islands in the central Pacific. He was in close contact and formed friendships with several Marquesans. They were not at all reserved in his presence and spoke freely of the more intimate details of life. Their openness and warmth gave him the opportunity to closely observe their patterns of culture, including their behavior with infants and children.

Linton noted that the nursing period was very short since the Marquesans believed that nursing makes a child difficult to raise and "not properly submissive. . . . No swaddling clothes were used. The infant was simply laid on bark-cloth, not on the bed but on the stone floor inside the house. The bark-cloth was changed from time to time as needed.

"There was no particular effort at anal control for small children until they were a year or so old. The adult merely changed the bark cloth on which the child lay. Later the child might be picked up, carried a short distance, and held out to perform its functions. With adults the excretory functions were private; they usually sought retirement in the bushes."[70]

## French Polynesia – the Marquesans (Kirkpatrick)

Research on early interactions in the Marquesas Islands was conducted on 'Ua Pou in the 1970s. John Kirkpatrick worked on the island in 1975–77, and Mary Martini made her observations there in 1976–77. They reported that for the first 2 or 3 months of life, an infant is cared for almost exclusively by the mother. After that, infants are introduced to other caregivers, and by the age of 5 or 6 months are in the care of a number of people.

"By four months, when the baby can sit with minimal support, he is entrusted to the care of other children in the household and is passed around brusquely, and typically is cared for while facing away from the caregiver. For example, feeding is done from behind as the infant sits on a caregiver's lap. The undiapered baby is held away from the caregiver when the caregiver thinks he will urinate. All routine caregiving activities are performed while the baby faces outward. . . . The 12- to 18-month-old . . . begins to understand to go outside to urinate and defecate."[71]

## India

In their book *Babies Celebrated*, Fontanel and D'Harcourt give a short but colorful description of infant potty training in India. An Indian mother forms a little toilet seat for her baby when she "seats the baby comfortably on her perfectly angled shins, propped up on her upturned feet, and thus kept away from the mud and filth of the ground. . . . When the mother senses that her baby needs to eliminate waste, she sits the child on her shins and makes little hushing sounds of encouragement . . . from one continent to another—in the absence of all baby furniture—the same positions have been invented."[72]

## India – the Lepchas

The Lepchas are a Mongoloid people living in the state of Sikkim. They inhabit the southern and eastern slopes of Mount Kinchenjunga in the Himalayas. The following account was published in 1938.

"The teaching of sphincter control is meant to start at the age of three months when the children are taken out on to the balcony at regular intervals; they should learn to cry when they want to be taken out and by the time they can crawl should be able to crawl there by themselves. This is, however, an ideal rather than a real statement; sphincter control and bodily cleanliness are not regarded as of emotional importance, and some quite big children refuse to accept the discipline and excrete inside the house, especially if the house has bamboo flooring. Children aged three or over who cannot or will not learn sphincter control are considered to show a bad prognosis; when they grow up they 'will show forth a bad heart (disposition)'. If big children are dirty they may be given a smack or other slight punishment; but as often as not no notice will be taken and the dirt just cleared away by some older person. Only if the child spoils or dirties somebody else's property will he be severely punished. When a child can move about by itself it is taught to go outside to relieve itself; it is always accompanied by an older person till it is quite big to keep away the scavenging dogs and pigs. It is cleaned, and taught to clean itself with sticks and leaves."[73]

## India – the Sikhs

Whether in their home state of Punjab in the north of India, elsewhere in the country or even abroad, Sikh mothers generally begin toilet training in infancy. They quickly learn to sense when their babies need to go, through observation of, or advice from, more experienced women vis-à-vis intuition, timing or cues from baby. Infants are conditioned to have a bowel movement first thing in the morning. If smaller infants defecate more than once a day for some months, this pattern is taken into account. Urination frequency is gauged and anticipated in relation to feeding and sleeping times. The process is gentle. Force and punishment are not used.

In traditional Sikh society, babies do not wear diapers. From birth, they are taught modesty and wear underpants since the donning of special underwear is one of the 5 K's or religious requirements of baptized Sikhs.

Infants are never alone and are not left to cry. They are always soothed, entertained, held and cuddled. At times they are handled a little roughly or

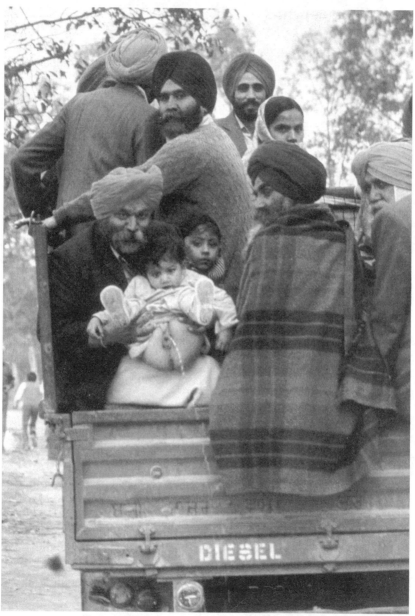

*Raghu Rai*

Improvising a "toilet place" on the road during a Sikh outing (1982).

have their cheeks squeezed and pinched, all out of love, joy or playfulness on the part of the adults. Extended families are still commonplace in villages, so a mother has plenty of help from other women and girls in the household during the day. Wealthier families with individual households have live-in housekeepers who also serve as nannies. A housekeeper may have children of her own who also help around the home. Babies spend most of their time in-arms, either sitting on their mother's lap or being carried by her or one of the other women in the home. After work, adoring fathers spend time with their little ones. Despite the continual physical contact between adults and infants, caregivers and babies alike remain clean and dry most of the time, including at night.

The whole family sleeps in one room. Sturdy cots the size of a single bed are the norm. The baby usually sleeps on the mother's chest or right next to her, without diapers. A mother is so attuned to her baby that she automatically wakes up during the night when it is time for her baby to go. Sikhs arise before dawn for their prayers, so if a mother is ill, others will be up early to assist with the baby.

The most common positions used during infancy are the classic in-arms squatting position (depicted on the following page and also in Part 1 Chapter 3, "The In-Arms Phase") and the two by Bibiji on next two pages. A mother will either squat and hold her baby in position in her arms or else sit on the floor or ground and use her feet to form a toilet seat for the baby.

Most claim their babies are toilet trained around the age of 6 to 9 months. In the mind of a mother, the argument that a baby is not toilet trained if he still needs some physical assistance to get to the bathroom and into position to evacuate is flawed and preposterous. She knows that her baby is aware of elimination and has (at least partial) control over evacuation. A mother is only too happy to do her part in helping her child. She would never consider letting her child go in his pants, just as adults would never want to go in their own pants.

Cleanliness in the form of a daily morning sponge bath is part of the Sikh doctrine, and this habit is instilled from birth. Bathrooms are small and plain, typically consisting of a faucet, a bucket and a drain. Many villagers depend on someone to remove the excrement from their bathroom floor. The plumbing, if any, in most villages consists of open gutters. Once children walk, they can easily find a place to squat and go in an open gutter outdoors. Some middle class families have Turkish (squat-style) toilets. The wealthiest can afford Western-style toilets in addition to a more simple and traditional bathroom. Whatever type of toilet is available in the dwelling, it

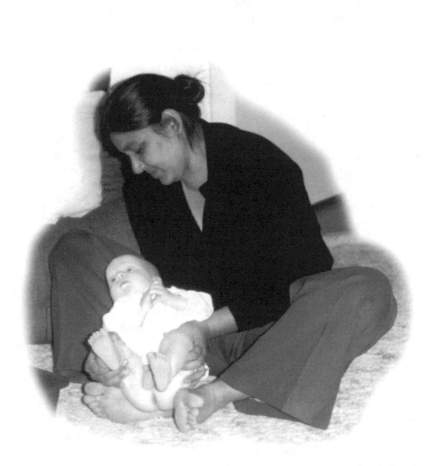

*Laurie Boucke*

3 months old — Baby faces away from caregiver,
baby's bottom rests on adult's feet,
adult's leg and arm supports baby's head and back (1979).

*Laurie Boucke*

3 months old — Baby faces caregiver, baby's bottom
rests on adult's feet, adult's hands support
baby's head and back (1979).

is easier for a small child to squat and go on the bathroom floor or outdoors than to climb and balance on a toilet.

Infant toilet training is the standard method used throughout the country (by Hindus, Muslims, etc., as well as Sikhs). In addition, this same
method is used throughout heavily populated neighboring countries such as
Pakistan, Bangladesh and Sri Lanka.

## Indonesia – the Alorese

Alor is a small and obscure island in Indonesia, about 50 miles long and
30 miles wide, north of Timor. Cora Du Bois reached Alor in 1938 and published *The People of Alor* in 1944. Her tome contains detailed information
on the child-raising practices of the Alorese.

"After completing birth, the mother picks up the child, wraps it in the
softest piece of woven or bark cloth available, and joins the group of friends
and visitors in the living room. People present suggest various names; those
of maternal and paternal grandparents are preferred. If a child begins to urinate or to nurse after a name is suggested, that is the one adopted. . . .

"No effort is made during infancy to teach the child to talk. . . . Toilet
training, too, is completely disregarded during the prewalking period. Adults
exhibit no anger or disgust when a child soils the carrying shawl or the body
of the person caring for it. The caretaker cleans up after the child with the
most casual matter-of-factness, wiping off its buttocks with a bit of leaf, a
corn husk, or a bamboo sliver.

"Toilet training is taught gradually and easily. When the child can walk
and 'when it is old enough to understand,' the mother makes a point of
taking it with her morning and evening when she defecates either in the
privy or outside at the edge of the village. Also, the child is watched and
told to withdraw whenever it needs to eliminate. Mothers report that children learn within a few months to use the proper places and to clean themselves with leaves. Children are sometimes careless in cleaning themselves
and as a result may suffer a certain amount of anal irritation.

"A child who is slow in establishing toilet habits may irritate the mother;
then she may shout at him or rap him on the head with her knuckles. However, since sphincter control is instituted relatively late it seems to be a
source of little annoyance. Children certainly by the age of three, or five at
the latest, are thoroughly trained. I have no data on play with excreta—

which does not mean that this does not occur, but it may mean that the problem does not obtrude itself.

"Bladder control, or at least modesty about urination, seems to come slightly later than sphincter control. I judge this to be the case since it is not unusual to see children of between three and five years standing at the edge of a group and casually urinating without anyone's paying much attention to it. A comparable lack of sphincter control was observed only twice and both times it brought angry scolding from adults."[74]

## Indonesia – the Balinese

Margaret Mead and Frances Macgregor explain in their 1951 photographic study of Balinese childhood that the normal place for a child under 15–18 months is in human arms or otherwise physically close to its caregiver, by means of a sling. An infant's first experience of clothing is the sling which is used to bind baby and mother together. The sling also serves as a diaper, a shawl for warmth, a pillow, a towel and a wrapper and carrier for the baby.

"Elimination is treated very lightly. No fuss at all is made over urination by an infant. . . . Little babies experience only the shout for the dog that is to clean them up, or the attention of the dog when they are placed on the ground. As they learn to walk steadily, they toddle a little away from a group and squat, and the distance gets greater as they get older. . . . Children slowly learn to regard defecation as mildly shameful. . . . A child's chief learning from the culturally imposed elimination habits is to watch where it is and to move away from inappropriate spots. It never has to go far, so that the emphasis on foresight and self-control, which American children learn and generalize to other areas of life, is missing."[75]

## Japan

The village of Taira in Okinawa, Japan, is the focus of one of the studies in the 1963 book *Six Cultures*. Thomas and Hatsumi Maretzki explain that although babies are diapered and swaddled until they are about a year old, mothers begin a form of toilet training during this time.

"When the infant is anywhere from 22 days to 10 months old, the mothers start trying to anticipate urination before the baby wets his diapers. Each mother trains herself to the child's particular cues, squirming, peculiar facial expressions, and so on, or keeps a kind of mental time check. Holding the infant in a semi-sitting position out over the edge of the porch, and supporting him under his knees with her hands and at his back with her chest, she coaxes gently, repeating 'shi-shi' until he urinates onto the ground outside. If the mother is successful in her efforts, she hugs, kisses, and praises the infant. On the other hand, if she does not reach him in time and he is already wet, she will hold the child over the wet diaper and say 'shi-shi.' This is to ensure that he has fully eliminated, or if the interval between diaper checks has been long, to make certain that he does not need to urinate again before putting on a fresh change. In these instances she does not praise unless the infant does urinate or eliminate at her coaxing, but she does not punish him for urinating in his diapers."

Mothers appeared to believe that children are incapable of toilet learning at this early age. Their main concern seemed to be the number of diapers they had to wash or buy. More serious toilet training begins after the child learns to walk, with completion reported at 2 and 3 years of age. Overall, toilet training is a relatively casual affair. [76]

## Kurdistan

In 1951, doctoral candidate William Murray studied the Kurds living in the town of Rowanduz, Iraq. His thesis on Kurdish life in Rowanduz, published in 1953, provides a general description of the local method of infant toilet training.

"Toilet training begins early, at five or six months, by the repetition of a nonsense word which signifies evacuation and is accompanied by the initial use of a pot. Gradually utilization of the latrine and its ewer of water is learned. After two or three years the mother and others of the family begin to punish a child who soils himself."[77]

## Micronesia – the Ifaluk

Ifaluk is an atoll in the Caroline Islands, part of the Trust Territory of the Pacific Islands. Information was gleaned during a 6-month study on the island in 1947–48. Ifaluk, population 250 at the time, was chosen for study because it had had a minimum of outside influence.

"The [newborn] baby itself is wrapped in cloth, as a kind of diaper, and is then covered completely with another cloth. . . . When the baby soils itself, the diaper is replaced with a clean one, and excrements are carried to the ocean, and the soiled diaper is washed.

"The infant wears swaddling clothes until it has learned to crawl. When an adult holds an infant on his lap, he usually holds the cloth under the infant so that he should not be soiled should the infant choose to defecate or urinate. This precaution is necessary because sphincter control is not taught the child until it can walk and talk; that is, not until he can understand the demand, and has mastered the motor behavior to carry it out. The infant's faeces [sic] are disposed of in the lagoon, whereas its urine is merely wiped up. Not only is there no attempt made to toilet-train the infant, but the adults do not convey to the infant by means of facial expressions or gestures any exaggerated abhorrence for excrement. Adults themselves, however, are ashamed of excretory processes, but do not view excrement as dangerous or harmful, nor as material with which to work evil magic. And this attitude, of course, is reflected in their reaction to the excretory behavior of their infants. For example, while I was sitting in a house with a young man and his infant daughter, the daughter defecated on the bare thigh of her father. He gave no overt indications of disgust or anger, but laughingly called to his wife to remove the faeces from his thigh.

"Once the child learns to walk and to talk, however, he is not only trained in sphincter control, but he learns that his parents are concerned about his bowel movements. He is taught to defecate in the lagoon, not in the house or on land. If he does not readily learn to use the lagoon he is reprimanded and shamed, though not beaten. Any person, parents and stranger alike, will rebuke a child for polluting the ground or the house. The parents often invoke the authority of the chiefs in chastising the child. 'Somebody come this place (that is, to our house), very bad this place (because of the excrement). Chief come, he angry to this place. You no afraid chief?' My observations indicated that few, if any, children rebel against this training, and I observed none who did not observe the practice of repairing to the lagoon, after they had been so taught.

"The attitude towards urine is much more lax. Children who do not as yet wear clothes may urinate on the ground, but not in the house, with impunity.

"The theory behind this indulgence is that the baby is completely innocent, and is not responsible for its behavior. ('No savvy nothing.') This theory is consistent with the lack of punishment of the child . . . The generally accepted adult view of the infants, one may conclude, is that the infant is a powerless, innocent creature, who must neither be restrained nor punished. The resultant adult behavior is one of indulgence, and little attempt is made to train the child until he can walk and/or talk."

Puritanism and a sense of shame play significant roles among the Ifaluk. These "puritanical attitudes are displayed with reference to excretory behavior. All people excrete in the lagoon, and though their faces are in public view their behavior is concealed. But if a person, even of their own sex, sees them urinating or defecating on land, with genitalia exposed, they are terribly ashamed. If a man must urinate, and other men are present, he bends down on his haunches, so that his penis is concealed. If a person is in a group and must defecate or urinate, he will not tell where he is going when he leaves. He says, 'I am going over there.'"

A "verbal taboo applies to excretory references as well. No mention may be made of them in mixed company, not even in the presence of one's own wife."[78]

## Micronesia – Truk Islands (Fischer)

Ann Fischer studied child-rearing practices on Romonum Island, Chuuk State, in Micronesia from 1946–49. Her 1950 report details the role of the Trukese mother and its effect on child training. The topic of toilet training is included in her publication.

Mothers are very sensitive to their children's elimination schedule. "Time and again the mother will put the child off the mat just before it urinates. One mother stated that she knew her child would urinate right after it awakened, and after it ate. The mother, seated on the floor, stretches her legs out in front of her and places the child with its head on her knees and its body lying along her legs toward the ankles. The child urinates in this position. After it is placed in this manner, the mother makes a sound with lips moving which sounds like 'pspspsps.' There is a special Trukese word for this sound, and it is always used when the child urinates at the direction of its mother. Supposedly it represents the sound of flowing urine, and should give the child the idea that it is now time to urinate. This direction is not always obeyed by the child, and accidents do occur on the mat. In this case, the mother wipes up the urine with a towel or rag and does not express concern over it. . . .

"Most Trukese children begin to go outside the house to eliminate when they are between two and three years old. Between three and four years of age they begin to take the more difficult step to the *penco*, the outdoor privy built over the sea for sanitation. . . . All in all, the toilet training of the child is not extremely severe nor extremely lenient. After he is one year old the child may begin to show some concern over pleasing his elders in this respect, and it is during this time that he is told what is desired of him although never in severe terms."[79]

## Micronesia – Truk Islands (Gladwin & Sarason)

In another study of the people of Romonum on the island of Truk, authors Thomas Gladwin and Seymour Sarason state, "Because there is no early emphasis on the control of elimination and [a child] is asked to observe the social norms at a time when he is able to do so readily, toilet training never becomes a problem either for parents or for children.

"Babies are not diapered and in fact seldom clothed, but practically no attempt is made to train them not to urinate or defecate in the house. Mothers will take small babies out of the house when they awake or at other times when they may be expected to urinate, and will carry them out also if they begin to defecate, if this is convenient; but if it is not, the feces are simply cleaned up off the mat or the mother's legs or wherever they may be with no apparent concern. The child's buttocks are usually cleaned with the mother's finger and rinsed with water. Later, when the child can walk, he will be gently directed outside when he eliminates, but a lapse is not punished."

In most other training situations, Trukese children are punished in two ways: by having food withheld and by beatings.[80]

## New Guinea – the Arapesh and the Manus

Margaret Mead studied primitive peoples in the South Seas between 1925 and 1933. In *Growing up in New Guinea*, she mentions toilet training in relation to the concepts of privacy, shame and embarrassment. "But the Manus' conception of social discipline is as loose as their standards of physical training are rigid. They demand nothing beyond physical efficiency and respect for property except a proper observance of the canons of shame. Children must learn privacy in excretion almost by the time they can walk; must get by heart the conventional attitudes of shame and embarrassment."[81]

In *Sex and Temperament in Three Primitive Societies*, Margaret Mead wrote, "[W]hen an [Arapesh] infant urinates or defecates, the person holding it will jerk it quickly to one side to prevent soiling his or her own person. This jerk interrupts the normal course of excretion and angers the child. In later life, the Arapesh have notably low sphincter-control, and regard its loss as the normal concomitant of any highly charged situation."[82]

## New Guinea – the Kwoma

The Kwoma live in the Peilungua Mountains of New Guinea. Anthropologist John Whiting spent 7 months among the Kwoma in 1936. He describes the Kwoma as "short, stocky, negroid people with long heads, dark frizzly hair, medium thick lips, and skin color varying from light to dark brown." In his book, he provides fairly detailed information on the Kwoma method of toilet training.

"Bladder and colon tensions give an infant little trouble. He simply evacuates when the pressure becomes strong enough. The mother makes no attempt at toilet training while the child is still an infant; she simply learns to anticipate his bowel and bladder movements, quickly lifting him from her lap and holding him over the earth floor. The feces are then wiped up with a leaf. Sometimes the mother does not lift the child quickly enough and he urinates on her leg. In such cases the leaf is again used, and the child is not held accountable for the mistake.

"Cleanliness training begins at approximately the same age as weaning. The mother is comparatively gentle in teaching her child toilet habits. She tells him that adults go outside near the garbage heap to urinate and that he is big enough to do likewise. Similarly, she points out that adults do not defecate in the house but in the household latrine. She takes the child with her to the latrine and holds him while he relieves himself until he has learned to do this without assistance. When I asked an informant whether a mother punishes her child if he persistently defecates in the house, he answered: 'No, of course not. He is her own child, isn't he? Why should she punish him? It is her duty to clean up after him if he defecates in the house.' Although this may express the theoretical position of the Kwoma native, in actual practice the infant is more recalcitrant, and the mother less patient, than the statement would indicate.

"Cleanliness habits are usually already established by the time a boy or girl reaches childhood. Informants stated that if a slip occurs it is the child's own business except that he is forced to clean up after himself."[83]

## Oman

In *Behind the Veil in Arabia* (1982), Unni Wikan portrays the lives of the Soharis of Oman, with an emphasis on the study of women. Of particular interest is the way in which the standards of segregation become entrenched and internalized in women. Although segregation is instilled in children from birth, it does not play a role in toilet training.

"Swaddling is common in the winter. The baby is wrapped in a large piece of cloth that covers all of his body, except for the head and buttocks. Training the infant to control his bowel movements begins as early as between four and six months of age (bladder control is considered of less importance) and thus the buttocks must be left uncovered.

"When the child begins to talk, around the age of two or three, he is expected to ask to be taken to the toilet, and he is scolded if he fails to do so. Until then, failures have been sanctioned with no more than discontent glances from the mother. After repeated mishaps, he may be threatened with spanking or the red-hot iron (*wasum*), or (since the inception of the hospital) injections."[84]

## Philippines – the Tarongans

William and Corinne Nydegger describe life in Tarong, an Ilocos barrio in the Philippines, in one of the studies of *Six Cultures*. Infants are never left to cry and are normally held unless they are asleep. During the day, a basketry hammock is sometimes used to rock a child to sleep, but the tiniest commotion prompts the caregiver to pick up and rock the baby in her lap. Clothing consists of a short shirt or dress. No diapers or underwear are worn.

"The infant is covered loosely, if at all, below the waist. When he urinates, the puddle is wiped up or the cloth is changed; if the mother's clothing is wet, it is ignored. While interviewing or chatting with mothers of infants, we noticed that in almost all instances of the child's wetting the mother, her response was to merely shift the child to a dry part of the lap and shift the wet portion of the skirt so that it would dry. There was no verbal or facial recognition of the incident. . . . Precautions are taken, however, against the mother's clothes being soiled by feces. A folded cloth is kept under the buttocks of infants, and after defecation, the cloth is replaced. . . . At 6 months or so, training is begun by moving the child to a corner of the kitchen porch over the waste-puddle for both urination and defecation.

"Toilet training is intensified some time before weaning, usually at about 1½ years when the child is able to understand simple verbal instruction and express his need to urinate or defecate . . . bowel, like bladder control, is attained with no apparent resistance." By age 2, children use the outhouse to defecate. Bladder control is accomplished at the very latest by age 3.[85]

## Taiwan (Diamond)

In her 1969 book, Norma Diamond explains how toilet training is done in the Taiwanese village of K'un Shen. "Carrying the child on her back, the mother soon becomes sensitized to motions or cries indicating that the child is about to urinate or defecate and she removes it from her back and holds it over the ground or a ditch to relieve itself. Toilet training thus begins at a very early age, for when the child urinates the mother makes a whistling sound. Soon, she begins holding the child and making the whistling sound to encourage it to urinate."

More serious toilet training begins around the end of the first year. Once children can walk, they have no problem continuing on their own, in part because they wear split pants. All they have to do to stay clean and dry is squat. Most children finish toilet training by the time they are 2. As soon as they are old enough to understand, they are encouraged to squat over the nearest ditch or on the dirt floor. Use of the outhouse is not encouraged until they are about 4 or 5 years old.[86]

## Taiwan (Gallin)

Bernard Gallin and his wife conducted research in Hsin Hsing village, Taiwan, for 16 months in 1957–58. Their study of sociocultural change in this Taiwanese peasant village covered the time frame 1900–1959. After World War II, the extended family gave way to the individual family unit.

Babies rarely cry for very long since they are never left alone and receive a lot of attention and affection. They are often cared for by older siblings.

"Toilet training, like weaning, is not considered a problem by the villagers. It is not emphasized until the child is considered ready for this new stage—that is, until he is physically capable of controlling the sphincter and bladder and able to understand what is expected of him. By the time the child is six-or-seven-months-old, his diaper is replaced by training pants—pants slit open at the crotch. However, toilet training does not begin until the child is almost two-years-old, walking, and beginning to talk and understand what he is told. At this time he is taught to ask to be taken to an inconspicuous spot to perform. Eventually, he will go there by himself. If the child has a lapse, he is slapped on the hand. Village mothers note that toilet training is usually accomplished in about a week after it is begun and that the child usually offers little resistance."[87]

## Taiwan (Wolf)

Margery Wolf observed and studied rural Taiwanese women in 1959–1961. Taiwanese mothers consider it dangerous to carry an infant very much before the age of at least 6 weeks. Infants spend most of their time on the family bed or in a bamboo crib on wheels, which is rolled around the house. After about 6 weeks, a baby is tied on her mother's back with a long strip of cloth that swaddles the baby and binds her to the mother.

"Toilet training is not something that arouses much concern or interest among Taiwanese mothers. The intimate contact between mother and child during the first few months allows the mother to 'know' her baby very well. Mothers claim to be able to identify the restless movements the child makes before she urinates and to use this signal to spread the child's legs and hold her away from their own body. The mother accompanies this act with a whistling noise so that in time the child associates the sound with the activity and empties her bladder on command. Diapers are used only at night, and many mothers claim even these can be dispensed with after six weeks. Mothers say they can keep a dry bed by holding the baby over the edge several times each night (the advantage of earth or concrete floors) and whistling. Bowel control is equally undramatic. When a child can walk she is encouraged to go to a garbage heap or drainage ditch. Accidents are not punished, unless one counts the looks of disgust by an older sister who has to clean it up. Undoubtedly the great number of acceptable toilet areas takes the emotional pressure off both mother and child."[88]

## Tibet

Anne Maiden and Edie Farwell provide details on life before conception and through early childhood in their 1997 book *The Tibetan Art of Parenting*. They include a general description of Tibetan toilet training in their work.

"Toilet training often begins with association by sound. The mother makes a specific sound and then the child slowly identifies that sound with the need to use the toilet pot. Soon the child learns to make these sounds, and in response the mother points to a place for the child to go, or bring the pot herself. By one-and-a-half or two years old, the child does this independently."[89]

## Turkey

A 1970 report from secluded villages of Eastern Anatolia does not give an age for beginning toilet training. Diapers are not used, "the child being put to sleep in his cradle bundled up with a type of soil that soaks up the urine." The wet soil is dried in the sun and used again in the same way. "Occasionally a kind of wooden apparatus is fitted to the child's genital area, the urine passing through a pipe to a receiving cup on the floor." Children wear dresses without underwear so as to make it easy to eliminate. Defecation is a private function which is performed out of sight while urination is performed casually in public. As soon as they can walk, toddlers are taken by older children to specified defecation locations. "Appropriate toilet behavior is regulated by shaming, and the children seem to learn quickly and sensitively about what is required of them. Here too, as observed by anthropologists, bodily possessions carry the bodily identity which it is superstitiously believed can be used for evil purposes by their enemies."[90]

chapter 4

# polar regions, the americas & beyond

## Arctic Regions –
## Greenland, Siberia and Aleutians

Joëlle Robert-Lamblin is a director of research at the National Center for Scientific Research in Paris, France. As an anthropologist, she has traveled to the Arctic many times since 1967, including 11 scientific missions to Greenland, a stay in the Aleutians and four expeditions to Siberia. In December 1999, she was able to give me a general overview of infant toilet training in the Far North.

"It's basically the mother who deals with toilet training. She makes sounds and gives encouragement to prompt her baby to eliminate. She never scolds or punishes her baby in this regard. Toilet training is gentle and carried out by joyful and affectionate enticement."[91]

## Arctic Regions – the Inuit of Canada (Damas)

David Damas spent a year, during 1962–63, with the Copper Eskimos of the Northwest Territories in Canada. He provides a general description of the toilet training practices in *The Copper Eskimo*.

"Toilet training is patiently but persistently pursued. The child is removed several times during the day and stimulated to urinate. The child is never reprimanded for defecating or urinating inside the mother's coat when he is carried."[92]

## Arctic Regions – the Inuit of Canada (Robbe)

The 1998 book *Babies Celebrated (Bébés du monde)* includes observations and photos of the Inuit. Among the Inuit, a deep and warm hood is used as a baby bag. When the mother "feels that her baby has to urinate, she takes the child out of the hood, often with the help of another woman. According to Bernadette Robbe, when the mother goes on a long trip, she slips lichen or rabbit skin into her anorak to serve as a diaper. There is not one specific material that is always used—mothers take what they find, according to the season. In spite of the restrictions of the region, each woman is inventive enough to improvise solutions, which are then repeated if they work well. However, the baby is not always put into the mother's hood—in some areas in the East Asian Arctic, when the weather is nice and the women sit outside to sew or just talk, they slip their babies into their large waders. With only his or her head sticking out of these seven-league boots, the little one begins to discover the world."[93]

## Arctic Regions – the Utkuhikhalingmiut of Canada

In 1963, Jean Briggs went to the Canadian Northwest Territories to make a 17-month anthropological field study of the Utkuhikhalingmiut or "Utku." The 20–35 Utkuhikhalingmiut Eskimos were the sole inhabitants of an area of 35,000 square miles.

The toilet training method of the Utku is briefly described in a footnote of the book. "The toilet training that is considered such a critical experience in the life of a *kapluna* [Caucasian] child does not appear to be a crisis for the Utku child, who from the time he is born is held over a can at appropriate moments: when he wakes, after (and sometimes while) he eats, before he goes to sleep, and in general whenever he shows signs of discharging. I did not observe the transition from this stage to the next, in which the child learns to call attention to his need for the can. Allaq told me that children learn a verbal signal by themselves, by imitating slightly older children, and this seems quite in line with the autonomy that children are granted in other areas of their development."[94]

## Belize – the Maya

Michael and Debi Pearl conducted missionary work among the Maya in Belize for a period of three months in 1983. During their stay, they observed various aspects of the Mayan lifestyle. One practice in particular caught their attention —the fact that mothers did not use any diapers on their babies.

"While on mission trips in Central America, I noticed that the tribal women did not put diapers on their babies. I found this interesting and started asking questions. Occasionally, mothers would slide their babies out of their back slings and sit them on the tops of their feet. The babies, being put in that position, then relieved themselves on the ground."[95]

The Pearls were so impressed that they used this method on their own children. Their account, entitled *No Greater Joy*, can be found in Part 2, Chapter 8, of this book.

## Bolivia – the Siriono

Anthropologist Allan Holmberg spent about 12 months with small groups of Siriono Indians in Bolivia during the years 1940–1942. At that time, the total population of the Siriono was about 2,000. They lived as semi-nomadic aborigines and inhabited the tropical rainforest area of northern and eastern Bolivia. By the time Holmberg arrived, many had abandoned aboriginal life and were living in servitude on cattle ranches and farms, and many who had been captured as children in the forests grew up as servants. In 1946, Dr. Holmberg wrote his doctoral dissertation on the Siriono Indians.

Among the Siriono, toilet training is a very gradual process. "[F]rom the time one is a child until one assumes the role of an adult, life is relatively carefree and undisciplined. In fact, this pattern of freedom so carries on throughout adult life that it can be truly said of the Siriono that they are a highly undisciplined people.

"An infant receives no punishment if he urinates or defecates on his parents. Almost no effort is made by the mother to train an infant in the habits of cleanliness, until he can walk, and then they are instilled very gradually. Of course, if a mother hears her infant fart or feels that he is about to defecate on her, she holds him away from her body so as not to be soiled, but about the only punishment that an infant is subjected to by defecating on her is that of being set aside for a while until she cleans up the mess.

"Children who are able to walk, however, soon learn by imitation, and with the assistance of their parents, not to defecate near the hammock. When they are old enough to indicate their needs, the mother gradually leads them further and further away from the hammock to urinate and defecate, so that by the time they have reached the age of three they have learned not to pollute the house. Until the age of four or five, however, children are still wiped by the mother, who also cleans up the excreta and throws them away. Not until a child has reached the age of six does he take care of his defecation needs alone.

"Little training is given a child in the matter of urination. Contact with urine is not regarded as harmful, and I frequently observed mothers who did not even move when babies on their laps urinated. Since no clothes are worn by either the mother or the child, the urine soon dries or can readily be washed off."[96]

## Bolivia & Brazil – the Chácobos and the Matis

Philippe Erikson holds a Ph.D. in ethnology and is a professor at l'Université de Paris X-Nanterre. He has worked extensively with the Matis in Brazil and the Chácobos in Bolivia.

"There are over 400 different Amerindian groups in the Amazon basin, making it difficult to generalize. Yet one has the impression that most of these cultures have very much in common with each other. In any case, the information I'm providing on infant toilet training applies mainly to the Matis in Brazil and somewhat to the Chácobos in Bolivia.

"This topic is not one of my specialties, but my impression is that the Amerindian method of toilet training is very casual, mainly a matter of handling the situation until a child can walk and take care of business on his own. Mothers are relaxed about elimination. This also holds true for pets, of which there are many. People carry small marmoset monkeys on their heads, and when accidents sometimes happen, it's no big deal.

"If a baby 'goes' inside the house, the mother simply cleans up after the child. As far as I know, women are the only ones who clean up after children. I have never seen fathers help in this regard. I do not recall seeing a mother get angry at a baby about elimination. Also consider that in the tropics, people tend to get diarrhea, so even adults often have little choice as to where they will go. Diarrhea is so prevalent that the Matis sing magic chants to prevent children from getting it. They chant special verses while slapping a child's buttocks with a grub. A typical chant invokes the child in question by name followed by, 'Show me your back so I can beat your rear end so you won't have diarrhea.'

"Outdoors, with the climate, bugs, etc., waste material all disappears in a matter of hours so there is no outdoor mess to worry about. Dogs also help clean up excrement. This is reminiscent of Haudricourt's theory that dogs were domesticated because of their usefulness as scavengers and house-cleaners.

"Children are visually exposed to excretion at an early age in forest-dwelling societies. One point to consider is that toddlers have more opportunities of seeing their mothers in action than in societies such as ours where people lock themselves in the bathroom and don't take their babies along. Of course, women will sometimes hand their baby to someone in order to have privacy, but this is not always possible.

"The Amazonian peoples I have lived with are very casual when it comes to mentioning excretion. No euphemisms are used such as *petit coin* in French. They just say something like, 'Wait a second, I'm going to shit.' If you meet someone on a trail and (s)he asks where are you going, you can answer, 'I'm going for a shit.'

"The Matis live in long-houses while the Chácobo live in individual ones. The floors are either dirt or palm wood (which is full of holes). It does not matter at all if a baby eliminates in a dwelling. The Matis, like most (if not all) Amazonian peoples, bathe several times a day, perhaps another reason for not being uptight about elimination.

"Supernatural beliefs play a role in toilet behavior. The most striking aspect of Amazonian toilet behavior has to do with the contrast between the extreme caution when it comes to adults and the very relaxed attitude in the case of babies. Grownups are very careful not to leave their feces lying around because it could be used against them by witches. (Some people such as the Machiguenga in Peru go as far as burying their feces). They are also very careful not to urinate on trails (even trails which are rarely ever used or miles from any house) because someone else might step on it and be harmed (their feet might itch). These considerations are important regarding adult defecation but barely come into play in the case of children.

"Another ethnographic detail of interest is that during major rituals, i.e., tattooing ceremonies, the initiates are separated by gender, boys on one side and girls on the other, but each group must stick together as a unit for a while and only go out at night. One of the things they do collectively is going out for their daily defecation.

*Philippe Erikson*

Matis Indian children at the evening campfire.
(Rio Itui, Amazonia, Brazil, 2000)

"The Cashinahua, living along the border of Brazil and Peru (mainly in Peru), consider urine and feces as two of the five spirits of an individual. The other three are the eye spirit, body spirit and dream spirit. The urine and feces spirits are volatile, meaning they don't last long and certainly disappear after death."[97]

## Brazil – the Tenetehara

Fieldwork was conducted by Charles Wagley and his team of assistants in the Brazilian rainforest during the period 1941–42 and later in 1945. At that time, the Tenetehara Indians were merging into Brazilian rural life.

"During the first year, parents pay little attention to sphincter and bladder control of the child. Several times each day the mother places the infant on the ground to urinate or to defecate. She then simply calls an older child to sweep up the feces on a banana leaf and to throw it into the nearby underbrush. At night the mother, without even leaving her hammock, holds a child out over the floor to urinate or even to defecate. After the child is able to walk, however, she sometimes shames it when it soils the hammock or the house floor. Older siblings or cousins usually take a two or three-year-old child just outside the house for such necessities. These older children laugh at the child who does not ask to be taken outside, and both adults and older children shame the child who urinates or defecates in the house in front of the family. Although several people told us that it was customary to 'spank the child lightly' (on the buttocks) when it continued to lack sphincter and bladder control after it was walking, we did not observe one instance of such punishment for these reasons. Instead we often saw children three or four years old defecate on the floor of a Tenetehara house without being punished at all.

"Children are soon, however, made to feel ashamed of these body functions and by the time they are adult, they are not only ashamed to urinate or defecate in view of a person of the opposite sex but also in the company of people of the same sex. Men on hunting trips move a distance away from their companions to urinate and go to infinite trouble for privacy for excretory functions. The same is true for women with other women. The attitudes of personal shame in regard to sphincter and bladder functions are passed on to children during the first three or four years of their life—not by corporal punishment but by ridicule and shame."[98]

## Canada – the Kwakiutl

The Kwakiutl of Vancouver Island are described in Clellan Ford's 1941 book about the life of a Kwakiutl chief. A general description of toilet training is provided.

"When it was old enough to talk, the mother or father would take the child out of the house and down to the beach to defecate. Somewhat earlier, it was taught to urinate in the chamber vessel, and this is said to have been readily accomplished without punishment. The child was taught the verb 'to urinate' and learned first to tell his mother his want and then to go by himself. Children were not punished for wetting the bed; this, it was thought, would have had no effect since children do not know what they are doing in their sleep. They were, however, repeatedly asked to wake up in the night if they wanted to use the chamber vessel."[99]

## Mexico – the Maya

In the village of Pustunich, Yucatán Peninsula, toilet training is gradual and permissive. The field date of this report was 1964. When a baby eliminates, it is held out at arm's length. "An attempt is made to get the child outside first, though floors are usually dirt. Its pants or huipil are then changed." There is no punishment used during approximately the first 18 months. "Little concern is given to soiling the hammock, as it is string mesh, dries fast, and is easily washable."

As a child learns to walk, he is taken outdoors to eliminate whenever other family members themselves "feel the need." As the child's understanding increases, family members talk with him, admonish him to leave the house when he needs to urinate or defecate, and encourage him to communicate his elimination needs to them. Once he indicates that he understands what is desired of him, he will be punished (slapped) for soiling the floor, hammock or clothing.

Toddlers wear only the huipil (traditional Mayan blouse), without any pants, which allows accidents with minimal soiling of clothing. Parents expect accidents and "try to avert them by learning the child's moods."[100]

## Paraguay – the Ache

Anthropologist Kim Hill of the University of New Mexico has lived part-time with and observed the Ache Indians for 20 years. When I asked him in December 1999 about infant elimination training among the Ache, Hill explained, "Babies simply urinate or defecate whenever they want and often all over the person holding them. This does not bother the Ache much at all. Only when they are quite a bit older (maybe 18 months) does training start to encourage them to move a few steps away from others when they want to eliminate."[101]

## United States – the Apache

The lifestyle and cultural patterns of the Apache of Arizona are described in detail by Grenville Goodwin in his 1942 book *The Social Organization of the Western Apache*. The author began his fieldwork in 1929 and was in close touch with the Apache for over 10 years.

The material was gleaned in large part from stories told to the author by 34 old Apache Indians. In the course of telling a story, they would sometimes qualify their sources, "This I am telling you was told me by my grandmother, and before she told it to me she heard it from her grandmother, and before that her grandmother heard it from another old person. You white people have written books, but everything we know about our people is written in our heads."

Children learned right and wrong mainly by observation and imitation. Mythology also played a part, particularly the coyote tales in which Coyote was tied to any kind of incorrect behavior. Children were often told to be careful and not to do as Coyote did.

Goodwin states that he did not specifically study the Apache method of toilet training. "On the few occasions observed, when babies and small children soiled, the Apache took it as a matter of course, and no remarks of disgust or anger were made. When one old woman, sitting on her own bed, placed her hand by mistake in a mess which her two-year-old great-grand-daughter had made on her blanket, she merely cleaned it off, remarking that when children were about such things happen. On another occasion, a man stepping in some human feces quite close to the door of a wickiup, attributed it to a small child, saying, 'You have to watch out for this in a camp where there are small children.' A little girl two years and nine months old, visiting in my house for several days, with her mother and father and two older sisters, more than once wet or soiled the floor, but when she did this she usually went behind a barrel in one corner of the room where she was partially out of sight. Her mother cleaned up after her good-naturedly and without remark, but, if she happened to see what the little girl was up to, she hurriedly carried her outside the house and let her relieve herself there unconcealed.[102]

## United States – the Hopi

The Hopi Indians are descendants of prehistoric cliff dwellers and inhabit mesas in northern Arizona. Wayne Dennis lived in a native house with his wife and daughter during the summer months of 1937 and 1938 in order to observe and study the Hopi. His book *The Hopi Child*, published in 1940, describes the Hopi pattern of child care and the behavior which issues from this pattern.

Dealing with the function of elimination starts with wrapping the infant and placing him in the cradleboard. "He is placed on a blanket. A piece of cotton cloth is placed over his chest and passed between the chest and the arms so that the arms will not be brought against bare flesh. Rags are placed under the buttocks and between the legs. Nowadays diapers are sometimes used in place of the rags. Then one side of the blanket is brought over one arm of the infant and passed between the chest and the arm of the opposite side and tucked under the infant's body. The other side of the blanket is passed over both arms, which are extended along the body of the infant, and it too is tucked under the infant. Thus wrapped, the infant is placed upon the cradleboard.

"The baby is bound to the cradle during the first day. This is done by lacing strings (formerly buckskin thongs) through holes provided at the side of the cradle, or by tying strips of cloth around both child and cradle. The ties are passed over the legs also, so that they can be flexed only slightly. The purpose of this binding is to ensure that the child will be straight and of good carriage.

"The child is taken off the cradle only for changing the soiled cloths and for bathing. He is put to the breast and nursed while on the board. When he has gone to sleep, the board is placed on the floor or on a bed. At night, the cradleboard rests beside the mother.

"Formerly the rags which were the primitive antecedent of diapers were dried in the sun and rubbed clean with fresh dry sand, although periodically they were washed. At present soap and water are used as the cleaning agents, and, as was noted earlier, modern diapers are used by some mothers. However, no other element of American baby clothes has yet come into use. Aside from rags or a diaper, the child within the blankets is naked.

"No toilet training is attempted until the child is able to walk, and to understand some words. He is then told to go outside when he needs to defecate and urinate. To the beginner, this means literally just outside the door, although older children go to a corner of the plaza, and adults go outside of the village. If the child fails to go out of doors at the proper time, he is spanked.

"At a slightly later age he is supposed to tell his mother when he needs to eliminate during the night, but he is not expected to avoid all bedwetting until he is two years of age."[103]

## United States – the Navaho

Dr. Clyde Kluckhohn of Cambridge University observed, interviewed and studied the Navaho in the late 1930s and early 1940s. Navaho babies were kept tightly wrapped up to the neck in a number of cloths (usually old flour or sugar sacks) and on a cradleboard. Use of the cradleboard started anywhere from as soon as the navel healed, after the umbilical cord fell off, to 1 month of age. The cradleboard contained one or more small holes in the lower part to allow urine to drain. The hours spent on the cradleboard steadily decreased as the child grew older. Some parents freed the child at the onset of crawling or scooting while others waited until the child could walk independently.

Navaho diapers were originally made from cliff-rose bark which was rubbed together to make straw. This material is very absorbent. After drying it in the sun, it is nearly odorless and can be used again and again. Later, cloth replaced the straw. Wet cloths were dried (not washed) and reused. Soiled cloths had the fecal matter scraped off, then were dried and reused in the cradle. Babies were changed at bath time (every day or every other day) plus a few other times a day, depending on individual family circumstances.

Training in most areas of life, including elimination, was gradual, gentle and delayed during the first 2–3 years of life. There was basically no sphincter discipline used for a year or more and only very gentle discipline thereafter.

"Babies under six months often urinate or defecate while nursing, and this not infrequently occurs with older children as well. These occurrences are accepted as a matter of course until the child talks or at least responds to words. At most the mother will interrupt the nursing briefly in order to clean her clothes or protect herself with additional dry cloths.

"Not until he can talk and understand is pressure put on a child to learn Navaho conventions of excretion. If a child who can walk and talk (or at least respond to speech) starts to urinate inside the hut, he is told to go outside to do this, and an older child will gently lead him out. At first elimination is permitted just outside the door; later the child is expected to go away into the bushes or behind a rock ledge. For a long time he is not punished for lapses or accidents but encouraged to act like his elders. Before going to sleep at night, he is taken out and is also advised not to eat or drink much for some time before going to bed. No special 'baby words' are used with children in referring to urine or feces.

"Navaho clothing for children is such that 'accidents' seldom render the garments completely unfit for further wear without washing. Neither sex ordinarily wears underwear." Little boys wear split pants, and little girls wear skirts.

"It is important to realize that bowel control is not expected of the Navaho child until he is old enough to direct his own movements and merely accompany an elder at night and in the morning. The mother or an older sister takes the child out in the morning when she herself goes to defecate and tells the little one to imitate her position and her actions. . . . After a time, the youngster who continues to wet or soil himself is teased or scolded by his relatives. In some families the buttocks of older children are slapped, though ordinarily Navaho children are switched on the legs, not on the buttocks. Even babies of under two who urinate or defecate within the hogan will be observed to have a slightly guilty look. Some children who are about to perform give an advance signal (such as a hand on the buttocks) which is recognized by the family, and they are hurriedly taken outside.

"Little feeling of disgust for urine or feces is inculcated. There is no exaggerated emphasis upon the unpleasantness of odors or consistency of excreta. A little girl of four will scrape out the diapers of her young brother in a perfectly matter-of-fact manner. Indeed, once a diaper is dry, she may use it for a head covering. Feces within the hogan are usually covered with sand or dirt and carried out in a shovel, but they may also be scraped into the firepit or under a stove. Adults do avoid stepping in urine or excreta, but their behavior conveys the notion that these materials are merely mildly unpleasant—not disgusting and certainly not shameful. When a baby urinates or defecates in someone's lap (which frequently occurs) the event is taken very calmly.

"In short, the two evacuation activities of the child are uniquely free from parental interference for a long time. Whatever may be the sensations associated with evacuation or retention of urine and feces, the processes are subject for some time to the impulses of the child, unmixed with parental punishment."[104]

## United States – the Papago

In 1949, Jane Chesky wrote about life on the Papago Indian Reservation in southern Arizona. The Papago call themselves "the Desert People" and use a gentle approach with babies, as evidenced in this condensed excerpt. "The keynote of a Papago infant's training is indulgence. The baby goes wherever his mother does. His slightest whimper brings her to him immediately, to talk to him or pick him up. Papago babies are nursed whenever they cry from hunger or when they can be quieted in no other way. Weaning comes later; several instances were found in which the youngest child of a family nursed four or five years, but the older children were weaned at from eighteen to thirty months. General patterns of child-training are based on the belief that a little child should be happy and therefore he should be humored as often as possible. Corporal punishment of any sort is seldom used on children under five."

Toilet training starts when a child can walk and understand instructions. The exact age is hard to determine since parents don't know their children's birthdays. Babies use diapers when in public but are usually bare-bottomed at home. There is no negative reaction when a baby urinates on the dirt floor or in the yard. When he can walk, his mother begins taking him to the bushes away from the dwelling and tells him to urinate there. His brothers and sisters take him there whenever they go to the bushes, and he learns mainly by imitation. "He soon becomes aware of the extreme modesty of his relatives during elimination, and by the time he is three and a half or four years old he knows that he is supposed to go to the bushes with members of his own sex." If he soils himself after this time, his mother makes a face and shows disapproval by saying "dirty" or "nasty" or else warns him that wild animals or ghosts will get him. "It is significant that, in using threats of the supernatural or the enemy, the mother sidesteps responsibility for the denial; it is not she who refuses the baby but an outside agency potentially harmful to them both."[105]

## Venezuela – the Warao

The Warao Indian culture and way of life focus on canoes. The name of the tribe means "boat people." Boys and young men receive extensive training in both the craft and spiritual aspects of canoes. "Behavior offensive to the canoe, or rather to the spirit of the canoe, called Masisikiri, can occur as early as during a child's infancy. . . . The child first learns to refrain from urinating or (worse still) defecating in or near the canoes." Toilet training is gentle, and no one gets upset if a child has accidents in the house. "But both mother and father will not tolerate similar defilement of a large canoe and the child is scolded severely. Usually they are told to stay away from it altogether."[106]

## Venezuela – the Yequana

Jean Liedloff provides a brief but colorful glimpse into the toilet training attitudes of the Yequana in her 1977 book *The Continuum Concept*. Further information on Liedloff and the concept can be found in Chapter 16, Part 1, "Compatible Lifestyles & Philosophies."

"When he wets or defecates, [his mother] may laugh, and as she is seldom alone, so do her companions, and she holds the infant away from her as quickly as she can until he finishes. It is a sort of game to see how fast she can hold him away, but the laughter is louder when she gets the worst of it. Water sinks into the dirt floor in moments and excrement is cleared away immediately with leaves.

"Later, when house training takes place, the toddler is chased outside if he sullies the hut floor." This is an act of positive learning rather than a form of punishment. The child realizes that the disapproval is not aimed at him but at his act, and this motivates him to modify his behavior.[107]

## Elsewhere

### "Toilet Training Age in Some Primitive Societies"

In their 1953 book *Child Training and Personality*, Whiting and Child list rough estimates of the "age at toilet training" for several primitive societies. The following societies toilet train their babies between the ages of 4 months and 2 years:

| | |
|---|---|
| Tanala | 0.3 |
| Chagga | 0.8 |
| Marquesans | 1.0 |
| Comanche | 1.2 |
| Manus | 1.2 |
| Ontong-Javanese | 1.2 |
| Hopi | 1.5 |
| Kwakiutl | 1.5 |
| Pukapukans | 1.7 |
| Slave | 1.7 |
| Alorese | 1.8 |
| Papago | 1.9 |
| Dahomeans | 2.0 |
| Lesu | 2.0 |
| Wogeo | 2.0 [108] |

## "Cross-Cultural Codes 2"

In their 1971, *Cross-Cultural Codes 2*, Barry and Paxson found that the following societies use infant or early elimination training:

* 0–6 months
  Hausa, Egyptians, Kurd, Toda, Lepcha, Garo, Burmese, Tanala, Bribri, Goajiro, Haitians, Cayapa, Amahuaca

* 7–12 months or onset of crawling
  Russians, Uttar Pradesh, Negri Sembilan, Javanese, Ingalik, Gros Ventre, Huichol, Chagga, Lebanese[109]

## "Lap Children" – Infants aged 0–1 Year

Margaret Mead classified children into four age groups based on her research on childhood in six societies. The first is the lap child, from birth to 1 year of age. Next comes the knee child which consists of toddlers from 2–3 years of age. The yard child is the preschooler aged 4–5 years, and the community child is 6–10 years old.

"Since the lap children in most of our samples are in close physical contact with their mothers during both day and night (they sleep in body contact with their caretakers), much of their communication with caretakers is nonverbal. Caretakers learn to read the cues of their charges. . . . The best demonstration of this kinesthetic style of communication is the caretaker's ability to foresee the lap child's need to urinate or defecate; the caretaker then holds the baby out before it soils the caretaker's clothes. In contrast, the style of communication of American mothers is more verbal and less kinesthetic."[110]

# List of IPT Countries

For reference purposes, here is a list of some of the countries where infant potty training is used. The list is by no means complete. Readers with experience or knowledge of other locations are invited to contact the author by e-mail at infantpotty@hotmail.com or by mail at White-Boucke Publishing, PO Box 400, Lafayette CO 80026, USA.

## Africa

Algeria, Botswana, Cameroon, Central African Republic, Egypt, Ethiopia, Ghana, Ivory Coast, Kenya, Madagascar, Mali, Nigeria, Senegal, South Africa, Sudan, Tanzania, Togo, Uganda, West Africa, Zaire

## Asia and Oceania

Afghanistan, Bangladesh, Cambodia, China, India, Indonesia, Iran, Iraq, Japan, Korea, Kurdistan, Lebanon, Malaysia, Micronesia, Myanmar (Burma), Nepal, New Guinea, Oman, Pakistan, Philippines, Polynesia, Sikkim, Singapore, Sri Lanka, Taiwan, Thailand, Tibet, Turkey, Vietnam

## Central & South America and Caribbean

Argentina, Belize, Bolivia, Brazil, Costa Rica, Dominican Republic, El Salvador, Guatemala, Honduras, Jamaica, Mexico, Nicaragua, Panama, Paraguay, Peru, Venezuela, West Indies

## Europe

Bulgaria, Czech Republic, Romania, Russia, Slovakia, Turkey

## Polar Regions

Alaska (Inupiat, Eskimos), Aleutians, Canada (Inuit, Kwakiutl, Netsilik and Utkuhikhalingmiut), Greenland, Siberia

chapter **5**

# onward

*nfant Potty Training* was written in large part for parents who are curious about this method. The book provides clear guidelines and numerous illustrative photos. The research and other information presented here demonstrate that the method is possible; it is gentle, safe and effective; it has been with us for centuries; and it is practiced by millions around the world today.

This book was also written in an effort to prevent practicing parents from feeling alone, estranged and unsure of themselves. Perhaps the facts, anecdotes, testimonials and photos will help alleviate any fears acquired through popular yet unproven developmental theories. Western mothers and fathers feeling isolated in using this method can find support and inspiration in their own or neighboring communities if they but reach out to elders, immigrants and other practicing parents. The transcultural and transgenerational currents are always flowing. Looking back at my own experience of 20 years ago, I was an American living in Holland and learned infant elimination training from an Indian Sikh mother passing through Holland on her way back to her adopted homeland of Kenya.

The book is also for parents who independently discovered this method on their own or who intuitively figured it out after receiving little more than a general description. Perhaps this tome will serve as an affirmation of what some readers already know.

It is hoped that this book will instill confidence and encourage parents to have faith in their abilities. Babies can sense doubt, and doubt creates blockage, hinders progress and slows success. One of the main messages of this book is for parents to relax about toilet training, no matter what method is used. A relaxed mother is able to better communicate and to more fully enjoy her baby. Parents must never pressure a baby and should always bear in mind that this method may take as long as any other.

This method is not about convenience, control or ego; it is about your relationship with your baby, communication, observing baby's natural elimination timing, responding to signals and "being there" on time for your baby. It is about a trusting and intimate interchange within the mother-infant dyad and the father-infant dyad.

Above all, this book is meant to educate and to increase awareness about this wonderful way of communicating so amazingly with infants. Your baby is ready if you are.

# NOTES

**PART 1 - THE CONCEPT & THE METHOD**

## Chapter 2 – Philosophy
1. Brazelton & Cramer, 1990.
2. Brazelton & Cramer, 1990.
3. Brazelton & Cramer, 1990.
4. Montessori, 1966.
5. Messmer, 1997.

## Chapter 3 – The In-Arms Phase
6. I first heard the term "the in-arms phase" from Jean Liedloff's writings and believe she is the originator of this expression.
7. Sears, 2001.

## Chapter 4 – The Potty Phase
8. Lorentzen, e-mail to the author, 1999.
9. Wilde, e-mail to the author, 2002.
10. Wang, e-mail to the author, 2002.
11. Fietser, from internet bulletin board, 2001.
12. Bradfisch, 2002.
13. Michel, 1999.
14. deVries, 1999.
15. Walker, 1978.

## Chapter 5 – Signals & Cues
16. Sears & Sears, 1993.
17. Tronick, 1989.

18. Ainsworth & Bell, 1969, in Small, 1998.
19. Appleton et al., 1975.
20. Brazelton & Cramer, 1990.
21. Wolff, 1969.
22. Small, 1998.
23. Volterra & Erting, 1990.
24. Stewart & Luetke-Stahlman, 1998.
25. Kisor, 1990.
26. Volterra & Erting, 1990.
27. Petitto & Marentette, 1991.
28. Petitto & Marentette, 1991.
29. Volterra & Erting, 1990.
30. Volterra & Erting, 1990.

**Chapter 6 – Nighttime**
31. Baas, e-mail to the author, 2002.
32. Sonna, 2003.

**Chapter 7 – Parental Attitude**
33. Lorentzen, e-mail to the author, 1999.
34. Lorentzen, e-mail to the author, 2000.

**Chapter 9 – Stage by Stage**
35. Clark, 1977.
36. D'Odorico & Levorato. In Volterra & Erting, 1990.
37. Clark, 1977.
38. Sonna, 2003.

**Chapter 10 – Late-Starters: 6 Months & Older**
39. Sonna, 2003.

**Chapter 11 – Doctors & Other Experts**
40. deVries, 1999.
41. Brazelton, 1999.
42. deVries & deVries, 1977.
43. deVries & deVries, 1977.
44. Ainsworth, 1967.
45. Ball, 1971.
46. Gersch, 1978.
47. Ravindranathan, 1978.
48. Smeets et al., 1985.
49. Fischer, 1990.
50. Schaefer & DiGeronimo, 1997.
51. Gablehouse, 2000.

52. Bakker & Wyndaele, 2001.
53. Sonna, e-mail to the author, 2002.
54. Rugolotto, e-mail to the author, 2002.
55. Dr. Lamb graduated from University of North Texas Health Science Center at Fort Worth, completed her residency at University of Southern California, then worked at Cook Childrens Medical Center in Fort Worth before moving to Idaho in 1999.
56. Van Pelt, 1996.
57. Hamilton, e-mail to the author, 2000.

**Chapter 12 – Diapers**
58. Brecevic, 1998.
59. Milder, 1997.
60. Greene, 1999.

**Chapter 13 – Environmental Issues**
61. MacEachern, 1990.
62. Lamb, 1990.
63. Vallely, 1990.
64. MacEachern, 1990.
65. Richer, 1999.
66. Brecevic, 1998.
67. Vallely, 1990.
68. Stortenbeek, letter to the author, 1991.
69. Vallely, 1990.
70. Vallely, 1990.

**Chapter 14 – Conventional Training**
71. University of Wisconsin, 1996.

**Chapter 15 – Dispelling the Myths**
72. *Mothering* magazine, 1998.
73. Hamilton, e-mail to the author, 2000.

**Chapter 16 – History & Theories**
74. Bagellardo, 1472, referenced from Beekman, 1977.
75. Stone, 1979.
76. Fontanel & D'Harcourt, 1997.
77. Fontanel & D'Harcourt, 1997.
78. Ball, 1971.
79. Locke, 1693 (in 1989 edition).
80. Greenleaf, 1978.
81. Greenleaf, 1978.
82. Verdi, 1870, referenced from Beekman, 1977.

83.   Beekman, 1977.
84.   Holt, 1894, referenced from Beekman, 1977.
85.   Dennett, 1912, referenced from Hull, 1967.
86.   Tweddell, 1913.
87.   West, 1914.
88.   Hull & Hull, 1919, referenced from Brackbill & Thompson, 1967.
89.   West, 1921.
90.   Griffith, 1921.
91.   Pouliot, 1921, in Fontanel & D'Harcourt, 1996.
92.   Dennett, 1922.
93.   Baker, 1923.
94.   Smith, 1924.
95.   Watson, 1928.
96.   Wolfenstein, 1953, referenced from Brackbill & Thompson, 1967.
97.   Litchfield & Dembo, 1930.
98.   Faegre & Anderson, 1930.
99.   Eliot, 1932.
100.  Hoffman & Hoffman, 1964.
101.  Law, 1938.
102.  Aldrich & Aldrich, 1938.
103.  Dunham & Crane, 1938.
104.  Whipple, Crane & Dunham, 1942 & 1945.
105.  Caldwell, 1964, referenced from Hoffman & Hoffman, 1964.
106.  Faegre, 1951.
107.  Douglas & Blomfield, 1958.
108.  Fontanel & D'Harcourt, 1997.
109.  Messmer, 1997.
110.  Ball, 1971.
111.  Montagu, 1971.
112.  Blurton-Jones, 1972.

**Chapter 17 – Compatible Lifestyles & Philosophies**

113.  Sears & Sears, 1993.
114.  Klaus et al., 1995.
115.  Pearce, 1977.
116.  Sears & Sears, 1993.
117.  Liedloff, 1977.
118.  Arco, 1978.

### PART 2 - TESTIMONIALS - U.S.A.

**Chapter 10 - No Greater Joy**
1. Pearl & Pearl, 1997.
2. Pearl & Pearl, 1994.

### PART 3 - TESTIMONIALS - AROUND THE WORLD

**Chapter 1 - Africa**
1. In many countries, cow and buffalo dung is shaped into patties and baked in the sun. The dung is a useful commodity in third world countries, with a variety of uses. Once it has been treated, it is not considered unhygienic.

**Chapter 13 - Taiwan**
2. Olson, e-mail to the author, 2002.
3. Wang, e-mail to the author, 2002.
4. Strawn, e-mail to the author, 2002.

### PART 4 - CROSS-CULTURAL STUDIES

**Chapter 1 - Cross-Cultural Comparisons**
1. Fontanel & D'Harcourt, 1998.
2. Fontanel & D'Harcourt, 1998.
3. Mead, 1939.
4. Tronick et al., 1987.
5. Konner, 1977, referenced from Leiderman et al., 1977.
6. LeVine, 1977, referenced from Leiderman et al., 1977.
7. LeVine, 1970, referenced from Paden & Soja, 1970.
8. LeVine, 1980, referenced from Fantini & Cárdenas, 1980.
9. LeVine, 1980, referenced from Fantini & Cárdenas, 1980.
10. Kilbride et al., 1970.
11. Yarrow et al., 1977.
12. Goldberg, 1972.
13. Tronick et al., 1987.
14. Small, 1998.
15. Counts, 1985.
16. Briffault, 1931; Geber, 1998 (It was later determined that the testing methods used by Geber and others were partially flawed due to issues of measurement); Epelboin, e-mail to author, 2000.
17. Warren, 1972.

18.  Super, 1981, referenced from Triandis & Heron, 1981.
19.  Kilbride, 1980.
20.  deVries & Super, 1979.
21.  deVries & deVries, 1977.
22.  deVries, 1999.
23.  Landers, 1989, referenced from Nugent et al., 1989.
24.  Keefer et al., 1989, referenced from Nugent et al., 1989.
25.  Keefer et al., 1989, referenced from Nugent et al., 1989.
26.  Ainsworth, 1967.
27.  Kilbride et al., 1970.
28.  Ainsworth, 1967.
29.  Konner, 1977, referenced from Leiderman et al., 1977.
30.  Super, 1973, referenced from Kilbride, 1980.
31.  Kilbride, 1980.
32.  Kilbride, 1980.
33.  Fontanel & D'Harcourt, 1998.
34.  Konner, 1976, referenced from Lee & DeVore, 1976.
35.  Hopkins, 1976.
36.  deVries, 1999.
37.  Goldsmith, 1984.
38.  Small, 1998.
39.  Small, 1998.
40.  Small, 1998.

**Chapter 2 – Africa**
41.  Konner, 1976, referenced from Lee & DeVore, 1976.
42.  Konner, 1977, referenced from Leiderman et al., 1977.
43.  Konner, 1972, referenced from Blurton-Jones, 1972.
44.  Pearce, 1977.
45.  Konner, e-mail to the author, 1999.
46.  Marshall, 1965, referenced from Gibbs, 1965.
47.  Super & Harkness, 1982, is one such report.
48.  deVries, 1987.
49.  deVries & deVries, 1977.
50.  LeVine, 1963, referenced from Whiting, 1963.
51.  Sangree, 1965, referenced from Gibbs, 1965.
52.  Linton, 1933.
53.  Linton, 1939.
54.  Wanono, e-mail to the author, 1999.
55.  Herskovits, 1938.

56. Cohen, 1967.
57. Epelboin, e-mail to author, 2000.
58. Rabain, e-mail to the author, 1999.
59. Cederblad, 1970.
60. Raum, 1940.
61. Fontanel & D'Harcourt, 1998.
62. Ainsworth, 1967.
63. Ainsworth, 1967.
64. Ainsworth, 1967.
65. Ainsworth, 1967.
66. Kilbride & Kilbride, 1990.
67. Geber, 1998.
68. Pearce, 1977.
69. Stork, 1999.

**Chapter 3 – Asia**
70. Linton, 1939.
71. Martini & Kirkpatrick, 1981.
72. Fontanel & D'Harcourt, 1998.
73. Gorer, 1938.
74. Du Bois, 1944.
75. Mead & Macgregor, 1951.
76. Maretzki, 1963, referenced from Whiting, 1963.
77. Murray, 1953, referenced from HRAF, 1999.
78. Burrows & Spiro, 1954.
79. Fischer, 1950, referenced from HRAF, 1999.
80. Gladwin & Sarason, 1953, referenced from HRAF, 1999.
81. Mead, 1930.
82. Mead, 1935.
83. Whiting, 1941.
84. Wikan, 1982.
85. Nydegger, 1963, referenced from Whiting, 1963.
86. Diamond, 1969.
87. Gallin, 1966, referenced from HRAF, 1999.
88. Wolf, 1972, referenced from HRAF, 1999.
89. Maiden & Farwell, 1997.
90. Sumer, 1970.

**Chapter 4 – Polar Regions, South America & Beyond**
91. Robert-Lamblin, e-mail to author, 1999.
92. Damas, 1972.

93.  Fontanel & D'Harcourt, 1998.
94.  Briggs, 1970.
95.  Pearl & Pearl, 1997.
96.  Holmberg, 1985.
97.  Erikson, e-mail to author, 1999.
98.  Wagley, 1949.
99.  Ford, 1941.
100. Press, 1975, referenced from HRAF, 2002.
101. Hill, e-mail to author, 1999.
102. Goodwin, 1942.
103. Dennis, 1940.
104. Kluckhohn, 1947, in Roheim, 1947.
105. Chesky, 1949.
106. Wilbert, 1976, referenced from HRAF, 2002.
107. Liedloff, 1977.
108. Whiting & Child, 1953.
109. Barry & Paxson, 1971. In some cases the data was meager,
     based on a single instance or weak inference. The findings do
     not include babies who learn by imitation.
110. Whiting & Edwards, 1988.

# REFERENCES

Ainsworth, Mary D. Salter. *Infancy in Uganda*, Johns Hopkins Press, pp. 77–78, 83–84, 1967.

Ainsworth, Mary D. Salter, and Steven M. Bell. "Some Contemporary Patterns of Mother-Infant Interactions in the Feeding Situation," 1969. In Meredith F. Small, *Our Babies, Ourselves*, Doubleday, 1998.

Aldrich, C. Anderson, and Mary M. Aldrich. *Babies Are Human Beings*, Macmillan, 1938.

Appleton, Tina, Rachel Clifton and Susan Goldberg. "The Development of Behavioral Competence in Infancy." In Frances Degen Horowitz, ed., *Review of Child Development Research*, vol. 4, University of Chicago Press, 1975.

Arco Publishing Company. *Peoples of Africa*, Arco, 1978.

Baas, Lois. E-mail to the author re: infant potty training, Mar.–Apr. 2002.

Bagellardo, Paolo. *Book on Infant Diseases*, 1472. In Daniel Beekman, *The Mechanical Baby,* Lawrence Hill, 1977.

Baker, S. Josephine. *Healthy Babies: A Volume Devoted to the Health of the Expectant Mother and the Care and Welfare of the Child*, Little, Brown, and Company, 1923.

Bakker, E. and J. J. Wyndaele. "Changes in the Toilet Training of Children during the Last 60 Years: The Cause of an Increase in Lower Urinary Tract Dysfunction?" *British Journal of Urology International* 86:248–252, 2000.

Balikci, Asen. *The Netsilik Eskimo*, Natural History Press, 1970.

Ball, Thomas S. "Toilet Training an Infant Mongoloid at the Breast," *California Mental Health Digest* 9:80–85, 1971.

Barry, Herbert III, and Leonora M. Paxson. "Infancy and Early Childhood: Cross-Cultural Codes 2," *Ethnology* 10:466–508, 1971.

Beekman, Daniel. *The Mechanical Baby,* Lawrence Hill, 1977.

Blurton-Jones, N. G., ed. *Ethological Studies of Child Behaviour*, Cambridge University Press, 1972.

Boucke, Laurie. *Trickle Treat: Diaperless Infant Toilet Training Method*, White-Boucke Publishing, 1991.

Brackbill, Yvonne, and George G. Thompson, eds. *Behavior in Infancy and Early Childhood*, The Free Press, 1967.

Bradfisch, Friederike. E-mail to the author re: infant potty training, Feb.–Mar. 2002.

Brazelton, T. Berry. "Housecall with T. Berry Brazelton," http://www.babycenter.com, 1999.

Brazelton, T. Berry, and Bertrand G. Cramer. *The Earliest Relationship: Parents, Infants, and the Drama of Early Attachment*, Adison-Wesley, 1990.

Brecevic, Candace. "The Diaper Debate," http://www.diaperingdecisions.com, 1998.

Briffault, Robert. *The Mothers: The Matriarchal Theory of Social Origins*, Macmillan, 1931.

Briggs, Jean L. *Never in Anger: Portrait of an Eskimo Family*, Harvard University Press, 1970.

Burrows, Edwin G., and Melford E. Spiro. *An Atoll Culture: Ethnography of Ifaluk in the Central Carolines*, Human Relations Area Files, 1954.

Caldwell, Bettye M. "The Effects of Infant Care." In Martin L. Hoffman and Lois Wladis Hoffman, eds., *Review of Child Development Research*, vol. 1, Russell Sage, 1964.

Cederblad, Marianne. "A Child Psychiatric Study of Sudanese Arab Children." In E. James Anthony and Cyrille Koupernik, eds., *The Child in His Family*, Wiley-Interscience, 1970.

Chesky, Jane. "Growing up on the Desert." In Alice Joseph, Rosamond B. Spicer and Jane Chesky, *The Desert People: A Study of the Papago Indians,* University of Chicago Press, 1949.

Clark, David A. "Times of First Void and First Stool in 500 Newborns," *Pediatrics* (60) 4:457–459, Oct. 1977.

Cohen, Ronald. *The Kanuri of Bornu*, Holt, Rinehart and Winston, 1967.

Counts, Dorothy A. "Infant Care and Feeding in Kaliai, West New Britain, Papua New Guinea." In Leslie B. Marshall, ed., *Infant Care and Feeding in the South Pacific*, Gordon and Breach, 1985.

Damas, David. *The Copper Eskimo*, Holt, Rinehart and Winston, 1972.

Dennett, Roger H. *The Healthy Baby: The Care and Feeding of Infants in Sickness and in Health,* Macmillan, 1922.

Dennis, Wayne. *The Hopi Child*, Appleton-Century, 1940.

deVries, Marten W. "Babies, Brains and Culture: Optimizing Neurodevelopment on the Savanna," *Acta Pædiatrica Suppl* 429:43–8, 1999.

_____. "Cry Babies, Culture, Catastrophe: Infant Temperament among the Masai." In Nancy Scheper-Hughes, ed., *Child Survival: Anthropological Perspectives on the Treatment and Maltreatment of Children,*" Reidel (with kind permission of Kluwer Academic Publishers), 1987.

deVries, Marten W., and Rachel M. deVries. "Cultural Relativity of Toilet Training Readiness: A Perspective from East Africa," *Pediatrics* 60:170–177, 1977.

deVries, Marten, and Charles M. Super. "Contextual Influences on the Neonatal Behavioral Assessment Scale and Implications for Its Cross-Cultural Use." In *Monographs of the Society for Research in Child Development,* Serial no. 177, vol. 43, nos. 5–6, University of Chicago Press, 1979.

Diamond, Norma. *K'un Shen: A Taiwan Village*, Holt, Rinehart and Winston, 1969.

D'Odorico, L., and M. C. Levorato. "Social and Cognitive Determinants of Mutual Gaze between Mother and Infant." In V. Volterra and C. J. Erting, eds., *From Gesture to Language in Hearing and Deaf Children*, Springer-Verlag, 1990.

Douglas, J. W. B., and J. M. Blomfield. *Children under Five*, George Allen & Unwin, 1958.

Du Bois, Cora. *The People of Alor: A Social-Psychological Study of an East Indian Island*, University of Minnesota Press, 1944.

Dunham, Ethel C., and Marian M. Crane. *Infant Care*, U.S. Dept. of Labor, Children's Bureau, GPO, 1938.

Eliot, Martha May. *Infant Care*, U.S. Dept. of Labor, Children's Bureau, GPO, 1929; 1932.

Epelboin, Alain. E-mail to the author re: Senegal and Central African Republic, Dec. 1999–Mar. 2000.

Erikson, Philippe. E-mail to the author re: Amerindians and Matis of Brazil, Dec. 1999–Jan. 2000.

Faegre, Marion L. *Infant Care*, U.S. Dept. of Labor, Children's Bureau, GPO, 1951.

Faegre, Marion L., and John E. Anderson. *Child Care and Training*, University of Minnesota Press, 1930.

Fantini, Mario D., and René Cárdenas, eds. *Parenting in a Multicultural Society*, Longman, 1980.

Field, Tiffany M., Anita M. Sostek, Peter Vietze and P. Herbert Leiderman, eds. *Culture and Early Interactions*, Lawrence Erlbaum, 1981.

Fischer, Ann M. *The Role of the Trukese Mother and Its Effect on Child Training*, Pacific Science Board, 1950.

Fischer, Paul. Letters to the Editor, "Early Toilet Training," *The Journal of Family Practice* 30:262, 1990.

Fontanel, Béatrice, and Claire D'Harcourt. *Bébé du monde* , Éditions de la Martinière, 1998; English edition, *Babies Celebrated*, Trans. Jack Hawkes, Harry N. Abrams, 1998.

_____. *Épopée des bébés, une histoire des petits d'hommes* , Éditions de la Martinière, 1996; English edition, *Babies: History, Art, and Folklore*, Trans. Lory Frankel, Harry N. Abrams, 1997.

Ford, Clellan S. *Smoke from Their Fires: The Life of a Kwakiutl Chief*, Yale University Press, 1941.

Gablehouse, Barbara. "The Potty Project for Babies," Five Star Parenting, 2000.

Gallin, Bernard. *Hsin Hsing, Taiwan: A Chinese Village in Change*, University of California Press, 1966.

Geber, Marcelle. *L'enfant africain dans un monde en changement, étude ethno-psychologique dans huit pays sud-africains*, Presses Universitaires de France, 1998.

_____. "The Psycho-motor Development of African Children in the First Year, and the Influence of Maternal Behavior," *Journal of Social Psychology* 47:185–195, 1958.

Gersch, Marvin J. Letter to the Editor, "Early Toilet Training," *Pediatrics* 61:674, 1978.

Gibbs, James L. Jr., ed. *Peoples of Africa*, Holt, Rinehart and Winston, 1965.

Gladwin, Thomas, and Seymour B. Sarason. *Truk: Man in Paradise*, (Viking Fund Publications in Anthropology, No. 20, 1953), by permission of the Wenner-Gren Foundation for Anthropological Research, New York, 1953.

Goldberg, Susan. "Infant Care and Growth in Urban Zambia," *Human Development* 15:77–89, 1972.

Goldsmith, Judith. *Childbirth Wisdom*, Congdon & Weed, Inc., 1984.

Goodwin, Grenville. *The Social Organization of the Western Apache*, University of Chicago Press, 1942.

Gorer, Geoffrey. *Himalayan Village: An Account of the Lepchas of Sikkim*, Michael Joseph, 1938.

Greene, Alan. Re: diaper rash. In Carlos E. Richer, "I have been told that cloth diapers are better for the skin of my baby . . .?". http://www.giga.com/~cricher/FAQ.htm, 1999.

Greenleaf, Barbara Kaye. *Children through the Ages: A History of Childhood*, McGraw-Hill, 1978.

Griffith, J. P. Crozer. *The Care of the Baby: A Manual for Mothers and Nurses*, W. B. Saunders, 1921.

Hamilton, Jacqueline. E-mail to the author re: infant potty training, Aug. 1999 & Mar. 2000.

Herskovits, Melville J. *Dahomey: An Ancient West African Kingdom*, vol. 1, J. J. Augustin, 1938.

Hoffman, Martin L., and Lois Wladis Hoffman, eds. *Review of Child Development Research*, vol. 1, Russell Sage, 1964.

Holmberg, Allan R. *Nomads of the Long Bow: The Siriono of Eastern Bolivia*, Waveland Press, 1985.

Holt, Luther Emmett. *The Care and Feeding of Children*, 1894 & 1903. In Daniel Beekman, *The Mechanical Baby,* Lawrence Hill, 1977.

Hopkins, Brian. "Culturally Determined Patterns of Handling the Human Infant," *Journal of Human Movement Studies* 2:1–27, 1976.

Hull, Clark L., and Bertha Iutzi Hull. "Conflict between Overlapping Learning Functions." In Yvonne Brackbill and George G. Thompson, eds., *Behavior in Infancy and Early Childhood*, The Free Press, 1967.

Human Relations Area Files (HRAF). Toilet training, Yale University, sourced via the Internet, Nov. & Dec. 1999 and April 2002.

Kardiner, Abram. *The Individual and His Society: The Psychodynamics of Primitive Social Organization*, Columbia University Press, 1939.

Keefer, Constance H., Suzanne Dixon, Edward Z. Tronick and T. Berry Brazelton. "Cultural Mediation between Newborn Behavior and Later Development: Implications for Methodology in Cross-Cultural Research." In J. Kevin Nugent, Barry M. Lester and T. Berry Brazelton, eds., *The Cultural Context of Infancy: Biology, Culture, and Infant Development*, vol. 2, Ablex, 1989.

Kilbride, Philip Leroy. "Sensorimotor Behavior of Baganda and Samia Infants: A Controlled Comparison," *Journal of Cross-Cultural Psychology* 11:131–152, 1980.

Kilbride, Philip Leroy, and Janet Capriotti Kilbride. *Changing Family Life in East Africa*, Pennsylvania State University Press, 1990.

Kilbride, Philip Leroy, Janet E. Kilbride and M. C. Robbins. "The Comparative Motor Development of Baganda, American White, and American Black Infants," *American Anthropologist* 72:1422–1428, 1970.

Kisor, Henry. *What's That Pig Outdoors? A Memoir of Deafness*, Hill and Wang, 1990.

Klaus, Marshall H., John H. Kennell and Phyllis H. Klaus. *Bonding: Building the Foundations of Secure Attachment and Independence*, Merloyd Lawrence, 1995.

Kluckhohn, Clyde. "Some Aspects of Navajo Infancy and Early Childhood," 1947. In Geza Roheim, ed., *Psychoanalysis and the Social Sciences*, vol. 1, International Universities Press, 1947.

Konner, Melvin J. "Aspects of the Developmental Ethology of a Foraging People." In N. G. Blurton-Jones, ed., *Ethological Studies of Child Behaviour*, Cambridge University Press, 1972.

————. "Infancy among the Kalahari Desert San." In P. Herbert Leiderman, Steven R. Tulkin and Anne Rosenfeld, eds., *Culture and Infancy: Variations in the Human Experience*, Academic Press, 1977.

————. "Maternal Care, Infant Behavior and Development among the !Kung." In Richard B. Lee and Irven DeVore, eds., *Kalahari Hunter-Gatherers*, Harvard University Press, 1976.

————. E-mail to the author re: !Kung in Botswana, Dec. 1999.

La Leche League International. "FAQ on Normal Bowel Movements of Breastfed Babies," http://www.lalecheleague.org, 1999.

Lamb, Jan Leah. Interview with the author, June 1993 and e-mail to the author re: infant potty training, Nov.–Dec. 1999.

Lamb, Marjorie. *Two Minutes a Day for Greener Planet: Quick and Simple Things You Can Do to Save Our Earth*, Harper Paperbacks, 1990.

Landers, Cassie. "A Psychobiological Study of Infant Development in South India." In J. Kevin Nugent, Barry M. Lester and T. Berry Brazelton, eds., *The Cultural Context of Infancy: Biology, Culture, and Infant Development*, vol. 1, Ablex, 1989.

Law, May Elizabeth MacIver. *Baby Care: A Helpful Guide for Mothers on the Care of Infants*, J. B. Lippincott, 1938.

Lee, Richard B., and Irven DeVore, eds. *Kalahari Hunter-Gatherers: Studies of the !Kung San and Their Neighbors*, Harvard University Press, 1976.

Leiderman, P. Herbert, Steven R. Tulkin and Anne Rosenfeld, eds. *Culture and Infancy: Variations in the Human Experience*, Academic Press, 1977.

LeVine, Robert A. "A Cross-Cultural Perspective on Parenting." In Mario D. Fantini and René Cárdenas, eds., *Parenting in a Multicultural Society*, Longman, 1980.

_____. "Child Rearing as Cultural Adaptation." In P. Herbert Leiderman, Steven R. Tulkin and Anne Rosenfeld, eds., *Culture and Infancy: Variations in the Human Experience*, Academic Press, 1977.

_____. "The Relative Absence of Separation Anxiety and Related Affects." In John N. Paden and Edward W. Soja, eds., *The African Experience*, Northwestern University Press, 1970.

LeVine, Robert A., and Barbara B. LeVine. "Nyansongo: A Gusii Community in Kenya." In Beatrice Blyth Whiting, ed., *Six Cultures: Studies of Child Rearing*, John Wiley, 1963.

Liedloff, Jean. *The Continuum Concept*, Knopf, 1977.

Linton, Ralph. "Marquesan Culture." In Abram Kardiner, *The Individual and His Society*, Columbia University Press, 1939.

_____. *The Tanala: A Hill Tribe of Madagascar*, vol. XXII, Field Museum of Natural History, 1933.

_____. "The Tanala of Madagascar." In Abram Kardiner, *The Individual and His Society*, Columbia University Press, 1939.

Litchfield, Harry R., and Leon H. Dembo. *Care of the Infant and Child: A Book for Mothers and Nurses*, Waverly Press, 1930.

Locke, John. *Some Thoughts Concerning Education*, Clarendon Press, 1989.

Lorentzen, Vanessa. E-mail to the author re: infant potty training, Aug.–Dec. 1999 & Jan.–Apr. 2000.

MacEachern, Diane. *Save Our Planet: 750 Everyday Ways You Can Help Clean up the Earth*, Dell Trade Paperback, 1990.

Maiden, Anne Hubbell, and Edie Farwell. *The Tibetan Art of Parenting*, Wisdom Publications, 1997.

Maretzki, Thomas W., and Hatsumi Maretzki. "Taira: An Okinawan Village." In Beatrice Blyth Whiting, ed., *Six Cultures: Studies of Child Rearing*, John Wiley, 1963.

Marshall, Lorna. "The !Kung Bushmen of the Kalahari Desert." In James L. Gibbs Jr., ed., *Peoples of Africa*, Holt, Rinehart and Winston, 1965.

Martini, Mary, and John Kirkpatrick. "Early Interactions in the Marquesas Islands." In Tiffany M. Field, Anita M. Sostek, Peter Vietze and P. Herbert Leiderman, eds., *Culture and Early Interactions*, Lawrence Erlbaum, 1981.

Mayo Clinic. "Choosing diapers." http://www.mayohealth.org, 1996.

Mead, Margaret. *From the South Seas: Studies of Adolescence and Sex in Primitive Societies*, W. Morrow, 1939.

_____. *Growing up in New Guinea: A Comparative Study of Primitive Education*, Blue Ribbon Books, 1930.

_____. *Sex and Temperament in Three Primitive Societies*, W. Morrow, 1935.

Mead, Margaret, and Frances Cooke Macgregor. *Growth and Culture: A Photographic Study of Balinese Childhood*, G. P. Putnam's Sons, 1951.

Michel, Robert S. "Toilet Training," *Pediatrics in Review* 20:240–245, 1999.

Milder, John. "Choosing Diapers," National Association of Diaper Services, http://www.diapernet.com/choose.htm, 1997.

Montagu, Ashley. *Touching: The Human Significance of the Skin*, Columbia University Press, 1971.

Montessori, Maria. *The Secret of Childhood*, Fides, 1966.

Mont-Reynaud, Randy. E-mail to the author re: mother training and Vietnam, July–Dec. 1999.

*Mothering.* "Your Letters," Nov.–Dec. 1998.

Murray, William M. *Rowanduz: A Kurdish Administrative and Mercantile Center,* Ph.D. dissertation, University of Michigan, 1953.

Nugent, J. Kevin, Barry M. Lester and T. Berry Brazelton, eds. *The Cultural Context of Infancy: Biology, Culture, and Infant Development*, Ablex, 1989.

Nydegger, Corinne. "Tarong: An Ilocos Barrio in the Philippines." In Beatrice Blyth Whiting, ed., *Six Cultures: Studies of Child Rearing*, John Wiley, 1963.

Olson, Katambra. E-mail to the author re: infant potty training, Mar. 2002.

Paden, John N., and Edward W. Soja, eds. *The African Experience*, Northwestern University Press, 1970.

Pearce, Joseph Chilton. *Magical Child: Rediscovering Nature's Plan for Our Children,* Dutton, 1977.

Pearl, Michael, and Debi Pearl. *No Greater Joy*, vol. 1, Michael and Debi Pearl, 1997.

———. *To Train up a Child*, Michael Pearl, 1994.

Petitto, Laura Ann, and Paula F. Marentette. "Babbling in the Manual Mode: Evidence for the Ontogeny of Language," *Science* 251:1483–1496, 1991.

Pouliot, L. *Hygiène de maman et de bébé* , 1922. In Béatrice Fontanel and Claire D'Harcourt. *Bébés du monde* , Éditions de la Martinière, 1998; English edition, *Babies Celebrated*, Trans. Jack Hawkes, Harry N. Abrams, 1998.

Press, Irwin. "Tradition and Adaptation: Life in a Modern Yucatan Maya Village," Greenwood Press, 1975.

Rabain-Jamin, Jacqueline. E-mail to the author re: the Wolof of Senegal, Dec. 1999.

Raum, Otto Friedrich. *Chaga Childhood: A Description of Indigenous Education in an East African Tribe*, Oxford University Press, 1940.

Ravindranathan, S. Letter to the Editor, "Early Toilet Training," *Pediatrics* 61:674, 1978.

Richer, Carlos E. http://www.giga.com/~richer/FAQ.htm, 1999.

Roark, Anne C. "Parenting: Mother of Invention," *Los Angeles Times*, 24 July 1988.

Robert-Lamblin, Joëlle. E-mail to the author re: the Arctic (Aleutians, Greenland and Siberia), Dec. 1999.

Roheim, Geza, ed. *Psychoanalysis and the Social Sciences*, vol. 1, International Universities Press, 1947.

Rugolotto, Simone. E-mail to the author re: infant potty training, Apr. 2002.

Sameroff, Arnold J., ed. *Monographs of the Society for Research in Child Development*, serial no. 177, vol. 43, nos. 5-6, University of Chicago Press, 1979.

Sangree, Walter H. "The Bantu Tiriki of Western Kenya." In James L. Gibbs Jr., ed., *Peoples of Africa*, Holt, Rinehart and Winston, 1965.

Schaefer, Charles E. *Childhood Encopresis and Enuresis,* Jason Aronson, 1993.

Schaefer, Charles E., and Theresa Foy DiGeronimo. *Toilet Training without Tears*, Signet, 1997.

Scheper-Hughes, Nancy, ed. *Child Survival: Anthropological Perspectives on the Treatment and Maltreatment of Children,"* Reidel, 1987.

Sears, William. "Toilet-Training: Tips to Tell Potty Times," http://www.AskDrSears.com, 2001.

Sears, William, and Martha Sears. *The Baby Book,* Little, Brown and Company, 1993.

Small, Meredith F. *Our Babies, Ourselves*, Doubleday, 1998.

Smeets, Paul M., Giulio E. Lancioni, Thomas S. Ball and Dorette S. Oliva. "Shaping Self-initiated Toileting in Infants," *Journal of Applied Behavior Analysis* 18:303–308, 1985.

Smith, Richard M. *The Baby's First Two Years*, Houghton Mifflin, 1924.

Sonna, Linda. *The Everything Potty Training Book*, Adams Media, 2003 (pre release copy).

_____. E-mail to the author re: infant potty training, Feb.–Apr. 2002.

Stewart, David A., and Barbara Luetke-Stahlman. *The Signing Family: What Every Parent Should Know about Sign Communication*, Gallaudet University Press, 1998.

Stone, Lawrence. *The Family, Sex and Marriage in England 1500–1800*, Harper & Row, 1979.

Stork, Hélène E. *Introduction à la psychologie anthropologique*, Armand-Colin, 1999.

Stortenbeek, Willem. Correspondence with the author re: diseases spread via diaper waste in landfills, Nov. 1991 and e-mail to the author, Mar. 2000.

Strawn, Katie. E-mail to the author re: infant potty training, Mar. 2002.

Sümer, Emel A. "Changing Dynamic Aspects of the Turkish Culture and Its Significance for Child Training." In E. James Anthony and Cyrille Koupernik, eds., *The Child in His Family*, Wiley-Interscience, 1970.

Sun, Min. E-mail to the author re: infant potty training, Apr. 2002.

Super, Charles M. "Cross-Cultural Research on Infancy." In Harry C. Triandis and Alastair Heron, eds., *Handbook of Cross-Cultural Psychology: Developmental Psychology*, Allyn and Bacon, 1981.

_____. "Patterns of Infant Care and Motor Development in Kenya," *Kenya Education Review* 1:64–69, 1973.

Triandis, Harry C., and Alastair Heron, eds. *Handbook of Cross-Cultural Psychology: Developmental Psychology*, vol. 4, Allyn and Bacon, 1981.

Tronick, Edward Z., and Jeffery F. Cohn. "Infant-Mother Face-to-Face Interaction: Age and Gender Differences in Coordination and the Occurrence of Miscoordination," *Child Development* 60:85–92, 1989.

Tronick, Edward Z., Gilda A Morelli and Paula K. Ivey. "The Efe Forager Infant and Toddler's Pattern of Social Relationships: Multiple and Simultaneous," *Developmental Psychology* 28:568–577, 1992.

Tronick, Edward Z., Gilda A. Morelli and Steve Winn. "Multiple Caretaking of Efe (Pygmy) Infants, *American Anthropologist* 89:96–106, 1987.

Tweddell, Francis. *How to Take Care of the Baby: A Mother's Guide and Manual for Nurses*, Bobbs-Merrill, 1913.

University of Wisconsin. *Picture of Health: Parents' Guide to Toilet Teaching*, Dept. of Outreach Education, University of Wisconsin Board of Regents, 1996.

Vallely, Bernadette. *1001 Ways to Save the Planet*, Ivy Books, 1990.

Van Pelt, Katie. *Potty Training Your Baby*, Avery, 1996.

Verdi, Tullio Suzzara. *Maternity, A Popular Treatise for Young Mothers*, 1870. In Daniel Beekman, *The Mechanical Baby*, Lawrence Hill, 1977.

Volterra, V., and C. J. Erting, eds. *From Gesture to Language in Hearing and Deaf Children*, Springer-Verlag, 1990.

Wagley, Charles, and Eduardo Galvao. *The Tenetehara Indians of Brazil: A Culture in Transition*, Columbia University Press, 1949.

Walker, Eugene C. "Toilet Training, Enuresis, Encopresis." In Phyllis R. Magrab, ed., *Psychological Management of Pediatric Problems*, vol. 1, University Park Press, 1978.

Wang, Angie. E-mail to the author re: "no" phase, Feb.–Mar. 2002.

Wanono, Nadine. E-mail to the author re: the Dogon of Mali, Nov. 1999–Jan. 2000.

Warren, Neil. "African Infant Precocity," *Psychological Bulletin* 78:353–367, 1972.

Watson, John B. *Psychological Care of Infant and Child,* Norton, 1928.

West, Mrs. Max. *Infant Care*, U.S. Dept. of Labor, Children's Bureau, GPO, 1914; 1921.

Whipple, Dorothy V., Marian M. Crane and Ethel C. Dunham. *Infant Care*, U.S. Dept. of Labor, Children's Bureau, GPO, 1942; 1945.

Whiting, Beatrice Blyth, ed. *Six Cultures: Studies of Child Rearing*, John Wiley, 1963.

Whiting, Beatrice Blyth, and Carolyn Pope Edwards. *Children of Different Worlds: The Formation of Social Behavior*, Harvard University Press, 1988.

Whiting, John W. M. *Becoming a Kwoma: Teaching and Learning in a New Guinea Tribe*, Yale University Press, 1941.

Whiting, John W. M., and Irvin L. Child, eds. *Child Training and Personality: A Cross-Cultural Study*, Yale University Press, 1953.

Wikan, Unni. *Behind the Veil in Arabia: Women in Oman*, Johns Hopkins University Press, pp. 76 & 78, 1982.

Wilbert, Johannes. "To Become a Maker of Canoes: An Essay in Warao Enculturation," UCLA Latin American Center Publications, University of California, 1976.

Wilde, Rosie. "Upright Baby Kinesiology," http://seafish.freeyellow.com/index.html, 2001.

Wolf, Margery. *Women and the Family in Rural Taiwan*, HRAF, Stanford University Press, 1972.

Wolfenstein, Martha. "Trends in Infant Care." In Yvonne Brackbill and George G. Thompson, eds., *Childhood Behavior in Infancy and Early Childhood,* The Free Press, 1967.

Wolff, Peter H. "The Natural History of Crying and Other Vocalization in Early Infancy." In B. M. Foss, ed., *Determinants of Infant Behaviour IV,* Methuen, 1969.

Yarrow, Leon, Frank A. Pedersen and Judith Rubenstein. "Mother-Infant Interaction and Development in Infancy." In P. Herbert Leiderman, Steven R. Tulkin and Anne Rosenfeld, eds., *Culture and Infancy: Variations in the Human Experience*, Academic Press, 1977.

# INDEX